Personal Development
ALL-IN-ONE
FOR
DUMMIES®

By Rhena Branch, Mike Bryant,
Kate Burton, Peter Mabbutt, Jeni Mumford,
Romilla Ready, and Rob Willson

Edited by Gillian Burn

Personal Development All-in-One For Dummies®

Published by
John Wiley & Sons, Ltd
The Atrium
Southern Gate
Chichester
West Sussex
PO19 8SQ
England

E-mail (for orders and customer service enquires): cs-books@wiley.co.uk

Visit our Home Page on www.wiley.com

For general information on our other products and services, please contact our Customer Care Department within the U.S. at 800-762-2974, outside the U.S. at 317-572-3993, or fax 317-572-4002.

For technical support, please visit www.wiley.com/techsupport.

Wiley also publishes its books in a variety of electronic formats. Some content that appears in print may not be available in electronic books.

British Library Cataloguing in Publication Data: A catalogue record for this book is available from the British Library

ISBN: 978-0-470-51501-3 (PB)

Printed and bound in Great Britain by Bell & Bain Ltd, Glasgow

10 9 8 7 6 5 4 3

WILEY

About the Authors

Gillian Burn has over 25 years of experience in health and wellbeing. Her background covers nursing, midwifery, and health visiting, including experience working with the Flying Doctor Service in the Australian outback.

Gillian has an MSc in Exercise and Health and is a qualified master practitioner in Neuro-linguistic Programming, time line therapy®, and in creating healthy environments. She is a licensed instructor for Mind Mapping® techniques and speed reading with Tony Buzan, and a licensed instructor in Body Control Pilates® with the Body Control Pilates Academy.

Gillian is the Director of Health Circles Ltd (www.healthcircles.co.uk), providing training programmes and consultancy services focusing on improving health and quality of life for individuals and companies. Her workshops focus on training people to use their mind and bodies to increase energy and performance. This includes nutrition and exercise advice, understanding the mind and body connection, creating balance, and techniques to increase creativity and effectiveness.

Gillian also provides life coaching to help clients create a compelling future to reach their full potential and peak performance. Gillian aims to practice what she preaches! She rows on the River Thames and enjoys swimming, walking, yoga, and pilates.

Rhena Branch, MSc, Dip CBT, is an accredited CBT therapist and works with the Priory Hospital North London as a CBT therapist. She also has her own practice in north London and supervises on the Masters' course at Goldsmith College, University of London.

Mike Bryant is an African-American who has lived in England since 1984. Mike is a qualified psychiatric social worker, counsellor, and hypnotherapist and has also worked as an Information Technology and Project Manager. With extensive experience in both America and the United Kingdom, Mike has established a range of innovative mental health schemes in London as well as having provided senior service development consultancy to NHS Mental Health Trusts across England, Ireland, Scotland, and Wales as a Senior Consultant with the Sainsbury Centre for Mental Health (SCMH). While at SCMH, he published a range of papers and reports on mental health issues.

Mike currently lives in London with his wife and family and has a private practice as a counsellor and as hypnotherapist. You can find more information about Mike's practice at www.londonhypno.com.

Kate Burton is an NLP coach and trainer who enables individuals and organisations to focus their energy effectively. Her business career began in corporate advertising and marketing with Hewlett-Packard. Since then she has worked with many varied businesses across industries and cultures on how they can be great communicators. What she loves most is delivering custom-built training and coaching programmes. She thrives on supporting people in boosting their motivation, self-awareness and confidence. Her belief is that people all have unique talents, abilities and core values. The skill is about honouring them to the full.

Peter Mabbutt is Director of Studies at the London College of Clinical Hypnosis (LCCH) and lectures throughout the UK and overseas to both lay students and medical practitioners. He is responsible for the development of the LCCH's core courses and with his colleagues has introduced many new techniques and subjects to the curriculum, ensuring that it continues to meet the needs of the modern-day hypnotherapist.

With a background in psychopharmacology Peter co-authored a range of papers on tranquilisers, anxiety, and learning and memory before training with the LCCH to become a hypnotherapist. Peter has a specialist interest in the mind-body connection, weight control, the treatment of trauma, and hypertension.

Jeni Mumford is a coach and facilitator who applies whole-life coaching techniques to her work with people and within businesses. Before her own life-changing decision to become a coach, Jeni benefited from a 16-year career with the Hays group, spanning recruitment, sales operations, project management, and people development, where she was lucky enough to embark on a new challenging job role every 18 months or so. It was this experience of discovering that the grass is green wherever you are – if you take proper care of the lawn – that gave Jeni the conviction and motivation to build her purpose around inspiring people to attract and enjoy their own dream life and work. In her business Jeni uses best practice coaching techniques together with NLP, and is a licensed facilitator of Tetramap (a holistic model of behaviour) and Goal Mapping (a brain-friendly technique for identifying and maximising progress towards goals). She is addicted to learning and this helps her add value to her work with clients. But in her moments of brutal self-honesty Jeni will admit that quite a lot of the credit is down to the succession of cats who have owned her, from whom she has picked up a great deal about how to handle the ups and downs of life.

One of the things Jeni likes best about being a coach is that she feels she always gets as much if not more out of the experience than her clients and she can't thank them enough for the honour of seeing them move themselves from frustration to power. Honestly, it's enough to make you want to write a book about it. You can find out more about Jeni and her business at: www.reachforstarfish.com.

Romilla Ready is a Master Practitioner of Neuro-linguistic Programming, and is the director of Ready Solutions, which was founded in 1996. She runs professionally developed workshops across a range of areas and has trained clients in the UK and overseas, using her cross-cultural skills to build rapport between different nationalities. Romilla has been interviewed on local radio and has had articles on stress management and applications of NLP published in the press.

Rob Willson, BSc, MSc, Dip SBHS, has worked for the Priory Hospital North London for a number of years as a CBT therapist. Rob also teaches and supervises trainee therapists at Goldsmith's College, University of London, and has his own practice in north London. His first book was *Overcoming Obsessive Compulsive Disorder* (Constable & Robinson, 2005), co-written with Dr David Veale.

Rob has done numerous newspaper and radio interviews about CBT. More rarely he's appeared on television discussing understanding and treating body image problems. His particular interests include the research and treatment of obsessional problems, and applying CBT in group and self-help formats.

Publisher's Acknowledgements

We're proud of this book; please send us your comments through our Dummies online registration form located at www.dummies.com/register/.

Some of the people who helped bring this book to market include the following:

Acquisitions, Editorial, and Media Development

Project Editor: Daniel Mersey

Content Editor: Steve Edwards

Commissioning Editor: Alison Yates

Text Splicer: Helen Heyes

Executive Editor: Jason Dunne

Executive Project Editor: Martin Tribe

Cover Photos: © Bernd Kohlhas/zefa/Corbis

Cartoons: Rich Tennant
(www.the5thwave.com)

Composition Services

Project Coordinator: Jennifer Theriot

Layout and Graphics: Claudia Bell, Stacie Brooks, Joyce Haughey, Barbara Moore, Heather Ryan

Proofreaders: Susan Moritz, Brian H. Walls

Indexer: Aptara

Wiley Bicentennial Logo: Richard J. Pacifico

Publishing and Editorial for Consumer Dummies

> **Diane Graves Steele,** Vice President and Publisher, Consumer Dummies

> **Joyce Pepple,** Acquisitions Director, Consumer Dummies

> **Kristin A. Cocks,** Product Development Director, Consumer Dummies

> **Michael Spring,** Vice President and Publisher, Travel

> **Kelly Regan,** Editorial Director, Travel

Publishing for Technology Dummies

> **Andy Cummings,** Vice President and Publisher, Dummies Technology/General User

Composition Services

> **Gerry Fahey,** Vice President of Production Services

> **Debbie Stailey,** Director of Composition Services

Contents at a Glance

Table of Contents

Introduction

· ·

*W*elcome to *Personal Development All-in-One For Dummies*, your launch pad to understanding the basics of the key techniques and therapies available for personal development.

As a human (we're assuming you're not a cat if you're reading this book), at some stage in your life you're likely to experience some sort of emotional problem that you'd like to surmount and you're interested in arming yourself with the techniques to help you tackle those problems. Perhaps you're tired or fed-up with the way some things are for you now and want to find interesting and useful information to enhance your life. If so, this book is a great starting point.

About This Book

If you're embarking on a journey of self-help or self-improvement, this book provides an introduction to the most popular and widely used techniques for personal development by:

- ✔ Focussing on how to use the techniques yourself.

- ✔ Providing practical exercises for you to try out.

- ✔ Outlining different methods of approaching your particular goal or problem.

The techniques described in this book are applicable for all aspects of mental health – from positive thinking and goal setting, to tackling specific psychological problems such as anxiety and addiction.

You can read further details in other *For Dummies* books or see a practitioner if any of the methods in particular take your fancy. If you've read all there is to read in this book but still want more, check out the extra information in these *For Dummies* titles (all published by Wiley):

- ✔ *Cognitive Behavioural Therapy For Dummies* (Rob Willson and Rhena Branch)

- ✔ *Hypnotherapy For Dummies* (Mike Bryant and Peter Mabbutt)

> ✔ *Life Coaching For Dummies* (Jeni Mumford)
>
> ✔ *Neuro-linguistic Programming For Dummies* (Romilla Ready and Kate Burton)

Conventions Used in This Book

To make your reading experience easier and to alert you to key words or points, we use certain conventions in this book:

> ✔ *Italics* introduces new terms, and underscores key differences between words.
>
> ✔ **Bold** text is used to show the action part of bulleted and numbered lists.
>
> ✔ Case studies in the book are illustrative of actual clients we have treated and are not direct representations of any particular client.

What You're Not to Read

You can read this book cover to cover or skip through just reading the section that interest you the most. If you're not in the mood for games, you can skim read the sections accompanied by a 'Try This' icon (but maybe you'll revisit them a little later?). You can also glean plenty of information from this book without reading the sidebars (the grey boxes) – the detail in our sidebars is interesting but not crucial to understanding the rest of the book's content.

Foolish Assumptions

In writing this book we've made a couple of assumptions about you:

> ✔ You have a general interest in self-improvement and personal development techniques.
>
> ✔ You're looking for ways to become more the sort of person you'd like to be and you're looking for inspiration and practical guidance on how to take your living experience to new levels of achievement, happiness, and success.

✔ You've heard about a particular technique, or have had a technique suggested to you by an advisor, friend, doctor, or mental health professional as a possible treatment for your specific difficulties.

How This Book Is Organized

We've divided *Personal Development All-in-One For Dummies* into five separate books. This section explains what you'll find in each of these books. Each book is broken into chapters tackling key aspects and skills. The table of contents gives you more detail of what's in each chapter, and we've even included a cartoon at the start of each part, just to keep you happy.

Book 1: Essential Concepts of Personal Development

This book is an introduction to the four core methods included in Books II – V. The chapters within walk you through the basics of each aspect of personal development, guiding you through definitions and exploring the main skill sets and applications of each. If you're new to personal development, this book will help you decide which area to focus on first.

Book II: Neuro-linguistic Programming

By showing you how to monitor and adapt your thinking, Neuro-linguistic Programming (NLP) can help you break free from negative thoughts and cultivate more useful inner beliefs about yourself and your world. Neuro-linguistic Programming is a common sense system of everyday psychology that has enhanced millions of lives.

Book III: Cognitive Behavioural Therapy

Whether you're trying to fight anxiety and depression, beat addiction, or simply lose weight, the key to success is learning how to think differently. Cognitive behavioural therapy (CBT) is a practical, sensible, and effective approach to help you master your thoughts and think constructively.

Book IV: Hypnotherapy

If you think hypnosis is just for stage tricks and party games, think again; this book explains how hypnotherapy works and shows you how to use it to treat a wide range of problems. Whether you're seeking to overcome anxiety or depression, improve performance, lose weight, or beat an addiction, hypnotherapy can help you make the positive changes you need to achieve your goals.

Book V: Life Coaching

Life coaching uses a range of practical, effective, and purposeful techniques to help you challenge negative beliefs, find answers to your own questions, and create the life that you want. Whether you're looking to make a change, or simply achieve more balance in your life, this book explains what to expect from life coaching and shows you how to develop your own coaching techniques – enabling you to establish an action plan, stay focused, and be inspired to achieve what you want, in all aspects of life.

Appendix

The appendix presents you with blank forms to use alongside five of the exercises outlined in the text. Flicking through to the appendix, you'll see that each form comes with a reference to the relevant book and chapter to use it with.

Icons Used in This Book

When you flick through this book, you'll notice little icons in the margins. These icons pick out certain key aspects of personal development:

This icon highlights practical advice to get our personal development methods working for you.

This icon is a friendly reminder of important points to take note of.

This icon highlights personal development terminology that may sound like a foreign language but which has a precise meaning in the personal development world.

This icon suggests ideas and activities to enable you to practice personal development techniques, and give you more food for thought.

This icon marks things to avoid in your enthusiasm when trying out personal development skills.

Where to Go from Here

If you're most interested in life coaching (for example), head straight over to Book V, or if Neuro-linguistic Programming appeals, check out Book II. However, if you're not sure which type of help you're most interested in, or just fancy an overview of the entire subject, turn the next page and get stuck into Book I, explaining the basics of each form of personal development.

Good luck to you, and we wish you the best in finding the answers you're looking for.

Book I
Essential Concepts of Personal Development

"Very good answer! Now let me ask you another question..."

In this part . . .

This book explains the basic concepts behind Neuro-linguistic Programming, cognitive behavioural therapy, hypnotherapy, and life coaching – in short, it's a handy introduction to the rest of this title's content. If you're not sure what the difference is between them, this is the place to start; and if you're well aware of the differences between these disciplines, take a look at the chapters in this book to see how they interact or approach problems from different directions.

Here are the contents of Book I at a glance:

Chapter 1

Exploring the Key Themes of NLP

. . . .

. . . .

*I*ncreasingly, you will hear the subject of Neuro-linguistic Programming (NLP) mentioned as you go about your daily life – in corporations, colleges, and coffee shops. We wrote this book because our experience of NLP transformed our lives. We wanted to ignite the spark of curiosity in you about what is possible in NLP and with NLP. We also believed it was time for NLP to come away from academic- and business-speak to real-life plain English for all our friends out there. By friends we mean everyone and anyone, especially you the reader.

NLP has grown in popularity because it offers 'aha' moments. It simply makes sense. Yet the name itself ('Neuro' relates to what's happening in our minds, 'Linguistic' refers to language and how we use it, while 'Programming' tackles the persistent patterns of behaviour that we learn and then repeat) and the jargon associated with it present a barrier to the average person. Some describe NLP as 'the study of the structure of subjective experience'; others call it 'the art and science of communication'. We prefer to say that NLP enables you to understand what makes you tick; how you think, how you feel, how you make sense of everyday life in the world around you. Armed with this understanding, your whole life – work and play – can become magical.

In any communication between two people, or in this case, between man and beast, there's always more than one perspective. Sometimes we just can't grasp that because we can't see the way forward.

NLP is one of the most sophisticated and effective methodologies currently available to help you do just that. It centres on communication and change. These days we all need the skills to develop personal flexibility to the extreme. Tricks and gimmicks are not enough: we need to get real.

So welcome to the start of the journey and in this chapter you'll get a quick taster of the key themes of NLP.

What is NLP?

We're all born with the same basic neurology. Our ability to do anything in life, whether it's swimming the length of a pool, cooking a meal, or reading this book, depends on how we control our nervous system. So, much of NLP is devoted to learning how to think more effectively and communicate more effectively with yourself and others.

- ✔ **Neuro** is about your neurological system. NLP is based on the idea that we experience the world through our senses and translate sensory information into thought processes, both conscious and unconscious. Thought processes activate the neurological system, which affects physiology, emotions, and behaviour.

- ✔ **Linguistic** refers to the way human beings use language to make sense of the world, capture and conceptualise experience, and communicate that experience to others. In NLP, linguistics is the study of how the words you speak influence your experience.

- ✔ **Programming** draws heavily from learning theory and addresses how we code or mentally represent experience. Your personal programming consists of your internal processes and strategies (thinking patterns) that you use to make decisions, solve problems, learn, evaluate, and get results. NLP shows people how to recode their experiences and organise their internal programming so they can get the outcomes they want.

To see this process in action, begin to notice how you think. Just imagine that it's a hot summer's day. You go home at the end of the day and stand in your kitchen holding a lemon you have taken from the fridge. Look at the outside of it, its yellow waxy skin with green marks at the ends. Feel how cold it is in your hand. Raise it to your nose and smell it. Mmmm. Press it gently and notice the weight of the lemon in the palm of your hand. Now take a knife and cut it in half. Hear the juices start to run and notice the smell is stronger now. Bite deeply into the lemon and allow the juice to swirl around in your mouth.

Words. Simple words have the power to trigger your saliva glands. Hear one word 'lemon' and your brain kicks into action. The words you read told your brain that you had a lemon in your hand. We may think that words only describe meanings: they actually create your reality. You'll learn much more about this as we travel together.

A few quick definitions

NLP can be described in various ways. The formal definition is that it is 'the study of the structure of our subjective experience.' Here are a few more ways of answering the $64,000 question: 'What is NLP?'

- ✔ The art and science of communication
- ✔ The key to learning
- ✔ It's about what makes you and other people tick
- ✔ It's the route to get the results you want in all areas of your life
- ✔ Influencing others with integrity
- ✔ A manual for your brain
- ✔ The secret of successful people
- ✔ The way to creating your own future
- ✔ NLP helps people make sense of their reality
- ✔ The toolkit for personal and organisational change

Where it all started and where it's going

NLP began in California in the early 1970s at the University of Santa Cruz. There, Richard Bandler, a master's level student of information sciences and mathematics, enlisted the help of Dr John Grinder, a professor of linguistics, to study people they considered to be excellent communicators and agents of change. They were fascinated by how some people defied the odds to get through to 'difficult' or very ill people where others failed miserably to connect.

So NLP has its roots in a therapeutic setting thanks to three world-renowned psychotherapists that Bandler and Grinder studied: Virginia Satir (developer of Conjoint Family Therapy), Fritz Perls (the founder of Gestalt Psychology), and Milton H Erickson (largely responsible for the advancement of Clinical Hypnotherapy).

In their work, Bandler and Grinder also drew upon the skills of linguists Alfred Korzybski and Noam Chomsky, social anthropologist Gregory Bateson, and psychoanalyst Paul Watzlawick.

From those days, the field of NLP has exploded to encompass many disciplines in many countries around the world. It would be impossible for us to name all the great teachers and practitioners in NLP today.

So what's next for NLP? It's certainly travelled a long way from Santa Cruz in the 1970s. So many more pioneers have picked up the story and taken it forward – made it practical and helped transform the lives of real people like you and me. The literature on NLP is prolific. Today you'll find NLP applications amongst doctors and nurses, taxi drivers, sales people, coaches and accountants, teachers and animal trainers, parents, workers, retired people and teenagers alike.

Each generation will take the ideas that resonate in their field of interest, sift and refine them, chipping in their own experiences. If NLP encourages new thinking and new choices and acknowledges the positive intention underlying all action, all we can say is the future is bright with possibilities. The rest is up to you.

The Pillars of NLP: Straight up and Straightforward

The first thing to understand is that NLP is about four things, known as the pillars of NLP (see Figure 1-1). These four chunks of the subject are explained in the following sections.

- ✔ **Rapport:** How you build a relationship with others and with yourself is probably the most important gift that NLP gives most readers. Given the pace at which most of us live and work, one big lesson in rapport is how you can say 'no' to all the requests for your time and still retain friendships or professional relationships.

- ✔ **Sensory awareness:** Have you noticed how when you walk in someone else's home the colours, sounds, and smells are subtly different to yours? Or that colleague looks worried when they talk about their job. Maybe you notice the colour of a night sky or the fresh green leaves as spring unfolds. Like the famous detective Sherlock Holmes you will begin to notice how your world is so much richer when you pay attention with all the senses you have.

- ✔ **Outcome thinking:** You'll hear the word 'outcome' mentioned throughout this book. What this means is beginning to think about what it is you want rather than getting stuck in a negative problem mode. The principles of an outcome approach can help you make the best decisions and choices – whether it's about what you're going to do at the week-end, running an important project, or finding out the true purpose of your life.

✔ **Behavioural flexibility:** This means how to do something different when what you are currently doing is not working. Being flexible is key to prac-tising NLP; you'll find tools and ideas for this in every chapter. We'll help you find fresh perspectives and build these into your repertoire.

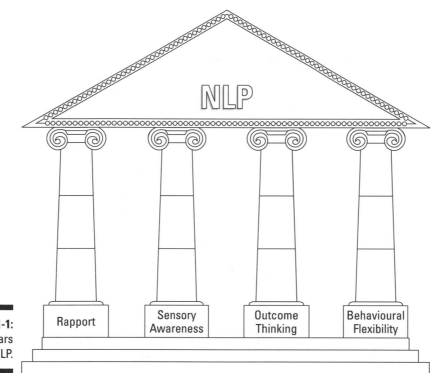

Figure 1-1:
The Pillars
of NLP.

Let's just give an example here of what this might mean every day. Suppose you have ordered some goods by mail. It could be a software package to store all your names, addresses, and phone number of friends or clients. You load it on your computer, use it a few times, and then mysteriously it stops working. There's a bug in the system, but you've already invested many hours in the installation and entering all your contacts. You phone up the supplier and the customer service people are unhelpful to the point of rudeness.

You need to bring out all your skills in building *rapport* with the customer service manager before anyone will listen to your complaint. You'll need to *engage your senses* – particularly your ears as you listen carefully to what the supplier is saying, and notice how to control your feelings and decide on your best response. You will need to be very clear about your *outcome* – what do you want to happen after you make your complaint? For example, do you want a full refund or replacement software? And finally you may need to be *flexible in your behaviour* and consider different options if you don't achieve what you want the first time.

Models and Modelling

Neuro-linguistic Programming (NLP) began as a model of how we communicate to ourselves and others and was developed by Bandler and Grinder based on their study of great communicators. So NLP says a lot about models and modelling.

NLP works by modelling excellence in every field. The premise begins like this: If you can find someone who's good at something, then you can model how they do that and learn from them. This means that you can learn to model whoever you admire – top business leaders or sports personalities, the waiter at your favourite restaurant, or your hugely energetic aerobics teacher.

NLP does not change the world – it simply helps you change the way that you observe/perceive your world. NLP helps you build a different map that helps you to be more effective.

Modelling excellence is another theme you'll hear discussed. The NLP approach is that anything somebody else can do is learnable if you break the learning into small enough component parts. It's an empowering perspective and also an encouragement to convert large overwhelming projects into lots of small ones – like eating an elephant.

NLP Presuppositions

NLP presuppositions are no more than generalisations about the world. In this chapter, we explain some of the presuppositions that we consider to be most influential out of several that have been developed by the founders of NLP and offer them for your consideration.

The map is not the territory

One of the first presuppositions is that *the map is not the territory*. This statement was published in 'Science and Sanity' in 1933 by Korzybski, a Polish count and mathematician. Korzybski was referring to the fact that you experience the world through your senses (sight, hearing, touch, smell, and taste) – the territory. You then take this external phenomenon and make an internal representation of it within your brain – the map.

This internal map you create of the external world, shaped by your perceptions, is never an exact replica. In other words, what is outside can never be the same as what is inside your brain.

Take one analogy; as I (Romilla) sit in my conservatory, writing, I am looking out at the oak tree in the garden. The representation that I make of it, when I close my eyes, is completely different from the actual tree in the garden. Not being a botanist I may not notice features a botanist would observe. Just because I cannot see those features, and therefore they do not exist in my internal representation, does not mean they do not actually exist. Or try another analogy; if you were driving in London, with your London street map, the 'roads' shown in the map book are completely different to the roads you are actually driving along; for a start the tube stations you drive past are in three dimensions and colour, whereas they are shown as a blue circle with a red line through it on the map.

Your senses bombard you with 2,000,000 bits of information per second but your conscious mind can only deal with between five and nine pieces of information at any given moment so there is an awful lot of information that is filtered out. This filtration process is influenced by your values and beliefs, memories, decisions, experiences, and your cultural and social background to allow in only what your filters are tuned in to receive.

People respond according to their map of the world

You respond according to the map of the world you hold in your head. The map is based on what you believe about your identity and on your values and beliefs as well as your attitudes, memories, and cultural background.

Sometimes the map of the world someone operates from may not make sense to you. However a little understanding and tolerance could help enrich your life.

There is no failure, only feedback

This is a very powerful assumption to live your life by. Everyone makes mistakes and experiences setbacks. You have a choice between allowing yourself to be waylaid by your undesirable results or learning the lessons that have presented themselves, dust yourself off and have another shot at jumping the hurdle.

When you're faced with 'failure', you can use this NLP presupposition to find the opportunities for growth by asking yourself the following questions.

Think of something you 'failed' at and ask yourself:

- ✔ What am I aiming to achieve?
- ✔ What have I achieved so far?
- ✔ What feedback have I had?
- ✔ What lessons have I learned?
- ✔ How can I put the lessons to positive use?
- ✔ How will I measure my success?
- ✔ Then pick yourself up and have another go!

The meaning of the communication is the response it elicits

No matter how honourable the intentions of your communications, the success of the interaction depends on how the message is received by the listener not by what you intended. In other words, the meaning of the communication is the response it elicits.

This is yet another very powerful assumption about communication. It places the onus of responsibility to get your message across squarely at your door. Once you adopt this presupposition you are no longer able to blame the other person for any misunderstandings. If the response you get is not what you expected then you, as a student of NLP, will have the tools to use your senses to realise that the other person is missing the point. You will also have the flexibility to do things differently, through your behaviour and your words.

If what you are doing is not working, do something different

So simple and yet you don't always modify your behaviour. After all, it's a lot easier wandering through life wishing change on other people and . . . you can enjoy all the angst you get from thinking those horrible thoughts about someone else. (We're being facetious.)

You cannot not communicate

Have you ever smiled at someone, said something really polite but been thinking, 'Oh! Just drop dead'? No? Just as well, because we, the authors, would bet the way you held your body or gritted your teeth wouldn't have fooled anyone. We are sure that if the person on the receiving end of the message has learned NLP, or has even some sensory acuity, they would detect the lack of warmth in your eyes, the grimace in your smile, or the snarl in your voice. So even though you don't say 'Drop dead', you're still communicating that message.

This is also shown in a fascinating study, pioneered by Professor Albert Mehrabi, established that, when talking about feelings and attitudes, what you say has a very small impact compared to the tone you use and how you hold your body. The influences, in percentage terms, were as follows:

- Verbal 7%
- Tonality 38%
- Physiology 55%

Individuals have all the resources they need to achieve their desired outcomes

We love this one! It's so positive. What this phrase means is that everyone has the potential to develop and grow. The important point to make here is you may not have *all* the internal resources you need but that you do have the internal resources to acquire new internal and external resources.

The mind and body are interlinked and affect each other

Holistic medicine works on the premise that the mind affects the body and the body affects the mind. In order to maintain a healthy human being a medical practitioner has to do more than just suppress the symptoms. She has to examine the mind and body and treat both together.

Recent research has shown just how integrated the mind-body connection is. Neurotransmitters are chemicals that transmit impulses along your nerves. They are the means by which your brain communicates with the rest of your body. Each thought you think reaches out to the farthest, miniscule cell in your body via neurotransmitters. Further research has discovered that the same neurotransmitters that are found in the brain can also be produced by your internal organs. So the idea that messages are initiated and transmitted in straight lines along the neurons is no longer true; these messages can be initiated and transmitted by your organs too. Dr Pert, of the National Institute of Mental Health, refers to the 'bodymind' – the mind and body working as an integrated whole, because at the level of the neurotransmitter there is no separation between the mind and the body.

Final words on presuppositions

One great way to increase your understanding of NLP is to explore your basic assumptions, or presuppositions, about life. Whatever you currently think about different people and problems, how you communicate and what's important, sometimes it helps to take a new perspective. This may trigger some new action or behaviour.

Remember: There is no correct answer. As you get a flavour for each of the presuppositions, consider them carefully. You don't have to agree with every one of them. You can simply try them on for size and see, hear, and feel what that does.

Chapter 2

Understanding Cognitive Behavioural Therapy

*C*ognitive behavioural therapy, or CBT, is growing in popularity as an efficient and long-lasting treatment for many different types of psychological problem. If the word 'psychological' sends you running from the room screaming, try to consider the term referring to problems that affect your emotional rather than your physical sense of wellbeing. At some point in your life, something's going to go a bit wrong with your body. So why on earth do humans assume that their minds and emotions should be above the odd hiccup, upset, or even more serious difficulty?

This book gives you a comprehensive introduction to the theory and application of CBT techniques. Although we don't have the space to go into nitty-gritty specifics about how to use CBT to overcome every type of emotional or psychological problem, we do try to lead you in a helpful direction. We believe all the CBT principles and strategies outlined in this book can improve your life and help you to stay healthy, regardless of whether you've worked with or are currently working with a psychiatrist or other psychological professional.

In addition, whether you think your problems are minimal, you're living the life of Riley, you feel mildly depressed, or you've had years of uncomfortable psychological symptoms, CBT can help you. We ask you to be open-minded and to use the stuff in this book to make your life better and fuller.

Cognitive behavioural therapy – more commonly referred to as *CBT* – focuses on the way people think and act to help them with their emotional and behavioural problems.

Many of the effective CBT practices we discuss in this book should seem like everyday good sense. In our opinion, CBT does have some very straightforward and clear principles and is a largely sensible and practical approach to helping people overcome problems. However, human beings don't always act according to sensible principles, and most people find that simple solutions can be very difficult to put into practice sometimes. CBT can maximise on your common sense and help you to do the healthy things that you may sometimes do naturally and unthinkingly in a deliberate and self-enhancing way on a regular basis.

In this chapter we take you through the basic principles of CBT and show you how to use these principles to better understand yourself and your problems.

Defining CBT

Cognitive behavioural therapy is a school of *psychotherapy* that aims to help people overcome their emotional problems.

- ✔ **Cognitive** means mental processes like thinking. The word 'cognitive' refers to everything that goes on in your mind including dreams, memories, images, thoughts, and attention.

- ✔ **Behaviour** refers to everything that you do. This includes what you say, how you try to solve problems, how you act, and avoidance. Behaviour refers to both action and inaction, for example biting your tongue instead of speaking your mind is still a behaviour even though you are trying *not* to do something.

- ✔ **Therapy** is a word used to describe a systematic approach to combating a problem, illness, or irregular condition.

A central concept in CBT is that *you feel the way you think*. Therefore, CBT works on the principle that you can live more happily and productively if you're thinking in healthy ways. This principle is a very simple way of summing up CBT, and we have many more details to share with you later in the book.

Combining science, philosophy, and behaviour

CBT is a powerful treatment because it combines scientific, philosophical, and behavioural aspects into one comprehensive approach to understanding and overcoming common psychological problems.

- ✔ **Getting scientific.** CBT is scientific not only in the sense that it has been tested and developed through numerous scientific studies, but also in the sense that it encourages clients to become more like scientists. For example, during CBT, you may develop the ability to treat your thoughts as theories and hunches about reality to be tested (what scientists call *hypotheses*), rather than as facts.

- ✔ **Getting philosophical.** CBT recognises that people hold values and beliefs about themselves, the world, and other people. One of the aims of CBT is to help people develop flexible, non-extreme, and self-helping beliefs that help them adapt to reality and pursue their goals.

  Your problems are not all just in your mind. Although CBT places great emphasis on thoughts and behaviour as powerful areas to target for change and development, it also places your thoughts and behaviours within a *context*. CBT recognises that you're influenced by what's going on around you and that your *environment* makes a contribution towards the way you think, feel, and act. However, CBT maintains that you can make a difference to the way you feel by changing unhelpful ways of thinking and behaving - even if you can't change your environment. Incidentally, your environment in the context of CBT includes other people and the way they behave towards you.

- ✔ **Getting active.** As the name suggests, CBT also strongly emphasises behaviour. Many CBT techniques involve changing the way you think and feel by modifying the way you behave. Examples include gradually becoming more active if you're depressed and lethargic, or facing your fears step by step if you're anxious. CBT also places emphasis on *mental behaviours*, such as worrying and where you focus your attention.

Progressing from problems to goals

A defining characteristic of CBT is that it gives you the tools to develop a *focused* approach. CBT aims to help you move from defined emotional and behavioural problems towards your goals of how you'd like to feel and behave. Thus, CBT is a goal-directed, systematic, problem-solving approach to emotional problems.

Making the Thought–Feeling Link

Like many people, you may assume that if something happens to you, the event *makes* you feel a certain way. For example, if your partner treats you inconsiderately, you may conclude that she *makes* you angry. You may further deduce that their inconsiderate behaviour *makes* you behave in a particular manner, such as sulking or refusing to speak to her for hours (possibly even days; people can sulk for a very long time!).

CBT encourages you to understand that your thinking or *beliefs* lie between the event and your ultimate feelings and actions. Your thoughts, beliefs, and the meanings that you give to an event, produce your emotional and behavioural responses.

So in CBT terms, your partner does not *make* you angry and sulky. Rather, your partner behaves inconsiderately, and you assign a meaning to her behaviour such as 'she's doing this deliberately to upset me!' thus *making yourself* angry and sulky.

Emphasising the meanings you attach to events

The *meaning* you attach to any sort of event influences the emotional responses you have to that event. Positive events normally lead to positive feelings of happiness or excitement, whereas negative events typically lead to negative feelings like sadness or anxiety.

However, the meanings you attach to certain types of negative events may not be wholly accurate, realistic, or helpful. Sometimes, your thinking may lead you to assign extreme meanings to events, leaving you feeling disturbed.

Psychologists use the word 'disturbed' to describe emotional responses that are unhelpful and cause significant discomfort to you. In CBT terminology, 'disturbed' means that an emotional or behavioural response is hindering rather than helping you to adapt and cope with a negative event.

For example, if a potential girlfriend rejects you after the first date (event), you may think 'This proves I'm unlikeable and undesirable' (meaning) and feel depressed (emotion).

CBT involves identifying thoughts, beliefs, and meanings that are activated when you're feeling emotionally disturbed. If you assign less extreme, more helpful, more *accurate* meanings to negative events, you are likely to experience less extreme, less disturbing emotional and behavioural responses.

Thus, on being rejected after the first date (event), you could think 'I guess that person didn't like me that much; oh well – they're not the one for me' (meaning), and feel disappointment (emotion).

Acting out

The ways you think and feel also largely determine the way you *act*. If you feel depressed, you're likely to withdraw and isolate yourself. If you're anxious, you may avoid situations that you find threatening or dangerous. Your behaviours can be problematic for you in many ways, such as the following:

- ✔ **Self-destructive behaviours,** such as excessive drinking or using drugs to quell anxiety, can cause direct physical harm.

- ✔ **Isolating and mood-depressing behaviours,** such as staying in bed all day or not seeing your friends, increase your sense of isolation and maintain your low mood.

- ✔ **Avoidance behaviours,** such as avoiding situations you perceive as threatening (attending a social outing, using a lift, speaking in public), deprive you of the opportunity to confront and overcome your fears.

Learning Your ABCs

When you start to get an understanding of your emotional difficulties, CBT encourages you to break down a specific problem you have using the *ABC format*, in which:

- ✔ **A** is the *activating event*. An activating event means a real *external* event that has occurred, a future event that you anticipate occurring, or an *internal* event in your mind, such as an image, memory, or dream.

  The 'A' is often referred to as your 'trigger'.

- ✔ **B** is your *beliefs*. Your beliefs include your thoughts, your personal rules, the demands you make (on yourself, the world, and other people), and the meanings that you attach to external and internal events.

- ✔ **C** is the *consequences*. Consequences include your emotions, behaviours, and physical sensations that accompany different emotions.

Figure 2-1 shows the ABC parts of a problem in picture form.

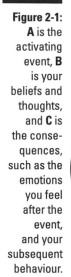

Figure 2-1:
A is the activating event, **B** is your beliefs and thoughts, and **C** is the consequences, such as the emotions you feel after the event, and your subsequent behaviour.

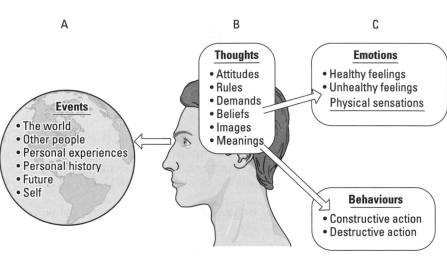

Writing down your problem in *ABC form* – a central CBT technique – helps you differentiate between your thoughts, feelings, and behaviours, and the *trigger* event. We give more information about the ABC form in Chapter 3, and you can find a blank ABC form at the back of the book.

Consider the ABC formulations of two common emotional problems, anxiety and depression. The ABC of anxiety may look like this:

- ✔ **A:** You imagine failing a job interview.
- ✔ **B:** You believe: 'I've got to make sure that I don't mess up this interview, otherwise I'll prove that I'm a failure.'
- ✔ **C:** You experience anxiety (emotion), butterflies in your stomach (physical sensation), and drinking to calm your nerves (behaviour).

The ABC of depression may look like this:

- ✔ **A:** You fail a job interview.
- ✔ **B:** You believe: 'I should've done better. This means that I'm a failure!'
- ✔ **C:** You experience depression (emotion), loss of appetite (physical sensation), and staying in bed and avoiding the outside world (behaviour).

You can use these examples to guide you when you are filling in an ABC form on your own problems. Doing so will help ensure that you record the actual facts of the event under 'A', your thoughts about the event under 'B', and how you feel and act under 'C'. Developing a really clear ABC of your problem can make it much easier for you to realise how your thoughts at 'B' lead to your emotional/behavioural responses at 'C'.

Characterising CBT

We give a much fuller description of the principles and practical applications of CBT in the rest of this book. However, here's a quick reference list of key characteristics of CBT. CBT:

- Emphasises the role of the personal meanings that you give to events in determining your emotional responses.

- Was developed through extensive scientific evaluation.

- Focuses more on how your problems are being *maintained* rather than on searching for a single root cause of the problem.

- Offers practical advice and tools for overcoming common emotional problems.

- Holds the view that you can change and develop by thinking things through and by trying out new ideas and strategies.

- Can address material from your past if doing so can help you to understand and change the way you're thinking and acting now.

- Shows you that some of the strategies you're using to cope with your emotional problems are actually maintaining those problems.

- Strives to normalise your emotions, physical sensations, and thoughts rather than to persuade you that they're clues to 'hidden' problems.

- Recognises that you may develop emotional problems *about* your emotional problems, for example feeling ashamed about being depressed.

- Highlights learning techniques and maximises self-help so that ultimately you can become your own therapist.

Getting complicated

Sticking to the simple ABC formulation in which A+B=C can serve you well. But if that seems a little simplistic, you can consider the more complicated formulations shown here:

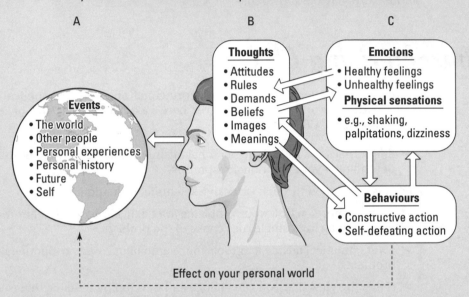

A

B

C

Thoughts
- Attitudes
- Rules
- Demands
- Beliefs
- Images
- Meanings

Emotions
- Healthy feelings
- Unhealthy feelings

Physical sensations
- e.g., shaking, palpitations, dizziness

Events
- The world
- Other people
- Personal experiences
- Personal history
- Future
- Self

Behaviours
- Constructive action
- Self-defeating action

Effect on your personal world

This diagram shows the complex interaction between your thoughts, feelings, and behaviours. Although your thoughts affect how you feel, your feelings also affect your thinking. So, if you're having depressed thoughts, your mood is likely to be low. The lower your mood, the more likely you are to act in a depressed manner and to think pessimistically. The combination of feeling depressed, thinking pessimistically, and acting in a depressed manner can, ultimately, influence the way you see your personal world. You may focus on negative events in your life and the world in general and therefore accumulate more negative As. This interaction between A, B, and C can become a vicious circle.

CBT pays a lot of attention to changing both unhealthy thinking patterns and unhealthy patterns of behaviour.

Chapter 3

Examining Hypnotherapy

*H*ypnosis is a subject everyone has an opinion about, but few people have ever directly experienced. Hypnotherapy, on the other hand, is a topic that leaves many people baffled or completely blank. So what exactly *is* the difference between hypnosis and hypnotherapy? That's one of questions this book answers.

An important point to understand is that hypnosis and hypnotherapy are not the same thing. Hypnosis has been around since humans began to speak and involves going into a trance. Hypnotherapy uses the hypnotic trance to help you achieve a goal, or create a positive change in your thinking, to help solve a problem. Whereas hypnosis is centuries old, hypnotherapy, like other talking therapies, is a relatively recent practice.

This book helps you understand how hypnosis works. It also discusses the various problems and symptoms hypnotherapy can effectively treat, and shows you how you can put hypnotherapy to use for you.

Understanding the Terms

Hypnosis is a powerful technique. It can help you change negative beliefs and achieve your goals, treat serious emotional problems, and alleviate a range of medical conditions.

You may hear about a work colleague who was cured of smoking in a single session, or a friend of a friend whose lifelong phobia was permanently removed by a hypnotherapist. A hypnotherapist can also show you how to practise self-hypnosis in order to achieve a seemingly infinite variety of personal goals.

This section explains what hypnosis and hypnotherapy are about. It gives you a clear understanding of what is involved, the difference between hypnosis and hypnotherapy, and some of the amazing benefits possible.

Getting to grips with the basics of hypnotherapy

First things first. We want to reassure you right up front that hypnosis is safe.

Being hypnotised is not dissimilar to being sleepy or in a daydream. And, as we explain in the 'Sliding into trance' subsection, you've been in a trance probably every day of your life; hypnotherapy is simply a method of putting your trance state to work solving your problems.

When you're in a hypnotic trance, you are completely aware of the words being spoken to you by the hypnotherapist. And, should a fire alarm go off – or any other physically threatening situation arise – you will immediately take yourself out of trance to respond.

Hypnosis carries an element of risk as do all therapies and activities. But, as long as your hypnotherapist is properly qualified, and operates within a professional code of conduct and ethics, you needn't worry.

In the following subsections, we sort out the jargon and the basic terms used in hypnotherapy.

Discovering the differences between hypnosis and hypnotherapy

The first useful thing to distinguish is the difference between hypnosis and hypnotherapy. We really want you to understand that there is a big difference between the act of hypnotising someone (hypnosis) and the amazing changes that can happen with the help of a qualified hypnotherapist (hypnotherapy). We hope that after you read this section you will never confuse a stage hypnotist (the person you see getting laughs on TV) with a hypnotherapist (the person who helps you stop smoking, lose weight, or recover from a life-long phobia).

Stage hypnosis is not hypnotherapy

Stage hypnosis is a form of entertainment. It is not a way to receive help for your problems or to achieve your aspirations. We do not recommend that you become personally involved in stage hypnosis as there is no personal care for your individual needs. It's a stage act where the main aim is to get laughs – at your expense if you get on stage!

Many, many people get involved in stage hypnosis with no bad after-effects. However, some former stage participants have suffered emotional problems afterwards. This is an area of great debate as to whether these people were already predisposed to emotional problems, or if stage hypnosis had a negative influence.

An interesting book that involves a critical look at stage hypnosis is *Investigating Stage Hypnosis* by Tracie O'Keefe and Katrina Fox (Extraordinary People Press).

- ✔ **Hypnosis** is a state of mind connected to deep relaxation, narrowed focus, and increased suggestibility. Hypnosis is an intermediate state between sleep and wakefulness.

  Hypnosis can be likened to the state you are in when you act intuitively instead of intellectually. During hypnosis, you basically ask your inner drill sergeant to take a break while your clever, artistic self comes forward. And believe us, everybody has both aspects within them!

- ✔ **Hypnotherapy** is hypnosis used for therapeutic purposes. Hypnotherapy applies the technique of hypnosis to encourage your unconscious mind to find solutions to problems.

Hypnosis is a state of consciousness. Hypnotherapy is a therapy. Hypnosis itself is not therapy. The therapy part of a hypnotherapy session occurs after hypnosis has been used to induce your trance. Then the hypnotherapist makes suggestions that help your unconscious mind achieve your goals or remove your problems. Just as there are many avenues to hypnosis, including self-hypnosis and self-induced trances (see the next section), there are many different hypnotherapy techniques and applications.

Sliding into trance

Trance is a state of mind that involves a selective focus of attention. You are in a natural trance state several times each day, usually when you're relaxing.

Examples of times you may slip into a trance include:

- ✔ Being fully involved in reading a book
- ✔ Going window shopping at your favourite stores
- ✔ Becoming anxious or fearful about an upcoming event
- ✔ Playing with an imaginary friend as a child
- ✔ Zoning out while exercising
- ✔ Fantasising about an old love interest

Trance states occur naturally and regularly. Hypnosis utilises these states to access your unconscious mind (see the next section) in order to help you more easily achieve your goal or solve your problem.

The following are the main trance states, and some of the traits a hypnotised person may experience while in each state, listed from light to deep levels:

- ✔ **Light trance:** Eyes closed, relaxed face muscles, deepened breathing.
- ✔ **Medium trance:** Head and body slump, reduced awareness of surroundings, slower responses, deepening of light trance state.
- ✔ **Deep trance:** Deepening of medium trance state, deeper abdominal breathing.
- ✔ **Somnambulism:** A very rare trance state in which a hypnotised person may experience sensations as if awake. Commonly known as sleepwalking, this is a very rare condition. This state is counterproductive in hypnosis because the person is in too deep a state to retain the hypnotherapy suggestions in either their conscious or unconscious memory!

At increasingly deeper levels of trance, you become more open to your unconscious mind and more receptive to hypnotic suggestions from the hypnotherapist. We discuss the importance of these therapeutic hypnotic suggestions throughout this book.

Examining states of mind

Conscious and unconscious are terms that describe aspects of your mind. Though impossible to prove as a reality, these concepts are widely accepted in the Western world. The *conscious* mind thinks quantitatively using words, numbers, and logical and sequential thinking. The *unconscious* mind, on the other hand, uses images, memories, feelings, intuition, dreams, and abstract, non-sequential thinking.

If you think of your mind as a spectrum, at one end of the spectrum is the super-alert state you're in when you're frightened or excited. At the other end of the spectrum is deep sleep. Figure 3-1 shows the spectrum of consciousness, from the unconscious to conscious states. In the middle of this consciousness spectrum is everyday alert states of mind, in which you're relatively focused on what you are doing. The left of this point, towards the unconscious end, represents an everyday trance state, such as daydreaming.

Interestingly, the word 'hypnosis' comes from Hypnos, the Greek god of sleep. So perhaps the *extreme* left end of the spectrum would be coma, but we're trying to be uplifting here!

Book I

Essential Concepts of Personal Development

Figure 3-1: The spectrum of consciousness.

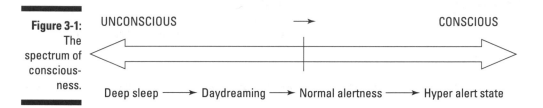

In this admittedly superficial model of human consciousness, the unconscious mind resides somewhere between daydreaming and deep sleep. Conversely, consciousness resides at all points to the right of the midway point.

No doubt this very simple model will have many scientists in dismay but, if nothing else, it should help you to understand one important thing: that consciousness and unconsciousness are two sides of the same coin. There isn't an either/or aspect to it, but only shades of grey.

Table 3-1 gives you another way to understand the differences between the conscious and unconscious mind.

Table 3-1	Traits of the Conscious and Unconscious Mind
Conscious Mind	*Unconscious Mind*
Logical	Intuitive
Sequential thoughts	Random thoughts
Easily accesses short-term and some long-term memories	Can access most lived memories and experiences since childhood
Uses words/numbers	Uses images/feelings
Analytical	Creative

So, although you may think that your conscious mind is in control most of the time, your hypnotherapist accesses your unconscious mind in order to help you to change your negative thinking, or solve your problems.

Why access the unconscious mind? Because, although your conscious mind is excellent at logical, sequential, and analytical thinking, it can also be quite fixed. Your conscious mind may also develop unhelpful defences in its attempt to protect itself. The unconscious mind is a more flexible friend, and can easily change old habits and defences maintained by your conscious mind.

Finding Help with Hypnosis

Hypnotherapy can help you cope with a wide range of issues, including:

- Increasing confidence
- Breaking bad habits such as smoking, nail-biting, bed-wetting, and so on
- Removing phobias
- Managing pain
- Enhancing performance in artistic, academic, and athletic fields
- Controlling weight and improving eating habits
- Correcting eating disorders
- Curtailing excessive alcohol use

Chapter 4

Introducing Life Coaching

In This Chapter

▶ Defining life coaching

▶ Finding your own happiness

▶ Coaching yourself through life

▶ Working out your current life priorities

*P*eople talk lots of hokum about life coaching. Life coaching television programmes, magazines, and newspaper columns range in quality from the powerful and inspirational through to the downright misleading and dangerous. True life coaching isn't about some guru telling you how you should live. Yes, you may be tempted to bask in the comfort of an 'expert' who can fix your life, your fashion sense, your body flaws, and your emotional angst. But these fixes are too often like an elegant sticking plaster. Changes don't last, unless a real change has come from deep within you. True life coaching enables you to call on your very own inner guru, any time, any place, with or without the support of another human being.

This chapter explains how coaching can work its magic for you and how it can help you manage the changes in your life, not just right now, but through all of the shifting priorities of your journey.

A Brief Definition of Life Coaching

Here's our definition of life coaching:

A purposeful conversation that inspires you to create the life you want.

You have conversations all the time (unless you're a hermit in a cave). Your conversations are either chit-chat to pass the time and get along with people, or purposeful talks where you clarify thought processes, resolve problems, reach agreements, and commit to actions.

Life coaching uses dialogue as well to move you along in the right direction. When you engage in a purposeful conversation with your coach – who is either a skilled professional, or simply that part of *you* that already *is* your coach – you cut through all the chit-chat and get to the root of everything. You may discuss the following topics, for example:

- ✔ Why you act in the way that you do.
- ✔ Which beliefs about yourself stop you from taking certain actions.
- ✔ What your options really are.
- ✔ How you can best go about getting the right results for you.
- ✔ How you can maintain your motivation.

Coaching conversations leave you refreshed, inspired, and ready for action.

Life coaching can help you form the questions that lead to answers that are right for you, which is a lot better than taking someone else's answers. Many books claim that they can guide you to The Magic Formula for Happiness, Success, and Fulfilment in life, but this book is a little different. Here, we guide you to the source of your *own* magic formula. The answers aren't 'out there' – you already have them all and life coaching shows you how and where to find them.

Living Your Ideal Life

John Lennon wrote, 'Life is what happens when you are making other plans.' I bet you often feel that you're so busy doing all the things you have to do that you never get a chance to enjoy the fruits of your labours – or simply 'be'.

Your happiness in life hinges on maintaining a delicate balance:

- ✔ ***Doing* the tasks and filling the roles you have to fulfil each day.** These tasks are things that maintain you and keep your life running smoothly, such as your job, shopping, mowing the lawn, and loading the dishwasher. The 'doing' category also includes the big things you do and achieve, such as running a marathon or honing a skill.

- ✔ *Having* **the things you enjoy in your life.** These 'things' may be material possessions, such as a house, a fancy car, or a pair of designer shoes. Or they can be intangibles like security, peace of mind, and love.

- ✔ *Being* **content and enjoying your experiences from all that you do and have.** 'Being' means having a sense of who you are – a feeling of being comfortable in your own skin. You often sense that you are 'simply being' in those quiet (and maybe rare) moments with yourself when you feel that you are the right person, in the right place, at just the right time.

When these three aspects of your life are in tune with each other, your life feels just right.

Life coaching doesn't turn your life into a super-charged roller-coaster of an experience – unless that's what you really want. It does help you to work out your unique gifts and your true priorities and it does support you in eliminating anything blocking you from doing, having, and being what you want. And life coaching provides that sprinkling of magic action dust that can transform your current life into something even better than your wildest dreams, because those dreams are rooted in your ideal reality.

Getting ready for change

Perhaps you picked this book off the shelf because you're totally fed up with where you are in your life. Or you may have a nagging feeling that more potential for happiness and fulfilment is out there for you. Obviously you're ready for change – after all, you don't want your life to stay exactly the same, so that means change, right?

The results you get from coaching depend to a large part on where you are in terms of readiness and willingness to change, and although you may feel that you want to change, you may not be quite ready to do so.

Most New Year's resolutions fail because the goals you set aren't always linked into your state of readiness. Unless you've done the work to seriously consider your options, and prepared the ground for action, your laudable resolution to lose 20 pounds, or give up smoking, or find the man/woman of your dreams is likely to lose momentum well before the end of January. If that's the case, nothing is wrong with you, you just haven't geared yourself up to sustain your promise to yourself.

Here are the stages you need to work through for any change to be effective:

1. **Drag yourself out of the Bogs of Denial.** If you bought this book you're probably not in denial about an aspect of your life that you want to change. Through coaching you may find that you're stubbornly resisting change in another aspect of your life. Denial is a tough phase, not least because its existence is hard to recognise in yourself. You need to look for the clues in your communication with other people. Do you get defensive when people say that you smoke or drink too much, or are working too hard? If you do, you may be in some state of denial. You can stay in denial just as long as it takes for you to see the need for change, but this book can help you get out of the bogs quicker.

2. **Take a good look around the Plateau of Contemplation.** After you climb out of the Bogs of Denial, you can't just rush into making changes; although many people do, if they get a sharp enough shock about the behaviour or thing that needs to change. Usually, you want to play around with the *idea* of change. You may start admitting, even if only to yourself, that perhaps you're a bit of a workaholic and promise yourself to address your work/life balance sometime sooner or later. You look around at your options and possible choices and you weigh up your desire to change against the things that are keeping you stuck. Reading this book can really help you take strides along the Plateau of Contemplation. After you communicate your intent to some trusted people, you're ready for the next stage.

3. **Assemble the Kit Bag of Preparation.** Consider your plan of action. How can you go about making changes in your life? What tools do you need? Who can support you? You don't need to stay too long at this stage – all planning and no action get a similar result to all action and no planning, and that's not the result you want! But the preparation needs to be right for you, whether that be emptying the house of all forms of chocolate temptation if you decide you want to lose weight, or drawing up a full-blown, all-singing, all-dancing project plan complete with bells and whistles. The coaching approach of exploring your options is invaluable here to ensure that you can check off the items you need for your change.

4. **Climb the Mountain of Action.** You're all prepared and you're ready to go! You're firing on all cylinders and you feel like an unstoppable force. You appreciate all the benefits of having worked through the first three stages now, because your strength, will, and resolve increase with every step towards your goal. Take note of what happens along the way, and expect a few sidesteps, too, in order to move forward.

5. **Claim the Flag of Consolidation.** Your life change only becomes embedded when you work out how to maintain it over time. Perhaps you'll fall back into an earlier stage of change (such as back into contemplation) from time to time – that's a normal part of consolidation. Think of this relapse as a way of fully integrating your changes into your life for the long term. Coaching is wonderful at maintaining and renewing your promise to yourself to change, not simply when doing so is easy.

Presenting the passport for your coaching journey

You already have everything you need to get started on the process of changing your life. The gifts that you may discover on your coaching journey are ones that you already have, although you may not yet recognise them. These gifts fall into three main areas:

- ✔ **You are unique and no one but you is so well equipped to create the life you want.** Consider what you need to live a whole and full life.

  You have to put yourself first, without being selfish, in order to be of service to anyone else.

- ✔ **You are infinitely resourceful.** You're capable of more than you usually achieve. Allow yourself to take control of your life, and you get even better results.

- ✔ **You have choices and freedom.** Even at times when you feel a little trapped by circumstances, you can take responsibility for your own attitude towards those barriers. You can trust your senses and tap into what helps you make the right choices in the future.

Tuning In to Your Inner Coach

You can move your life forward with the help of your very own inner coach. You may know this inner coach already, but we're guessing that you don't yet give it the respect it deserves. And the reason you don't is because you've spent far too long listening to the whining voice of your inner critic. Well, it's time to make a change and let your inner coach come out to play! You can start by understanding more about these two aspects of yourself.

Introducing your split personality!

Your inner critic loves to talk, warning you of all the terrible consequences of everything you do. Your inner critic speaks from your past, and selectively recalls only those things that went wrong – when you failed an exam, when you didn't get the date with the love of your life, and when you were made redundant. So your inner critic tries to make your present and your future safe and problem-free by wrapping you in cotton wool and persuading you to take as little action in the present as possible so you don't trip up. And yet all the negative conversations you have with your inner critic make you feel miserable and stifled in that cotton wool instead of all warm and cosy. And that's not the worst. Your inner critic is quite prepared to use nasty tactics to hold you back from living out your dangerous dreams for yourself. It distorts and stretches reality so that it focuses only on what you think you *can't* do or be. Your inner critic is not afraid to speak its mind and tell you you're not good enough, you're too fat, or too stupid.

The good news is that you also have an inner coach, cheering you on to have a go and celebrating your progress. The inner coach speaks from your future. That version of you who knows how it all turns out and is bursting to tell you that everything is going to be just fine! Yes, you had some hard challenges along the way and even periods when you felt deeply unhappy or frustrated. But your inner coach looks back along your life and sees a great deal more to celebrate – lots of fun and growth and love and happiness. Even what you thought were catastrophes turned out to be blessings in disguise. For example, getting made redundant resulted in a total career change where you discovered your true calling. And how lucky that the love of your life didn't agree to that date, because you then went on to meet the *real* love of your life, someone who you didn't, at that time, find remotely interesting!

The job of your inner coach is to encourage you to create a great future by taking positive action in your present. Your inner coach wants to tell you that you can trust yourself, because as long as you take positive action, everything will be okay. You can work out how to deal with any false steps along the way and, instead of feeling miserable and stifled wrapped up in all that cotton wool, you can feel energised and free, breathing in the fresh air and looking forward to your next adventure.

You may not hear the voice of your inner coach very often because that of your inner critic is so strident and ever-present. And when you do hear your inner coach, your inner critic is quick to slap down the wisdom, labelling the viewpoint as 'unrealistic' or even 'self-indulgent'.

Inner critics are fantastic at their jobs and convince us that worry, cynicism, and doubt are the only real things to be guided by, and that optimism and self-belief are delusions. But both voices come from you and both perspectives have value, in the right proportions. Sometimes your inner critic points out something useful that you really need to take account of. (Inner critics do often start with a grain of truth to lure you into a dialogue where they can really go for the full guilt trip.)

You may not even know that your inner coach has a voice you can trust – you may simply let your inner critic run on autopilot so that the inner coach never gets a chance to fly the plane. You can get far better results in your life if you switch their roles so that your inner coach is the captain of the plane and your inner critic has a turn only in support and under strict supervision!

Giving yourself the gift of your own good opinion

Your inner coach – just like a professional coach if you decide to work with one – supports you in the following ways:

- Encourages you to set challenging and inspiring goals for your life that are in tune with your values
- Believes you can do it!
- Expects the best from you and knows you can meet that expectation
- Explores options with you
- Helps to generate action steps that work for you
- Keeps you moving forwards
- Celebrates your accomplishments along the way
- Delights in the positive results you get for yourself

Your inner critic, on the other hand, seeks to do the opposite of all that and delights in the times when you indulge in self-sabotage, keeping you stuck in loops that go nowhere.

Who would you rather listen to?

Turning up the volume on the voice of your inner coach

The first step in engaging with your inner coach is letting its voice come through loud and clear amid all the white noise created by your inner critic. Try this activity:

1. **Set aside 15 minutes in a place where you won't be disturbed.** Let your thoughts wander freely for a few moments, maybe bringing your attention to something you have experienced recently, perhaps a project at work or an exchange with a friend or loved one.

2. **Start to listen to the voices that come through.** Can you hear the voice of your inner critic? What does it sound like? What does it say? How often does it use negative language? Do you hear a lot of 'should', 'ought', or 'must'? Is it taunting, mocking, strident, bitchy, sarcastic? Or is it sorrowful, fed-up, depressed, dejected? Or something else entirely?

3. **Now imagine a voice that is the opposite.** How does it sound? What does it say? Is it a voice you know and love or one that is delightfully fresh to you? If you turn up the volume on this voice, how do you feel? Does your inner critic complain? If so, let it fade away and fizzle out all by itself and keep turning up the volume on the voice of your inner coach. What new insights does it offer you? What feelings does it produce for you?

4. **Practise this activity frequently.** Fifteen minutes a day over a period of time can soon have you tuning in at will to what your inner coach has to say.

When Jo came to coaching, she found that writing in her journal most effectively helped her to recapture the voice of her inner coach. It also did the trick for taming her inner critic. Whenever she felt an inner critic attack coming on, she stopped and found a few moments to write out what she was feeling. The crazy, spiteful words of her inner critic often seemed ridiculous written out on the page in black and white. Within 5 or 10 minutes of doing this she found herself starting to write down the wisdom coming from her inner coach. She said that for her, writing out the dialogue in her head acted almost like a meditation and she was always able to get back into the swing of things feeling refreshed and energised.

Identifying Your Current Priorities for Coaching

Knowing where to start with applying coaching techniques to the elements of your life may seem hard. Sometimes you get a clear sense that one particular area, your work or career for example, is the one that requires the most attention. At other times you have the general feeling that all areas of your life need a good overhaul or boost of momentum.

This section enables you to really home in on the area of your life in which coaching can provide the biggest and most immediate benefits. You can keep coming back to this section to take a rain check every so often, because one thing's for sure – your priorities change over time, and that's just as it should be.

Dividing up your life into handy compartments may seem simplistic. Your life is full of connections and consequences, so you don't really move attention from your career to finance issues to relationships throughout your day, even if your diary indicates that you're at work from 8 a.m. until 6 p.m., with a lunch appointment with your accountant, and an evening spent with your family. All areas of your life intrude on and complement each other. However, when applying coaching techniques dividing these distinct areas of your life into separate compartments is helpful so that you can be very specific about the changes you want to make and the actions you need to take. You can then think about the impact the changes may have on other areas of your life.

Working out what's really important to you (your core values in life) gives you a great entry point into coaching, because doing so can highlight common themes or specific areas of your life that are out of kilter. Read Chapter 1 of book 2 for more about identifying your core values.

The following activity helps you to identify your compelling current priority for life coaching If you haven't identified one yet.

1. **In Table 4-1, mark in the second column (A) how important each factor is to you.** Three ticks indicate that the factor is very important to you, two ticks mean that it is moderately important to you, and one tick means that it's not very important to you.

Table 4-1	Identifying Areas for Coaching	
	A. How important is this to me?	**B. How satisfied am I with this right now?**
Career and work		
I enjoy my work and get satisfaction from it		
I receive appropriate recognition for my work		
I have enough opportunities to develop myself in my work		
Money and wealth		
I am financially secure		
I have enough money to live the kind of lifestyle that I want		
I am creating wealth for my future		
People and relationships		
I enjoy loving family relationships		
I have close and supportive friendships		
I have access to beneficial networks and communities		
Health and wellbeing		
I take care of my health to prevent illness		
I am fit, strong, flexible, and energetic		
I am emotionally and mentally resilient		
Learning and growing		
I have enough fun and leisure in my life		

	A. How important is this to me?	B. How satisfied am I with this right now?
I am constantly learning and developing myself		
I have a sense of purpose and meaning in my life		

2. **Consider what areas, if any, have appeared as priorities for you.** You may be surprised that one or two areas don't warrant three or even two ticks. Or maybe everything has three ticks for you, but you have a sense that some ticks carry more importance for you than others. Don't worry; that's natural. But have a sense of what, when push comes to shove, are the factors that most sustain you.

3. **Consider each statement in the light of your current level of satisfaction.** Mark three ticks in the third column (B) if you're very satisfied, two ticks if you're moderately satisfied, and one tick if you're not very satisfied.

4. **Look at your results and see how many three-tick matches you have.** Well done if you have a total of six ticks in some areas (the combined ticks in the two columns) – this shows that you're getting high satisfaction from an area of your life that is very important to you.

Are you getting a high level of satisfaction from an area that is quite low in importance to you? That's okay – but perhaps you can consider whether you can shift the balance a little so that your higher-priority areas get some more attention. Or maybe this highlights that something great is going on in your life that you've begun to take for granted.

Look out for the areas that only get one or two ticks on a satisfaction level. These are your more urgent priority areas of focus as you apply coaching techniques to your life.

Book II
Neuro-linguistic Programming

"No, it hasn't anything to do with my presentation. But wait until you see how I hold everyone's attention with it sitting next to me at the podium."

In this part . . .

Some describe Neuro-linguistic Programming (NLP) as the study of the structure of subjective experience; others call it the art and science of communication. We prefer to say that NLP enables you to understand what makes you tick; how you think, how you feel, how you make sense of everyday life in the world around you. Armed with this understanding, NLP gives you 'aha' moments, when everything makes sense. (In case you're curious, 'Neuro' relates to what's happening in our minds, 'Linguistic' refers to language and how we use it, while 'Programming' tackles the persistent patterns of behaviour that we learn and then repeat).

Here are the contents of Book II at a glance:

Chapter 1

Taking Charge of Your Life

· ·

In This Chapter

▶ Controlling your memory

▶ Walking the path to excellence

▶ Getting to grips with your unconscious mind

▶ Using your tracking system

▶ Benefiting from beliefs and values

▶ Imagining your own future

· ·

*Y*our memories can be a wonderful gift or a terrible scourge. They can cradle you softly in strands of silk or bind you in coils of razor wire. Your memories can propel you to your dreams or keep you trapped in the past. However, with the help of NLP, and by understanding how you can program your mind, *your past need not create your future.*

This chapter is all about making you the driver not the passenger in the story of your life. So let's get rolling. It's time to have fun.

Taking Control of Your Memory

Your memories are recorded as pictures, sounds, and feelings and by adjusting the buttons on these qualities you can enhance positive memories and take the sting out of negative memories. You can start off by flexing your taking-control-of-your-memory muscles with the following very simple exercises.

In the first exercise, you find out how to recall and manipulate a positive memory so that you can feel good, or even better, at will. Follow these steps:

1. **Think of a day when you were truly happy.**

2. **Notice what you see, hear, and feel when you bring back the memory.**

3. **If the memory is a picture adjust its quality by making it bigger, brighter, and bringing it closer. If you're observing yourself, try stepping into the picture to see if this makes you feel even better.**

4. **Notice any sounds that may have been in the memory at the time. Does making them louder, moving them to inside or outside your head increase the positive feelings?**

5. **Notice the feelings you have, if any. Where in your body are you experiencing them? Do they have a colour, texture, or weight? Does moving the location of the feelings or changing their colour, texture, and weight alter these feelings? Adjust these parameters to enhance the feelings.**

By completing this exercise you have manipulated the qualities of the experiences you have had and more importantly, you have seen that you *can* change the structure of your memories in order to diminish the affect of negative experiences and re-experience and heighten joyful ones.

Of course, not all memories are good ones. This second exercise will show you how you can change the qualities of an unpleasant memory. By changing the attributes of the negative memory, you will be able to release negative emotions which may still be holding you in their grasp. Follow these steps:

1. **Think of a memory that is only marginally unpleasant.** For this exercise, and until you become more practised at NLP techniques, think of a memory that is only marginally unpleasant. Please leave heavy duty memories like traumas to when you are with a trained therapist.

2. **Notice the pictures, sounds, and any feelings that the memory brings up.**

3. **If you are in the picture, step out of it to become an observer.** Imagine you are behind a film camera, filming yourself acting out the memory with which you are working.

4. **Change any sounds so that they're softer or perhaps make people in the picture speak like Mickey Mouse.** So if there are sounds like sirens or crying, you can make them softer or if you hear someone saying something unpleasant, you can have them talk to you in a silly cartoon voice.

5. **Adjust the quality of the picture.** Make it smaller, darker, and in black and white; move it far away from you until it's a dot and almost invisible. You may want to send it into the sun and watch it disappear in a solar flare. By carrying out this step, you experience destroying the hold the memory previously had on you.

Changing the memory does not mean the event did not occur. It does, however, mean that you have a choice over how the memory affects you today and the impact it has on your tomorrows.

The Path to Excellence

The human brain is a learning machine that needs to be kept occupied. If it isn't, it can dwell on the negative and get its owners into all kinds of trouble. As a human being, you can use all your ingenuity to direct your brain in to helping you achieve your goals. If you can create a compelling, irresistible future your brain will help you to align your behaviour in a way that will get you to your outcome quickly and easily. *The first step is working out what you want.*

Book II

Neuro-linguistic Programming

Fast forward the years and looking back at your life now, make a list of the dreams you would dare to live if you had all the money and influence in the world and you knew you couldn't fail.

So you may decide that you want material things like a huge nest egg, a big house, nice cars, or you may decide you want to be influential in the political arena.

Knowing what you want

When Alice (*Alice's Adventures in Wonderland* by Lewis Carroll) asks the Cheshire Cat, 'Would you tell me, please, which way I ought to walk from here?', without any clear idea of where it is she wants to go, she just wants to go somewhere, the Cheshire Cat responds that Alice is sure to get somewhere if she just walks long enough. And like Alice, imagine what would happen next time you go to a train station and ask for a ticket to somewhere.

For you want to move forward and achieve your goals, you need to be very clear about what it is you *do* want. So often in life, you get caught up in what it is you don't want and spend an awful lot of energy, both physical and emotional, in avoiding the undesirable result.

To figure out what you want and put your energies toward achieving it, sit down and write your own obituary. You can then decide on the legacy you want to leave to posterity and the actions you would take to fulfill the legacy. There you can discover that your unconscious mind is a wonderful ally in assisting you to achieve the goals you want . . . and don't want!

A client who came to see me (Romilla) as she was trying to 'escape' from her second marriage said, 'I am bad with relationships.' On working through her issues, we discovered that she had lost her much adored grandfather as a very young child. The trauma of this particular event had gone very deep into her psyche and her fear of loss had been driving her to end her relationships before she could experience the pain of loss again. Because the client was focusing, at a subconscious level, on what she didn't want – pain of loss – her unconscious mind was assisting her in maintaining behaviours that made her avoid the pain. Unfortunately it created other problems. For her to get the relationship she craved, she had to think about and design exactly what she wanted in a relationship and focus on creating it in her life.

One way to discover what you really want is to go way into your future. Imagine you are a grey-haired grandparent. You're sitting on a rock, under the stars, with a roaring campfire in front of you and at your feet are your grand-children, demanding another story about your life. Would you want to tell them of the time you missed the chance to fulfil a dream because you were too scared, too influenced by someone else's 'you can't'? Or would you want to tell them that, despite all the odds and in keeping with your values, you did something spectacular?

Creating well-formed outcomes

NLP builds on the SMART approach by making you use all of your senses to design a goal, to fine tune it to being more than just Specific, Measurable, Achievable, Realistic, and Timed. This process requires you to answer a series of questions that really help you explore the hows, whys, and where-fores of your desired outcome. By following the process you will really begin to understand your true motives for wanting your goals and you will be able to weigh up the pros and cons of success versus failure! A fairly common example of a well-formed outcome may be you want a better paid job.

When your desired outcome meets the following criteria, NLP says it satisfies the well-formedness conditions. For every result you want to achieve, we suggest that you ask yourself the following questions:

- ✔ Is the goal stated in the positive?
- ✔ Is it self-initiated, maintained and within my control?
- ✔ Does it describe the evidence procedure?
- ✔ Is the context clearly defined?
- ✔ Does it identify the needed resources?
- ✔ Have I evaluated whether it is ecological?
- ✔ Does it identify the first step I need to take?

The 4-point formula for success

The formula for success consolidates what you have discovered in creating at least one well-formed outcome. This formula can be applied to lifetime goals as effectively as to short-term ones. Remember: It is much easier to hit a target that is clearly defined and visible. Robin Hood would never have won Maid Marion if he didn't aim for the bull's eye!

To hit the target, follow these steps:

1. **Know your outcome.**

   It is important to specify precisely what it is you want. You can use the outcome frame to fine tune the desired outcome and satisfy the well-formedness conditions. See the earlier sections for details.

2. **Take action.**

   Unless you take that first step, and then the following ones, nothing will happen to help you towards your outcome, no matter how clearly they are defined.

3. **Have sensory awareness.**

   If you have the awareness to see, hear, and feel what isn't working, you can modify your behaviour to steer you towards the desired outcome. Chapter 6 will show you how you can develop sensory awareness.

4. **Have behavioural flexibility.**

   This ties in beautifully with the NLP presupposition: 'In interactions among people, the person with the most flexibility of behaviour can control the interaction.' Or you could say...'If it ain't working, do something different.'

If you always do what you've always done, you'll always get what you always got.

Spinning the Wheel of Life

This section will help you to identify whether you have a balanced life and, if there is scope for improvement, which areas need to be worked on in order to get balance in your life, simply and effectively.

In the diagram of the wheel in Figure 1-1, if you were to label the wedges of the wheel with the words that mean the most to you about areas in your life, those that are important to you, what would you choose? Typically people

Book II

Neuro-linguistic Programming

choose to include work and career (including the home), finances and money, friends and family, relationships, personal growth and learning, fun and recreation, spirituality, and physical environment.

Taking the centre of the wheel as 0 and the outer edge as 10, rank your level of satisfaction with each life area by drawing a straight or curved line to create a new outer edge. The new perimeter of the circle represents your personal wheel of life (see Figure 1-1 for an example). The ideal situation would obviously have all the sections at 10, giving you a beautifully round wheel, like the one in the diagram.

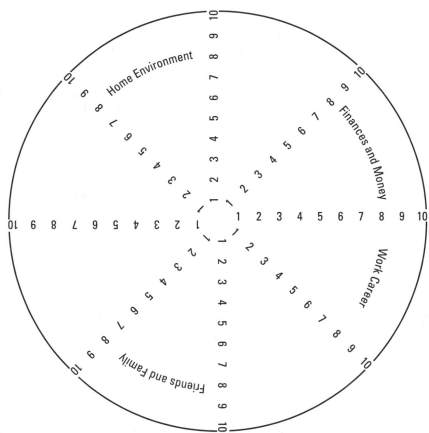

Figure 1-1:
An example
of a Wheel
of Life.

Think of a goal as an appointment with a desired outcome and write it down. If there was only one thought you take from this book to make you more successful, it is to write down your goals, commit to actions to achieve them, and work on your plans every single day.

Pick some areas in your life you would like to have goals in. This may be a little involved and we invite you to take your time and savour each stage because what you are really doing here is *designing the future you will want to live*. Basically, you're going to create your own dream diary and fill it with your own dreams and goals. Follow these steps:

1. **Find yourself a wonderful file that you will enjoy working with every day; get some colourful dividers, too.**

2. **Draw and fill in a Wheel of Life (refer to Figure 1-1).**

3. **Pick each area in your life which you may want to design or re-design and label each divider with the area you want to work at.**

   You may decide to just work on one or two areas to start with.

4. **Think of some goals for each area.**

   Consider both long-term (lifetime, five years, or more) and short-term (six months to a year) goals.

5. **Apply the *well-formed outcome* process to your goals.**

   Refer to the section 'Getting smarter than SMART' earlier in this chapter.

6. **Write down your goals and include the date by which you want to have achieved them.**

7. **Break the goals down into monthly, weekly, and daily goals and write them in your diary along with their dates.**

   You may want some more dividers (best to keep them the same colour).

8. **Each night before you go to sleep (this only takes a few minutes) look at your dreams and make a list of what you will do the next day in order to meet your goals.**

Book II

Neuro-linguistic Programming

Understanding The Unconscious Mind

You may decide consciously that you want to get a goal. If your unconscious mind is not on board, it will assist you by fulfilling its own agenda – which may be contrary to what you consciously think you want. Imagine what you could achieve if you were in rapport with your unconscious mind and able to go in the direction that would get you to your goal quickly.

In order to direct the unconscious mind, you need to open up communication channels between your conscious and your unconscious mind. This rapport is developed by finding a quiet time for meditation or relaxation and examining the memories presented to you by your unconscious mind.

Conscious and unconscious

In NLP terms, your conscious mind is that part of your mind which has awareness of things around and within you at any given moment in time, which, according to research conducted by George Miller in 1956, is a meagre 7±2 chunks of information. This is your short-term memory which can hold thoughts from minutes to hours. You use this part of your brain when you hold a telephone number in memory long enough to make that call. The rest is your unconscious or subconscious mind. The conscious mind can be compared to the tip of an iceberg and the unconscious mind to the nine-tenths of the iceberg which is submerged underwater.

Your conscious and unconscious mind excel at different things (see Table 1-1). Knowing what each is best suited for can help you to recognise if you are better at using your logical left brain more or your creative right brain more. You may then decide to focus on aspects of your mental development, for instance learning to draw, if you are more left brained, or learning applied mathematics, if you are more right brained. Certainly learning to meditate will develop the traits of both and get them communicating better.

Table 1-1	Comparing the Conscious and Unconscious Mind
The conscious mind excels at	*The unconscious mind is better at*
Working linearly	Working holistically
Processing sequentially	Intuition
Logic	Creativity
Verbal language	Running your body
Mathematics	Taking care of your emotions
Analysis	Storing memories

This is not a sexist thing

Did you know that your brain has a left and a right half which are joined together by the corpus collosum? Generally, women have a thicker corpus collosum than men, which enables them to multi-task better.

Oh! And by the way, if someone calls you thick . . . thank them. They're simply complimenting you on the density of the network connecting your brain cells which makes you more intelligent.

Your quirky unconscious mind

As with any friend and their little foibles, your unconscious mind has some interesting quirks with which it would be useful for you to become acquainted so you can get on with it better. The ideal would be to have your conscious and unconscious minds working as one.

By getting your unconscious mind on board, working with you instead of against you, you will be able to achieve much more in life, like setting and achieving compelling goals seemingly effortlessly.

Your unconscious cannot process negatives

Your unconscious can't process negatives. It interprets everything you think as a positive thought. So if you think, 'I don't want to be poor,' your unconscious mind focuses on the 'poor' and, because it doesn't do negatives, the thought becomes 'I want to be poor.' Being poor then becomes the goal in your unconscious mind and like a young child, desperate to please, it helps you behave in a way that will keep you poor. Obviously not what you wanted!

That's why stating your goals in the positive is so important. In this instance, instead of thinking 'I don't want to be poor,' you'd think 'I want to be wealthy.'

Your unconscious needs direction

In order to direct the unconscious mind, you need to open up communication channels between your conscious and your unconscious mind. This rapport is developed by finding a quiet time for meditation or relaxation and examining the memories presented to you by your unconscious mind.

The Reticular Activating System (RAS) – Your Tracking System

There are approximately 2 billion pieces of data coming in through your five senses every second. To maintain your sanity, this deluge is filtered through a network of cells in your brain so that only a very minute proportion of the information gets through to the rest of the brain. This network is called the Reticular Activating System or RAS for short. The RAS works like an antenna, noticing stimuli and alerting your brain to pay attention. The RAS lets in only data that meets at least one of the following criteria:

✔ It is important to your *survival*.

For example when you are in a deep sleep but wake up because you hear a strange noise in the house or if you are jay walking and in a daydream you will be alerted to traffic bearing down on you.

✔ It has *novelty* value.

Remember the last time you decorated a room? Initially you had this feeling of real pleasure each time you walked into the room as you saw the wallpaper with fresh eyes. Then after a few weeks you might have noticed that a painting was askew or an ornament not quite central and not necessarily the pattern on the wallpaper or the colour of the paint. That is because the novelty had worn off.

✔ It has a high emotional content.

The survival aspect also applies to others than yourself and you will be alert instantly if your baby's breathing changes but sleep through your husband's snoring or mumbling in his sleep.

Can you remember the last time you misplaced a loved one in a shopping centre and you were searching high and low, promising to do all kind of horrible things to him for getting lost? And then it's as if the crowd fades into obscurity as you catch a glimpse of your loved one in the distance and you zero in on them with nothing but relief. If no emotional connection with the misplaced person existed, he would just be another body in the crush. But because he is a loved one, he stands out like a beacon.

Effectively the RAS operates on stimuli that are above its threshold of observation. Mundane and daily routines slip below this threshold. It helps you to notice things that are relevant to your current goals.

Can you remember making a list and sticking it on the wall. You may have noticed it for a while and then no longer seen it even though you may have walked past it several times a day. This is because the list no longer had novelty value and was allowed to slip below the threshold for observation.

We're sure you know of chronically unlucky people, those who say things like, 'I never win anything' or 'Lucky breaks don't come my way'. These are the people whose belief systems stop them from seeing opportunities. If an opportunity was to jump up and slap them in the face, they would say, 'That's too good to be true' as they skirted the opportunity. Then there are those who always land on their feet. The lucky people are the ones who are open to possibilities. This way of thinking will have them seeking success out of failure because their belief systems dictate they deserve to win.

Your beliefs will affect the threshold level of the RAS. Someone who believes that he is a poor speller may not 'see' an advertisement for a reporter's job, even though this shortcoming can be helped with spelling technology and he may be much better at investigating stories than someone who may not have a hang-up over their spelling ability and who applies for the job.

By being aware of your beliefs, you can identify how these beliefs may be stopping you from achieving your goals. Think of a time when you really wanted to do something but, for whatever reason, couldn't find the opportunity to achieve your goal. Now examine your beliefs. You may discover that these beliefs were stopping you from noticing openings that could have enabled you to achieve your goal.

How Memories Are Created

Memories are normally created when information from the RAS is sent to the part of the brain called the amygdala, where it is given an emotional weighting before being passed on to the hippocampus. The hippocampus evaluates the data against that held in long-term memory and presents it to the cortex for analysis and re-filing back into long-term memory. Figure 1-2 shows you where these strangely named brain parts are located.

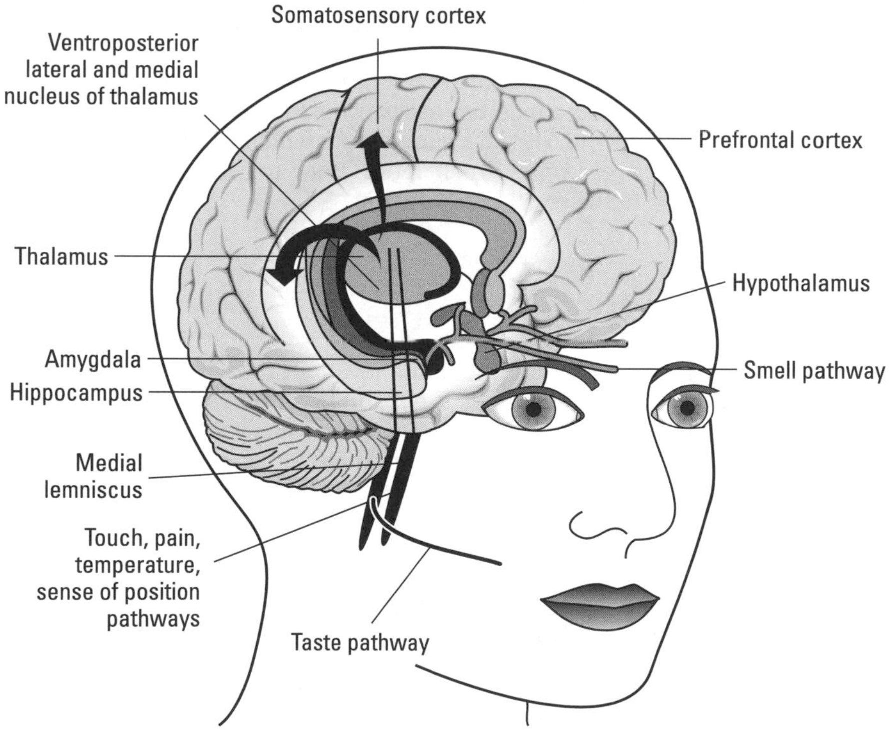

Somatosensory cortex

Ventroposterior lateral and medial nucleus of thalamus

Prefrontal cortex

Thalamus

Hypothalamus

Amygdala

Hippocampus

Smell pathway

Medial lemniscus

Touch, pain, temperature, sense of position pathways

Taste pathway

Figure 1-2: Finding your way around the human brain.

Post Traumatic Stress Disorder (PTSD)

The general public first became aware of Post Traumatic Stress Disorder (PTSD) when films about veterans from the Vietnam War started to be made. Today the news coverage has made us much more aware that PTSD is common among people who work in the emergency services as well as people who are the unfortunate victims of war and crime.

PTSD occurs when the amygdala receives input with a very high emotional value, gets in a panic and cannot send the information to the hippocampus. Because of this, the traumatic event gets trapped within the amygdala and the hippocampus is not able to present the memory to the neocortex for evaluation, which means the brain cannot make sense of the event. As the amygdala is the organ primarily involved with your survival, in PTSD sufferers it stays in the constant state of arousal, causing flashbacks and high levels of anxiety.

Virginia Woolf wrote *Mrs Dalloway* in the early twenties and her portrayal of Septimus Smith clearly identifies him as suffering from post traumatic stress after the horrors of World War One. Unfortunately, at the time, conventional medicine was relatively inexperienced at dealing with psychological problems. Patients like Septimus Smith were advised to have plenty of rest in order to recuperate and were given advice such as 'pull yourself together, man.'

Phobias and PTSD are part of a group of *anxiety disorders*. Both have a similar structure, in that a memory stays trapped in the amygdala. Fortunately these days we have the NLP fast phobia cure which can be very useful in helping people recover from both anxieties. Head to the section 'The NLP fast phobia cure' later in this section for details.

Phobias

The experts have differing opinions about the origins of phobias. Some psychologists say phobias are the result of a trauma, such as having a frog dropped down your back, others that phobias are a learned response, when a two-year-old is confronted by a cobra and becomes phobic as a result of the reactions of the adults around her. Flick through to 'The NLP fast phobia cure' (next in this chapter) for help in overcoming phobias.

The NLP fast phobia cure

The fast phobia cure allows you to re-experience a trauma or phobia without experiencing the emotional content of the event or having to face the trigger that would normally set off the phobic response. You should ensure that you work in an environment where you know yourself to be completely safe, in the presence of another person who can help to keep you grounded.

This means that you examine an experience while you are doubly dissociated from the memory, creating a separation between you (in the now) and the emotions of a trauma or a phobic response. In the following list, the double dissociation is done through having you watch yourself in a cinema theatre (dissociation), while watching yourself on a cinema screen (double dissociation):

1. **Identify when you have a phobic response to a stimulus or a traumatic or unpleasant memory that you wish to overcome.**

2. **Remember that you were safe before and are safe after the unpleasant experience.**

3. **Imagine yourself sitting in the cinema, watching yourself on a small, black-and-white screen.**

4. **Now imagine floating out of the you that is sitting in the cinema seat and into the projection booth.**

5. **You can now see yourself in the projection booth, watching yourself in the seat, watching the film of you on the screen.**

6. **Run the film in black–and white, on the very tiny screen, starting before you experienced the memory you wish to overcome and running it through until after the experience when you were safe.**

7. **Now freeze the film or turn the screen completely white.**

8. **Float out of the projection booth, out of the seat and into the end of the film.**

9. **Run the film backwards very quickly, in a matter of a second or two, in full colour, as if you are experiencing the film, right back to the beginning, when you were safe.**

10. **You can repeat steps 8 and 9 until you are comfortable with the experience.**

11. **Now go into the future and test an imaginary time when you might have experienced the phobic response.**

Book II

Neuro-linguistic Programming

Beliefs and Values Make a Difference

You may have heard someone say, 'Those teenagers today, they have no values.' Everyone has values; they are just different for different people and different groups of people. Your values and beliefs are unconscious filters that you use to decide what bits of data coming in through your senses you will allow in and what bits of data you will keep out. You know what that means, don't you? That the unconscious nine-tenths of your brain has been sitting there on the quiet, building up all sorts of beliefs and making all sorts of decisions about you and your environment and . . . you aren't even aware of them.

The power of beliefs

Your beliefs can, when allowed to go to the extreme, have the power of life and death over you. Your beliefs can help you to health, wealth, and happiness or keep you unwell, poor, and miserable.

The beliefs we are talking about here are distinct from religious beliefs – these beliefs are the generalisations you make about your life experiences. These generalisations go on to form the basis of your reality which then directs your behaviour. You can use one empowering belief, for example, to help you to develop another belief to the next level of achievement. So 'I am a really good speller' can help you develop the belief that you enjoy words and are really quite articulate. This might lead you to believe that you can tell stories and suddenly you find that you have the courage to submit a short story to a magazine and . . . all of a sudden you are a published author.

Just as you have positive, empowering beliefs, you can also have negative, disempowering beliefs. If you had the misfortune of being bullied at school, you may have developed a belief that people, in general, are not very nice. This might make you behave quite aggressively toward people when you first meet them. If some people then respond in a similarly aggressive way their behaviour could well re-enforce your belief that 'people aren't very nice'. You may not even notice when someone responds in a friendly manner because your belief filters are not geared to notice nice people.

Be aware that a limiting belief may be lurking if you find yourself using words or hearing words like can't, should, shouldn't, could, couldn't, would, ought, and ought not. As Henry Ford said, 'He can who thinks he can, and he can't who thinks he can't. This is an inexorable, indisputable law.'

Being impacted by others' beliefs

The really scary thought is that other people's preconceptions can place false limitations on you, especially if the other people are teachers, bosses, family, and friends.

A very interesting study conducted with a group of children who had been tested and found to be of average intelligence illustrates how a teacher's belief can enhance or hinder a child's learning ability.

The students were split into two groups at random. The teacher for one group was told that the students in the group were gifted, whereas the teacher for the other group was told that these students were slow learners. Both groups of children were retested for intelligence a year later. The intelligence score for the group where the teacher thought the students were gifted was higher than when previously tested; whereas the group where the teacher had been told the students were slow learners scored lower on the intelligence test than they had done before.

Sadly these limitations are not just the domain of overcrowded schools but exist in homes where parents shoehorn their children into an 'acceptable' position. Other examples include when your friends remind you to be careful of changing a secure job to pursue a dream, or if a boss whose communication style is different to yours has a detrimental affect on your career progression. Not only are some of these people perceived to know more than you, you may even have placed them on a pedestal.

It may be difficult for a child to overcome the shortcomings of a teacher without parental assistance and even more so the restrictions of a parent or family environment. As an adult, you can weigh up the pros and cons of the advice you are being given by seeing it from the other person's point of view. Once you understand the reasons for the other person's opinion, you can choose to follow their advice or not and, last but not least, you can always learn to utilise your boss's communication style in order to get your message across and so progress your career.

Changing beliefs

Some beliefs you hold may empower you. Other beliefs can limit the way you think and hold you back. The good news is that beliefs can and do change. Take the example of the four-minute mile. For years sportsmen did not believe it was possible to run a mile in four minutes. Roger Bannister achieved this in May 1954. Soon after, even this record was broken several times over.

One way of changing a belief is to adjust its submodalities. This is a really useful process as it can help you loosen the hold a limiting belief can have on you and re-enforce the effects of a positive belief to develop a more empowering belief about which you are less confident. Suppose you can't help but be drawn to people and have long been told that being subjective is bad – changing your belief to 'I'm good with people' can make a huge difference to your confidence when dealing with others. Similarly, if you know you are good at art, this belief can help you branch into a more technical, art-based career like computer graphics.

To practise manipulating or changing your beliefs, follow these steps:

1. **Think of a belief you know to be true, for example 'I am a really considerate driver.'**

   If you cannot think of a belief, ask yourself if you believe the sun will rise in the morning? Even behind all those clouds?

2. **Did you get a picture, have a feeling, and/or hear a sound? What were the qualities of the picture or feeling or sound?**

3. **Now think of a belief that you would like to change because it is not serving you well: 'I can't park straight!'**

4. **Superimpose the qualities of the belief you know to be true on those of the belief you would like to change.**

   Say the picture of what you know to be true is bright, big, in three dimensions, close, and straight in front of you and the picture of a belief you want to change is small, dark, in two dimensions, and far away. Make the picture of the belief you want to change bright, big, in three dimensions, close, and straight in front of you.

   Similarly, think of the qualities of any sounds and feelings you get for the belief you know to be true. Are the qualities of the sounds and feelings of the belief you want to change different?

As a member of the human race what beliefs are holding your 'isms' (sexism, ageism, racism) in place and whose 'isms' are you allowing to keep yourself boxed in?

A cluster of beliefs is called a belief system. A belief or belief system can support a particular value. Values are the *why* you do something. Beliefs direct your behaviour which then helps you fulfil a value – provided of course there are no conflicts created by your unconscious mind. To find out more about values, head to the next section, 'Values'.

Values

Values are the 'hot buttons' that drive all your behaviours and are your unconscious motivators and de-motivators. It is because of your values that you do something. After you have done it, you use these values to judge whether the deed is either good or bad. For instance, if you value honesty you may decide to pick up a wallet you find in the street for safe-keeping and feel good about handing it over to the police.

Values affect the choice of your friends and partners, the types of goods you purchase, the interests you pursue, and how you spend your free time. Just like your beliefs, your values also influence the filters that the RAS operates (see the section earlier in this chapter 'The Reticular Activating System (RAS) – Your Tracking System' for more information about RAS and how it works).

Your life has many facets. You are probably a member of a family, a team at work, and maybe you belong to a club in your pursuit of a hobby, just to name a few. Each of these areas of your life, family, work, leisure, and so on will have its own values hierarchy, with the most important value at the top. The values at the top of the hierarchy are usually more abstract than those further down and exert the most influence in your life.

Means to an end values

Values can either be *ends* values or *means* values, with means values occurring further down the hierarchy, acting as the rungs in a ladder that enable you to reach your ends value. Means values are those which need to be fulfilled in order to get you to your final, ends value. Freedom is harder to quantify than, say, money. In the example you can have money without having freedom, but to have freedom you need money. So freedom – ends value – is dependent on money – means value.

Your values can either drive you toward pleasure or away from pain.

Toward Values	*Away from Values*
Love	Guilt
Freedom	Sadness
Health	Loneliness
Happiness	Anger

Values with *away from* tendencies are indicative of negative emotions, negative decisions, or emotional traumas that may be exerting an influence on your life. These can be released using techniques such as Time Line Therapy The main purpose of any such technique is to learn the lessons that may be of value from the negative events in order for the unconscious mind to release the trapped emotions. Essentially Time Line Therapy works on the principle that your memories are arranged along a time line, and by changing a memory along this time line you can release the hold of some memories, which in turn will help you gain more control over your reactions to events and have more choices in your life.

Creation of values

Your values are essentially formed over three periods in your life.

- The **imprint** period occurs from the time of your birth to when you are approximately seven years old. During this time you learn largely unconsciously from your parents.

- The **modelling** period occurs between the ages of eight and 13 when you learn by consciously and unconsciously copying friends. Some of your most important values, core values, are formed when you are around ten years old.

- The **socialisation** period occurs between the ages of 14 and 21 years. It is during this time that you learn values that affect your relationships.

Eliciting your values

If there are areas in your life that you think could do with some improvement, you can examine your values to get a clue that may enable you to make positive change. By following the suggestions in these steps, you may discover what's holding you back from getting what you want.

1. **Pick an area (or context) in your life that you're not happy with or want to improve.**

   For instance, are you living or working in an environment that you don't like and want to make more enriching?

2. **Make a list of what is important to you in this context.**

   You will notice that the first few values will come to mind very quickly. Stay with it and you will notice another batch of values will surface.

3. **Put these values in order of importance to you, with the most important appearing at the top.**

   If you have trouble rearranging the list, just ask yourself, 'If I could have A but not B, would this be OK?' If the answer is yes, A is of greater importance than B; if the answer is no, then B needs to be moved above A. For example, in the list of values below, which may relate to your job, you may decide that security is much more important to you than adventure:

   Success

   Power

   Achievement

   Adventure

   Security

Once you put all of these into an order of importance you will probably find the ones that surfaced later have greater significance for you.

4. **After you arrange your values, ask yourself if there is a value that would be useful for you to have in this area of your life but which is missing. Where would you slot it in the list of existing values?**

   For instance, if you value your job but you cannot get the level of success you want, it may be because you don't have fulfilment in your hierarchy. In fact by going through the above process you may decide it is more important to you to have:

   Success

   Fulfilment

   Achievement

   Adventure

   Security

Daydreaming Your Future Reality

Contrary to what your teachers may have told you when they saw you gazing out the classroom window, allowing your mind to wander can be a powerful first step in achieving your goals. By using the techniques described in earlier sections of this chapter, you can discover what your heart's desire is and take the first steps toward achieving it – all by daydreaming.

So give yourself permission to dream and play. What would you want to succeed at if Cinderella's fairy godmother came to you and gave you one wish? She would make sure you had all the influence, contacts, and resources you need to fulfil your heart's desire. Got your goal? Now follow these steps:

1. **Make a list of what is important to you about your goal, all the reasons why you want it, and put them in order of importance.**

   Are you surprised by your values? Did you realise something you thought important wasn't that important after all and did you think of a value that may have been missing in the beginning?

   If you're not sure how to do this, refer to the section 'Eliciting your values' earlier in this chapter.

2. **Now, while still daydreaming, imagine floating out of your body and into the future, to a time when you might have achieved this goal.**

3. **Notice the pictures, sounds, and feelings and manipulate them.**

   Can you make these stronger, more vibrant, and then even more so?

4. **From the place in the future, turn and look back to now and let your unconscious mind notice what it needs to know about and help you do in order for you to achieve your goal.**

   Remember to notice what the first step would be!

5. **When you've savoured the dream fully, come back and *take that first step*!**

You may surprise yourself!

Chapter 2

Creating Rapport

· ·

In This Chapter

▶ Defining rapport

▶ Understanding the basics of rapport

▶ Working with multiple perspectives

▶ Using metaprograms

· ·

*R*apport is like money. You only realise you have a problem when you haven't got enough of it. Rapport is not a technique that you turn on and off at will. It should flow constantly between people. Rule one of communication: establish rapport before expecting anyone to listen to you. And this is the case with anybody and any situation, whether with a teacher, pupil, spouse, friend, waitress, taxi-driver, coach, doctor, therapist, or business executive.

Rapport sits at the heart of NLP as another central pillar, or essential ingredient, that leads to successful communication between two individuals or groups of people. You do not need to like someone to build rapport with him or her. It is a mutually respectful way of being with others and a way of doing business at all times.

Don't kid yourself that you can pull it instantly out of the bag for a meeting or problem-solving session. True rapport is based on an instinctive sense of trust and integrity. This chapter will help you to spot situations when you do and don't have rapport with another person. We'll encourage you to focus on building rapport with people whom it might be valuable for you to have it, and we'll share with you some special NLP tools and ideas to enable you to build rapport.

Recognising Rapport

The word rapport derives from the French verb *rapporter*, translated as 'to return or bring back'. The English dictionary definition is 'a sympathetic relationship or understanding'. It's about making a two-way connection. You know you've made such a connection when you experience a genuine sense of trust and respect with another person, when you engage comfortably with someone no matter however different they are to you, and when you know that you are listening and being listened to.

There's no magic pill to learn rapport. It's something you learn intuitively – otherwise robots and aliens would have the leading edge on us humans. So, in order for you to understand how you personally build rapport and what is important to you in different relationships, let's begin by making some comparisons.

1. **First think for a moment about someone you have rapport with.** What signals do you send out to them and receive back that allow you to know that you're on the same wavelength? How do you create and maintain that rapport?

2. **Now, as a contrast, think for a moment about someone you do not have rapport with, but would like to.** What signals do you send out to them and receive back that allow you to know that you're not on the same wavelength? What gets in the way of creating and maintaining rapport with that person?

3. **Based on your experience with the first person, what might you do differently in your behaviour with the second person that can help you build a stronger relationship?**

You might think that the first person (the one you have rapport with) is naturally easy to get on with and the second (the one you don't yet share any rapport with) is just a difficult person. Yet, by being more flexible in your behaviour or thoughts about the second person, you may well find that you can build rapport with them through some simple stages. It may be that you need to take more time to get to know them and what's important to them rather than expecting them to adapt to you and your style. You'll find more tips on doing so in this chapter.

Basic Techniques for Building Rapport

Having rapport as the foundation for any relationship means that when there are tough issues to discuss, you can more easily find solutions and move on.

Fortunately, you can learn how to build rapport. Rapport happens at many levels. You can build rapport all the time through:

- ✔ The places and people you spend time with
- ✔ The way you look, sound, and behave
- ✔ The skills you have learned
- ✔ The values that you live by
- ✔ Your beliefs
- ✔ Your purpose in life
- ✔ Being yourself

Book II

Neuro-linguistic Programming

Seven quick ways to sharpen your rapport

For starters, try some immediate ways to begin building rapport; for more advanced rapport-building techniques keep reading:

- ✔ Take a genuine interest in getting to know what's important to the other person. Start to understand them rather than expecting them to understand you first.
- ✔ Pick up on the key words, favourite phrases and way of speaking that someone uses and build these subtly into your own conversation.
- ✔ Notice how someone likes to handle information. Do they like lots of details or just the big picture? As you speak, feed back information in this same portion size.
- ✔ Breathe in unison with them.
- ✔ Look out for the other person's intention – their underlying aim – rather than what they do or say. They may not always get it right, but expect their heart to lie in the right place.
- ✔ Adopt a similar stance to them in terms of your body language, gestures, voice tone and speed.
- ✔ Respect the other person's time, energy, favourite people and money. They will be important resources for them.

The communication wheel and rapport building

Classic research by Professor Mehrabian of the University of California at Los Angeles (UCLA) looked at how live communication was received and responded to. His figures suggested that your impact depends on three factors – how you look, how you sound, and what you say. His research broke it down as illustrated in the communication wheel here: 55 per cent body language, 38 per cent quality of the voice and 7 per cent actual words spoken (see Figure 2-1).

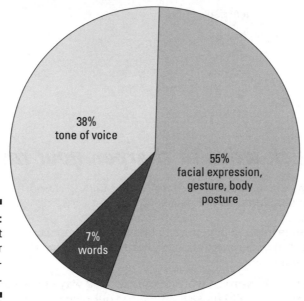

Figure 2-1:
The impact
of your
communi-
cation.

38%
tone of voice

55%
facial expression,
gesture, body
posture

7%
words

Clearly, first impressions count. Do you arrive for meetings and appointments hot and harassed or cool and collected? When you begin to talk, do you mumble your words in a low whisper to the floor or gaze directly and confidently at your audience before speaking out loud and clear?

In terms of building rapport – *you* are the message. And you need all parts of you working in harmony: words, pictures, and sounds. If you don't look confident – as if you believe in your message – people will not listen to what you are saying.

Rapport involves being able to see eye-to-eye with other people, connecting on their wavelength. So much (93 per cent) of the perception of your sincerity comes not from what you say but how you say it and how you show an appreciation for the other person's thoughts and feelings.

When you are in rapport with someone, you can disagree with what they say and still relate respectfully with him or her. The important point to remember is to acknowledge other people for the unique individuals that they are. For example, you may well have different political or religious views to your colleagues or clients, but there's no need to fall out about it. It's also likely that there are several choices about what's favourite to eat for supper and you can agree to differ with your family on that one, too.

Hold on to the fact that you simply wish to differ with their opinion and this is no reflection on the person. NLP makes a distinction between beliefs and values at one level, and identity at a higher level. A person is more than what they say, do, or believe.

Matching and mirroring

Book II

Neuro-linguistic Programming

When you are out and about in bars and restaurants, even the staff cafeteria (if you're lucky enough to get meals at work), have you noticed how two people look when there's rapport between them? Without hearing the details of the conversation you can see it's like a dance. People naturally move in step with each other. There's a sense of unison in their body language and the way they talk – elegantly dovetailing their movements and speech. NLP calls this matching and mirroring.

Matching and mirroring is when you take on someone else's style of behaviour and their skills, values, or beliefs in order to create rapport with them.

By contrast, think of a time when you've been the unwilling witness to an embarrassingly public argument between a couple, or a parent and child in the street or supermarket. Not quite a punch-up, but almost. Even with the volume turned off, you soon feel what it's like when people are totally out of synchronisation with each other just from their body posture and gestures. NLP calls this *mismatching*.

Matching and mirroring are ways of becoming highly tuned in to how someone else is thinking and experiencing the world. It's a way of listening with your whole body. Simple mirroring happens naturally when you have rapport.

What NLP suggests is that you can also deliberately match and mirror someone to build rapport until it becomes natural. To do this, you will need to match:

- ✔ Voice tonality (how you sound) or speed
- ✔ Breathing rates
- ✔ Rhythm of movement and energy levels
- ✔ Body postures and gestures

When rapport helps you say 'no'

You may have a teddy bear style of behaviour. Perhaps you're one of those people who prefer to say 'yes' to everything, to be helpful and pleasing to the boss, clients, and family. You'll be the first person to put your hand up in committee meetings, the one who organises the school jumble sale or charity dinner, who drives the kids around, and you're always the one who ends up having to do the tasks. Learning to say 'no' sometimes is essential learning if you're to protect yourself from overload. Consider James's story:

At work, how tempting it is for a manager to ask the willing worker to take on more. As a maths teacher who loves his job, James was finding it increasingly hard to say: 'I'm not going to take that on.' He felt he was letting people down by saying 'no' and was in danger of making himself seriously ill through overwork. He learned that by simply matching the body language of his head of department, it was easier for him to smile and say very politely: 'I'd love to do that, and yet my time is already fully committed. If you want me to take on extra responsibility you must decide what you'd like me to stop doing to make time for this.' In this way he refused to take on a greater load than he could possibly handle.

Beware the fine line between mimicry and moving in rhythm with someone. People instinctively know if you are making fun of them or being insincere. If you decide you'd like to check out mirroring for yourself, do it gradually in no-risk situations or with foreigners who you'll never see again. Don't be surprised though if it works and the strangers want to become your friends!

Pacing to lead

Building great relationships requires that you pace other people. As a metaphor, NLP compares pacing people to running alongside a train. If you tried to jump straight on to a moving train, it's likely you'd fall off. In order to jump on a moving train you would have to gather speed by racing alongside it until you were moving at the same speed before you could jump on. (And please, never actually try jumping on to a moving train!)

In order to lead somebody, to influence them with your point of view, remember to pace them first. This means really listening to them, fully acknowledging them, truly understanding where they have come from – and being patient about it.

Additional important advice from NLP to build rapport is to: Pace . . . pace . . . and pace again before you . . . lead. Pacing is how NLP describes your flexibility to respectfully pick up and match other people's behaviours and vocabulary, where you are actively listening to the other person. Leading is when you are attempting to get the other person to change by subtly taking them in a new direction.

In business, companies that succeed in introducing major change programmes do so in measured steps. This allows changes to gradually become accepted by employees. People are unwilling to be led to new ways of working until they have first been paced – listened to and acknowledged. The most effective leaders are those who pace their people's reality first.

Watch effective salespeople in action and you'll see how they master the art of pacing the customer and demonstrate genuine interest. (By effective, we're thinking of those who sell a genuine product with integrity rather than the shark approach.) They listen, listen, and listen some more about what the customer's needs are, what they really want, before trying to sell them anything. People resent being sold to, but they love to be listened to and to talk about what's important to them. An antiques dealer friend has perfected this art over many years, gently guiding his customers by his genuine affection for the articles he sells from his own home, and sharing his expertise.

When I (Kate) last bought a car, I went to six different showrooms where salespeople were hasty to sell the virtues of their car without showing any interest in how it fitted in with my lifestyle. The successful salesperson had superb interpersonal skills as well as the right product. He paced me well, listening carefully, treating me with respect (unlike those who assumed the buying decision would be made by my husband), and trusted me to take the keys and take it for a spin immediately. As I drove along, he gently gathered the information he needed to match the right model of car to my buying criteria, realising I wasn't going to accept a hard direct sell.

Building rapport in virtual communication

Fifteen years ago, the Internet and email tools were confined to the research labs and those nerdy types. Regular business transactions involved lots of letters and faxes, mostly filed in hard copy: it was OK to jump in the car to drive and visit suppliers and colleagues in other offices. Today life's different. Of course, we still write and phone, the paperless office remains elusive, and the percentage of electronic transactions has shot through the roof. If the computer goes down and we can't email for an hour, we feel lost and helpless.

Virtual teams who hold virtual meetings have entered the workplace. We have also the phenomenon of virtual management, of multi-cultural project teams that sit across global networks and work remotely thanks to the technology – conference calls, email and video-conferencing. In fact, a recent survey of 371 managers by British business management school, Roffey Park, showed that 46 per cent of managers currently work in virtual teams and 80 per cent said that virtual management arrangements were increasing.

In this environment of reduced face-to-face contact, you lose the nuances of facial expressions, the body language and subtlety of getting to know the colleague at the next desk as you work closely with others. At its best, the virtual team spells freedom and flexibility of working practices, diversity, and a richness of skills. At its worst, it's lonely, isolated, and ineffective.

For all, the challenge of virtual working to build rapport is greater than before. Little wonder that people are being recruited more for soft skills – the ability to influence and negotiate – than for technical competence. Following are ten ways to develop rapport over the phone and teleconferences.

- ✔ Make sure that all the locations are connected and can hear each other on the phone. Introduce and welcome people with a roll call.

- ✔ Work to a clear agenda. Set outcomes for the call and agree these with all participants.

- ✔ Check you've had input from a mix of people. If necessary, encourage the quieter individuals to take part. Say, for example: 'Mike, what are your thoughts on this?'

- ✔ Discourage small talk or separate chats at different sites. One discussion, one meeting, one agenda.

- ✔ Speak more slowly and precisely than in face-to-face meetings. Remember you can't get clues from the body language.

- ✔ Listen for the style of language – check if people have visual, auditory, or kinaesthetic preferences and match your language style to theirs as we suggest in Chapter 6 – Seeing, Hearing, and Feeling Your Way to Better Communication.

- ✔ Get attention before making your point (otherwise the first part of the message gets lost). Begin with phrases like: 'I have something I'd like to mention here . . . it's about . . . '

- ✔ Use people's names more than in face-to-face meetings. Address questions to people by name and thank them for their contribution by name.

- ✔ As you listen to the conversation, visualise the person at the other end of the phone line (you may even like to have a photo of them in front of you).

- ✔ Continually summarise and check understanding of points and decisions.

How to break rapport and why

There will be times when you choose to *mismatch* people for a while and break rapport. Mismatching is the opposite of matching or mirroring. To mismatch somebody you aim to do something dissimilar to them. This might be to dress very differently, speak in a different tone or at a different speed, adopt a different physical posture, or behave quite differently to them.

Three changes enable you to break rapport in the short term:

- ✔ **How you look and move physically**. You may want to physically move away from someone, break eye contact, or use a facial expression to communicate your message. Raised eyebrows say a lot. Turning your back is even more powerful. So, beware of doing this inadvertently!

- ✔ **How you sound**. Change your voice intonation or volume. Take it louder or softer, high or low. Remember the power of silence.

- ✔ **The words you say.** Remember that useful little phrase: 'No, thank you.' Sometimes it's the hardest to say, so practise it for when you need it. In multi-cultural settings, switching to your native language when you've been working in a common language is another clear way of saying, 'I need a break now.'

Book II

**Neuro-
linguistic
Programming**

There are plenty of times when you may want to say 'thank you' and 'goodbye for now'. Notice which come easily to you and where you could use some practise.

- ✔ **You are closing a deal.** Salespeople momentarily break connection with a customer at the point of signing a contract. They'll walk away and leave the customer to look at the paperwork alone rather than becoming connected to that final signing in the customer's eyes. This helps maintain rapport for the long term if buyer's remorse sets in.

- ✔ **You have enough information.** Maybe your brain has filled up for the moment and you're heading into sensory overload. You want time to think and digest what you have heard and to come back for the next instalment later.

- ✔ **You see someone else you'd like to talk to**. Perhaps you're at a drinks party and you've got stuck with the ultimate bore and there's someone much more attractive at the other side of the room.

- ✔ **You're tired.** All good things come to an end and it's good to know when it's time for the party to end and head home.

✔ **You're busy.** At any one time there will be a number of demands on your energy. Hold onto your own outcome rather than satisfying someone else's for them.

✔ **You're getting into tricky subjects**. Sex, politics, and religion are all good subjects to avoid in a business negotiation. They also cause lively dinner-party conversations where you may want to blow the whistle, call time out, and agree to differ as discussions get heated.

It's a skill to learn to break rapport and end a conversation, particularly if your best friend or mother wants to chat. Do it with consideration. Give clear feedback that you'd love to talk so long as it's contained to the right time of day, place, and length of time. You care about them as a person, so try and arrange a time to talk that suits you when work's over for the day.

The power of the 'but' word

There are times when something as small as a tiny word makes a huge difference between your ability to keep rapport and break it. NLP pays attention to such details in the pattern of conversation and so offers some useful clues for your influential communication. Work by NLP leaders like Robert Dilts has demonstrated that simple words like 'and' or 'but' make you focus your attention in different ways. When you adopt the 'but' word, people will remember what you said afterwards. With the 'and' word, people remember what you said before and afterwards.

Be aware that if you are making a comment to someone, they may only notice part of what you say. Consider the following example: 'The company has returned £5 million profit this financial year, but we're closing the San Francisco operation.' If you say it like this, people may only remember what you said after the 'but' word. Now consider the following: 'The company has returned £5 million profit this financial year, and we're closing the San Francisco operation.' If you say it like this, people remember what you said *before* and *after* the word 'and'.

Find out just how much little words make a difference in your daily communication with the 'Yes, but . . .' game for three or more players.

1. **Get your friends into a circle.**

2. **Person A begins *round one* with offering 'a good idea'.** (For example, 'It's a sunny day, how about if we take the afternoon off and head out to the beach?')

3. **Person B replies 'Yes, but . . .' and offers their own 'good idea'.**

4. Person C and all other team members offer their ideas in turn, always starting with 'Yes, but . . .'.

5. *Round two* continues with Person A offering a good idea.

6. Person B replies 'Yes, and . . .' and offers their own 'good idea'.

7. Person C and all other team members offer their ideas in turn, always starting with 'Yes, and . . .'.

Notice the difference?

Understanding Other Points of View

Book II

Neuro-
linguistic
Programming

Successful people enjoy the flexibility of being able to see the world in different ways. They take multiple perspectives, enabling themselves to explore new ideas. NLP offers various techniques to help people build rapport in very challenging relationships, especially where there is some kind of emotional conflict happening. These techniques are also used to explore new ways of building rapport, even in relationships that are only mildly troublesome or confusing.

Exploring perceptual positions

One of the ways that NLP helps you to build rapport with others is by distinguishing at least three different points of view. NLP calls these *perceptual positions*. It's rather like looking at a building from all angles – coming in at the front entrance, moving round to the back door, and then looking down with a bird's eye view from a helicopter overhead.

✔ **First position** is your own natural perspective, where you are fully aware of what you think and feel regardless of those around you. This can be a position of strength – when you're really clear about what you want and your own beliefs and values. It can also be incredibly selfish until you consciously become aware of what other people want.

✔ **Second position** is about shifting into someone else's shoes – imagining what it's like for them. You may already be really good at always considering others' needs. Mothers rapidly develop this skill in caring for new offspring. You put someone else's view first.

✔ **Third position** involves taking an independent position where you act as a detached observer noticing what is happening in the relationship. At its best, this is a mature position where you appreciate a situation from both sides. Sometimes it means you're reluctant to engage fully in a situation – you merely sit on the fence.

Mastery of all three perspectives puts you in a wise place to enjoy life to the full.

The NLP meta-mirror

The meta-mirror is an exercise developed by Robert Dilts in 1988 to bring together a number of different perspectives or perceptual positions. The basis of the meta-mirror is the idea that the problem you face is more a reflection of you, and how you relate to yourself, than about the other person. It's a way of allowing you to step back and see a problem you are facing in a new light – hence the idea of the mirror.

The meta-mirror will help you to prepare for, or review, a number of possible scenarios you face:

- ✔ A difficult conversation with a teenager or family member
- ✔ A presentation at work
- ✔ A meeting
- ✔ A contract negotiation
- ✔ Sensitive discussion with a partner or friend
- ✔ How you relate to your boss or a colleague at work
- ✔ Dealing with difficult clients

This exercise is based on the work of Robert Dilts and takes four perceptual positions. You may like to try this exercise with the help of a coach or friend to help you concentrate on the process so that you just work with your issue.

First choose a relationship you'd like to explore. Perhaps you'd like some insight into a difficult conversation or confrontation in the past or the future. Then lay out four spaces on the floor to denote four positions (see Figure 2-2). Pieces of paper or Post-it notes are fine. Notice that it's important to 'break state' between each position by physically moving between each move. Just shake your body a little!

Figure 2-2:
The NLP meta-mirror exercise.

1. Stand in *first position*, your point of view, imagining that you're look-ing at the other person in second position. Ask yourself: 'What am I experiencing, thinking, and feeling as I look at this person?'

2. Now shake that off and go to stand in *second position,* imagining you're that person looking back at yourself in first position. Ask your-self: 'What am I experiencing, thinking, and feeling as I look at this person?'

3. Now shake that off and stand in *third position*, that of the indepen-dent observer looking at both people in this relationship impartially. Looking at yourself in first position, how do you respond to that 'you' there?

4. Now shake that off and stand in a further external space, the *fourth position*. Think about how your thoughts in third position compared to your reactions in the first position and switch them around. For example, in the first position you may have felt confused, while in the third position you may have felt sadness. Whatever your reactions were, in your mind's eye switch them to the opposite positions.

5. Go back and revisit *second position*. Ask yourself: 'How is this differ-ent now? What has changed?'

6. Finish by coming home to *first position*. Ask yourself: 'How is this dif-ferent now? What has changed?'

Book II

Neuro-linguistic Programming

Understanding Metaprograms: Your Unconscious Mental Filters

Metaprograms are unconscious filters directing what you pay attention to, the way you process any information you receive, and how you then communi-cate it.

If you want to build rapport with someone quickly and you are forearmed, you may choose to dress like them, behave like them, or at least speak like them. And by that we don't mean you mimic someone's accent, rather that you use their vocabulary. By beginning to hear people's metaprograms you have the choice to use the same words and phrases as the person with whom you are interacting. Because people's use of metaprograms are mostly uncon-scious, by matching their metaprograms, what you say will have the added dimension of communicating with someone's unconscious mind at the same time as with their conscious mind.

In this section we introduce you to six metaprograms we hope you will find most useful in communicating more effectively, more quickly, and – as you experience the benefits of better communication – we hope you will be motivated to discover more about other metaprograms.

As children, you pick up metaprograms from your parents, teachers, and the culture you are brought up in. Your life experiences may change these learned programs as you get older. For instance, if you grow up being admonished for being too subjective, you may start practising detachment and learn to suppress your feelings. You could find this affects your choice of career. Instead of entering a caring profession you may decide to become someone who uses their intellect more. Your learning style may be influenced too and you learn to focus more on facts and figures. If you deliver training, you may depend more on drier, chalk-and-talk systems than on getting students more involved with touchy-feely experiments.

Of the many metaprograms that have been written about, we have chosen six that we think are the most useful to get you started. We selected the *global and detail* metaprogram as we believe that this is one that has great potential for conflict and by recognising another's capacity for operating at the global or detail end of the scale you may be able to avoid possible problems. By understanding the other five metaprograms you will be able to learn how you can motivate not only yourself but other people with whom you come in contact.

The metaprograms discussed in this section are:

- ✔ Proactive/Reactive
- ✔ Options/Procedures
- ✔ Toward/Away From
- ✔ Internal/External
- ✔ Global/Detail
- ✔ Sameness/Difference

As you think about metaprograms, keep these things in mind:

- ✔ Metaprograms are not an either/or choice as they operate along a sliding scale ranging from one preference to the other.
- ✔ Metaprograms are not a means to pigeonhole people.

There is no right or wrong metaprogram. It is simply that you run various combinations of metaprograms depending on the context of the communication and the environment in which you find yourself.

Metaprograms and language patterns

Everyone has patterns of behaviour which can be picked up from their language, long before the behaviour becomes apparent. Leslie Cameron-Bandler, among others, has conducted further research into the metaprograms developed by Richard Bandler. She and her student, Rodger Bailey, established that people who use similar language patterns portray similar patterns of behaviour. For example, people with an entrepreneurial flare may have similar patterns – outgoing, good at persuading people, strong belief in themselves, and so on – even though they may work in very different fields.

Imagine a gathering of the heads of the United Nations without any translators. There would be very little communication. A similar break down in communication can occur if you are unaware of the metaprograms the person you are trying to communicate with is operating. Learning about metaprograms allows you to become proficient in translating the mental maps people use to navigate their way around their experiences.

Book II

Neuro-linguistic Programming

Bandler and Grinder realised that people who used similar language patterns developed deeper rapport more quickly than people who used dissimilar ones. I am sure you have heard some English people who are non-French speakers complain that the French are unfriendly. Others who can speak French refute this. Metaprograms are a powerful way to establish rapport verbally by hearing the patterns someone is running and then responding with language that they can understand easily.

To help you understand the type of language that is characteristic of the various metaprograms, we've included in the following sections phrases that you're likely to hear with each metaprogram.

Proactive/Reactive

If you are more inclined to take action and get things moving you operate at the proactive end of the scale. If, however, you are inclined to take stock and wait for things to happen, you are probably more reactive. Following are more in-depth descriptions:

- ✔ **Proactive:** If you are proactive you will take charge and get things done. You are good at spotting solutions to situations which require constant fire-fighting. You may find yourself drawn to jobs in sales or working for yourself. You find yourself upsetting some people, especially if they are more reactive, as they will liken you to a bulldozer.

- ✔ **Reactive:** If you are more reactive you may be quite fatalistic. You will wait for others to take the lead or take action only when you consider the time to be right. You may need to be careful not to analyse yourself into a paralysis.

Toward/Away From

People either invest time, energy, and resources moving 'toward' or 'away from' something they find enjoyable or something they wish to avoid. The something is their values which they use to judge whether an action is either good or bad.

The *away from* people have a tendency to notice what could go wrong and are very useful to employ for maintaining production plants and aircrafts, managing crises, or in conducting critical analysis. These are the people who are motivated by the 'stick'. You can motivate *away from* people by threats of job losses and the negative consequences of not meeting financial targets.

People with *toward* metaprograms may be seen as naïve by the *away from* people because the former do not always think about and cater for potential problems in the pursuit of their goals.

Options/Procedures

If you are more of an *options* person, you enjoy trying out new ways of doing things. As a *procedures* person, you will display a preference for following set methodologies.

An *options* person loves variety. The analogy that springs to mind is that of offering a gourmet a smorgasbord or dim sum and letting him pick and savour the myriad delicacies on offer.

If you are a person with a preference for an *options* metaprogram you will be good at starting projects, although you may not always see them through.

If you have a *procedures* preference, you like to follow set rules and procedures, although you may prefer to have these created for you rather than design them yourself.

Once you have a working procedure you will follow it repeatedly, without modification. You may feel compelled to follow each step of a procedure to the end and feel cheated if circumstances prevent you from getting there.

You will stick to speed limits and take personal affront when other drivers drive along using a mobile phone or with only one hand on the steering wheel.

Internal/External

If you trust your judgement when it comes to making decisions or in knowing you have done a good job, you operate at the *internal* end of the scale for this metaprogram.

If you need feedback from other people to know how well you have done, you probably have more of an *external* preference.

Global/Detail

Some people find it easier to see the big picture when they start work on a project or when setting a goal. Others find it difficult to get a global perspective, but find it much easier to envisage the steps required to achieve the goals and prefer to work with smaller details.

Chunk size refers to the size of the task a person prefers to work with. A person with a *global* preference will break tasks into larger chunks than a *detail* person. A *detail* person will need to have a task chunked down into smaller, more manageable steps. The scale at which people work is referred to as the *chunk size*.

Book II

Neuro-linguistic Programming

If you are one of the people who prefer to work at a global or conceptual level and have trouble dealing with details, you will want a *big picture* outline of what you are about to be taught when you learn something new. If your presenter launches straight into the details of the subject, you may have difficulty in understanding the new topic. You find it easier to see the forest but get confused by the mass of trees. If you prefer working with the big picture, you may find yourself switching off or getting impatient with the amount of information that a *detail* person may give you.

If, on the other hand, you prefer eating the elephant a bite at a time, you have a predisposition for handling details. You may find it difficult to share the vision of someone who thinks globally. *Detail* people handle information in sequential steps and may have trouble getting their priorities right because they are unable to make the more general connections to other areas within which they are working. These people are very good in jobs that require close attention to detail, especially over a period of time, for instance on an assembly line or conducting a test in a laboratory.

Sameness/Sameness with Difference/Difference

If, when you learn or experience something new, you try and match the information to what you already know, you have a preference for *sameness*.

Or you could be someone who first notices the similarities in situations and becomes aware of the differences, in which case you have a *sameness with difference* preference.

If, on the other hand, you look at what is different to what you already know, you prefer sorting by *difference*.

As a *sameness* person, you have a head start when it comes to rapport because rapport is all about matching someone else's physiology and thinking – probably something you do automatically. You tend to delete a lot of incoming information if you cannot spot the similarities to previous situations. You may have difficulty in learning something new because you do not have hooks on which to hang the relevant information that is coming in. You are one of the people who does not like change, may even feel threatened by it, and find it difficult to adapt to changes in your work and home life. As a general rule, you only initiate major changes anywhere between 15 and 25 years. This means you probably move house or change jobs very infrequently.

As a *sameness with difference* person, you will first look for similarities in a situation and then you tend to spot the differences. You like the evolutionary approach to change, preferring a major change every five to seven years and you may resist sudden change.

If you operate a *difference* metaprogram, you thrive on change. You love a revolution in your life at least every 18 months and create change for the sake of change. As with *sameness* people, you too have a tendency to delete vast amounts of data, except in your case it is information in which you cannot spot the differences. Some people may find you difficult because of your tendency to always see the other side of the coin.

A close family member of Romilla sorts by differences. Until she learned about NLP, communications between Romilla and her family member were difficult, to say the least. Now Romilla really values his input. When working on a new project, she does all the brainstorming with other friends and family members. Once she has worked out a fairly solid idea, she approaches her contrary relative who is able to identify the errors and problems the rest of the brainstormers have overlooked. This process saves a lot of time that would otherwise have been wasted in trial and error.

To uncover a person's preferred metaprogram in a given context, you can ask, 'What is the relationship between this job and your previous job?'

A person who sorts for *sameness* may respond with, 'There's no difference, I'm still writing programs.'

A person who runs a *sameness with difference* metaprogram may respond, 'I'm still writing programs for the accounting suite, but now I have the responsibility of supervising three junior programmers.'

The *difference* person may respond with, 'I've been promoted to supervise junior programmers and everything is different.'

A little party game is to ask someone the relationship between the rectangles shown in Figure 2-3. Each rectangle is the same size, but don't tell the person this before asking them.

A person who is operating a *sameness* metaprogram may say, 'They're all rectangles' or 'the rectangles are the same size'.

A person who runs a *sameness with difference* metaprogram may respond with, 'They're all rectangles but one is positioned vertically'.

A person who has a *differences* metaprogram is likely to say, 'They're laid out differently'.

Figure 2-3:
The Sameness/ Sameness with Difference/ Difference party game.

If you do not have rectangles, bar mats, or coasters, you could use three, one pound coins and place two with their heads up and one with the tail up and ask about the relationship between the three coins.

People with a preference for *sameness* will use words like 'same', ''similar', 'in common', 'as always', ''static', 'unaltered', 'as good as', and 'identical'.

People who operate from a *sameness with difference* base will use words and phrases like 'the same except', 'better', 'improve', 'gradual', 'increase', 'evolutionary', 'less', 'although', 'same but the difference is'. In order to gain greater rapport with these people, you should emphasise things that are the same, followed by what is different, for example 'the work will be fairly similar to what you have done, however you will be involved with implementing new solutions.'

In order to influence someone who operates at the *difference* end of the spectrum, use words and phrases like 'chalk and cheese', 'different', 'altered', 'changed', 'revolutionary', 'completely new', 'no comparison', and 'I don't know if you'll agree or not . . .'

Combinations of metaprograms

You have a combination of metaprograms that you prefer to adopt when you are within your comfort zone. You should try to remember that this preference may change depending on the different circumstances you find yourself in. For instance, a project manager may combine *difference*, *proactive*, *detail*, and *toward* when at work but may choose to be more of a *sameness, reactive, global* person when at home.

It is also important to realise that certain combinations of metaprograms may fit certain professions better than others and that there are many more metaprograms which may be of use to you.

Would you want the pilot of your 747 to have a high *options*, *global* and *difference* metaprogram combination? I think I might be a little nervous of being in the hands of someone who might decide to skip a couple of the flight checks because the procedure was boring and it might be fun to see what would happen if he could get that red light to flash.

Would you want your prescription filled by a chemist who would like to test the result of adding a couple extra drops of the pretty blue liquid to your angina medicine?

The above examples are meant to illustrate that jobs work best when the profile of the person fits the parameters of their job.

You might decide the best metaprogram fit for a quality controller is for her to have a preference for *detail*, *away from*, and *procedures*.

Chapter 3

Reaching Beyond the Words People Say

*H*ave you ever invited someone, even yourself, to: 'Say what you mean and mean what you say?' If only speech was so easy.

You use words all the time as important tools to convey your thoughts and ideas – to explain and share your experiences with others. In Chapter 2, we explain that in any face-to-face communication, people take just part of the meaning from the words that come out of your mouth. Your body language – all those movements and gestures – and the tone of your voice transmit the rest.

Words offer just a model, a symbol of your experience; they can never fully describe the whole picture. Think of an iceberg – the tip above the surface is like the words you say. NLP says this is the *surface structure* of our language. Beneath the surface lies the rest of the iceberg – the home of the whole experience. NLP calls this the *deep structure*.

This chapter takes you from the surface structure and leads you into the deep structure so that you can get beyond the vague words of everyday speech to be more specific about what you mean. You'll meet the magic of the Meta Model, one of NLP's most important revelations that clarifies the meaning of what people say. No one gives a complete description of the entire thought process which lies behind their words; if they did, they'd never finish speaking. The Meta Model is a tool for you to get closer access to someone's experience that they code into speech.

It's been a hard day's work

Supper table talk in my (Kate) family often goes like this: 'So, has it been a hard day's work today?' In recounting the highlights of the day, our conversation invariably centres on what constitutes a hard day's work. Does a 12-hour-long stint in a warm, comfortable office surrounded by the latest computers and coffee-making devices qualify?

The question stemmed from watching a TV documentary of motorway maintenance men who work shifting traffic cones in the dead of night. We agreed that this really was hard work by comparison with the reality of a hard day for us as well as most of our friends and co-workers.

What's a hard day for you? In just one sentence, you can conjure up a wealth of different meanings. The qualities of the work experience if you're running a home or an office would be very different by comparison with the physical reality of, say, a firefighter tackling blazes or a builder constructing houses and exposed to the elements in all weathers.

A statement such as 'a hard day's work' will be interpreted in numerous different ways. To get to any one speaker's precise meaning requires access to more information– the facts that have been left out. As you read on in this chapter, you'll see how to gain easy access to relevant information to stop you jumping to the wrong assumptions about somebody else's experience.

Gathering Specific Information with the Meta Model

Richard Bandler and John Grinder, the founders of NLP, discovered that when people speak they naturally adopt three key processes with language, which they labelled as: *deletion*, *generalisation*, and *distortion*. These processes enable us all to explain our experiences in words to others without going into long-winded details and boring everyone to death.

These processes happen all the time in normal everyday encounters. We *delete* information by not giving the whole story. We make *generalisations* by extrapolating from one experience to another, and we *distort* reality by letting our imaginations run wild.

Figure 3-1 demonstrates the NLP model of how you experience the real world through your senses – visual (pictures), auditory (sounds), kinaesthetic (touch and feelings), olfactory (smell), and gustatory (taste). Your perception of reality is filtered or checked against what you already know through the processes of generalisation, distortion, and deletion. This is how you create your personal map or mental model of the real world.

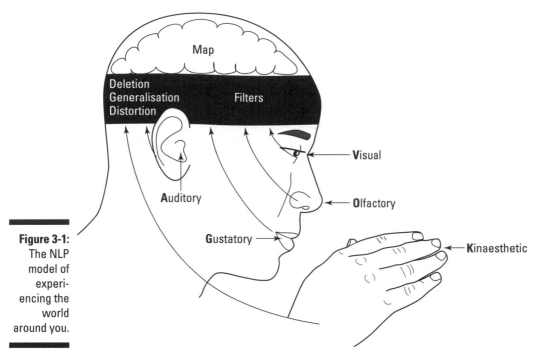

Figure 3-1:
The NLP model of experiencing the world around you.

Book II

Neuro-linguistic Programming

By watching and analysing two different, highly experienced therapists – at work talking to their clients – Bandler and Grinder came up with the NLP Meta Model as a way to explain the link between language and experience.

Bandler and Grinder were interested in finding the rules that determine how humans use language so that others could learn similar skills. They were influenced by their own knowledge of linguistics and the field of *transformational grammar*, and idea that set out ideas on how people describe and record their experiences in language. They published the results in 1975 in *The Structure of Magic*. Although the early work came from the field of psychotherapy – because they wanted to enrich the skills of 'people-helpers' – the models shed light equally well for you and I in ordinary situations where we're simply talking with friends, family, and colleagues.

The Meta Model offers a series of questions that enable you to overcome the deletions, distortions, and generalisations that people make. You'll recognise some of the questions. They'll be questions you naturally ask when you want to clarify meaning. But perhaps you haven't thought about them consciously before. Asked in a gentle way and with rapport, these questions let you gather more information to define a clearer picture of what is really meant.

Table 3-1 summarises some of the different ways in which we can delete, generalise, and distort an experience through the language we adopt. Don't worry about the names of the NLP patterns just yet. It's more important that you begin to tune your ears into what people actually say. As you learn to spot the main Meta Model patterns that you prefer yourself, and that others favour too, you're in a great position to respond appropriately. We offer some suggestions of what to say when you respond to gather the missing information that helps you to be sure of understanding what the other person really means.

Table 3-1	Meta Model Patterns	
NLP Meta Model Patterns	*Examples of the patterns you might hear*	*Questions to help you gather information or expand the other person's viewpoint*
Deletion		
Simple deletion	I've been out	Where specifically have you been?
	Help!	What do you want help with?
Unspecified verbs	She annoyed me	How specifically did she annoy you?
Comparisons	She's better than me	Better at what than you?
Judgements	You are wrong	Who says so and what are the facts?
Nominalisations	Our *relationship* isn't working	How do we not relate to each other?
	Change is easy	Changing what is easy?
Generalisation		
Modal operators of possibility	I *can't* . . . it's not possible	What stops you?
Modal operators of necessity	We *have to* do this . . . we *should, ought to*	What would happen if we didn't?
Universal quantifiers	He *never* thinks about my feelings	Never, ever?
	We *always* do it this way	Every single time? What would happen if we did it differently?
Distortion		
Complex equivalence	With a name like that, he must be popular	How does having this name mean that he is popular?

NLP Meta Model Patterns	Examples of the patterns you might hear	Questions to help you gather information or expand the other person's viewpoint
Mind reading	You're going to love this	How do you know that? Who says?
Cause and effect	His voice makes me angry	How does his voice make you angry?
	I made her feel awful	How exactly did you do that?

Book II

Neuro-linguistic Programming

Deletion – you're so vague

Deletions happen when you pay attention to some information coming in through your senses but are completely oblivious to other stimuli. Think of a nutty professor, so caught up in his work that he leaves home wearing his bedroom slippers.

When you are listening, you naturally ignore many extra sounds, saving you the effort of processing every single word. When you speak, you economise on all the details you could share. This is called deletion because something has been removed. Figure 3-2 shows some everyday examples of deletion.

Figure 3-2: The language of deletion.

"You were good."

"Just do it!"

"I don't know."

"This is important."

"I'm scared."

Just consider that your central nervous system is being fed some two million pieces of information every second. If every bit of this information had to be processed, imagine the time and energy you would need; an impossible task with full information overload!

To help you operate at peak efficiency, deletion delivers a valuable critical screening mechanism. Selective attention is deletion. Deletions in our language encourage us to fill in the gaps – to imagine – to make it up. If I say to you 'I bought a new car', then you will begin to guess more information. If I don't tell you what new car I've bought, then you will have your own ideas about what make it is, the colour, and age.

Abstract nouns and the wheelbarrow test

What we really like about the Meta Model is the way it helps you clarify vague statements. If you say to me 'Love is so painful', I would need more information from you to understand what was going on for you.

Abstract nouns – ones such as love, trust, honesty, relationship, change, fear, pain, obligation, responsibility, impression – are particularly hard to respond to. NLP calls these *nominalisations*. These are words where a verb (to *love*) has turned into a noun (*love*) which is hard to define in a way that everyone would agree on. In order to extract more meaning from your statement, I need to turn the noun back into a verb to help get more information and then

reply. My response to your statement above would be: 'How specifically is the way you love someone so painful?'

Imagine a wheelbarrow. If you think of a noun and can picture it inside the wheelbarrow, then it will be a concrete noun – a person, a flowerpot, an apple, a desk are all concrete examples. Nominalisations are the nouns that don't pass the wheelbarrow test. You can't put love, fear, a relationship, or pain in your wheelbarrow! Instead, when you rephrase these words as verbs, you put the action and responsibility back in them, which helps people explore more choices.

The downside of deletion is that it can restrict and limit our thinking and understanding. For example – we can develop the habit of deleting certain information and signals from others. Compliments and criticism are the classic example. Some people are experts at deleting compliments they receive and only noticing the criticism. So, too, they ignore success and only notice failure. If this rings a bell for you, then it's time to break the habit.

To gather deleted information, ask these useful questions:

> Who? What? When? Where? How?
>
> What precisely?
>
> What exactly?

Generalisation – beware the always, musts, and shoulds

You make a generalisation when you transfer the conclusions you came to from one experience to fit other similar situations or occurrences. Generalisations can be good; they help you to build a cognitive map of the world. If you didn't generalise, you would have to re-learn the alphabet and learn to put together individual letters like 'a+n+d' every time you came to read a book. Generalisations allow you to build on what you already know, without re-inventing the wheel.

Watch a young child getting on a two-wheeled bike for the first time. They pay tremendous attention to keeping their balance and steering it. Perhaps they'll need stabilisers for a time until they've mastered the skill. Yet, some weeks or months later, they're competent and don't have to re-learn each time they cycle away – they've generalised from one experience to the next.

Your ability to generalise from past experiences is another important skill that saves huge amounts of time and energy in learning about the world. These generalised experiences are represented by words. Think of the word 'chair'. You know what one is like: you've no doubt sat on many and seen it in different forms. As a child, you learned the word to represent a particular chair. Then you made a generalisation. So the next time you saw a chair, you could name it. Now whenever you see a chair, you understand its function.

The skill of generalisation can also limit our experience of options and differences in other contexts. When you've had a bad experience, then you may expect it to happen time and time again. A man who has experienced a string of unhappy romantic encounters may conclude 'All women are a pain' and decide that he's never going to meet a woman with whom he can live happily.

Romilla and I (Kate) were driving from a meeting on the motorway one afternoon when she ably demonstrated her natural ability to generalise and said: 'Gosh, have you noticed how *everyone's* driving my car?' Surprised, I asked how that could be the case. She pointed out to me that she had seen 15 new Mini Cooper cars in the last ten minutes. This was the car she had fallen in love with and she was deciding whether to buy it. All she could see everywhere were the possible colour combinations of this new car. I hadn't noticed one of them – I wasn't interested in a new car at all – just concentrating on getting through the traffic and out of London.

Think about the generalisations you hear about particular cultures or groups:

> British drink tea.
>
> Americans talk loudly.
>
> Scots are prudent with money.
>
> Italians are wild drivers.
>
> Unmarried mothers are a drain on society.
>
> Politicians can't be trusted.

Such rigid, black-and-white thinking that allows for no grey scale in between creates unhelpful generalisations about other people and situations. Stop and

Book II

Neuro-linguistic Programming

listen to what you say. And when you hear the verbal clues about generalisations in words like 'all', 'never', 'every', 'always' (Figure 3-3 shows several examples of everyday generalisations), then challenge yourself. Is *everyone* like that? Do *all* clients do that? Must we *always* do it this way?

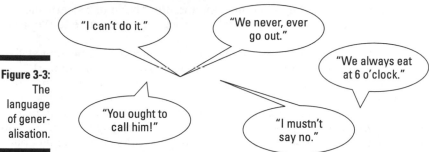

Figure 3-3:
The language of generalisation.

When you hear someone (or yourself!) generalising, ask these useful questions. They will make you stop and think about whether you are limiting your choices unnecessarily and encourage you to take a broader perspective.

What stops you?

Always? Never? Every?

So what happens if you do . . .?

Just imagine you could, what then?

To begin to explore your own thinking on what is possible and impossible, here's an easy exercise to play with in just ten minutes. Beware – it may change your life forever!

1. **Look at the following and jot down some of the statements you've made (to yourself as well as others) in the last week that start with these words:**

    'I always . . .'

    'I must . . .'

    'I should . . .'

    'I never . . .'

    'I ought to . . .'

    'I have to . . .'

2. **Now stop.**

3. **Go back to your list and for each statement ask yourself three questions:**

   'What would happen if I didn't . . .?'

   'When did I decide this?'

   'Is this statement true and helpful for me now?'

4. **Review your list in the light of the questions you asked.**

5. **Create a revised list for yourself that replaces the words 'I always', 'must', 'should never', 'ought to', and 'have to' with the words 'I choose to . . .'**

By completing this exercise you are examining some of the types of generalisations that you make (which NLP calls modal operators and universal quantifiers). Then, in step 3, you ask Meta Model questions to explore choices for yourself. By revising the statements in step 5, you put yourself back in control of your own decisions and behaviour.

Book II

Neuro-linguistic Programming

Distortion – that touch of fantasy

A distortion occurs when you misinterpret information coming in through your senses.

Disraeli was right when he said, 'Imagination governs the world'. Distortion, the process by which you change the meaning of the experience against your own map of reality, is one such example. Figure 3-4 shows some everyday examples of distortion.

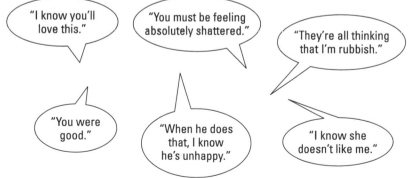

Figure 3-4:
The language of distortion.

"I know you'll love this."

"You must be feeling absolutely shattered."

"They're all thinking that I'm rubbish."

"You were good."

"When he does that, I know he's unhappy."

"I know she doesn't like me."

Tennis anyone?

There will be times when people want something so badly, that they will believe it to be true even when the evidence is against them. As a tennis coach, John Woodward finds that the most frustrating people in the junior tennis leagues are the competitive parents.

'They so desperately want their children to win that they become blind to the facts of the game. They see what they want to see, even if it's not true, to the extent that as they watch their children play matches, they'll give faulty line calls in favour of their own budding tennis star.

Grandparents are even worse! I once saw a grandfather attack his grandson's tennis opponent with his umbrella because he was convinced that his grandson had won a shot that everybody else saw as out.'

The problem with distortion, though, is that most people don't realise that the distortion doesn't necessarily represent the truth. Instead, it just represents their own perception. For example, have you ever come out of a meeting with a group of people and all had a different understanding of what happened? Or been to the cinema or theatre with a group of friends and come away with a completely different viewpoint about the message it conveyed when you chat to your friends about it? Distortion happens when you take one aspect of an experience and change it according to what is happening for you.

Creativity relies on the ability to distort reality in a way that makes new and interesting connections. Science fiction and cartoon strips distort in order to entertain as does art, poetry, and literature. A visit to the cinema or theatre, or reading a novel leaves you free to make your own meaning and connections. Distortion supports your ability to explore your own inner world, your dreams, and lets your imagination run wild.

At the same time, it can be unhelpful to be mind-readers. Mind reading is a further example of distortion. You can never know what someone else is truly thinking, even though they give out interesting clues. When negative distortion is combined with generalisation it can become quite debilitating. An example of this is a child who comes home from school and says: 'Everyone stares at me every time I walk into the classroom and they all think I'm stupid.'

Beware making judgements about what other people think until you have actually gathered specific information and reviewed the facts.

Here are some other useful questions to ask when you want to check for distorted meanings:

'Who says?'

'How do you know?'

'How exactly does x lead to y?'

Using the Meta Model

The Meta Model questions give you powerful verbal tools in business, in coaching, education, therapy, and in life. They let you use language to gain clarity and get closer to somebody's experience. You may want to adopt the Meta Model when you want to:

- ✔ **Get more information** to understand the objectives and scope of a new project.

- ✔ **Clarify the other person's meaning** to find out exactly what the other person has in mind. Are you both on the same wavelength or making assumptions that you really understand?

- ✔ **Spot your own and other people's limitations** to work through beliefs and habitual behaviour that can be unhelpful.

- ✔ **Open up more choices** to explore different ways of doing things for yourself and for others.

Book II

Neuro-linguistic Programming

Two simple steps

When you use the Meta Model, challenge distortions first, then generalisations, and then deletions. If you begin with deletions, you may get more information than you can handle.

To use the Meta Model, follow these simple steps:

1. **Listen to the words and spot the pattern** (distortion, generalisation, or deletion).

   Refer to the section 'Gathering Specific Information with the Meta Model' earlier in this chapter for an explanation of the language clues that will help you recognise which pattern is being used.

2. **Intervene with the right question.**

   For distortion, ask:

   - 'How do you know?'
   - 'What's the evidence?'

   For generalisation, ask:

   > 'Is that always the case? Every time? Never?'

   > 'What if . . .?'

   For deletion, ask

   > 'Tell me more . . .'

   > 'What, when, where, who, how?'

A couple of caveats

There's a way of asking questions that is considerate and valuable. There's another way that sounds like interrogation by the Spanish Inquisition. So here are some points to remember, *please* (we don't want you falling out with your best friend):

- Rapport always comes first.

- People need to trust before they're ready to open up on difficult issues. Pace their timing.

- Make sure you are clear about what you are trying to achieve – your outcome – as you ask questions, otherwise you will get overloaded with irrelevant information and you are not being helpful.

- Soften your voice and be sensitive in your questioning. Feed the questions gently into conversations and meetings rather than firing them like a market researcher in the street.

- Try the Meta Model out on yourself before you rush off to sort out your family and friends uninvited. Go steady. Like Tom in the following example, they may wonder what's happening and not thank you for your new-found interest.

On Friday nights Andrew winds down after a busy week working in the City with a beer at his favourite pub in the picturesque village where he lives. After taking an NLP training course, he was enthusiastic to try out the Meta Model. His drinking partner, Tom, an architect, talked about the week he'd had, and especially about a major argument he had had with a colleague over an important project.

As Tom began his tale with 'I'll never work with him again,' Andrew questioned the generalisation with: 'What never? Are you sure? What would happen if you did?'

Tom looked puzzled and responded with: 'Our partnership isn't going to work; communication has just broken down.'

Delighted to spot not one but two nominalisations in one sentence, Andrew jumped in with: 'How would you like to be a partner with this guy? And how might you be able to communicate?'

To which, Tom looked aghast and said: 'Look, you're normally on my side. What's going on?'

In his keenness to try out NLP, he'd forgotten to match and pace his friend and ease in gently with some subtle use of the Meta Model. All Tom really wanted that night was to have a good moan to a friend who would listen and sympathise.

Speaking So People Remember Your Message: Using Stories, Fables, and Metaphors

Stories get to the parts that other words don't reach. They speak to you at an unconscious level.

Through stories you can get your message across in a way that is much more effective than any logical argument. They connect to people's experiences, to their memories and their emotions. In NLP terms, stories help build rapport. They enable you to convey information indirectly, to pace someone's current reality and then lead them on to a new one. To move away from problems to different outcomes. To open up new possibilities. So when you are sitting comfortably, let us begin . . .

Book II

Neuro-linguistic Programming

Stories, metaphors, and you

Your brain is a natural pattern-matching machine and all the time you are matching and sorting. When you hear something new you go: 'Aha. This is like *this*. This reminds me of *that*.' Brains naturally recognise patterns. Stories and metaphors transport you to a different place and put you into a trance – a deeply relaxed state in which you are very resourceful and your brain naturally recognises patterns.

NLP defines metaphors broadly in terms of stories or figures of speech that imply a comparison. The reason NLP suggests that stories and metaphors work as valuable communication tools is because they distract the conscious mind and overload it with processing. Meanwhile the unconscious mind steps in to come up with creative solutions and the resources you need. Thus you're able to make new meanings and solve the problems.

The stories of your life

We live in a world of stories. And you too are an accomplished storyteller. Don't believe us? Consider this. When you recount the day's events to a friend or partner, you are telling a story. When you gossip on the telephone to your mates, or describe a business process to a client, you are telling a story. Events don't have to be make-believe to qualify as a story.

The travelling storyteller

Throughout history, people have told stories, myths, and legends, and used metaphors to communicate a message. The oral tradition preceded the written word and multi-media as a critical form of communication. Storytellers were typically travellers who would move from town to town, passing on important information by word-of-mouth. Without the luxury of email and PowerPoint, they used rhythm, rhyme, and visualisation to aid memory. The more fantastic and outrageous the story, the more you are likely to remember it.

Storytelling basics

Good stories whether they relate actual or imaginary events have four key ingredients. Think about a child's fairy story handed down through generations such as *The Wizard of Oz*, *Little Red Riding Hood*, or *Cinderella* and see if you can recognise these elements:

- The characters – you need a hero, plus goodies and baddies along the way
- The plot – the storyline of the journey that the hero takes
- A conflict – the challenge that the hero takes up or difficulty they face
- A resolution – the result or outcome that happens at the end of the tale (and hopefully it doesn't end in tears!)

Stories engage the left side of the brain to process the words and the sequence of the plots and the right side in terms of imagination, visualisation, and creativity.

Some stories are told solely to entertain, but you can use stories for a number of purposes:

- To focus concentration
- To illustrate a point
- To teach a lesson that people remember
- To sow new ideas
- To get people to recognise their own problems
- To make a complex idea simpler
- To change people's mood
- To challenge behaviour
- To have fun

Storytelling at work

Stories and metaphors work in business communication just as well as a social or religious context. We learn from others' experiences and take meaning from metaphors. Companies tell stories to:

- ✔ Communicate information
- ✔ Convey values of the organisation
- ✔ Educate people
- ✔ Give the listener the benefit of their wisdom
- ✔ Help teams to evaluate choices and make decisions

Book II

**Neuro-
linguistic
Programming**

Stories engage people more fully. This is why customer examples, testimonials, and case studies work so well to reinforce a business message. They're so much more powerful than a pure product promotion.

Powerful Metaphors

Just as people tell stories all day, your ordinary conversations will be richly embroidered with metaphors. Consider these examples:

'Look, it's a jungle out there!'

'He was putty in their hands.'

'She's a pain in the neck.'

'He's a breath of fresh air.'

'We could have cut the atmosphere with a knife.'

Some would say that, while a picture is worth a thousand words, a metaphor is worth one thousand pictures.

Metaphors in NLP

The word metaphor is derived from the Greek, and literally means 'to carry across'. A metaphor makes a comparison, a parallel between two sometimes unrelated terms. It can be a powerful and innovative way of describing a situation; it can help the listener to reflect on himself or herself; or see a difficult situation in a new light, providing a novel way of resolving it.

In NLP, metaphors are used in a broader sense than that defined in English grammar – they are used to help people move across from one context to another. NLP calls this movement *chunking sideways.* Chunking is about moving up and down levels of detail (up to the big picture or down to specifics) in order to communicate with somebody at the most appropriate level.

As Nick Owen describes in his book *The Magic of Metaphor* (Crown House Publishing, 2001): 'Metaphors are not simply poetic or rhetorical embellishments, but powerful devices for shaping perception and experience.'

In my (Kate) Watercress training business, I help people to build their presentations. On a particular workshop, Janet, one of the delegates, was looking at creative ways to liven up a presentation to a group of teenage children. As a careers advisor, Janet's work takes her into schools where she needs to inspire groups with all the options of apprenticeship schemes. At first, she stood up and explained the choices open to the kids in the hope they'd listen because of her strong enthusiasm and in-depth knowledge. Later, as she thought about ways of refining her presentation with stories and metaphors, Janet hit on the idea of using the metaphor of a mobile phone – something that all the kids could identify with. She compared all the various career routes and choices with the sophisticated functions of the latest phone model. In this way, she bridged the gap from the advisor to the student and found a way to develop a more compelling talk. Thanks to the appealing metaphor, she discovered a fresh approach to enliven her story and inspire the kids.

To practise creating metaphors and have a little fun at the same time, try this exercise. You need three people: Person A has a subject (like writing a book, for example) that they'd like to communicate in a different way. Follow these steps:

1. **Person A says: '<Topic> is like . . .'**

   Using the book writing example, Person A would actually say, 'Writing a book is like . . .'

2. **Person B thinks of an object . . . any object at all to complete the sentence 'Writing a book is like . . .'**

   Person B, for example, might say, 'an apple'.

3. **Person C makes the connection.**

   For example, they might say: '. . . because you can get your teeth into it.'

This exercise makes a good suppertime game. And you can use it to find a metaphor to help you communicate a message in a more memorable way.

Using metaphors to find new solutions

One of Robert Dilts tales in his book *Sleight of Mouth* is about the young man in a psychiatric ward suffering from the delusion that he is Jesus Christ. He spends his days unproductively, rambling around, annoying and ignored by the other patients. All attempts by the psychiatrists and their aides fail to convince the man of his delusion.

One day, a new psychiatrist arrives on the scene. After observing the patient quietly for some time, he approaches the young man. 'I understand that you have some experience as a carpenter,' he says. 'Well . . . yes, I guess I do,' replies the patient. The psychiatrist explains to the patient that they are building a new recreation room at the facility and need the help of someone who has the skills of a carpenter. 'We could sure use your assistance,' says the psychiatrist, 'That is, if you are the type of person that likes to help others.'

Book II

Neuro-linguistic Programming

And so the story ends well. The patient becomes drawn into a project, begins to interact with people again, and becomes able to leave the hospital and secure a stable job.

In this therapeutic story, the new psychiatrist connects with the client by working with his or her own metaphor. If the patient believes he is Jesus Christ, the psychiatrist accepts that and doesn't attempt to contradict. Instead the psychiatrist works with the patient's belief and adopts the same metaphor – Jesus the carpenter – to effect the cure.

Skilled therapists of all disciplines frequently work with the client's own metaphors to help shift problems. In the same way, you can work with other people's metaphors to aid communication in everyday conversation. This might be:

✔ To convey bad news like project delays or job changes

✔ To calm down an anxious teenager facing exams

✔ To explain a complicated subject to a group of people

✔ To encourage courage or confidence in a young child

Word plays on themes like weather and nature – rain and storms to sunshine and calm, or comparing a challenging situation to climbing a mountain or crossing a river – can defuse tension. Also, relating a message in terms of your friend's favourite sports – like golf, tennis, sailing, or football can help elicit shifts in thinking.

As an example, when your colleague at work tells you 'This project is a real nightmare,' you can gently drop words around sleep and dreaming into the conversation to gain more information or lead them to a more positive state of thinking. So you might feed some of the following types of language into the discussion: 'What aspects of the project are keeping you awake at night?', 'Are there some scary bits?', 'Perhaps people need to sleep on this for a while.', 'How would you like to get this put to bed?', and 'So in your wildest dreams, what would you see happening?'

Anthony is a therapist who works with clients with addictive behaviours. He told us: 'I had a client who told me about the pleasure she derived from her drinking until it got out of control. Initially she described the delight of her favourite tipple – the anticipation and smell of the first glass, how appealing it looked in the bottle, beautifully packaged and presented. But as she went on to describe the feelings of helplessness as the addiction overtook her, the alcohol was transformed into an ugly spirit that haunted and frightened her. Over a period of time, we were able to work with her story, develop the plot and re-work it to have a happier ending. She could then believe in a future where she could break free from the addiction that was overwhelming her life.'

Direct and indirect metaphors

NLP distinguishes between direct and indirect types of metaphors.

- ✔ A *direct* metaphor compares one situation with another where there's an obvious link in terms of the type of content. An example would be to compare learning a new software application with learning to drive. Both are about learning.

- ✔ An *indirect* metaphor makes comparisons which are not immediately obvious. So it might compare learning the software with cooking a meal or planning a holiday. Such indirect metaphors form the basis of the most creative advertising campaigns.

When I (Kate) set up a training venture with two partners, they held a brain-storming session to come up with a name that was memorable and different instead of the predictable 'ABC Associates'. They chose the name 'Watercress' as an indirect metaphor because of the subtle connotations of soft skills, a fresh approach, and building on hidden strengths.

Here's a group exercise that you can have fun with. It builds in the use of metaphors to encourage new thinking.

Get together a group of three people and follow these steps.

1. **One person (A) thinks of an issue they are currently trying to resolve. A describes their issue to B and C.**

Isometric metaphors

The hypnotherapist Milton Erickson had incredible successes with very sick people by telling them therapeutic stories while they listened in a very relaxed and receptive trance. The clients would then take their own meanings from the stories and apply these to their own situation to improve their own health.

Erickson's technique of these specially constructed stories that he'd tell to his clients is explained in NLP as an *isometric metaphor*. Isometric means *having equal dimensions or measurements*. Therapists will construct a story about a completely different subject that runs parallel to the structure of the client's problem and use it to lead the client to a desired resolution.

Book II

Neuro-linguistic Programming

2. **The other two people (B and C) each think of a different object. (This can be ordinary or obscure, such as a loaf of bread or pink sunglasses.)**

3. **First B then C tells a story to the other two. This can be any type of story they like; the only rule and the object in some way.**

Exercise source: thanks to Ian McDermott, ITS Training

Building Your Own Stories

In storytelling, the most compelling stories are those that come from someone's heart. In this section we've gathered ideas for you to develop your own repertoire of stories and build your skills as an engaging storyteller. Even if you've not thought of yourself as a storyteller before now, you'll soon see how to capture your own story ideas and organise your thoughts for maximum effect.

As you begin to create your own favourite stories, think about:

- ✔ How you will *start* the story and how you will *finish*. Some great starts lose their way (and their readers) long before the finishing post.

- ✔ What happens in the *middle* to give the dramatic interest – what are the interesting landmarks, battles, dilemmas, or conflicts on the way?

- ✔ Who are the *characters* – who is the hero and what about the supporting cast? How will you make them memorable?

- ✔ Build the content around a strong framework.

Using the personal story builder journal

Everyday experiences can form the basis of your own compelling stories. Here's a way to capture and record storylines that you can adapt later.

1. **Find a *situation* that has generated an emotion.** Write down the emotion generated.

   For example, joy, laughter, fear, anger, surprise, confusion, disbelief.

2. **Name the *characters*.**

   Which people were involved?

3. **Tell what happened by giving three key points of the *storyline*.**

4. **Tell what the *outcome* was; in other words, how did it end?**

5. **Describe something funny or *interesting* that was communicated.**

6. **Explain what you *learned* from this.**

7. **List your ideas for *developing* this story:** Identify where, when and to whom you will tell it.

Stories develop and change over time. Come back to the journal at regular intervals to extend your repertoire. Listen to speakers who inspire or entertain you and you may notice their storylines are quite simple. Feel free to record interesting stories you've heard others tell and put your spin on them to make them your own.

More ways to flex your storytelling muscles

Effective storytelling is a fabulous skill that it's worth learning – a well-told story captures the audience and remains with the people long after the other details of an event are forgotten. Here are some suggestions for you to hone your technique.

- Start with simple stories and then get more adventurous as your skills grow.

- Head for the children's library for all sorts of examples of folk and fairy tales that you can adapt well to any context. One of our clients describes *Alice in Wonderland* as the best business book ever written.

✓ Remember that when you tell a story the focus is on you. Practise and live with your story so that when you perform, you can command the audience's attention and gather everyone with you. Know the first lines and last lines by heart and simplify the structure to a few key points.

✓ Tell a humorous story with a deadpan serious face and you'll have so much more impact than when you smirk all the way through. The surprise element is powerful.

✓ Hold onto that essential ingredient of rapport to keep people listening.

✓ Arrange the time, the place, and the setting in which you tell the story. Make sure people are relaxed and comfortable. Campfire settings and flickering log fires make for perfect storytelling moments – as do seats under shady trees on a lazy summer's day.

✓ Think of your voice as a well-tuned musical instrument. Enjoy exploiting all your skills to play it to the full range of expression.

✓ Speaking from the heart rather than reading from a book or script is more powerful . . . and people will allow you to be less than word perfect.

✓ Stimulate your audience's senses so they can see vivid pictures, hear the sounds, get in touch with feelings, even smell and taste the delicious tale you've concocted for them. Delicious.

✓ Have a great beginning. For examples of memorable openers, head to the sidebar 'Hooking people in'.

Book II

Neuro-linguistic Programming

Chapter 4

Exploring the Amazing Power of Your Senses

*T*hink back a moment. In Book One we introduced you briefly to the four main pillars of NLP. One of these upstanding elements is what NLP labels *sensory awareness* or how we make meaning of the world and create our own reality by using our senses.

Just for a minute, imagine a special creature with highly developed personal antennae. Well, actually that's you. You come tumbling into the world as a new human baby with amazingly well-developed senses, all geared up to discover the secrets of the universe. Unless you were born with difficulties in some way, you arrive as a perfect mini learning machine with eyes, ears, a sense of smell, taste, and touch, plus that most distinctly human quality – the ability to experience an emotional connection with others.

Of course, life all starts very well and then around the age of nine or ten it begins to go downhill. Ever heard the term 'Use it or lose it'? Often, as human beings, we get a bit lazy about learning or stuck in a rut. Once we find we're good at one way of doing things, that's the way things can stay. We take the easy option, narrowing down the possibilities. This is what can happen with our sensory awareness. We get very good at one style of thinking and processing information and let the rest of our senses lie dormant in a rusty heap.

Leonardo da Vinci mused that the average human 'looks without seeing, listens without hearing, touches without feeling, eats without tasting, moves without physical awareness, inhales without awareness of odour or fragrance, and talks without thinking'.

What an invitation for personal improvement!

So as you move on, dear reader, let us encourage you to try out some new ways of engaging with the world, fine tuning those incredible senses, and notice what a difference it can make. Guess what? You can look forward to serious fun and learning along the way.

Seeing, Hearing, and Feeling Your Way to Better Communication

The NLP model describes the way that you experience the external world – and, by the way, it's called real life – through your five senses or modalities of sight, sound, touch, smell, and taste.

Notice what happens inside your head and body, for example, when I say: 'Think about a delicious meal you've enjoyed.' You might see a picture of the table spread with colourful dishes, hear the sound of knives and forks, a waiter telling you about today's specials, or a friend chatting in the kitchen. Perhaps you notice a warm and pleasant anticipation inside as the aromas of food drift your way, you hear the uncorking of a bottle of wine or feel a cool glass of water in your hand, and then there's the taste of the first mouthful. Mmm . . . a multi-sensory experience. And this is just thinking about it in your armchair.

Until now you might not have thought about *how* you think (the process), only *what* you think about (the content). However, the quality of your thinking determines the quality of your experience. So the *how* is just as important, if not more important, than the *what.* This section introduces you to some dimensions of your thought processes that you may never have considered before. As you open up your own awareness as to how you think and make sense of the world, some interesting things happen. You begin to notice that you can control how you think about a person or situation. You also realise that not everybody thinks like you do about even the everyday events that seem so clear and obvious to you. And in the process you may decide that life can be more rewarding if you begin to think differently by paying attention to different senses.

Filtering reality

As you experience reality, you selectively filter information from your environment in three broad ways known in NLP as visual, auditory, and kinaesthetic (VAK for short, and VAKOG if you include the olfactory and gustatory bits).

- Some see the *sights* and *pictures* – you'll have a clear picture of the *visual* dimension.

- Others of you *hear* the *sounds* – you'll be tuned into the *auditory* dimension.

- A third group *grasp* the *emotional* aspects or *touch* – you'll feel the *kinaesthetic* dimension as *body awareness*, and in this grouping we also include the sense of taste (gustatory) and of smell (olfactory).

In 'NLP-speak' the different channels through which we represent or code information internally using our senses are described as the *representational systems*. You'll hear NLPers talk about rep systems for short, VAK preferences or preferred thinking styles. Visual, auditory, and kinaesthetic make up the main rep systems. The actual sensory-specific words (such as 'picture', 'word', 'feeling', 'smell', or 'taste') we employ – whether nouns, verbs, or adjectives are called the *predicates*.

Book II

Neuro-
linguistic
Programming

Hearing how they're thinking

As human beings we naturally blend a rich and heady mix of these three main dimensions, yet we tend to have a preference for one mode over the others.

So how do you decide whether you or others have a preference for the visual, auditory, or kinaesthetic dimension? Here's a fun quiz for you – and we don't claim it's scientific. Try it out on yourself and with friends and colleagues to find out more about your primary representation system. It'll take just a couple of minutes.

1. For each of the following statements, circle the option that best describes you.

   1. I make important decisions based on:

   a) Following my gut feelings

   b) The options that sound best

   c) What looks right to me

   2. When you attend a meeting or presentation, it is successful for you when people have:

   a) Illustrated the key points clearly

   b) Articulated a sound argument

   c) Grasped the real issues

3. People know if I am having a good or bad day by:

a) The way I dress and look

b) The thoughts and feelings I share

c) The tone of my voice

4. If I have a disagreement I am most influenced by:

a) The sound of the other person's voice

b) How they look at me

c) Connecting with their feelings

5. I am very aware of:

a) The sounds and noises around me

b) The touch of different clothes on my body

c) The colours and shapes in my surroundings

2. Copy your scores from the question onto the grid below:

1a	K	4a	A
1b	A	4b	V
1c	V	4c	K
2a	V	5a	A
2b	A	5b	K
2c	K	5c	V
3a	V		
3b	K		
3c	A		

3. Add up how many Vs, As, and Ks you got.

4. See how you did!

Did you get mainly V, A, or K or was it evenly mixed? Check your preferences below and see whether what we say here makes any sense for you.

✔ **V – visual** – A visual preference may mean you will be able to see your way clearly, keep an eye on things, and take a long-term view. You may enjoy visual images, symbols, design, watching sport, physics, maths, and chemistry. You may need to have an attractively designed environment.

✔ **A – auditory** – An auditory preference may mean you will be able to tune into new ideas, maintain harmonious relationships, and sound people out. You may enjoy music, drama, writing, speaking, and literature. You may need to manage the sound levels in your environment.

✔ **K – kinaesthetic** – A kinaesthetic preference may mean you will be able to get to grips with new trends, keep a balance, hold tight onto reality. You may enjoy contact sports, athletics, climbing, working with materials – electronics or manufacturing. You may need to have a comfortable environment.

Within Britain and America it's estimated that visual is the dominant style for approximately 60 per cent of the population. This is hardly surprising given the bombardment of our visual senses.

Beware of labelling people as visuals, auditories, or kinaesthetics – a gross generalisation. Instead, think of them as preferences or behaviours rather than identities. Be mindful, too, that no one system is better or worse than any other. (You can't help but operate in the different modes, even if this happens unconsciously.) It's simply a different way of taking in and storing information as you experience the world about you. After all, everyone's unique.

Listen to the World of Words

In the early days of NLP, the founders, Richard Bandler and John Grinder, became fascinated by how people used language in different ways. The whole NLP notion of *representational systems* came out of their seminars and study groups when they identified patterns of speech linked to the VAK senses. We represent our experience through our senses, and NLP calls the senses representational systems.

The everyday language you use provides clues to your preferred representational system. In enhancing your own communication skills, listen to the types of words people use. You'll find clever clues as to what's going on inside their heads, whether they will be more responsive to pictures, words, or sounds. Table 4-1 demonstrates.

Book II

Neurolinguistic Programming

Table 4-1	VAK Words and Phrases	
Visual	*Auditory*	*Kinaesthetic*
Bright, blank, clear, colour, dim, focus, graphics, illuminate, insight, luminous, perspective, vision	Argue, ask, deaf, discuss, loud, harmony, melody, outspoken, question, resonate, say, shout, shrill, sing, tell, tone, utter, vocal, yell	Cold, bounce, exciting, feel, firm, flow, grasp, movement, pushy, solid, snap, touch, trample, weight
It appears that	The important question we are all asking is...	Driving an organisation
A glimpse of reality	So you say	We reshaped the work
We looked after our interests	I heard it from his own lips	Moving through
This is a new way of seeing the world	Who's calling the tune?	It hit home
Now look here	Clear as a bell	Get a feel for it
This is clear cut		Get to grips with
Sight for sore eyes	Word for word	Pain-in-the-neck
Show me what you mean	We're on the same wavelength	Solid as a rock
Tunnel vision	Tune into this	Take it one step at a time
	Music to my ears	
	That strikes a chord	

Eye accessing cues

Body language offers wonderful clues to people's preferred representational systems. How we breathe, our posture, body type, and voice tone and tempo tends to vary according to visual, auditory, and kinaesthetic styles. In the early days of NLP, Bandler and Grinder observed that people move their eyes in systematic directions depending on which representational system they are accessing. These movements are called *eye accessing cues*.

What this means is that when people move their eyes in response to a question, you can pretty much guess whether they are accessing pictures, sounds, or feelings. Why is this helpful, you may wonder? The answer is that you have a great chance of knowing, even without them uttering a word, which system they will use and how you can talk to them in a way that will make them respond positively to you. Table 4-2 outlines what eye movements are associated with which representational system.

Table 4-2		Accessing Cues	
Pattern	*Eyes move to the subject's*	*What's happening inside*	*Sample of language*
Visual constructed	Top right	Seeing new or different images	Think of an elephant covered in pink icing
Visual remembered	Top left	Seeing images seen before	Think of your partner's face
Visual	Blank stare ahead	Seeing either new or old images	See what's important
Auditory constructed	Centre right	Hearing new or different sounds	Listen to the sound of your name backwards
Auditory remembered	Centre left	Remembering sounds heard before	Hear your own door-bell ring
Auditory internal dialogue	Bottom left	Talking to oneself	Ask yourself what you want
Kinaesthetic	Bottom right	Feelings, emotions, sense of touch	Notice the temperature of your toes

Book II

Neuro-linguistic Programming

The following picture shows the kind of processing most people do when they move their eyes in a particular direction. A small percentage of the population, including about half of all left-handers, are reversed – their eye movements are the mirror image of those shown.

The picture in Figure 4-1 is drawn as if you are looking at someone else's face and shows how you would see their eyes move. So, for example, if they are moving up and to your right into the *visual remembered* position, your own eyes would be shifting up and to your left if you're trying it out on yourself as in a mirror.

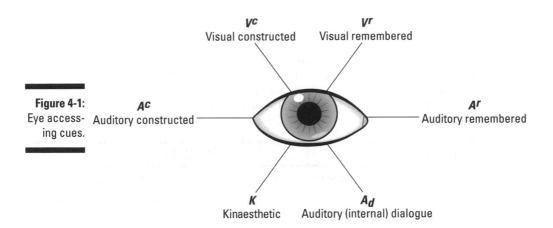

Figure 4-1:
Eye access-
ing cues.

Making the VAK system work for you

Once you become aware of VAK, then life gets more interesting. Here are some ideas on how you can pull it out of your new toolkit and use it to your advantage.

✔ **Influence a business meeting, training session, or presentation.** Remember that when you speak to a room full of people they will all have a preference for how they take in information and you don't know what that is. Unfortunately, people don't have a label on their foreheads to inform you about what they want to know and how they want to receive it – give me the picture, tell me the words, share your feelings about this subject. So what you need to do is ensure you connect with each and every person in the room by presenting your ideas with a variety of media. Vary your presenting style and aids to help the visuals see it with pictures, the auditories to hear it loud and clear, and the kinaesthetics to experience it with feeling.

✔ **Make home projects fun for all.** Recognise that each family member has a different way of thinking about a major project. Perhaps you'd like to extend the house, re-decorate a room, or re-design the garden. Not everybody wants to spend hours talking it through, with discussions that stretch late into the night. Your partner may want to pore over the drawings, while your kids will be motivated by the chance to just get in there and get their hands dirty with paint or earth.

✔ **Develop your goals so they're more real for yourself.** When you set goals in your personal or professional life, they will come alive if you really use all your senses. Think of what they will really look, sound, and feel like when you've achieved them and at every step along the way. NLPers get proficient at imagining all the fine details of their future experience – you'll hear the phrase 'putting up a movie screen' to describe how people can create their own dream. So if you want to motivate someone (or yourself) to push themselves out of their comfort zones, help them to explore what it will be like when the task is complete and the hard work is done.

✔ **Help children to learn better.** Thank goodness education has changed dramatically since we were at school and teachers now recognise that pupils all learn in different ways. As both parents and teachers, you need to support children to understand how they learn at their best – and appreciate that it may be different to the way you were taught or would like to learn. Visual learners will benefit from pictures, wall displays, and diagrams. Auditory learners need to hear what they are learning – through discussions, lectures, and music. Kinaesthetic learners benefit from practical sessions and role playing. They like a 'hands-on' approach. Teachers of groups of pupils need to provide a multi-sensory approach that caters for all styles. Children may be labelled as 'slow' when in fact the dominant teaching style does not fit with their preferred way to learn. All these principles apply to adult learners, too.

✔ **Increase the impact of the written word**. When you put pen to paper, words to screen – from a job description, to customer proposal, charity letter, product advertisement, or article for your local community newsletter – you'll need to broaden your vocabulary to cover all the modalities. To appeal to every reader, select words that include all three.

✔ **Connect with clients and colleagues on the phone.** Nowadays more and more business happens on the phone and with email rather than face-to-face. You may never get to even meet some of your clients or colleagues. Keep a pad by the phone and make a note of the kind of language they use – can you hear visual, auditory, or kinaesthetic language? As you listen, and then reply, phrase your sentence to match their preference.

One a day

As you read this chapter, you may have become more curious about yourself and those you spend time with – how you think and experience life around you. To enhance your skills further, you can explore your senses in different ways. Pick a sense theme for each day.

This could be an *olfactory* day, when you pay attention to every fragrance, smell, and aroma. Or a *visual* day, when you switch off the music and

focus on the sights, shapes, and pictures – see what's around you. A *touch* day can be fun, when you feel the textures around you or get in touch with your feelings at regular points in the day.

If you're a creature of habit who takes the dog for a walk every morning or drives the same route every day, notice what changes for you when you pay attention to just one sense at a time.

Book II

Neuro-linguistic Programming

Discovering How to Fine Tune Your Senses

Try this: Think of a really pleasant experience that you have had. You don't have to share the experience with us so you can let rip and really get into it. As you think of the experience, do you get a picture, feel a feeling, hear any sounds? It's terrific if you can do all three and OK if you can only manage one or two out of the three; we'll work with you to experience all three. Can you begin to intensify the experience? Great! Now can you ramp it up some more?

Welcome back! So, as you relived the experience, how did you intensify it? Did you make the picture brighter, bigger, more colourful, or perhaps you brought it in closer to you. Maybe you turned up the volume of any sounds you heard and if you had a feeling, you spread that feeling further through your body. You have just discovered how to play with your *submodalities*.

Because submodalities are the basic building blocks of the way you experience your world, a very slight change in a submodality can have a significant effect on the changing of the experience. What this means is that you have control over the way you choose to experience your world. You can choose to change your mind to heighten a pleasurable time or to remove the negative emotions from an unpleasant one. You can also learn to take yourself from an undesired state, such as confused, to a better state, such as understanding. In short, *you* can *choose* the meaning you give to what happens to you in life.

Submodalities are how you give meaning to your experiences – something is real or false, good or bad, and so on. You can use submodalities to change the intensity of the meaning. In the exercise at the start of the chapter, you gave your experience a meaning – it was pleasant. By changing the submodalities of the experience you were able to increase the experience and therefore the meaning of the experience – it became even more pleasant.

To associate or to dissociate

This section helps you experience how you can move in and out of your memories in order to offer you more choices over how you 'turn up' or 'turn down' your feelings. In our experience this is a very important submodality and one that needs a little extra clarification.

When you visualise yourself in a picture it is like watching yourself in a home movie. This is *dissociated*. Or you could actually be in the picture seeing out of your own eyes. This is *associated*. Being associated or dissociated into a picture can be an extremely important submodality when experiencing emotions as a result of the pictures you make.

Usually the emotions are heightened if you associate into the picture. Sometimes people find it difficult to either associate or dissociate. For instance, someone who has experienced a severe personal loss or been traumatised may find it hard to associate and may need to learn to do this.

To get the feel of being associated or dissociated, make a picture of yourself sitting in the front seat of a car. If you are dissociated, you will see a picture of yourself in the car, a little bit like watching yourself on television or looking at yourself in a photograph. If you want to associate into the picture, imagine opening the car door and sitting down. Now look out of your own eyes. The dashboard is in front of you. Can you see the texture and colour of the dashboard? Now look up at the windscreen. Is it splattered with the remnants of suicidal insects (or aliens, if you've seen *Men in Black*)?

Do you find it hard to dissociate? Picture yourself sitting in a car! Now imagine stepping out of the car and onto the pavement. Turn around and look back at the car and look at yourself sitting in the front seat. If you still cannot dissociate, pretend you are watching a movie and it's you there on the screen, in front of the car.

If you feel you aren't getting the hang of this, or any other exercise, feel free to leave it for the moment. You can always come back to it and give the exercise another go when you have more NLP embedded in your mind and muscle. Or you can find yourself an NLP practitioner or NLP practice group to work with in order to advance your skills.

Defining the details of your memories

If you are sitting down to read this book, you're probably unaware of the feel of the seat against your back and legs, although you are now because we mentioned it. Similarly, you are not always aware of the qualities of your memories until we ask you to remember a time when you were brushing your teeth, playing a game, reading a book, or cooking. Then you realise that there are a range of qualities to those memories. For instance, when reading the book – the picture you make of yourself, the book or the story, may have a frame around it. It may be in black and white. Perhaps you can hear the sound of distant traffic or of the pages turning. Maybe the book you were reading made you laugh and feel uplifted and happy. You can become aware of the qualities of the submodalities by paying attention to what you see, or hear, or feel when you think of an experience. The following sections present you with questions that can help you elicit the quality of the visual, auditory, and kinaesthetic submodalities.

Note: We have decided to focus on just the visual, auditory, and kinaesthetic submodalities in this chapter and put taste and smell aside just now. This is because we believe that culturally, unless you are a wine-, tea-, or coffee-taster, for example, these do not have the same emphasis that they do in some other cultures. Having said that . . . tastes and smells affect our emotional brain and you may find the smell of roasted chestnuts suddenly transporting you back to falling snows and Christmas carols.

Eliciting visual submodalities

You can define the quality of a picture in terms of where it is located in space as you look at it. For instance, it could be directly in front of you, to your left, to your right, or it could be slightly displaced to the top or bottom. If it is panoramic, it will look like you are standing in one spot and turning your head to look at the view in front of you. It will have other qualities of brightness, shape, and so on. You can discover how you make pictures in your head by thinking about the following qualities.

Visual Submodalities	*Questions to Discover Them*
Location	Where is it in space? Point to the picture. How close or how far away is it?
Colour/black-and-white	Is it in colour or is it black –and white?
Associated or dissociated	Is the picture associated or dissociated? Can you see yourself in the picture or are you looking out of your own eyes?
Size	Is the picture big or small? What size would you say the picture measures?
2- or 3-dimensional	Is the picture in 2- or 3-dimensions?
Brightness	Is the picture bright or dull?
Still or moving	Is the picture still or is it a movie? If a movie, how fast is the movement of the movie?
Shape	Is the picture square, round, or rectangular?
Framed or Panoramic	Does the picture have a border around it, or is it panoramic?
Focused or fuzzy	Is the picture in sharp focus or is it blurred?

Eliciting auditory submodalities

Like the pictures you make in your head, the sounds you hear have certain qualities to them. You may not be aware of the attributes of the sounds you hear until you focus your mind on them by thinking of the questions below.

Auditory Submodalities	Questions to Discover Them
Location	Where do you hear the sound? Is the sound inside your head or outside? Point to where the sound is coming from.
Words or sounds	Can you hear words or sounds? If words, is it the voice of someone you know?
Volume	Is the sound loud or soft? Is the sound a whisper or clearly audible?
Tone	If you hear a voice, what tone does it have? Is it deep, rich, nasal, rasping?
Pitch	Is the sound high- or low-pitched?
Mono or stereo	Can you hear the sound on both sides or is it one-sided? Is the sound all around you?
Constant or intermittent	Is the sound continuous or intermittent?
Rhythm	Does the sound have a beat or a rhythm to it?
Tempo	Is the sound you hear slow or fast?
Tune	Does the sound have a tune?

Book II

**Neuro-
linguistic
Programming**

Eliciting kinaesthetic submodalities

And guess what! Submodalities to do with feelings also have qualities that help to define them.

Kinaesthetic Submodalities	Questions to Discover Them
Location	Where is it in your body? Point to where you can feel the feeling.
Shape	Does the feeling have a shape?
Pressure	Does the feeling exert a pressure?

(continued)

Kinaesthetic Submodalities	Questions to Discover Them
Size	Does the feeling have a size? Is it big or small?
Quality	Does the feeling make you tingle? Is it spread out or knotted in one place?
Intensity	Is the feeling strong or weak?
Still or moving	Can you feel the feeling in one place or is it moving around your body?
Temperature	Is the feeling warm or cold?
Constant or intermittent	Is the feeling constant or intermittent?
Texture	Does the feeling have a texture to it?

When you are playing at changing the submodalities of a memory, it is important you make a list at the start, before you start changing submodalities around. Because if you start to get uncomfortable with the process at any point, you can put the picture, sounds, or feelings back to how they were. At the end of this chapter you will find a worksheet designed for that very purpose. Make as many copies as you need.

Always remember to ask yourself if it is OK to go ahead with making any change. If you discover a resistance, a feeling that makes you uncomfortable, acknowledge the feeling and thank your unconscious mind for making you aware of possible internal conflict. For example, when I (Romilla) was working on resolving grief with a client he did not want to let go of the pain of loss. He believed that if he let go of the pain he would forget his father. In fact, by releasing the pain he was actually able to remember his father more vividly. You may simply overcome the issue by some quiet time to yourself or you may need to talk to someone, an NLP practitioner perhaps.

Getting a little practice

Imagine you have a remote control with three sliding buttons labelled V for visual, A for auditory, and K for kinaesthetic. You can change the qualities of any pictures you make in your mind, sounds you hear in your head, or any feelings you feel in your body just by sliding the V, A, and K controls.

Why would you want to adjust the qualities of your memories? Supposing, years ago, you were rehearsing for a school play and your highly stressed teacher screamed at you, 'You stupid boy you, you blew that again!' Now you are in a job where you need to make some strong presentations to colleagues and clients. Yet every time you get started you begin to sweat and stammer and the voice in your head goes, 'You stupid boy you, you blew that again!' You may need to adjust the qualities of your memories because they get in the way of what you want to achieve. Imagine you slide the brightness control and the picture of the teacher gets dimmer. Then you slide the size control and the teacher gets smaller and becomes insignificant. Finally you adjust the volume control and the scream drops to a whisper. Now you find you can make presentations the way you always knew you could.

To see how effective changing submodalities can be, try this exercise, using the worksheet at the end of the chapter:

1. **Think of someone you like.**

2. **Remember the last time you spent real, quality time with them.**

3. **Record the qualities of the picture you see, any sounds you hear, and any feelings you get.**

4. **Change the picture you made, *one visual submodality at a time*; notice how each change affects the memory of your time together.**

5. **Change the sounds you hear, *one auditory submodality at a time*; notice how each change affects the memory.**

6. **Change any feelings that you are feeling, *one kinaesthetic submodality at a time*; notice how each change impacts the whole experience of your time together.**

Book II

Neuro-linguistic Programming

Making Real-Life Changes

In playing with the exercises so far, we hope you're beginning to have a pretty good idea of which submodalities have the most impact on you – your critical submodalities, those that can change other submodalities – your driver submodalities. And we hope you have the conviction now that you are in control of your experiences and can change them so you can choose how you feel. In the light of this knowledge and belief we invite you to experience real change in your life by working through the exercises in the following sections.

Just think, you can sit and program your mind on the train, in a traffic jam, or even over a boring meal with your in-laws (or should they be out-laws, just joking). And remember, practise makes perfect so get practising, safe in the knowledge that you can't get arrested for playing with your submodalities, even in public.

Changing a limiting belief

How often have you heard yourself say such things as, 'I can't do that', 'I'm no good at maths', or 'I should learn to cook properly'? These are all examples of limiting beliefs. Your beliefs are generalisations you make about yourself and your world. These can either disable you, holding you back, or empower you. Beliefs are really self-fulfilling prophesies which can start off just as a notion or a hint of an idea. Then your filters (metaprograms, values, beliefs, attitudes, memories, and decisions) begin aligning themselves like gates to only let in those 'facts' and experiences that will re-enforce your beliefs. For instance, let's say that you decided that you were a little more cuddly than you wanted to be and so you started on a diet. Perhaps you stuck to the diet for a few days but then temptation got the better of you. At this stage you got a hint of the notion that 'maybe I'm not good at following a diet'. Then you tried again and failed again until eventually you came to the limiting belief of 'I can't stick to a diet'.

1. **Think of a limiting belief you currently hold, one which you would like to change.**

2. **Think of a belief that you used to believe in but which, for you, is no longer true.**

   This can be a belief such as 'I am no longer a teenager'. It does not have to be a limiting belief that you may have overcome.

3. **Using the reference page at the end of this chapter, identify the submodalities of the belief which for you is no longer true.**

   For example when you think of a fictional character like the Tooth Fairy or Santa Claus, you may see her over to your right, in the distance, in colour, and very bright. You may get a warm, fluttery feeling in your chest and you hear the sound of a soft voice.

4. **Think of the limiting belief and put it into the submodalities of the belief you used to believe in.**

5. **When you think of your limiting belief, the submodalities, we would guess, are different.**

6. **Move the picture you get when you think of your limiting belief to the same position and distance you saw the Tooth Fairy at and give it the same colour and brightness. Then produce the same feelings in your body and listen for the same voice.**

Notice how your negative belief has changed, if it hasn't disappeared altogether!

Creating an empowering belief

Since beliefs are self-fulfilling prophecies it is useful to remember that you have control over choosing which ones you want to hold onto! In the previous exercise you learned how to let go of a limiting belief. Wouldn't it be really useful to learn how you can increase your choices in life by choosing to create a whole plethora of beliefs that will enable you to 'sing your song'?

1. **Think of a belief it would be really useful for you to have, we'll call it a desired belief.**

   It could be, for example, 'I deserve to be successful.'

2. **Think of a belief which *for you* is absolutely true.**

   For example – the sun will rise in the morning (yes, even behind those clouds).

3. **Using the reference pages at the end of this chapter, identify the submodalities of this absolutely true belief.**

   For example, when you think of the sun rising you may see it in front of you, about six feet away, in pale shimmering, orange colours and very bright. You may feel warm all over and hear bird songs.

4. **Put the desired belief into the exact same submodalities of the absolutely true belief.**

   Move the picture you get when you think of your desired belief to the same position and distance of the rising sun and give it the same colours and brightness. Then produce the same feelings of warmth and listen for the bird songs.

Getting rid of that backache

This process can be used for other unpleasant feelings, too.

1. **Calibrate your backache on a scale of 1 to 5.**

2. **Make a picture of the backache.**

3. **From the list at the end of the chapter, note the submodalities of the backache.**

4. **Change each attribute of the backache, one at a time.**

   If it has a colour, what happens when you give it a different colour, healing blue perhaps? What happens if you see that band of steel break up into strips of ribbon, fluttering in the wind? If there is a dull ache, can you change the feeling to a tingle? If it feels hot, can you change that feeling into one of a cool breeze blowing over the area? These changes should have already reduced the backache, if it hasn't already gone.

5. **Now imagine you are sitting in front of a movie screen, remove the backache from your body and project a picture of the backache on to the screen.**

6. **Make the picture on the screen smaller and smaller until it is the size of a balloon.**

7. **Now watch the balloon float up, up, and away into the sky and as you see the balloon floating away your backache is getting less and less.**

8. **As the balloon reaches the clouds and you calibrate your backache, it is just a 1.**

9. **As the balloon disappears from sight, the backache fades to just the faintest memory.**

Using the swish

This is a powerful technique for making lasting changes in habits and behaviours. The *swish*, as with a lot of NLP, is based on behavioural psychology. Assuming that learning to respond in a certain way results in you exhibiting a particular behaviour, then the swish teaches you a different way to respond in place of the unwanted behaviour. The idea behind using the swish is to use the learned pathways of the unwanted behaviour to create a new, desired pattern of behaviour. If you want to stop yourself biting your nails, think of what triggers the nail-biting and make a picture of the trigger. It may be you run your finger along a nail and find a jagged edge or it may be a response to getting nervous. The desired image is what you would rather have or see instead. In this case it may be a hand with perfect nails.

Identify the unwanted behaviour:

1. **Check with yourself that it is OK to go ahead with the change. Simply ask yourself: 'Is it OK?'**

2. **Identify the trigger that initiates the unwanted behaviour and make an associated picture. This is the cue picture.**

3. **Play with the image to discover the one or two critical submodalities.**

4. **Break state.**

   Break state means to change the state or frame of mind that you are in. You may stand up and give your body a good shake or move around the room when going from one phase of an exercise to another, allowing a natural break from the pictures and emotions of the first stage of the exercise.

5. **Think of the desired image. Create a dissociated image of you doing a preferred behaviour or looking a certain way.**

6. **Break state.**

7. **Recall the cue picture. Make sure you are associated into it and place a frame around it.**

8. **Create an image of the desired outcome.**

9. **Squash the desired image into a very small, dark dot and place it in the bottom left corner of the cue picture.**

10. **With a *swishhhh* sound, propel the small, dark dot into the big picture so that it explodes, covering the cue picture.**

11. **Break state.**

12. **Repeat the process several times.**

If you are more kinaesthetic than visual or auditory, you may find the swish more effective if you keep your hands far apart at the start of this exercise. Then as you *swishhhh* you bring your hands together quickly.

You have had a lot of experience now of playing with your submodalities and you know that you can change these to help you increase the choices in your life. You can use the process of putting *exhausted* into the submodalities of *relaxed* as you have done in the above exercises.

Book II

Neuro-linguistic Programming

Chapter 5

Opening the Toolkit

'I just don't know what came over me!' Familiar words? Ever had that feeling that your reactions to a situation have been way in excess of what was called for? Your feelings may have overtaken or even overwhelmed you. Perhaps you'd even say that you weren't quite yourself.

Ordinary people like you and us have emotional responses all the time. Some are great – falling in love, joy, and pleasure. Others are not so great – falling out of love, sadness, and pain. It's what makes life and work interesting and fun, as well as confusing and unpredictable. Often in our work, we talk to managers who sigh and wish that their colleagues would leave their emotions at home. And at home, many people would prefer that their partners would leave their workplace stresses at work.

Maybe you've witnessed situations when someone has 'blown a fuse' unexpectedly. Often this happens at what, on the face of it, seems the slightest provocation. Most of us can identify with the discomfort or agitation of being in a bit of a state. In fact, NLP adopts the term *state* to look at, and become more aware of, how you are at any moment in time.

Taken to extremes, these feelings of being overwhelmed and of being out-of-control can scare people. They can affect your career and your social life. People will question if such a person can be trusted in responsible situations or if they have to represent the company.

You'll be pleased to know that with the stabilising influence of the NLP toolkit, help is at hand to control yourself, your state at any one time, and the effect you have on other people. And once you discover how, it's pure magic.

NLP tools that help you create positive states in yourself are known as anchoring techniques. NLP defines an anchor as an external stimulus that triggers a particular internal state or response. People set and respond to anchors all the time. You know to stop the car at a red traffic light. You find that certain foods get you licking your lips.

You may be curious as to why anchors are helpful. The answer is that when you learn how to anchor, you can take all your positive and challenging experiences and memories and play around with them to make yourself more resourceful in the future.

The idea of anchoring in NLP came from modelling the techniques of Milton Erickson, the hypnotherapist. Erickson often used cues as triggers to help a person change his or her internal state outside the therapeutic setting.

Humans learn behaviour in response to a stimulus: it's not just dolphins who learn amazing tricks. From conception, babies are programmed to respond to certain stimuli. We constantly move and change our state in response to our environment with incredible flexibility in our behaviour.

Setting an Anchor and Building Yourself a Resourceful State

Our memories are stored as associations with our senses. Smells are particularly powerful anchors to times and events. So, for example, you smell a particular perfume and it transports you back to your first date and splashing on the cologne or aftershave. Or if you've ever been drunk on whisky, perhaps the smell of it alone will be enough to make you feel nauseous. We create positive and negative anchors for ourselves all the time.

How do you set an anchor? NLP teachers suggest various techniques. Ian McDermott and Ian Shircore describe the following simple three-step NLP technique for taking control of your own state by establishing resourceful anchors:

1. **Get clear about the positive state you would ideally wish to be in.**

   Your confident state may be bold or witty, energetic, anticipatory, enthusiastic. Be clear and specific in your own words to describe it.

2. **Recall a specific occasion in the past when you have been in that state.**

What you are looking for here is a comparable experience, even though the context can be very different.

3. **Relive it as vividly as you can.**

Engage fully with the experience – the sights, sounds, smells, the physical feelings, and internal sensations.

Once you have followed these three steps and you are in the highest positive state, it's the moment to set an anchor for yourself. Hand movements work well as a physical (kinaesthetic) anchor. Simply notice what your hands are doing as you engage with the experience and hold a distinct movement – such as a clenched grip, or thumb and first finger in a circle. (A handshake won't work because it's too mundane and habitual.) Alternatively, as an auditory anchor, listen for a sound. For those with a visual preference, see a picture that symbolises the positive state.

Book II

Neuro-linguistic Programming

When you need to get back into a positive state, you simply fire the anchor for yourself as a stimulus to change your state.

Anchors need to be:

- ✔ Distinctive – different to everyday movements, sounds, or pictures
- ✔ Unique – special for you
- ✔ Intense – set when you fully and vividly experience the peak of the state
- ✔ Timely – catching the best moment to make the association
- ✔ Reinforced – use it or you'll lose it. Anchoring is a skill to develop with practice.

Setting your own repertoire of anchors

One great way to work with NLP concepts is to find optimal states for yourself. Simply the best way for you to be yourself. This is a bit like having a repertoire of tennis or golf shots. Ask yourself what might be the best way:

- ✔ To learn effectively
- ✔ To perform at your best
- ✔ To relate to other people

Notice times in the past when you've been particularly successful in these areas. What was going on for you at the time? Where were you, who were you with, what were you doing at the time that was helpful? What was important to you?

Build a range of visual, auditory, and kinaesthetic anchors that make you feel good about yourself and other people. You may want to enlist the help of a friend and work with each other on this.

What are the triggers, the stimuli that affect you most at home or work? Make a note in the chart below (Figure 5-1) so that you begin to become aware of the times you're feeling good and less good. Your aim is to concentrate more on your positive experiences and change or let go of the negatives.

	AT HOME		AT WORK	
	Good	Bad	Good	Bad
V-Sights				
A-Sounds				
K-Touch/feelings				
O-Smells				
G-Tastes				

Figure 5-1:
A personal anchor chart.

Take some time to record some details of different experiences that make you feel good or bad. These can be seemingly insignificant everyday events and will be very individual.

You may feel good at home at the sight of a log fire or a vase of tulips on the table, the sound of your favourite CD, or the smell of a hot meal on the kitchen stove. Equally, the sight of your computer on a tidy desk, the buzz of the people, or the smell of a steaming hot drink may welcome you to work in the mornings.

Alternatively, if you flip when someone turns the TV up loud, or another email or piece of paper plops into your in-tray, you may need to find some strategies to switch the negatives into positives. Only when you identify what you like and what you don't like can you start steering the minute details of your daily experience in the best direction for you.

We've organised this chart by the different VAKOG senses (head to Chapter 4, for more on these). Here are some anchors to notice:

Visual – pictures, colours, decoration

Auditory – music, voices, birdsong, sounds

Kinaesthetic – textures, feel of the physical elements, and emotional vibes

Olfactory – smells, chemicals, scents

Gustatory – tastes, food and drink

Come back to this framework every few weeks or so to help you get more of what gives you pleasure. If you have a dominant sense – with more visual anchors than auditory ones, check if you're missing out and filtering information unnecessarily.

Your anchors will change over time. As you concentrate more and more on the things that give you pleasure, you may begin to notice that those that upset at first seem less relevant over time. Here's an exercise that you may want to turn into a healthy daily habit.

As you go through every day, pick out five events or experiences that have given you pleasure. Keep a private notebook of what's going well for you. Often it's the small things that make a difference – a pleasant conversation, a kind gesture, the smell of a bakery, or the sun breaking through the clouds. When you're feeling under pressure, refer to it and ensure that you spend at least part of every day on important things that matter to you.

Book II

Neuro-linguistic Programming

Changing negative anchors

Sometimes it's necessary to have a way of changing a negative anchor. As a simple example, you may want to change a destructive habit. A slimmer who reaches for the biscuit tin every time he has a cup of tea has created a negative anchor. Drink equals biscuit. Or an office worker who feels anxious each day when going into work because they once had an argument with their boss may be heading for a stress-related illness.

Desensitising yourself

One of the most common NLP approaches to releasing an anchor is by *desensitisation*. To do this you need to first get into a neutral or disassociated state – and then introduce the problem in small doses. So if the issue is the slimming one mentioned above, you'd need to get first into a strong state when you are able to say 'No, thank you' to fattening foods. Then practice being tempted while staying in the strong state. Essentially, it's about learning new habits.

Collapsing the anchor

Another strategy is to *collapse the anchor* by firing off two anchors simultaneously – the unwanted negative one plus a stronger positive one. What happens is that you are thrown into a state of confusion and a new, different state emerges. The pattern breaks, making way for a new one.

I (Romilla) have a client, Jane, who recently divorced and won custody of the couple's two young children. Jane felt uncontrollably angry every time her ex-husband called to make arrangements to visit the children. In turn, the children were becoming very anxious about weekend visits to their father and his new partner. Romilla enabled Jane to anchor a selection of different calm and positive states so that she could manage a strong and open dialogue with her ex-husband.

Stage anchors

For many people, public speaking represents speaking under severe pressure. A number of studies, borne out by our own experiences with clients, demonstrate that some people would actually rather die than stand up and speak in public! Apparently in the US, public speaking is the number one fear; in the UK, it's in second place to a fear of spiders.

We regularly work with clients who suffer performance anxiety which shows itself in hot sweats, loss of voice, stomach cramps, and upsets. When a dinner guest is invited to give an after-dinner speech, they often fail to enjoy the meal when faced with the prospect of entertaining the audience with their wit over the coffee, petit fours, and brandy.

If ever there was a reason to use anchoring to get back in control, this is it!

Using the Circle of Excellence

The NLP *circle of excellence* is a technique to help you summon up the confidence to perform a skill. So you can use it if you have a fear of public speaking, if you want to boost your confidence to play your best shot in sport, and in many other instances.

The circle of excellence is the classic NLP technique to practise with a partner if you are the after-dinner entertainment. It works best if you enlist a buddy or NLP practitioner who takes you sensitively through these steps while maintaining rapport with you, and not rushing.

First think of the situation where you are going to perform and imagine your own magic circle on the ground in front of you. Make it a generous circle of about three feet in diameter. These step-by step instructions take you in and out of your magic circle, telling you what to do at each stage, with the help of a partner.

Circle	*What to do*
* OUT	Identify your best state. Tell your partner what that state is.
	* Your partner says: 'Remember a time when you were xxxxxxxxxx' (use their words) . . . get back to it strongly . . . see what you saw then, hear what you heard.
* IN	Step into the circle and re-live that experience. (Make it vivid, be there in it.)
	* Feel what your hands are doing and hold or anchor that state with a hand movement.
* OUT	Step out of the circle and repeat the exercise with a second experience of your best state.
	* In order to prepare for the future event, your partner says: 'Think of a time when this state will be useful.'
* IN	With your hand in the anchored position, you move into the circle, and your partner asks you to see, hear, and feel how it can be now for you.
* OUT	Relax . . . you've got it!

Spatial anchoring is a way of influencing your audience through anchors. When you repeatedly do the same thing on stage in the same place, then people come to expect a certain behaviour from you according to where you move around stage. A lectern is a definite anchor – when you stand at the lectern, people expect you to speak.

When you are presenting, you can deliberately set up other expectations with the audience at different places on the stage. Perhaps you'll do the main delivery from the centre point of the stage, but you'll move to one side when you're telling stories and another when you deliver technical information. Very quickly, people learn to expect certain input from you according to where you position yourself.

Anchors may or may not work for you when you first try them. As with all the tools in this book, you'll learn fastest by taking an NLP class and working with an experienced practitioner. Whichever way you choose to develop your skills – on your own or with others – then simply give it a go. Let us encourage you to persist even if it seems strange at first. Once you take control of your own state, you expand your choices and it's worth it.

Book II

Neuro-linguistic Programming

Understanding Logical Levels

The NLP approach to change is that there is no single correct map of change at any one time. To survive and thrive, you need to acknowledge and embrace the fact that change is happening and put strategies in place to work with it rather than against it.

In this section we introduce you to a favourite model in NLP that has been developed largely thanks to the work of a man named Robert Dilts. This model is particularly helpful to apply in two ways:

- ✔ For understanding change for yourself as an individual
- ✔ For understanding change for organisations

NLP logical levels are a powerful way to think about change by breaking it down as a model into different categories of information (see Figure 5-2). (You'll also see them referred to in the NLP literature as a series of neurological levels.)

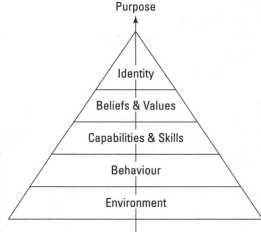

Figure 5-2:
The logical
levels of
change.

Although we've presented the levels to you in our diagram in a hierarchy, you may find it useful to look at them as a network of interrelationships or a series of concentric circles. All levels connect to each other. The device of the model simply creates some structure and understanding about how it all works.

In many cases it is easier to change at the lower levels on the diagram than the higher levels. So, for example, a company would find it easier to make changes to the building (environment), such as by painting the walls a different colour, than to change the culture or create a new identity for itself. Each level impacts those above and below it; the key value of the model is that it provides a structured approach to help understand what is happening.

Asking the right questions

As you begin to think about some change you'd like to make, you can ask yourself some questions at the different levels.

Book II

Neuro-linguistic Programming

- ✔ **Environment** refers to the factors which are external opportunities or constraints. Answers the questions **where?** and **when?** and **with whom?**

- ✔ **Behaviour** is made up of specific **actions** or reactions within the environment. Answers the question **what?**

- ✔ **Capabilities** are about the knowledge and skills, the 'how-tos' that guide and give direction to behaviour. Answers the question **how?**

- ✔ **Beliefs and values** provide the reinforcement (motivation and permission) to support or deny our capabilities. Answers the question **why?**

- ✔ **Identity** factors determine our sense of self. Answers the question **who?**

- ✔ **Purpose** goes beyond self-consciousness to relate to the bigger picture about mission to ask **what for or for whom?**

Taking logical levels step-by-step

You can use the logical levels to think about what's happening in the world around you, step-by-step. They'll help you to understand the structure and pattern as well as the content of different issues, events, relationships, or organisations, as we'll explain in the next few pages.

Let's just look at how you can apply this model when you're facing something like making a decision about change, or a dilemma that needs a solution. You can use the concept of logical levels to help you find the best way forward. Here's how the process works:

1. **First, you recognise that things are out of alignment.**

   You know this is the case when you're uncomfortable and you know that you want things to be different.

2. Discover where the change really needs to take place.

You do this by asking yourself certain questions that can help you identify where the change needs to occur. Each logical level has certain types of questions. Head to the section 'Finding the Right Lever for Change' to help you work through the individual logical levels.

3. Once you have identified the logical level, you bring that level back in alignment with the others.

At the lower levels of change, say at environment or behaviour, there may be some simple changes or habits you can adjust. Building your capability will take more time, while you may need to work with an individual coach (or business consultant in the organisational context) to help you examine your beliefs and values or develop a new identity for yourself.

Wherever you are operating on the levels of change, it's important to make sure you get the resources in place at the logical level above. To make lasting change at the environment level, you'll need to do the right things (behaviour). To develop capability, you'll need to have useful beliefs in place.

Environment

The environment is about time, place, and people. It's the physical context where you hang out. It's about finding the right time and the right place. If you want to become fluent in a new language, then the easiest way to learn would be to go and live in the country for a while, fully immerse yourself in the culture, ideally by living with the natives. You would be in the best place to learn. Similarly, if you wanted to learn a new software package, then it would make sense to move onto a project to work with a person or team that applied it in their business. Again, the environment would be conducive to learning, which is itself a type of change. The timing would also be critical – you cannot learn if the time is not right for you – maybe if you're tied up with other needs.

Some *environmental* questions to ask yourself when you sense that you are not in the right place or this is not the right time for you to get what you want:

- Where do you work best?
- Where in the world do you want to explore?
- What kind of home environment is right for you – modern, minimalist, or traditional?
- What kind of people do you like to have around you? Who makes you feel good, energised, and comfortable? Who makes you feel drained? Or do you prefer to work alone?
- What time of day do you feel good – are you up with the lark in the mornings or a night owl?

Questions such as these will give you the right kind of data so you can decide what environmental issues you can work on.

Behaviour

Your behaviour is all about what you actually say and do, what you consciously get up to. In NLP terms, behaviour refers to what you think about as well as your actions. It also points out that all your behaviour is aimed at a purpose, it has a positive intention for you.

Change at the behavioural level is easy to make when you have a real sense of purpose, it fits with your sense of identity, and your beliefs and values.

Some *behavioural* questions to ask yourself when you think that you may need to change your behaviours in order to get the results you want: Do your behaviours support your goals?

Book II

Neuro-linguistic Programming

- ✔ Do they fit with your sense of who you are?
- ✔ What do you do that makes life interesting and fun?
- ✔ What do you find yourself saying habitually? Can you detect any patterns?
- ✔ What do you notice about other people's words and sayings?
- ✔ How aware are you of people's behaviour – how they walk, the tone of their voice, and their smile?
- ✔ What colour changes do you observe in people as they talk?
- ✔ How does your breathing change and when?
- ✔ What body language do you adopt in different circumstances?
- ✔ What do you sound like?

Capabilities

Capabilities are your talents and skills. They lie within people and organisations as highly valuable assets. These are the behaviours that you do so well that you can do them consistently without any seemingly conscious effort. Things like walking and talking are skills you learned without ever understanding how you did that. You are a naturally great learning machine.

Other things you've learned more consciously. Perhaps you can fly a kite, ride a bicycle, work a computer, or play a sport or musical instrument. These are skills you will have deliberately learned. Perhaps you're great at seeing the funny side of life, listening to friends, or getting the kids to school on time. All valuable skills that you take for granted and others could learn. You're likely to remember the time before you could do these things, while you probably can't recall a time before you could walk or talk. Organisations build core competencies into their business processes, defining essential skills that are needed to make the company function at its best.

NLP focuses plenty of attention at the capability level, working with the premise that all skills are learnable. It assumes that anything is possible if taken in bite-size pieces or chunks. The HR director of one of the UK's most prestigious retailers told us recently: 'We recruit primarily on attitude: once this is right, we can teach people the skills they need to do the job.'

Yet even attitudes can be learned and changed so long as you find the desire, know-how and opportunity to learn. The question to hold on to is: 'How can I do that?' Bear this in mind for yourself as you go through every day. The NLP approach is that by modelling others and yourself, you become open to making changes and developing your own capabilities. If you want to do something well, first find someone else who can do it and pay close attention to all of their logical levels.

Here are some *capability and skills* questions to ask yourself when you want to make an assessment of your capabilities and see where you can learn and improve:

- ✔ What skills have you learned that you're proud of – how did you do it?

- ✔ Have you become expert at something that serves you less well – how did that happen?

- ✔ Do you know someone who has got a really positive attitude that you could learn from – how could you learn from them?

- ✔ Ask other people to say what they think you are good at.

- ✔ What next? What would you like to learn?

As you build capability, the world opens up for you. You are in a position to take on greater challenges or to cope better with the ones you struggle to face.

Beliefs and values

Beliefs and values are the fundamental principles that shape your actions. What *you* believe to be true is often going to be different to what *I* believe to be true. Here, we're not talking about beliefs in the sense of religion – rather your perception at a deep, often unconscious, level.

Likewise values are the things that are important to you, what motivates you to get out of bed in the morning, or not – criteria such as health, wealth, or happiness. Beliefs and values and the way we rank them in order of importance are different for each person. This is why it's so difficult to motivate a whole team of people with the same approach. One size does not fit all when it comes to beliefs and values.

Values are also rules that keep us on the socially acceptable road. I may seek money, but my values of honesty keep me from stealing it from other people. Sometimes there will be a conflict between two important values – such as family life and work. In terms of making change, understanding beliefs and values offers huge leverage. When people value something or believe it enough, it's an energising force for change. They are concentrating on what's truly important to them, doing what they really want to be doing, and becoming closer to who they want to be. They are in a place that feels right and natural for them. Beliefs and values drive us and influence the lower levels of capability, behaviour, and environment. Thus all the levels begin to come into alignment.

Here are some *beliefs and values* questions to ask yourself when you sense that there's a conflict at this logical level that is hindering you getting what you want:

- ✔ Why did you do that? Why did they do that?
- ✔ What factors are important to you in this situation?
- ✔ What is important to other people?
- ✔ What do you believe to be right and wrong?
- ✔ What has to be true for you to get what you want?
- ✔ When do you say 'must' and 'should' and 'must not' and 'should not'?
- ✔ What are your beliefs about this person or situation? Are they helpful? What beliefs might help me get better results?
- ✔ What would somebody else believe if they were in your shoes?

Book II

Neuro-linguistic Programming

Armed with the answers to these questions, you may want to work on your beliefs and values to ensure that they support you through difficult times. As you question your beliefs about yourself you may choose to discard some of them that no longer serve you well.

In business change management programmes, you often hear talk of 'winning the hearts and minds' of people. This means you need to address people's beliefs and values. Once the right beliefs are firmly in place, NLP suggests that the lower levels – such as capability and behaviour – will fall into place automatically.

Identity

Identity describes your sense of who you are. You may express yourself through your beliefs, values, capabilities, behaviours, and environment, yet you are more than this. NLP assumes that a person's *identity* is separate from their *behaviour* and recommends that you remain aware of the difference. You are more than what you do. It separates the intention that lies behind your action from your action itself. This is why NLP avoids labelling people. 'Men behaving badly', for example, does not mean the men are intrinsically bad, it's just bad behaviour.

There's a saying that one of our corporate clients quotes: 'Easy on the person. Tough on the issue.' This is a positive management style consistent with the NLP premise that people make the best choices open to them, given their own situation at any time.

If you want to give feedback to encourage learning and better performance, always give very specific feedback about what someone has said or done in terms of the *behaviour* rather than commenting at the *identity* level. So, instead of saying: 'John. Sorry mate, but you were just awful.' Try instead: 'John, it was difficult to hear you at the meeting because you looked at the computer all the time and had your back to the audience.'

Here are some *identity* questions to ask yourself when you have a sense of conflict around your identity:

- ✔ How is what you are experiencing an expression of who you are?
- ✔ What kind of person are you?
- ✔ How do you describe yourself?
- ✔ What labels do you put on other people?
- ✔ How would others describe you?
- ✔ Would other people think of you as you wish?
- ✔ What pictures, sounds, or feelings are you aware of as you think about yourself?

A greater awareness of self is a valuable insight in any journey of personal change. Too often people try to change others when changing themselves would be a more effective starting point.

Purpose

This 'beyond identity' level connects you to the larger picture when you begin to question your own purpose, ethics, mission, or meaning in life. It takes individuals into the realms of spirituality and their connection with a bigger order of things in the universe. It leads organisations to define their *raison d'être*, vision, and mission.

Man's survival amidst incredible suffering depends on true self-sponsorship that goes beyond identity. Witness the resilience of the Dalai Lama driven from Tibet or the story of Viktor Frankl's endurance of the Holocaust in his book *Man's Search for Meaning*.

As we become older and approaching different life stages, it's natural to question what we're doing with our lives. Sometimes there will be a trigger to inspire action and light up our passion. A friend and logistics manager in industry, Alan, travelled to Kenya on holiday and saw at first-hand the educational needs of the country. Thus began a powerful one-man campaign that took over his life and led him to create an international charity taking educational materials into Africa thanks to his personal passion to make a difference. On speaking to him about it, he would often say. 'I don't know why me. It's mad, but I just know I have to do this.' His purpose was stronger than his identity.

Here are some *purpose* questions to ask yourself when you want to check whether you are steering your life in the right direction for yourself:

- ✔ For what reason are you here?
- ✔ What would you like your contribution to be to others?
- ✔ What are your personal strengths that you can add to the bigger world out there?
- ✔ How would you like to be remembered when you die?

Book II

Neuro-linguistic Programming

In *The Elephant and the Flea,* management guru Charles Handy conveys the passion that comes from a sense of mission and underlying purpose. He talks of the entrepreneurs featured in *The New Alchemists*, another book by Handy and his wife, the portrait photographer Elizabeth Handy, as people who leap beyond the logical and stick with their dream:

> *Passion is what drove them, a passionate belief in what they are doing, a passion that sustained them through the tough times, that seemed to justify their life. Passion is a much stronger word than mission or purpose, and I realise that as I speak that I am also talking to myself.*

When you are operating in a purposeful way, notice how you are unstoppable – you will be in the best place to gain true alignment at all the logical levels.

Practical uses for logical levels

You can use logical levels to bring energy and focus to many different situations. Here are just a few examples:

- ✔ **Gathering and structuring information** – compiling a report, school essay, or any piece of writing.
- ✔ **Building relationships in a family** – exploring what all members of the family want for the family to work together. This is especially useful when dramatic change occurs in a family's structure such as happens in a divorce or remarriage.
- ✔ **Improving individual or corporate performance** – deciding where to make business changes that will help turn around a struggling company or one going through mergers and acquisitions.
- ✔ **Developing leadership and confidence** – stepping through the levels to get alignment and feel confident in leading a team or enterprise.

Figuring out other people's levels: Language and logical levels

The intonation in someone's language, the way they speak, can tell you at what level they are operating. Take the simple phrase: 'I can't do it here' and listen to where the stress is placed.

'*I* can't do it here' = statement about identity.

'I *can't* do it here' = statement about belief.

'I can't *do* it here' = statement about capability.

'I can't do *it* here' = statement about behaviour.

'I can't do it *here*' = statement about environment.

When you know the level that someone is operating at, you can help them to make change at that level. If they are working at the environmental level, the question to ask is: 'If not here, where can you do it?' If they are at the identity level, the question is: 'If not you, who can do it then?'

Chapter 6

Uncovering Your Secret Programs Behind Your Habits and Behaviours

*W*hen you woke up this morning did you brush your teeth first or did you shower first? When I (Romilla) was studying yoga with Swami Ambikananda, one of the tasks the class was set was to gain a greater understanding of the unconscious rituals that all of us have in our lives. Swami Ambikananda suggested we start our day by changing the sequence we had for getting dressed, eating breakfast, and preparing to go to work. Boy did that scramble the brain! It required real concentration to keep the rest of the day running smoothly. For me, at least, it felt like I had forgotten something crucial that day and my brain kept trying to remember what that was. It was a very uncomfortable experience.

Everyone has a strategy for everything and very few people are even aware that they do things on automatic pilot. The great thing now is that, once you realise you are running an ineffective strategy you will have the tools to change it and . . . you will also know how to find someone else's strategy that is working and model it.

As Tad James, creator of the Time Line Therapy(tm) technique, said, 'A strategy is any internal and external set (order, syntax) of experiences which consistently produces a specific outcome.'

You use strategies for all behaviours – feeling loved, loving your partner, parent, child, or pet, hating someone, getting irritable with your daughter, buying your favourite perfume, learning to drive, succeeding, failing, health, wealth, and happiness ad infinitum. In this chapter you will discover the mechanics of your behaviours, something that will put you in the driving seat of your life.

The Evolution of Strategies

The NLP strategy model has come about through a process of evolution. It started with Pavlov and his dogs and was enhanced by Miller, Galanter, and Pribram, who were cognitive psychologists, before being refined by NLP's founding fathers, Grinder and Bandler.

The TOTE model

Miller, Galanter, and Pribram built on the Stimulus-Response (S-R) model of behaviourism and presented the TOTE (Test, Operate, Test, Exit) model, which is illustrated in Figure 6-1. The TOTE model works on the principle that you have a goal in mind when you exhibit a particular behaviour. The purpose of your behaviour is to get as close to the desired outcome as possible. You have a test in order to assess whether you have reached your goal. If your goal is reached, you stop the behaviour. If it isn't reached, you modify the behaviour and repeat it, thereby incorporating a simple feedback and response loop. So if your outcome is to boil the kettle, the test is whether the kettle has boiled; if it hasn't then you carry on waiting for it to boil and test for the kettle having boiled and exit once it has.

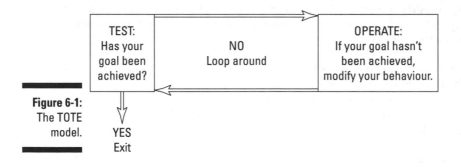

Figure 6-1:
The TOTE
model.

The NLP strategy model in action

This section shows how the NLP strategy model works for someone enacting a basic road rage strategy. The TOTE model (see Figure 6-2) is enriched by adding modalities to give you the NLP strategy model which can be used to understand how someone operates a particular pattern of behaviour.

Figure 6-2 shows how the NLP strategy model works.

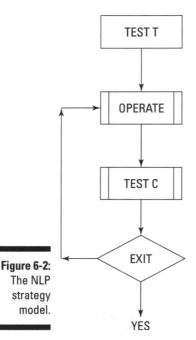

Figure 6-2: The NLP strategy model.

Book II

Neuro-linguistic Programming

✔ **Test T(rigger)** – is the initial trigger that starts off a strategy. This test is where you assess whether the information coming in from your senses complies with data necessary to fire off the strategy. If you are prone to road rage, the trigger may be that you see someone undertaking and pushing in front of you in a traffic jam (visual confirmation), but because you are in a good mood (no kinaesthetic confirmation) you choose not to run the strategy. However if you are in a bad mood (kinaesthetic confirmation), you fire your road rage strategy when you get the visual confirmation of someone undercutting you. The outcome is to make sure the driver in front knows exactly what you think of him and to thoroughly relish the feeling of giving in to the red mist of uncontrollable rage (kinaesthetic).

✔ **Operate** – is the process by which you gather the data that will help you carry out your strategy. So for your road rage strategy, you remember where the button for your horn is, where the light switch is, and which rude hand gesture you want to use. In this example you utilise the the visual modality as you visualise your arsenal to use for running your strategy. Although you do invoke the auditory digital modality as you recall all the juicy rude words you know. Then you launch yourself into your best road rage behaviour.

✔ **Test C(ompare)** – is where you compare the current data and situation to your outcome for running the strategy. Yes, you blew your horn (auditory); yes, you mouthed all your worst swear words (visual for the transgressor's benefit) and made the appropriate gestures (kinaesthetic for yourself and visual for the other driver). Yes, the red mist feels goooood as it holds you in its deadly embrace (kinaesthetic). But . . . Oh no! You didn't flash your lights (visual).

✔ **Exit** – is where you exit your strategy. In this example, because you didn't remember to flash your lights, you would loop around to continue operating the strategy and exit once you had flashed your lights at the offending driver.

When I (Romilla) did my NLP Master Program, the exercise on modelling involved breaking a board. This was a fairly solid piece of wood that I was terrified of failing to break. My strategy for 'psyching' myself up was to see the board breaking (visual), feel energy in my solar plexus, pulsing up my chest and down my arm (kinaesthetic), and say repeatedly, 'You can do it' (auditory digital). The way this fits into the TOTE model is:

1. Test 1– Stepping up to breaking the board is the trigger that starts this strategy.

2. Operate – Run my strategy for psyching myself up using the visual, kinaesthetic, and auditory digital representation systems (modalities).

3. Test 2 – Tested if I was psyched up.

4. Exit – Until I was ready, I looped around to operate the strategy, reinforcing my modalities. When I was ready I exited to the actual board break strategy.

Flexing your strategy muscles

You develop strategies all through your life. Most of the basic ones like walking, eating, drinking, and choosing and making friends are created when you are young. Some you develop as you come across new circumstances in life. Sometimes what you develop for yourself may not be as effective as a strategy that another person uses, because they started from a more informed platform or had a teacher. If you can recognise the fact that your strategy may have grounds for improvement, that's a useful tool. For instance if your colleague is earning more than you are, for the same job, is it because she can present her success in a better light to the boss?

Acquiring new capabilities

Chapter 5 explains the NLP concept of logical levels, basically the idea that you have different levels at which you operate: identity, values and beliefs, capabilities and skills, behaviour, and environment. Your strategies relate to your capabilities and skills level. Sometimes you can improve your strategies by acquiring new skills. In the example of the higher earning colleague mentioned at the start of this section, you can learn how she has built and maintains rapport with the boss. Maybe she makes sure she keeps the boss apprised of progress on her project. Maybe you could try out talking to the boss of your progress.

Book II

Neuro-linguistic Programming

Kay had always worked in an office where she felt safe and was confident of her abilities. When Kay decided to set up in business for herself, she discovered she had to learn a whole raft of new behaviours. Kay realised she had to learn to 'network' in order to spread the word of her new venture. Unfortunately, she would go to networking meetings and come away without really having achieved anything. She was quite vague about her objectives as she thought she was just going to meet new people who might prove useful in her business. She realised she would have to learn new strategies in order to connect successfully with new people. She did this by observing Lindsay, a friend of hers, who was very successful at introducing herself and making a connection with someone new. She started to adopt Lindsay's strategies (outlines of which are listed below with how Kay used each step) and found she was making successful, new contacts.

- ✔ **Think of the outcome you want from a networking event.** Kay decided she wanted to exchange cards with at least six people who could be useful to her and she could be useful to them, either in a business or social context.

- ✔ **Go up to someone and introduce yourself:**

  'Hello, I'm Kay and you are . . .?'

- ✔ **Ask questions to break the ice.** Kay's questions included:

  'This is my first time here. Have you been here before?'

  'How do you find these events?'

  'Have you travelled far?'

  'What line of business are you in?'

✔ **Stay focused on what the other person is saying as well as your outcome for the event.** Kay realised that she would get so caught up in the content of what the other person was saying she would forget to swap cards or would spend too much time with one person and forget to continue meeting people. She decided the way to stay focused on her goal was to hold the container with her cards in her left hand instead of putting it away in her handbag. This left her right hand free to shake hands, while keeping her mind on her goal.

Re-coding your programs

Strategies can be changed. In the road rage example earlier in this chapter, whose agenda were you fulfilling? Surely not yours? Particularly when you know how much physical damage anger and stress do to your body. How about developing another strategy that could go something like:

✔ **Test T** – Trigger: Someone undercutting you.

✔ **Operate** – Instead of accessing all your best rude words and gestures, think instead about the sun collapsing into a planetary nebula in about 5 billion years' time when all this angst will be completely pointless – and give yourself a quiet little smile and enjoy your life.

✔ **Test C** – Does your strategy for staying positive work? If so, move to last step, if not, return to previous step and try an alternative strategy.

✔ **Exit** – Choose to follow your own agenda and exit.

Chinese Qigong practitioners know that the 'internal smile' technique improves their immune system, gets the brain working more efficiently, and can reduce blood pressure, anxiety, and simple depression.

Understanding NLP by Time Lines

Time has a strange, elastic quality. It goes really fast when you are engaged in something interesting and stretches when you allow yourself to get bored. Are you one of the time-rich people who has all the time in the world or are you time-poor, always short of time? Perhaps having time, like money, depends on where you focus your attention. Although day and night for the rich, poor, young, and old is 24 hours, the perception of time is different. Some people are stuck in the past, others have their gaze firmly staring into the future, and some people just live in the moment.

Time also gives your memories meaning. You can change the meaning a memory has by changing its quality and its relationship to time. This allows you to release yourself of negative emotions and limiting decisions and gives you the means to create the future you would rather have, without the influence of disempowering past memories.

How Your Memories are Organised

Think of something you do on a regular basis. This means that you can remember doing it in the past, imagine or experience doing it in the present, and can imagine doing it in the future. Do you notice that the pictures have different locations? By going into the past to examine a memory and again into the future, although with a pit stop in the present, you have just experienced a little 'land-based' time travel. (You can experience the airborne variety in the next section, 'Discovering Your Time Line'.)

Book II

Neuro-linguistic Programming

Discovering Your Time Line

Memories are arranged in a pattern. Now, if you were asked to point to the direction the past memory came from, where would you point? Similarly, if you were to point to the picture of the thing you will do in the future, notice where you are pointing now. Could you also point to where your image for the present is? If you draw a line between the memory from the past, the one in the present, and the one in the future, you've created your very own *time line*.

People may identify their past as behind them and their future as in front of them. Some people may have a V-shaped line. Some may have their past to their left and their future to their right – this is interesting because the left is where most people move their eyes to when they want to remember something and the right is where they move their eyes to when they want to imagine something that isn't real, yet. Interestingly, some people arrange their time line geographically, with their past perhaps in Cornwall, Los Angeles, or Timbuktu and their present where they are currently residing. Their future may lie in the place they want to move to.

If you find it easier, draw an imaginary line on the ground and, trusting your unconscious mind, walk along the line, from where you feel your past is to where you feel your future is.

Walking along a time line can be difficult if spatial restrictions get in the way, for example if you are in a small room. This exercise will show you how you can visualise your time line in your head by 'floating up' from where you are relaxing in order to get a clear view of the time line stretching out below you.

1. **Think of an event that you experienced recently.**

2. **Now take a deep breath and just relax as deeply as you can.**

3. **Imagine yourself floating up, up above your present and way above the clouds, into the stratosphere.**

4. **Picture your time line way below you, like a ribbon, and you can see yourself in the time line.**

5. **Now float back over your time line until you are directly over the recently experienced event.**

6. **You can hover there as long as you like until you decide to float back to the present and down into your own body.**

Hope you enjoyed that trial flight. Remember the process as you'll be doing a lot of it.

Changing Time Lines

When you got your time line, where was it in relation to you? For instance, did the line run through your body as in the first two *in-time* diagrams (see Figures 6-3 and 6-4)? Or was it out in front of you so that you could see the whole of your time line laid out in front of you as in the *through-time* diagram (see Figure 6-5)?

In Time

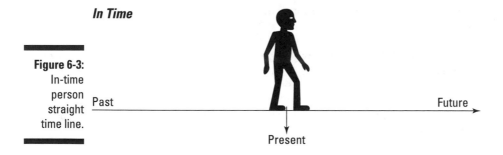

Figure 6-3:
In-time person straight time line.

Past

Future

Present

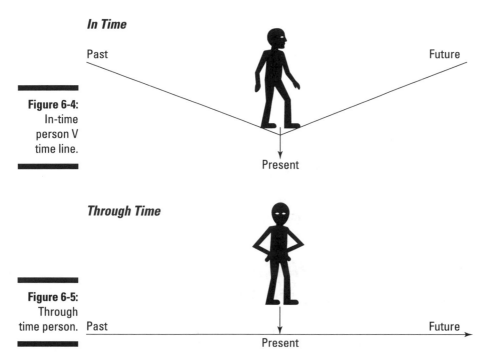

In Time

Past   Future

Present

Figure 6-4:
In-time
person V
time line.

Through Time

Figure 6-5:
Through
time person. Past   Future
Present

Book II

**Neuro-
linguistic
Programming**

The shape of your time line can influence various personality traits. If you have a through-time line, you will have an American-European model of time, which means you may have the following tendencies:

- Very aware of the value of time
- Goal-oriented
- Conscious of turning up for appointments on time
- Good at planning activities
- Able to keep your emotions separate from events
- Living in the now is difficult

As a person with an in-time line you may have the following abilities and tendencies:

- Creative
- Good at multi-tasking
- Feel your emotions very strongly
- Like to keep your options open
- Good at living in the moment

Travelling Along Your Time Line to a Happier You

Your time line is made up of a sequence of memories which have a structure to them; pictures are in colour, sounds can be loud or soft, and feelings can make you feel light or weigh you down. Your memories are created by your mind – if we witnessed an event at the same time as you, each of us would remember the event differently. As you travel your time line, examining your memories and understanding the lessons that need to be learned can release the hold the memories have on the present and you can change their structure, making them smaller, softer, or lighter. So your past need no longer cast a shadow on your present – or more importantly on your future.

Releasing negative emotions and limiting decisions

Negative emotions are emotions such as anger, fear, shame, grief, sadness, guilt, regret, and anxiety, to list just a few. Not only can such emotions have a powerful, undesired, physical affect on your body, they can have a devastating affect on the way you conduct your life.

A limiting decision is a decision made because once upon a time you decided you couldn't do something because you were too stupid, unfit, poor, or any number of other reasons; for example, 'I can never be slim' or 'I am bad at adding numbers'.

Negative emotions and limiting decisions reach far from your past to influence you in your present. If you can go into the past, by travelling back along your time line, and understand consciously what your unconscious mind was trying to protect you from, you will be able to release the emotions and decisions more easily.

Dealing with negative emotions can be, well, emotional. So before you attempt to use the techniques in this section to release negative emotions or understand your limiting decisions, keep these points in mind:

> ✔ In order to clear really heavy duty stuff such as very important emotional issues (such as the trauma of child abuse or divorce), we definitely recommend that you see a qualified NLP Master Practitioner or Time Line Therapist.

✔ This process is *not* for a trauma or phobia as you need a fully qualified therapist to ensure that your issues are dealt with professionally and sensitively and that you can handle resolving the trauma.

✔ It is better to work with someone else when working with time lines as they will be able to keep you grounded if you forget the exercise and succumb to the emotions you are experiencing. They can also ensure that you follow the steps in the exercise correctly.

The diagram shown in Figure 6-6 is very important to the following exercises as it clarifies the locations along your time line that you need to be aware of. It is particularly useful to people who are more visual, who make pictures in their heads.

Book II

Neuro-linguistic Programming

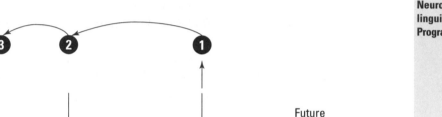

Figure 6-6: Locations on your time line.

✔ Location number 1 in the figure represents the position you float up to which is directly above the present on your time line.

✔ Location number 2 is directly above the SEE (Significant Emotional Event) or root cause.

✔ Location number 3 is still way above your time line but 15 minutes before the root cause.

This exercise introduces you to a process which will help you remove negative emotions that you may be holding onto, for instance you may be prone to inappropriate feelings of anger. Once you have mastered this technique you can use it for eliminating negative decisions that you may have made in the past, for example 'I can never be truly successful'. Please remember to keep an open mind to the answers that your unconscious mind presents.

1. **Find yourself somewhere safe and quiet to relax and think of a mildly negative emotion you may have experienced in the past.**

2. **Check with yourself if it is OK to learn from the event and release the emotion. When you relax, ask your unconscious mind, 'Is it OK for me to let go of anger?'**

3. **Ask your unconscious mind, 'What is the root cause of this problem, which, when disconnected from it will cause the problem to disappear? Was it before, during, or after my birth?'**

When you ask your unconscious mind if the root cause was before, during, or after your birth, please keep an open mind about the answer it gives you. Your unconscious mind absorbs a lot of information and makes a lot of decisions without your conscious awareness. Romilla's clients have been surprised with the responses they got.

4. **When you get the root cause, float way above your time line so that you can see your past and your future stretching below you.**

You are now at location 1 shown in Figure 6-6.

5. **Still above your time line, float back along your time line until you are above the SEE (location 2 in Figure 6-6), see what you saw, felt, and heard.**

6. **Ask your unconscious mind to learn what it needs to from the event in order for it to let go of the negative emotions easily and quickly.**

7. **Float to location 3 in Figure 6-6, which is above and 15 minutes *before* the SEE.**

8. **As you float above your time line at location 3, turn and face the present so that you can see the root cause in front of you and below you.**

9. **Give yourself permission to let go of all the negative emotions associated with the event and notice where the negative emotion is.**

Have all the other negative emotions associated with the event disappeared too?

10. **If other negative emotions remain, use each 'out' breath to release all the emotions that are associated with the SEE.**

11. **Stay at location 3 until you feel, or know, that all the negative emotions have dissipated.**

12. **When you are ready, and by that we mean when you feel you have released the negative emotion, float back to location 1.**

Go only as fast as your unconscious mind can learn from similar events and let go of all the associated emotions.

13. **Come back down into the room.**

14. **Just test – go into the future to when an event would have triggered the emotion you let go and notice that the emotion has gone.**

This exercise can also be used for getting rid of a limiting decision. For example, you may have decided to stay poor or unhealthy or made some other self-defeating decision. Follow the above process using the limiting decision in place of the negative emotion.

Finding forgiveness

With hindsight and maturity you can forgive someone in your past. This allows you to release all the energy you had invested in resentment, anger, or other emotions. You can then move on and have all that energy to be more creative or loving or anything wonderful you may want. One useful way to accomplish this is to understand the motives of a person who may have hurt you and realise that, because of their own issues, they were operating from a reality which provided them with a very limited choice.

As an example, imagine that you had a burning desire to become an actress and your parents gave you a hard time about it. Now acknowledge that they were actually showing parental concern for you. They were only doing their best for you with the resources they had at their disposal. Go back along your time line to when you can remember one such difficult time with your parents. You can then hover way above your time line while you learn any important lessons that you needed to be aware of. You can float down into the event and give your parents a hug and let them know you realise now that they were doing their best for you. If you find it easy, you can surround yourself in a bubble of light and just enjoy the feelings of love, compassion, and forgiveness.

Book II

Neuro-linguistic Programming

Healing along the time line

My (Kate) friend, Tara, shared an inspiring experience with me. Tara had suffered severely with blocked sinuses since she was 18. This condition was so bad that she needed antibiotics at least three or four times a year in order to alleviate the debilitating symptoms. By the time Tara attended a workshop on Time Line Therapy she had undergone four unsuccessful operations to clear her sinuses and been told by her doctors that she would either have to live with her illness or stay on steroids. During the workshop, Tara discovered her symptoms became particularly severe when she needed attention from a particular person, when she became overwhelmed by people and events, or when she needed nurturing. Tara explored the possibility that her physical behaviour was psychosomatic. By investigating any limiting beliefs and benefits she was getting from her illness, Tara realised that she had built a Gestalt around illness. She remembered that, as a child, her brother had received a lot of attention from their mother because he was asthmatic and the only time Tara got the attention was when she had tonsillitis. Tara's father also suffered with chronic sinusitis and Tara found that her illness gave her something in common with her father. She also believed that she could not clear her disease by herself. Tara accepted that she could get attention from people without being ill, that she could ask for TLC (tender loving care) and that it was OK to admit to feelings of being overwhelmed. She went back along her time line to where she believed the first SEE happened. She realised that this was where she first became jealous of the attention her brother got. She was able to let go of the Gestalt associated with this event and has been free of sinusitis and antibiotics since March 2002.

When you travel back along your time line and find an event that involves you when you were young, you can embrace the younger you, reassure him or her that all will be well, surround yourselves with light and let yourselves be healed. Now, imagine bringing all that joy and relief along your time line, right into the present.

Getting rid of anxiety

Anxiety is simply a negative emotion about a future event. You learnt that you can remove a negative emotion or limiting decision by going to *before* the event which has created the emotion or when you made the decision (see the section 'Releasing negative emotions and limiting decisions' earlier for details). Anxiety can be removed by going into the future *beyond* the successful conclusion of the event about which you are anxious.

Imagine what you would see, hear, and feel when the event which is causing you to feel anxious has been truly successful. Then, when you travel forward, above your time line to beyond the successful conclusion of the event, you will find that the anxiety no longer exists. Using Figure 6-7 as a reference, follow these steps:

1. **Find yourself somewhere safe and quiet to relax and think of an event about which you are feeling anxious; now check with your unconscious mind if it is OK for you to let go of the anxiety.**

2. **Now float way above your time line so that you can see your past and your future stretching below you.**

3. **Still above your time line, float forward along your time line until you are above the event about which you are feeling anxiety.**

4. **Ask your unconscious mind to learn what it needs to from the event in order for it to let go of the anxiety easily and quickly.**

5. **When you have the information needed, float further into the future, along your time line until you are 15 minutes after the *successful conclusion* of the event about which you were feeling anxious.**

6. **Turn a look toward now and notice that you are calm and no longer anxious.**

7. **When you are ready, float back to your present.**

8. **Just test – go into the future to the event about which you were anxious and confirm that the anxiety no longer exists.**

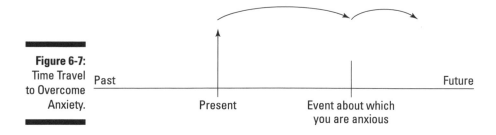

Figure 6-7:
Time Travel
to Overcome
Anxiety.

Past — Present — Event about which you are anxious — Future

Making a Better Future

Book II

**Neuro-
linguistic
Programming**

Once you know how to travel your time line, think how wonderful it would be to take some goals that are so compelling that they are irresistible and put them into your future?

Always check your motives in setting and obtaining your goals in order to ensure they fit within all areas of your life. By really examining your reasons, you will ensure there are no hidden negative emotions driving you, for instance if you are focusing on making a lot of money you may want to know that the desire stems from wanting to be comfortably secure and able to help those less fortunate than yourself and not because you are trying to escape from a poverty stricken childhood. Checking your motives will also help you identify any lurking, unconscious fears, for example 'If I am rich people will only want to be friends because of my money, not because they like me'. Analysing these fully will help crystallise your exact reasons for your desire and you can take steps to overcome any unconscious issues.

1. **Find yourself somewhere safe and quiet to relax and design your goal.**

2. **Float way above your time line so that you can see your past and your future stretching below you.**

3. **Still above your time line, float forward along your time line until you are above the time by which you want to have achieved your goal.**

4. **Turn and look back to** *now* **and allow all the events along your time line to align so that they support your goal, noting any actions you may have to take along the way.**

5. **When you are ready, float back to your present and back down into the room.**

Book III
Cognitive Behavioural Therapy

The 5th Wave   By Rich Tennant

In this part . . .

Cognitive Behavioural Therapy (CBT) is a scientifically tested and verified psychotherapeutic method of overcoming common emotional problems. It helps you to identify your problems and set specific goals for how you would rather be living your life, gives you techniques to identify errors in the way you may be thinking and to adopt more helpful thoughts, attitudes, philosophies, and beliefs. It also gives you information that can help you to understand, normalise, and address some common human problems. You are not alone. Many of the problems you may be experiencing such as depression, anxiety, anger, and obsessions are in fact very common.

Here are the contents of Book III at a glance:

Chapter 1

Correcting Your Thinking

In This Chapter

▶ Spotting pitfalls in human thought

▶ Correcting your thinking

▶ Managing your thoughts and attention

▶ Meditating mindfully

*O*ne of the messages of CBT is that the thoughts, attitudes, and beliefs you hold have a big effect on the way you interpret the world around you and on how you feel. So, if you're feeling excessively bad, chances are that you're thinking badly – or, at least, in an unhelpful way. Of course, you probably don't *intend* to think in an unhelpful way, and no doubt you're largely unaware that you do.

Thinking errors are slips in thinking that everyone makes from time to time. Just as a virus stops your computer from dealing with information effectively, so thinking crrors prevent you from making accurate assessments of your experiences. Thinking errors lead you to get the wrong end of the stick, jump to conclusions, and assume the worst. Thinking errors get in the way of, or cause you to distort, the facts. However, you do have the ability to step back and take another look at the way you're thinking and set yourself straight.

Months or years after the event, you've probably recalled a painful or embarrassing experience and been struck by how differently you feel about it at this later stage. Perhaps you can even laugh about the situation now. Why didn't you laugh back then? Because of the way you were thinking at the time.

Identifying Classic Pitfalls in Human Thought

To err is most definitely human. By understanding the thinking errors we outline in this section, you can spot your unhelpful thoughts and put them straight more quickly. Get ready to identify and respond in healthier ways to some of the most common 'faulty' and unhelpful ways of thinking identified by researchers and clinicians.

Catastrophising: Turning mountains back into molehills

Catastrophising is taking a relatively minor negative event and imagining all sorts of disasters resulting from that one small event.

Consider these examples of catastrophising:

- ✔ You're at a party and you accidentally stumble headlong into a flower arrangement. After you extract yourself from the foliage, you scurry home and conclude that everyone at the party witnessed your little trip and laughed at you.

- ✔ You're waiting for your teenage daughter to return home after an evening at the cinema with friends. The clock strikes 10:00 p.m., and you hear no reassuring rattle of her key in the door. By 10:05 p.m., you start imagining her accepting a lift home from a friend who drives recklessly. At 10:10 p.m., you're convinced she's been involved in a head-on collision and paramedics are at the scene. By 10:15 p.m., you're weeping over her grave.

- ✔ Your new partner declines an invitation to have dinner with your parents. Before giving him a chance to explain his reasons, you put down the phone and decide that this is his way of telling you the relationship's over. Furthermore, you imagine that right now he's ringing friends and telling them what a mistake it was dating you. You decide you're never going to find another partner and will die old and lonely.

Catastrophising leads many an unfortunate soul to misinterpret a social faux pas as a social disaster, a late arrival as a car accident, or a minor disagreement as total rejection.

Nip catastrophic thinking in the bud by recognising it for what it is – just thoughts. When you find yourself thinking of the worst possible scenario, try the following strategies:

- ✔ **Put your thoughts in perspective.** Even if everyone at the party did see your flower-arranging act, are you sure no one was sympathetic? Surely you aren't the only person in the world to have tripped over in public. Chances are, people are far less interested in your embarrassing moment than you think. Falling over at a party isn't great, but in the grand scheme of things it's hardly society-page news.

✔ **Consider less terrifying explanations.** What other reasons are there for your daughter being late? Isn't being late for curfew a common feature of adolescence? Perhaps the movie ran over, or she got caught up chatting and forgot the time. Don't get so absorbed in extreme emotions that you're startled to find your daughter in the doorway apologising about missing the bus.

✔ **Weigh up the evidence.** Do you have enough information to conclude that your partner wants to leave you? Has he given you any reason to think this before? Look for evidence that contradicts your catastrophic assumption. For example, have you had more enjoyable times together than not?

✔ **Focus on what you can do to cope with the situation, and the people or resources that can come to your aid.** Engaging in a few more social encounters can help you put your party faux pas behind you. You can repair a damaged relationship – or find another. Even an injury following an accident can be fixed with medical care.

No matter how great a travesty you create in your mind, the world's unlikely to end because of it even if the travesty comes to pass. You're probably far more capable of surviving embarrassing and painful events than you give yourself credit for – human beings can be very resilient.

All-or-nothing thinking: Finding somewhere in between

All-or-nothing or *black-or-white thinking* is extreme thinking that can lead to extreme emotions and behaviours. People either love you or hate you, right? Something's either perfect or a disaster. You're either responsibility-free or totally to blame? Sound sensible? We hope not!

Unfortunately, humans fall into the all-or-nothing trap all too easily:

✔ Imagine you're trying to eat healthily in order to lose weight and you cave in to the temptation of a doughnut. All-or-nothing thinking may lead you to conclude that your plan is in ruins and then to go on to eat the other 11 doughnuts in the pack.

✔ You're studying a degree course and you fail one module. All-or-nothing thinking makes you decide that the whole endeavour is pointless. Either you get the course totally right or it's just a write-off.

Book III

Cognitive Behavioural Therapy

Consider the humble thermometer as your guide to overcoming the tendency of all-or-nothing thinking. A thermometer reads degrees of temperature, not only 'hot' and 'cold'. Think like a thermometer – in degrees, not extremes. You can use the following pointers to help you change your thinking:

✔ **Be realistic.** You can't possibly get through life without making mistakes. One doughnut doesn't a diet ruin. Remind yourself of your goal, forgive yourself for the minor slip, and resume your diet.

✔ **Develop 'both–and' reasoning skills.** An alternative to all-or-nothing thinking is *both–and reasoning*. You need to mentally allow two seeming opposites to exist together. You can *both* succeed in your overall educational goals *and* fail a test or two. Life is not a case of being either a success or a failure. You can *both* assume that you're an OK person as you are *and* strive to change.

All-or-nothing thinking can sabotage goal-directed behaviour. You're far more likely to throw in the towel at the first sign of something blocking your goal when you refuse to allow a margin for error. Beware of 'either/or' statements and global labels such as 'good' and 'bad' or 'success' and 'failure'. Neither people nor life situations are often that cut and dry.

Fortune-telling: Stepping away from the crystal ball

Often, clients tell us after they've done something they were anxious about that the actual event wasn't half as bad as they'd predicted. Predictions are the problem here. You probably don't possess extrasensory perceptions that allow you to see into the future. You probably can't see into the future either with a crystal ball. And yet, you may try to predict future events. Unfortunately, the predictions you make may be negative:

✔ You've been feeling a bit depressed lately and you aren't enjoying yourself like you used to. Someone from work invites you to a party, but you decide that if you go you won't have a good time. The food will unpalatable, the music will be irksome, and the other guests are sure to find you boring. So, you opt to stay in and bemoan the state of your social life.

✔ You fancy the bloke who sells you coffee every morning on the way to the office, and you'd like to go out with him on a date. You predict that if you ask him, you'll be so anxious that you'll say something stupid. Anyway, he's bound to say no thanks – someone that attractive must surely be in a relationship.

✔ You always thought that hang-gliding would be fun, but you've got an anxious disposition. If you try the sport, you're sure to lose your nerve at the last minute and just end up wasting your time and money.

You're better off letting the future unfold without trying to guess how it may turn out. Put the dustcover back on the crystal ball and leave the tarot cards alone, and try the following strategies instead:

✔ **Test out your predictions.** You really never know how much fun you might have at a party until you get there – and the food could be amazing. Maybe the chap at the coffee shop has got a partner, but you won't be sure until you ask.

✔ **Be prepared to take risks.** Isn't it worth possibly losing a bit of cash for the opportunity to try a sport you've always be interested in? And can't you bear the possibility of appearing a trifle nervous for the chance to get to know someone you really like? There's a saying 'a ship is safe in a harbour, but that's not what ships are built for'. Learning to live experimentally and taking calculated risks is a recipe for keeping life interesting.

✔ **Understand that your past experiences don't determine your future experiences.** Just because the last party you went to turned out to be a dreary homage to the seventies, the last person you asked out went a bit green, and that scuba-diving venture resulted in a severe case of the bends doesn't mean that you'll never have better luck again.

Typically, fortune-telling stops you from taking action. It can also become a bit of a self-fulfilling prophecy. If you keep telling yourself that you won't enjoy that party, you're liable to make that prediction come true. Same goes for meeting new people and trying new things. So, put on your party gear, ask him out for dinner, and book yourself in for some hang-gliding.

Mind-reading: Taking your guesses with a pinch of salt

So, you think you know what other people are thinking, do you? With *mind-reading*, the tendency is often to assume that others are thinking negative things about you or have negative motives and intentions.

Here are some examples of mind-reading tendencies:

✔ You're chatting with someone and they look over your shoulder as you're speaking, break eye contact, and (perish the thought) yawn. You conclude immediately that the other person thinks your conversation is mind-numbing and that he'd rather be talking to someone else.

✔ Your boss advises that you book some time off to use up your annual leave. You decide that he's saying this because he thinks your work is rubbish and wants the opportunity to interview for your replacement while you're on leave.

Book III

Cognitive Behavioural Therapy

✔ You pass a neighbour on the street. He says a quick hello but doesn't look very friendly or pleased to see you. You think that he must be annoyed with you about your dog howling at the last full moon and is making plans to report you to environmental health.

You can never know for certain what another person is thinking, so you're wise to pour salt on your negative assumptions. Stand back and take a look at all the evidence to hand. Take control of your tendency to mind-read by trying the following:

✔ **Generate some alternative reasons for what you see.** The person you're chatting with may be tired, be preoccupied with his own thoughts, or just have spotted someone he knows.

✔ **Consider that your guesses may be wrong.** Are your fears really about your boss's motives, or do they concern your own insecurity about your abilities at work? Do you have enough information or hard evidence to conclude that your boss thinks your work is substandard? Does it follow logically that 'consider booking time off' means 'you're getting the sack'?

✔ **Get more information (if appropriate).** Ask your neighbour whether your dog kept him up all night, and think of some ways to muffle your pet next time the moon waxes.

You tend to mind-read what you fear most. Mind-reading is a bit like putting a slide in a slide projector. What you *project* or imagine is going on in other people's minds is very much based on what's already in yours.

Emotional reasoning: Reminding yourself that feelings aren't facts

Surely we're wrong about this one. Surely your feelings are real hard evidence of the way things are? Actually, no! Often, relying too heavily on your feelings as a guide leads you off the reality path. Here are some examples of emotional reasoning:

✔ Your partner has been spending long nights at the office with a co-worker for the past month. You feel jealous and suspicious of your partner. Based on these feelings, you conclude that your partner's having an affair with his co-worker.

✔ You feel guilty out of the blue. You conclude that you must have done something wrong otherwise you wouldn't be feeling guilty.

When you feel emotional reasoning taking over your thoughts, take a step back and try the following:

1. **Take notice of your thoughts.** Take notice of thoughts such as 'I'm feeling nervous, something must be wrong' and 'I'm so angry, and that really shows how badly you've behaved', and recognise that feelings are not always the best measure of reality, especially if you're not in the best emotional shape at the moment.

2. **Ask yourself how you'd view the situation if you were feeling calmer.** Look to see if there is any concrete evidence to support your interpretation of your feelings. For example, is there really any evidence that something bad is going to happen?

3. **Give yourself time to allow your feelings to subside.** When you're feeling calmer, review your conclusions and remember that it is quite possible that your feelings are the consequence of your present emotional state (or even just fatigue) rather than indicators of the state of reality.

The problem with viewing your feelings as factual is that you stop looking for contradictory information – or for any additional information at all. Balance your emotional reasoning with a little more looking at the facts that support and contradict your views.

Overgeneralising: Avoiding the part/whole error

Overgeneralising is the error of drawing global conclusions from one or more events. When you find yourself thinking 'always', 'never', 'people are . . .', or 'the world's . . .', you may well be overgeneralising.

You might recognise overgeneralising in the following examples:

✔ You feel down. When you get into your car to go to work, it doesn't start. You think to yourself, 'Things like this are always happening to me. Nothing ever goes right', which makes you feel even more gloomy.

✔ You become angry easily. Travelling to see a friend, you're delayed by a fellow passenger who cannot find the money to pay her train fare. You think, 'This is typical! Other people are just so stupid', and you become tense and angry.

✔ You tend to feel guilty easily. You yell at your child for not understanding his homework and then decide that you're a thoroughly rotten parent.

Situations are rarely so stark or extreme that they merit terms like 'always' and 'never'. Rather than overgeneralising, consider the following:

- **Get a little perspective.** How true is the thought that nothing *ever* goes right for you? How many other people in the world may be having car trouble at this precise moment?

- **Suspend judgement.** When you judge all people as stupid, including the poor creature waiting in line for the train, you make yourself more outraged and are less able to deal effectively with a relatively minor hiccup.

- **Be specific.** Would you be a *totally* rotten parent for losing patience with your child? Can you legitimately conclude that one incident of poor parenting cancels out all the good things you do for your little one? Perhaps your impatience is simply an area you need to target for improvement.

Shouting at your child in a moment of stress no more makes you a rotten parent than singing him a great lullaby makes you a perfect parent. Condemning yourself on the basis of making a mistake does nothing to solve the problem, so be specific and steer clear of global conclusions.

Labelling: Giving up the rating game

Labels, and the process of labelling people and events, are everywhere. For example, people who have low self-esteem may label themselves as 'worthless', 'inferior', or 'inadequate'.

If you label other people as 'no good' or 'useless', you're likely to become angry with them. Or perhaps you label the world as 'unsafe' or 'totally unfair'? The error here is that you're globally rating things that are too complex for a definitive label. The following are examples of labelling:

- You read a distressing article in the newspaper about a rise in crime in your city. The article activates your belief that you live in a thoroughly dangerous place, which contributes to you feeling anxious about going out.

- You receive a poor mark for an essay. You start to feel low and label yourself as a failure.

- You become angry when someone cuts in front of you in a traffic queue. You label the other driver as a total loser for his bad driving.

Strive to avoid labelling yourself, other people, and the world around you. Accept that they're complex and ever-changing. Recognise evidence that doesn't fit your labels, in order to help you weaken your conviction in your global rating. For example:

- ✔ **Allow for varying degrees.** Think about it: The world isn't a dangerous place but rather a place that has many different aspects with varying degrees of safety.

- ✔ **Celebrate complexities.** All human beings – yourself included – are unique, multifaceted, and ever-changing. To label yourself as a failure on the strength of one failing is an extreme form of overgeneralising. Likewise, other people are just as complex and unique as you. One bad action doesn't equal a bad person.

When you label a person or aspect of the world in a global way, you exclude potential for change and improvement. Accepting yourself as you are is a powerful first step towards self-improvement.

Making demands: Thinking flexibly

Albert Ellis, founder of rational emotive behaviour therapy, one of the first cognitive-behavioural therapies, places demands at the very heart of emotional problems. Thoughts and beliefs that contain words like 'must', 'should', 'need', 'ought', 'got to', and 'have to' are often problematic because they're extreme and rigid.

The inflexibility of the demands you place on yourself, the world around you, and other people often means you don't adapt to reality as well as you could. Consider these possible examples:

- ✔ You believe that you *must* have the approval of your friends and colleagues. This leads you to feel anxious in many social situations and drives you to try and win everyone's approval.

- ✔ You think that because you try very hard to be kind and considerate to others, they really *ought* to be just as kind and considerate in return. Because your demand is not realistic – sadly, other people are governed by their own priorities – you often feel hurt about your friends not acting the way you do yourself.

- ✔ You believe that you *absolutely should* never let people down. Therefore, you rarely put your own welfare first. At work, you do more than your fair share because you don't assert yourself, and so you often end up feeling stressed and depressed.

Book III

Cognitive Behavioural Therapy

Holding *flexible preferences* about yourself, other people, and the world in general is the healthy alternative to inflexible rules and demands. Rather than making demands on yourself, the world, and others, try the following techniques:

- ✔ **Pay attention to language.** Replace words like 'must', 'need', and 'should' with 'prefer', 'wish', and 'want'.

- ✔ **Limit approval seeking.** Can you manage to have a satisfying life even if you don't get the approval of everyone you seek it from? Specifically, you'll feel more confident in social situations if you recognise your *preference* for approval rather than viewing approval as a dire need.

- ✔ **Understand that the world doesn't play to your rules.** In fact, other people tend to have their own rulebooks. So, no matter how much you value considerate behaviour, your friends may not give it the same value. If you can give others the right to not live up to your standards, you'll feel less hurt when they fail to do so.

- ✔ **Retain your standards, ideals, and preferences, and ditch your rigid demands about how you, others, and the world 'have to' be.** So keep acting consistently with how you *would like* things to be rather than becoming depressed or irate about things not being the way you believe they *must* be.

When you hold rigid demands about the way things 'have got to be', you have no margin for deviation or error. You leave yourself vulnerable to experiencing exaggerated emotional disturbance when things in life just don't go your way.

Mental filtering: Keeping an open mind

Mental filtering is a bias in the way you process information, in which you acknowledge only information that fits with a belief you hold. The process is much like a filter on a camera lens that allows in only certain kinds of light. Information that doesn't fit tends to be ignored. If you think any of the following, you're making the 'mental filtering' thinking error:

- ✔ You believe you're a failure, so you tend to focus on your mistakes at work and overlook successes and achievements. At the end of the week, you often feel disappointed about your lack of achievement – but this is probably largely the result of you not paying attention to your successes.

- ✔ You believe you're unlikeable, and *really* notice each time your friend is late to call back or seems too busy to see you. You tend to disregard the ways in which people act warmly towards you, which sustains your view that you're unlikeable.

To combat mental filtering, look more closely at situations you feel down about. Deliberately collecting evidence that contradicts your negative thoughts can help you to correct your information-processing bias. Try the following:

✔ **Examine your filters closely.** For example, are you sifting your achievements through an 'I'm a failure' filter? If so, then only failure-related information gets through. If you look for a friend's achievements over the same week without a filter, you'd be likely to find far more success.

✔ **Gather evidence.** Imagine you're collecting evidence for a court case to prove that your negative thought isn't true. What evidence do you cite? Would, for example, an assertion that you're unlikeable stand up in court against the proof of your friends behaving warmly towards you?

If you only ever take in information that fits with the way you think, you can very easily end up thinking the same way. The fact that you don't see the positive stuff about yourself, or your experiences, doesn't mean it isn't there.

Disqualifying the positive: Keeping the baby when throwing out the bathwater

Disqualifying the positive is related to the biased way that people can process information. Disqualifying the positive is a response to a positive event that transforms into a neutral or negative event in your mind.

The following are examples of disqualifying the positive:

✔ You convince yourself that you're worthless and unlovable. You respond to a work promotion by thinking, 'This doesn't count, because anyone could get this sort of thing.' The result: Instead of feeling pleased, you feel quite disappointed.

✔ You think you're pathetic and feel low. A friend tells you you're a very good friend, but you disqualify this in your mind by thinking, 'She's only saying that because she feels sorry for me. I really am pathetic.'

Hone your skills for accepting compliments and acknowledging your good points. You can try the following strategies to improve your skills:

✔ **Become aware of your responses to positive 'data'.** Practice acknowledging and accepting positive feedback and acknowledging good points about yourself, others, and the world. For example, you could override your workplace disappointment by recognising that *you're* the one who got the promotion. You can even consider that the promotion may well have been a result of your hard work.

✔ **Practice accepting a compliment graciously with a simple thank you.** Rejecting a sincerely delivered compliment is rather like turning down a gift. Steer your thinking towards taking in positive experiences. When others point out attributes you have, start deliberately making a note of those good points.

Book III

Cognitive Behavioural Therapy

If you frequently disqualify or distort your positive attributes or experiences, you can easily sustain a negative belief, even in the face of overwhelming positive evidence.

Low frustration tolerance: Realising you can bear the 'unbearable'

Low frustration tolerance refers to the error of assuming that when something's difficult to tolerate, it's 'intolerable'. This thinking error means magnifying discomfort and not tolerating temporary discomfort when it's in your interest to do so for longer-term benefit.

The following are examples of low frustration tolerance:

✔ You often procrastinate on college assignments, thinking, 'It's just too much hassle. I'll do it later when I feel more in the mood.' You tend to wait until the assignment's nearly due and it becomes too uncomfortable to put off any longer. Unfortunately, waiting until the last moment means that you can rarely put as much time and effort into your coursework as you need to in order to reach your potential.

✔ You want to overcome your anxiety of travelling away from home by facing your fear directly. And yet, each time you try to travel farther on the train, you become anxious, and think 'This is so horrible, I can't stand it', and quickly return home, which reinforces your fear rather than helping you experience travel as less threatening.

The best way to overcome low frustration tolerance is to foster an alternative attitude of *high frustration tolerance*. You can achieve this way of thinking by trying the following:

✔ **Pushing yourself to do things that are uncomfortable or unpleasant.** For example, you can train yourself to work on assignments even if you aren't in a good mood, because the end result of finishing work in good time, and to a good standard, outweighs the hassle of doing something you find tedious.

✔ **Giving yourself messages that emphasise your ability to withstand pain.** To combat a fear of travel, you can remind yourself that feeling anxious is really unpleasant, but you *can* stand it. Ask yourself whether, in the past, you've ever withstood the feelings you're saying you presently 'can't stand'.

Telling yourself you can't stand something has two effects. First, it leads you to focus more on the discomfort you're experiencing. Second, it leads you to underestimate your ability to cope with discomfort. Many things can be difficult to tolerate, but rating them as 'intolerable' often makes situations seem more daunting than they really are.

Personalising: Removing yourself from the centre of the universe

Personalising involves interpreting events as being related to you personally and overlooking other factors. This can lead to emotional difficulties, such as feeling hurt easily or feeling unnecessarily guilty.

Here are some examples of personalising:

- ✔ You may tend to feel guilty if you know a friend is upset and you can't make him feel better. You think, 'If I was really a good friend, I'd be able to cheer him up. I'm obviously letting him down.'

- ✔ You feel hurt when a friend you meet in a shop leaves quickly after saying only a hurried 'hello'. You think, 'He was obviously trying to avoid talking to me. I must have offended him somehow.'

You can tackle personalising by considering alternative explanations that don't revolve around you. Think about the following examples:

- ✔ **Imagine what else may contribute to the outcome you're assuming personal responsibility for.** Your friend may have lost his job or be suffering from depression. Despite your best efforts to cheer him up, these factors are outside your control.

- ✔ **Consider why people may be responding to you in a certain way.** Don't jump to the conclusion that someone's response relates directly to you. For example, your friend may be having a difficult day or be in a big hurry – he may even feel sorry for not stopping to talk to you.

Book III

Cognitive Behavioural Therapy

Getting intimate with your thinking

Figuring out which thinking errors you tend to make the most can be a useful way of making your CBT self-help more efficient and effective. The simplest way of doing this is to jot down your thoughts whenever you feel upset and note what was happening at the time. Remember the maxim: When you feel bad, put your thoughts on the pad! See Chapter 3 for more on managing unhelpful thoughts by writing them down.

You can then review your thoughts against the list of thinking errors in this chapter and write down next to each unhelpful thought which thinking error you may be making. With practice you can get better at spotting your thinking errors – and in all probability, you may notice that you're more prone to making some errors than others; therefore, which alternative styles of thinking to develop.

You may also become aware of patterns or themes in the kinds of situations or events that trigger your negative thoughts. These can also help you to focus on the areas in which your thoughts, beliefs, and attitudes need most work.

Because you really aren't the centre of the universe, look for explanations of events that have little or nothing to do with you.

Tackling Toxic Thoughts

In your endeavours to become your own CBT therapist, one of the key techniques you use is a tool known as an *ABC form*, which provides you with a structure for identifying, questioning, and replacing unhelpful thoughts using pen and paper.

The way you think affects the way you feel. Therefore, changing your unhelpful thoughts is a key to feeling better.

In this section, we give you two versions of the ABC form: one to get you started with identifying your triggers, thoughts, and feelings, and another that takes you right through to developing alternative thoughts so you can act differently in the future.

Using ABC self-help forms to manage your emotions

Getting the hang of the ABC form is often easier if you break down the process into two steps. The first step is to fill out the first three columns (*Activating* event, *Beliefs* and thoughts, *Consequences*) of the form, which you can find further on in this chapter (ABC Form I). This gives you a chance to focus on catching your *negative automatic thoughts* (NATs) on paper and to see the connection between your thoughts and emotions.

Using the ABC form is great, but if you don't have one to hand when you feel an upsetting emotion, grab anything you can write on to scribble down your thoughts and feelings. You can always transfer your thoughts to a form later. As has been said by many a CBT therapist: When you feel bad, stick it on the pad!

Making the thought–feeling link

A crucial step in CBT is to make the *thought–feeling link* or *B-to-C connection*; that is, seeing clearly for yourself the connection between what goes through your mind and your resulting emotions. When you see this connection, it can help you to make much more sense of why to challenge and change your thoughts.

Becoming more objective about your thoughts

One of the biggest advantages of writing down your thoughts is that the process can help you to regard these thoughts simply as hunches, theories, and ideas – rather than as absolute facts.

The more negative the meaning you give to an event, the more negative you'll feel, and the more likely you'll act in a way that maintains that feeling. Crucially, when you feel negative, you're more likely to generate negative thoughts. See how easily you can get caught in a vicious circle? Just one of the reasons to take your negative thoughts with a bucket of salt!

Stepping through the ABC Form 1

So, time to embark on this major CBT self-help technique (see Figure 1-1). The basic process for completing the ABC form is as follows:

1. **In the 'Consequences' box, point 1, write down the emotion you're feeling.**

   Therapy's about becoming emotionally healthier and acting in a more self-helping or productive way. So, when you're filling out the ABC form, the most important place to start is with the emotion you're feeling.

   Emotions and behaviour are *consequences* (C) of the interaction between the *activating event or trigger* (A) and the *beliefs or meanings* (B) in the ABC model of emotion.

   Examples of emotions you may choose to list in the 'Consequences' box include:

   - Anger
   - Anxiety
   - Depression
   - Envy
   - Guilt
   - Hurt
   - Jealousy
   - Shame

   Fill out an ABC form when you feel emotionally upset, when you've acted in a way that you want to change, or when you feel like acting in a way that you wish to change.

2. **In the 'Consequences' box, point 2, write down how you acted.**

   Write down how your behaviour changed when you felt your uncomfortable emotion. Examples of the behaviour that people often identify as their actions in this box include:

   - Avoiding something
   - Becoming withdrawn, isolated, or inactive
   - Being aggressive

Book III

Cognitive Behavioural Therapy

- Binge-eating or restricting food intake

- Escaping from a situation

- Putting off something (procrastination)

- Seeking reassurance

- Taking alcohol or drugs

- Using safety behaviours, such as holding on to something if you feel faint

3. **In the 'Activating Event' box, write down what triggered your feelings.**

   The A in ABC stands for *activating event or trigger*, which are the things that triggered your unhelpful thoughts and feelings. Activating events or triggers to put in this box can include:

   - Something happening right now

   - Something that occurred in the past

   - Something that you're anticipating to happen in the future

   - Something in the external world (an object, place, or person)

   - Something in your mind (an image or memory)

   - A physical sensation (increased heart rate, headache, feeling tired)

   - Your own emotions or behaviour

   An activating event can be pretty much anything. Use your feelings – rather than whether you think the event is important – as a guide to when you should fill out a form.

   To keep your ABC form brief and accurate, focus on the specific aspect of the activating event that you're upset about. Use the table of emotions in Chapter 2 to help you detect the themes to look out for if you're unsure about what may have triggered your thoughts and feelings.

4. **In the 'Beliefs' box, write down your thoughts, attitudes, and beliefs.**

   Describe what the event (whatever you've put in the 'Activating Event' box) meant to you when you felt the emotion (what you've written under point 1 in the 'Consequences' box).

   The thoughts, attitudes, and beliefs you put in 'Beliefs' box often pop up reflexly. They may be extreme, distorted, and unhelpful – but they may *seem* like facts to you. Some examples of these NATs include:

   - Here I go again, proving that I'm useless!

   - I should've known better!

   - Now everyone knows what an idiot I am!

   - This proves that I can't cope like normal people do!

Thoughts are what count, so think of yourself as a detective and set out to capture suspect thoughts. If your thoughts are in the form of a picture, describe the image, or what the image means to you – write them down in the 'Beliefs' box.

We think not only in words but also in pictures. People who are feeling anxious frequently describe that they see *catastrophic images* going through their mind. For example, if you fear fainting in a restaurant, you may get an image of yourself on the restaurant floor with staff fussing over you.

5. **In the 'Thinking Error' box, consider what your thinking errors may be.**

One of the key ways to become more objective about your thoughts is to identify the *thinking errors* that may exist in the thoughts you list in this box.

Questions that you might ask yourself in order to identify your thinking errors include:

- Am I jumping to the worst possible conclusion? (Catastrophising)

- Am I thinking in extreme – all-or-nothing – terms? (Black-and-white thinking)

- Am I using words like 'always' and 'never' to draw generalised conclusions from a specific event? (Overgeneralising)

- Am I predicting the future instead of waiting to see what happens? (Fortune-telling)

- Am I jumping to conclusions about what other people are thinking of me? (Mind-reading)

- Am I focusing on the negative and overlooking the positive? (Mental filtering)

- Am I discounting positive information or twisting a positive into a negative? (Disqualifying the positive)

- Am I globally putting myself down as a failure, worthless, or useless? (Labelling)

- Am I listening too much to my negative gut feelings instead of looking at the objective facts? (Emotional reasoning)

- Am I taking an event or someone's behaviour too personally or blaming myself and overlooking other factors? (Personalising)

- Am I using words like 'should', 'must', 'ought', and 'have to' in order to make rigid rules about myself, the world, or other people? (Demanding)

- Am I telling myself that something is too difficult or unbearable or that 'I can't stand it' when actually it's hard to bear but it *is* bearable and worth tolerating? (Having a low frustration tolerance)

Book III

Cognitive Behavioural Therapy

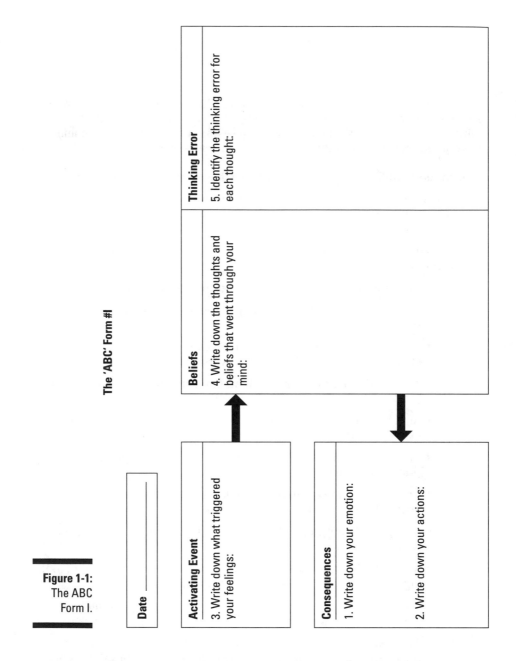

Figure 1-1:
The ABC
Form I.

The 'ABC' Form #I

Date _____

Activating Event

3. Write down what triggered your feelings:

Beliefs

4. Write down the thoughts and beliefs that went through your mind:

Thinking Error

5. Identify the thinking error for each thought:

Consequences

1. Write down your emotion:

2. Write down your actions:

Creating constructive alternatives: Completing the ABC Form II

When you feel more confident about identifying your As, Bs, Cs, and thinking errors, you can move on to the ABC form II (see Figure 1-2). This second form helps you question your unhelpful thoughts in order to reduce their intensity, generate and rate the effects of alternative thoughts, and focus on acting differently.

The first five steps for completing the ABC form II (see the example later in this section) are the same as those for the ABC form I. Then come five more steps. You can find a blank version of the ABC form II in the Appendix. In the ABC form II, column A is the Activating Event, column B is Beliefs, column C is for Consequences, column D is Dispute, and column E is Effect.

6. **Examine your negative thoughts more closely.**

   Ask yourself the following questions in order to examine and weaken your unhelpful thoughts:

   - Can I prove that my thought is 100 per cent true?

   - What are the effects of thinking this way?

   - Is my thought wholly logical or sensible?

   - Do people whose opinions I respect agree that this thought's realistic?

   - What evidence exists against this thought?

   - Is my thought balanced, or extreme?

   - Is my thought rigid or flexible?

   - Am I thinking objectively and realistically, or are my thoughts being biased by how I feel?

   Consider long and hard your negative or unhelpful thoughts in the light of the preceding questions. Don't simply give glib 'yes' or 'no' answers. Instead, think things through and perhaps write down your challenges to your unhelpful thoughts in column D. See the list of questions and prompters at the bottom of the ABC form II, which can help you further with this.

7. **Generate alternatives for each of your unhelpful thoughts, attitudes, and beliefs.**

   This step is critical as it's your alternative thoughts that will help you to feel better! In column D, write down a flexible, non-extreme, realistic, and helpful alternative for each thought, attitude, or belief that appears in column B. The following questions may help you to generate some alternatives:

   - What's a more helpful way of looking at the situation?

   - Do I encourage friends to think in this way?

   - When I'm feeling OK, how do I think differently?

   - Have any past experiences shown me that another possible outcome exists?

   - What's a more flexible or less extreme way of thinking?

- What's a more realistic or balanced way of thinking that takes into account the evidence that does *not* support my thought?

- What do I need to think in order to feel and act differently?

Some thoughts are more stubborn than others, and you won't turn your thinking around completely in one go. Wrestling with NATs for a while before they weaken is typical and appropriate. Think of yourself as *training* your mind to think more flexibly and constructively over a period of time.

Some intrusive thoughts, images, and doubts can be made worse if you engage with them. If you have obsessive-compulsive disorder (OCD), health anxiety, body dysmorphic disorder (BDD), worry, or a jealousy problem, be sure to develop the capability to live with doubt, and allow catastrophic thoughts to pass through your mind rather than challenging them. So if you think you need to learn to live with doubt, or to tolerate upsetting, intrusive thoughts in general, we suggest steering clear of using ABC forms for these problems.

8. **In column E, rate the effects of your alternatives on your feelings.**

   Rate your original feelings 0–100 per cent. Also note whether you experience any alternative healthier emotions such as:

   - Concern

   - Annoyance

   - Sadness

   - Remorse

   - Disappointment

   - Sorrow

You won't always notice a great deal of change in how you feel at first, so keep persevering!

9. **Develop a plan to move forward.**

   The final step on the ABC form II is to develop a plan to move forward. Your plan may be to conduct a behavioural experiment to help you gather more information about whether your thoughts are true or realistic, or to behave differently in a specific situation.

Keeping your old ABC forms can be a rewarding record of your progress, and a useful reminder of how to fill them in if you need to use one again in the future. Many of our clients look back over their ABC forms after they feel better and tell us: 'I can't believe I used to feel and think like that!'

The 'ABC' Form #II

Figure 1-2:
An example of a filled-in ABC Form II.

Date March 18th

Activating Event (Trigger). 2. Briefly write down what triggered your emotions. (e.g. event, situation, sensation, memory, image)	Beliefs, thoughts, and attitudes about A. 3. Write down what went through your mind, or what A meant to you. B's can be about you, others, the world, the past, or the future.	Consequences of A+B on your emotions and behaviours. 1. Write down what emotion you felt and how you acted when you felt this emotion.	Dispute (question and examine) B and generate alternatives. The questions at the bottom of the form will help you with this. 4. Write an alternative for each B, using supporting arguments and evidence.	Effect of alternative thoughts and beliefs (D). 5. Write down how you feel and wish to act as consequence of your alternatives at D.
Returning to work for the first time after being off sick.	*Things will have changed and I won't know what to do (Fortune Telling). People will ask me awkward questions about why I've been off sick and I won't know what to say (Catastrophising). They'll think I'm crazy if they find out I've had depression (Catastrophising, Mind Reading).*	**Emotions** e.g. Depression, guilt, hurt, anger, shame, jealousy, envy, anxiety. Rate intensity 0–100. *Anxiety 70%*	*I don't know whether things have changed. Even if they have I've coped with changes many times before. I'm sure my colleagues will help. Possibly one or two people will ask, and I can just keep my answers short. Mostly everyone will be glad to have me back. I've no reason to think they'll think I'm crazy. When Peter was off with stress people were mostly supportive and understanding. When Helen called last week she seemed to treat me just the same as normal.*	**Emotions** Re-rate 0–100. List any healthy alternative emotion e.g. Sadness, regret, concern. *Anxiety 40%*
		Behaviour e.g. Avoidance, withdrawing, escape, using alcohol or drugs, seeking reassurance, procrastination *Running over in my mind what I'll say to everyone.*		**Alternative Behaviour or Experiment** e.g. Facing situation, increased activity, assertion *Wait and deal with things when I get there, and stop trying to work it out in advance.*

Disputing (Questioning and Examining) and Generating Alternative Thoughts, Attitudes, and Beliefs: 1. Identify your 'thinking errors' at **B** (e.g. Mind Reading, Catastrophising, Labelling, Demands etc.). Write them next to the appropriate 'B'. 2. Examine whether the evidence at hand supports that your thought at **B** is 100% true. Consider whether someone whose opinions you respect would totally agree with your conclusions. 3. Evaluate the helpfulness of each **B**. Write down what you think might be a more helpful, balanced and flexible way of looking at **A**. Consider what you would advise a friend to think, what a role model of yours might think, or how you might look at **A** if you were feeling OK. 4. Add evidence and arguments that support your alternative thoughts, attitudes and beliefs. Write as if you were trying to persuade someone you cared about.

Book III

Cognitive Behavioural Therapy

An ABC a day keeps the doctor at bay!

If you want to master any skill, remember these three words: *Practice, practice, practice!* You may not need to fill out an ABC form everyday. Other days, you may need to complete more than one form. The point is, that practicing ABC forms regularly is worthwhile because:

- Practice helps change disturbing feelings and the thoughts that underpin them.

- Sinking a new thought into your head and heart takes repetition.

- By completing forms on paper, you can become increasingly able to challenge unhelpful thoughts in your head – although you may still need to do it on paper sometimes.

As you progress in your ability to overcome difficulties and develop your CBT self-help skills, you may still find the ABC form useful when you're hit with a biggy. And remember: If you can't work out your unhelpful thinking on the hoof, do sit down and bash it out on paper.

Directing and Redirecting Your Attention

Traditionally, CBT has tended to concentrate many of its techniques on helping people change the *content* of their thinking – from a negative to a more realistic thought, for example. However, modern CBT has begun to tackle another area of human psychology – how we focus our attention.

This section does not discuss *what* you think, but does discuss *how* you manage your thoughts and attention. We introduce *task concentration training* and *mindfulness*, two techniques for managing problematic thoughts and exerting some power over your attention. This section has two main messages:

- For the most part, your thoughts, no matter how distressing and negative, are not the real problem. Rather, the importance or meaning you attach to those thoughts is what causes you the problem. If you view the notion, 'I'm a hopeless case', as a thought rather than a fact, you can greatly lessen its impact.

- When you have an emotional problem, your mind tends to attach unhelpful meanings to aspects of yourself, the world around you, and other people. You can also tend to *overfocus* on particular aspects of these unhelpful meanings. Fortunately, you can develop the ability to steer your attention towards, and away from, any features of your experience you choose, which can help improve your mood and reduce anxiety.

Training in task concentration

Becoming adept at redirecting your attention away from yourself (this includes your bodily sensations, thoughts, and mental images), in certain situations, is the essence of *task concentration*. Rather than thinking about yourself, you focus your attention towards your external environment and what you're doing.

Task concentration involves paying less attention to what's going on inside of you and more attention to what's happening outside of you.

Task concentration can be particularly useful in situations that trigger anxiety in you. Task concentration can help you to counterbalance your tendency to focus on threats and on yourself when you feel anxious.

Choosing to concentrate

The point of task-concentration exercises is not to lessen your overall concentration, but to concentrate harder on different aspects of the external environment. Some tasks require you to focus your attention on certain behaviours – such as listening to what another person is saying during a conversation, or attempting to balance a tray of drinks as you walk through a crowded room.

In other situations, you may feel anxious but you don't have a specific task to attend to. In such a situation, for example, while sitting in a crowded waiting room, you can direct your attention to your surroundings, noticing other people, the features of the room, sounds, and smells.

With practice, you can be both task- and environment-focused rather than self-focused, even in situations that you regard as highly threatening.

The following exercises aim to increase your understanding of how paying attention to sensations and images limits your ability to process information around you. The exercises will also help you realise that you can attend to external task-related behaviours. In other words, you can master *choosing* what you pay attention to in situations when your anxiety is triggered.

Intentionally directing your attention away from yourself does not mean distracting yourself from your sensations or suppressing your thoughts. Sometimes, people try to use thought suppression as a means of alleviating uncomfortable sensations and anxiety. However, suppression usually works only briefly, if at all.

Concentration exercise: Listening

For this exercise, sit back-to-back with someone else, perhaps a friend or your therapist. Ask the person to tell you a story for about two minutes. Concentrate on the story. Then, summarise the story: Note how much of your attention you direct towards the task of listening to the other person, towards yourself, and towards your environment – try using percentages to do this. Your partner can give you feedback on your summary to give you some idea how you did.

Book III

Cognitive Behavioural Therapy

Now do the exercise again, but this time round sit face-to-face with the story-teller and make eye contact. Ask the person to tell you a story, but on this occasion consciously distract yourself by focusing on your thoughts and sensations, and then redirect your attention towards the storyteller. Summarise the story, and note (using percentages again) how you divide your attention between yourself, listening to the other person, and your environment.

Repeat the storytelling activities, sitting back-to-back and then face-to-face, several times until you become readily able to redirect your attention to the task of listening after deliberate distraction through self-focusing. Doing so helps you to develop your ability to control where you focus your attention.

Concentration exercise: Speaking

Follow the same steps for this speaking exercise as you do for the listening exercise, as we describe in the preceding section. Starting with your back to the back of the other person, tell a two-minute story, focusing your attention on making your story clear to the listener.

Next, position yourself face-to-face with the listener, making eye contact. Deliberately distract yourself from the task of storytelling by focusing on your feelings, sensations, and thoughts. Then, refocus your attention towards what you're saying and towards the listener, being aware of her reactions and whether she understands you.

Again, using percentages, monitor how you divide your attention among yourself, the task, and your environment.

Concentration exercise: Graded practice

For this exercise, prepare two lists of situations. For your first list, write down five or so examples of situations you find non-threatening. As you write down the situations, practise distracting yourself by focusing on your internal sensations and thoughts. Now read back through the list of these situations, but this time try refocusing your attention outwards. For your second list, write down ten or so examples of situations you find threatening. Arrange the situations in a hierarchy, starting from the least anxiety-provoking and graduating up to the most anxiety-provoking. Now you can work through your hierarchy by deliberately entering the situations, while practicing task concentration until you reach the top of your list. This means you can start to master your anxiety in real-life situations.

Concentration exercise: Taking a walk

For this exercise, walk through a park, paying attention to what you hear, see, feel, and smell. Focus your attention for a few minutes on different aspects of the world around you. First, focus your attention mainly on what you can hear. Then shift your attention to focus on smells, and then on to the feel of your feet on the ground, and so on. You can move your attention around to different sensations, which can help you tune your attention into the outside world.

After you've practised directing most of your attention to individual senses, try to integrate your attention to include all aspects of the park. Try to do this for at least 20 minutes. Really let yourself drink in the detail of your surroundings. Discover what hooks your attention. You may be drawn to water or have a keen interest in birds, plants, or perhaps even woodland smells. Notice how you feel much more relaxed and less self-conscious as you train your attention on the world around you.

Tuning in to tasks and the world around you

If you're suffering from anxiety, you're probably self-focused in social situations and fail to notice the rest of the world. On top of feeling unnecessarily uncomfortable, your self-focus means that you're likely to miss out on a lot of interesting stuff. Luckily, you can change your attention bias and overcome much of your anxiety.

You can also use re-training your attention onto the outside world to help interrupt yourself from engaging with the stream of negative thoughts that accompanies depression, which will help you to lift your mood.

Here's an example of how you can use task-concentration techniques to overcome anxiety, specifically social phobia.

Harold was particularly worried that people would notice that he blushed and sweated in social situations. He believed that people would think he was odd or a nervous wreck. Harold constantly self-monitored for blushing and sweating and tried very hard to mask these symptoms of his anxiety.

Here's a list of Harold's list of situations, with each situation becoming gradually more challenging:

1. Having dinner with his parents and brother.

2. Socialising with his three closest mates at a local pub.

3. Using public transport during quiet periods.

4. Eating lunch with colleagues at work.

5. Going to the cinema with a friend.

6. Walking alone down a busy street.

7. Socialising with strangers at a party.

8. Going to the grocery shop alone.

9. Going to the gym alone.

10. Initiating conversation with strangers.

Book III

Cognitive Behavioural Therapy

11. Using public transport during busy periods.

12. Eating alone in a restaurant.

13. Going for an interview.

14. Offering his opinion during work meetings.

15. Giving a presentation for work.

Harold used the principles of task concentration to increase his ability to focus deliberately on chosen external factors in non-threatening situations. When Harold was at the pub with his mates, he focused his attention on what his friends were saying, other people in the pub, the music, and the general surroundings. Harold also deliberately distracted himself by focusing on whether he was blushing and sweating, and then he refocused his attention again.

Harold then used the same techniques in more-threatening situations. In the grocery store, Harold found that the more he focused on his blushing and sweating, the more anxious he felt and the less able he was to pack up his shopping. When he paid attention to the task of packing his groceries, made eye contact with the cashier, and even made a bit of small talk, Harold's anxiety symptoms reduced, and he became more aware of what he was doing and what was going on around him.

Harold worked diligently through his hierarchy of feared situations and now feels much more confident and relaxed in social situations.

Becoming More Mindful

Mindfulness meditation, commonly associated with Zen Buddhism, has become popular in the past few years as a technique for dealing with depression, and managing stress and chronic pain. Evidence shows that mindfulness meditation can help reduce the chance of problems such as depression returning, and adds another weapon into your armoury against emotional problems.

Being present in the moment

Mindfulness is the art of being present in the moment, without passing judgement about your experience. The mindfulness process is so simple – and yet so challenging. Keep your attention focused on the moment that you're experiencing *right now*. Suspend your judgement about what you're feeling, thinking, and absorbing through your senses. Simply observe what's going on around you, in your mind, and in your body without doing anything. Just allow yourself to be aware of what's happening.

Mindfulness literature talks about the way your mind almost mechanically forms judgements about each of your experiences, labelling them as good, bad, or neutral depending on how you value them. Things that generate good and bad feelings within you get most of your attention, but you may ignore neutral things or deem them to be boring. Mindfulness meditation encourages awareness of the present moment with an uncultured mind, observing even the seemingly mundane without judgement. The whole experience is a bit like looking at the world for the first time.

When you meet someone you know, try to see her through fresh eyes. Suspend your prior knowledge, thoughts, experiences, and opinions about her. You can try this with acquaintances or people you know very well, such as family members and close friends.

Try mindfulness exercises when you're in the countryside or walking down the street. Whether the surroundings are familiar to you or not, try to see the details of the world around you through fresh eyes.

Letting your thoughts pass by

You can develop your mindfulness skills and use them to help you deal with unpleasant thoughts or physical symptoms. If you have social anxiety for example, you can develop the ability to *focus away* from your anxious thoughts.

Watching the train pass by

Imagine a train passing through a station. The train represents your thoughts and sensations (your 'train of thought'). Each carriage may represent one or more specific thoughts or feelings. Visualise yourself watching the train pass by without hopping onto any carriage. Accept your fears about what other people may be thinking about you without trying to suppress them or engaging with them. Simply watch them pass by like a train through a station.

Standing by the side of the road

Another version of the exercise is to imagine that you're standing on the side of a reasonably busy road. Each passing vehicle represents your thoughts and sensations. Just watch the cars go by. Observe and accept them passing. Don't try to hitch-hike, redirect the flow of traffic, or influence the cars in any way.

Discerning when not to listen to yourself

One of the real benefits of understanding the way that your emotions influence the way you think, is to know when what you're thinking isn't likely to be helpful or very realistic. Being mindful means learning to experience your thoughts without passing judgement as to whether they are true or not.

Book III

Cognitive Behavioural Therapy

Given that many of the negative thoughts you experience when you're emotionally distressed are distorted and unhelpful, you're much better off letting some thoughts pass you by, recognising them as *symptoms* or *output* of a given emotional state or psychological problem. Chapter 2 covers the *cognitive consequences* of emotions, giving you an idea of the types of thoughts that can occur as a consequence of how you're feeling.

Becoming more familiar with the thoughts that tend to pop into your head when you feel down, anxious, or guilty makes it easier for you to recognise them as thoughts and let them come and go, rather than treating them as facts. This familiarity gives you another skill to help manage your negative thoughts in addition to challenging or testing them out in reality.

Incorporating mindful daily tasks

Becoming more mindful about little everyday tasks can help you to strengthen your attention muscles. Essentially, everything you do throughout the day can be done with increased awareness. For example, think about the following:

- ✔ Washing-up mindfully can help you experience the process more fully. Notice the smell of the washing-up liquid, the temperature of the water, and the movement of your hands.

- ✔ Eating mindfully can give you a more enjoyable eating experience. Slow down the speed you eat, and pay attention to the texture of the food, the subtlety of the flavours, and the appearance of the dish.

Chapter 2

Overcoming Obstacles to Progress

. . . .

In This Chapter
▶ Considering your emotions and feelings
▶ Progressing with positive principles
▶ Getting to grips with anxiety
▶ Tackling depression

. . . .

This chapter aims to introduce you to some of the key differences between the unhealthy negative emotions you may experience and their healthy counterparts. The information we offer also helps you to discover ways to identify whether you're experiencing a healthy or an unhealthy emotional response.

Exploring Emotions and Naming Your Feelings

If someone asks you how you feel, you may have difficulty describing exactly which emotion you're feeling. You may not be sure what name to give to your internal experience, or perhaps you're feeling more than one emotion at the same time.

Don't get caught up on words! When you start to make a distinction between healthy and unhealthy feelings, what you call them isn't terribly important. The main point is to be able to analyse your thoughts and behaviours, and to take notice of where your attention is focused (CBT refers to this as *attention focus*). These three areas are ultimately your most reliable guides as to which type of emotion you're experiencing.

For the sake of clarity, therapists can often encourage people to use different words for unhealthy and healthy alternatives to common feelings. For example, you could use the word 'anger' to describe an unhealthy emotion and 'annoyance' to describe the healthy counterpart.

Some people find it simpler to choose a descriptive word for their emotion and to add the term 'healthy' or 'unhealthy' to that word. Whatever way you prefer to describe your emotions is okay – the important bit's understanding the category each emotion falls into. Different people have different ways of describing things. Think about how you'd describe an oil painting compared with the way a friend or art critic may talk about it. Similarly, people describe emotional states in diverse ways. You, a friend, and a psychotherapist (someone highly skilled in discussing emotions) may all use very different words to describe the same type of feeling.

If you're not used to talking about the way you feel, you may have a hard time finding the words to reflect your feelings.

The following is a reference list of common human emotions and their synonyms, which you can use to increase your vocabulary of *emotive* (relating to emotions) terminology. This list is not broken down into healthy and unhealthy emotions.

- **Angry:** aggressive, annoyed, bad-tempered, complaining, confounded, cross, displeased, enraged, fractious, fuming, furious, hostile, ill-tempered, incensed, irritated, livid, miffed, peevish, prickly, resentful, testy, touchy, truculent.

- **Anxious:** agitated, apprehensive, bothered, concerned, edgy, fearful, fretful, frightened, jumpy, nervous, nervy, panicky, restless, tense, troubled, uneasy, vexed, worried.

- **Ashamed:** belittled, debased, defamed, degraded, discredited, disgraced, dishonoured, humiliated, mortified, scorned, smeared, sullied, tarnished, undignified, vilified.

- **Disappointed:** crestfallen, deflated, dejected, discouraged, disenchanted, disheartened, disillusioned, dismayed, gutted, let down, thwarted.

- **Embarrassed:** awkward, diminished, discomfited, humiliated, ill at ease, insecure, self-conscious, small, timid, uncomfortable, unconfident, unsure of oneself.

- **Envious:** green with envy, malevolent, malicious, Schadenfreude, sour, spiteful.

- **Guilty:** answerable, at fault, blameworthy, condemned, culpable, deplorable, indefensible, inexcusable, in the wrong, liable, reprehensible, unforgivable, unpardonable.

- ✔ **Hurt:** aggrieved, broken-hearted, cut to the quick, cut up, damaged, devastated, gutted, hard done by, harmed, horrified, injured, marred, offended, pained, wounded.

- ✔ **Jealous:** bitter and twisted, distrustful, doubtful, green-eyed, sceptical, suspicious, wary.

- ✔ **Love:** (we threw this one in just to lighten the mood) admiring, adoring, affectionate, besotted, blissful, crazed, devoted, enamoured, esteemed, fond, head over heels, infatuated, keen, loved-up, love-struck, mad about, on cloud nine, smitten, struck by cupid's arrow, worshipping.

- ✔ **Sad:** bereft, blue, depressed, distraught, distressed, down, downcast, downhearted, grief-stricken, heartsick, inconsolable, melancholic, mournful, shattered, sorrowful, tearful.

One benefit of understanding the difference between healthy and unhealthy emotions is that you give yourself a better chance to check out what you're thinking. If you recognise that you're experiencing an unhealthy emotion, you're then in a position to challenge any faulty thinking that may be leading to your unhealthy emotional response. Disputing and correcting thinking errors can help you to experience a healthy, negative emotion instead of an unhealthy feeling.

Understanding the anatomy of emotions

Figure 2-1 shows the complex processes involved in human emotion. Whenever you feel a certain emotion, a whole system is activated. This system includes the thoughts and images that enter your mind, the memories you access, the aspects of yourself or the surrounding world that you focus on, the bodily and mental sensations you experience, physical changes such as appetite, your behaviour, and the things you *feel like* doing.

As the diagram shows, these different dimensions interact in complex ways. For example, training your attention on possible threats is likely to increase the chance of anxious thoughts popping into your mind, and vice versa. Not sleeping well may increase the chances of you being inactive; continued inactivity can further disrupt your usual sleeping pattern. The advantage of understanding this system of emotion as presented in Figure 2-1, is that it gives you plenty of opportunity to make changes. Changing even one aspect of the system can make changing other parts easier.

An example of change is becoming more active if you've been inactive, which may alleviate your feelings of depression and make it easier for you to challenge your depressive, pessimistic thinking. Being prescribed antidepressant

Book III

Cognitive Behavioural Therapy

medication, which works by effecting brain chemistry, can take the edge off your depression. Use of antidepressants can make it easier for you to train your attention *away* from your negative thoughts and uncomfortable symptoms and *towards* possible solutions to some of your practical problems.

Deciphering between healthy and unhealthy versions of negative emotions can be challenging, especially when the process is new to you. Think of Table 2-1 as your emotional ready reckoner for the characteristics of both healthy and unhealthy emotions. Everything you may need to identify the emotion you're experiencing is in this table. Plus, if you do identify that an emotion you're experiencing is unhealthy, you can implement the thoughts, attention focuses, and behaviours of the healthy version to aid you in feeling better.

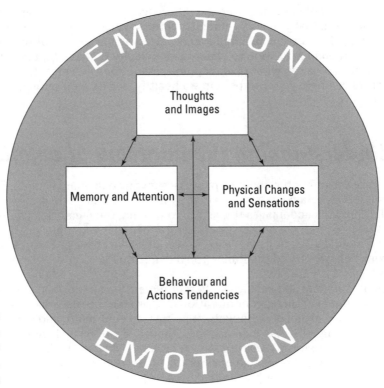

Figure 2-1:
The anatomy
of emotion.

Table 2-1		Healthy and Unhealthy Emotions		
Emotion	*Theme*	*Thoughts*	*Attention Focus*	*Behaviour/ Action Tendencies*
Anxiety (unhealthy)	Threat or danger	Has rigid or extreme attitudes	Monitors threat or danger excessively	Withdraws physically and mentally from threats
		Overestimates degree of threat		Uses super-stitious behav-iour to ward off threat
		Underestimates ability to cope with threat		Numbs anxi-ety with drugs or alcohol
		Increases threat-related thoughts		Seeks reassurance
Concern (healthy)	Threat or danger	Has flexible and preferential attitudes	Doesn't see threat where no threat exists	Faces up to threat
		Views threat realistically		Deals with threat constructively
		Realistically assesses ability to cope with threat		Doesn't seek unneeded reassurance
		Doesn't increase threat-related thoughts		
Depression (unhealthy)	Loss or failure	Has rigid and extreme attitudes	Dwells on past loss/ failure	Withdraws from others
		Sees only nega-tive aspects of loss/failure		
	Ruminates on unsolv-able problems	Neglects self and living environment		

Book III

Cognitive Behavioural Therapy

(continued)

Table 2-1 *(continued)*

Emotion	Theme	Thoughts	Attention Focus	Behaviour/ Action Tendencies
		Feels helpless	Focuses on personal flaws and failings	Attempts to end feelings of depression in self-destructive ways
		Thinks future is bleak and hopeless	Focuses on negative world events	
Sadness (healthy)	Loss or failure	Has flexible and preferential attitudes	Doesn't dwell on past loss/failure	Talks to significant others about feelings about loss/ failure
		Sees both negative and positive aspects of loss/failure	Focuses on problems that one can change	Continues to care for self and living environment
		Is able to help self	Focuses on personal strengths and skills	Avoids self-destructive behaviours
		Is able to think about future with hope	Balances focus between positive and negative world events	
Anger (unhealthy)	Personal rule is broken or self-esteem is threatened	Has rigid and extreme attitudes	Looks for evidence of malicious intent in other person	Seeks revenge
		Assumes other person acted deliberately	Looks for evidence of offensive behaviour beng repeated by other people	Attacks other person physically or verbally

Emotion	Theme	Thoughts	Attention Focus	Behaviour/ Action Tendencies
		Thinks of self right and other as person as wrong	Takes anger out on innocent person, animal, or object	
		Cannot see other person's point of view		Withdraws aggressively/ sulks
				Recruits allies against other person
Annoyance (healthy)	Personal rule broken or self-esteem is threatened	Has flexible and preferential attitudes	Looks for evidence that other person may not have malicious intent	Doesn't seek revenge
		Considers other person may not have acted deliberately	Doesn't see further offence where it may not exist	Asserts self without physical/verbal violence
		Considers that both self and other person may be right to some degree		Doesn't take out feelings on innocent parties
		Is able to see other person's point of view		Remains in situation, striving for resolution (doesn't sulk)
				Requests other person to change their offensive behaviour

(continued)

Book III

Cognitive Behavioural Therapy

Table 2-1 *(continued)*

Emotion	Theme	Thoughts	Attention Focus	Behaviour/ Action Tendencies
Shame (unhealthy)	Shameful personal information has been publicly revealed by self or others	Overestimates shamefulness of information revealed	Sees disapproval from others where it doesn't exist	Hides from others to avoid disapproval
		Overestimates degree of disapproval from others		May attack others who have shamed self, in attempt to save face
		Overestimates how long disapproval will last		May try to repair self-esteem in self-destructive ways
				Ignores attempts from social group to return to normal
Regret (healthy)	Shameful personal information has been publicly revealed by self or others	Is compassionately self-accepting about information revealed	Focuses on evidence that self is accepted by social group despite information revealed	Continues to participate in social interaction
		Is realistic about degree of disapproval from others		Responds to attempts from social group to return to normal
		Is realistic about how long disapproval will last		

Emotion	Theme	Thoughts	Attention Focus	Behaviour/ Action Tendencies
Hurt (unhealthy)	Other person treats one badly (self is undeserving)	Has rigid and extreme attitudes	Looks for evidence of other person not caring or being indifferent	Stops communicating with other person/sulks
		Overestimates unfairness of other's behaviour		Punishes other person through silence or criticism, without stating what one feels hurt about
		Thinks other person doesn't care		
		Thinks of self as alone and uncared for		
		Dwells on past hurts		
		Thinks other person must make first move towards resolution		
Disap- pointment (healthy)	Other person treats one badly (self is undeserving)	Has flexible and preferential attitudes	Focuses on evidence that other person does care and isn't indifferent	Communicates with other person about feelings
		Is realistic about degree of unfairness of other's behaviour		Tries to influence other person to act in fairer manner

(continued)

Table 2-1 *(continued)*

Emotion	Theme	Thoughts	Attention Focus	Behaviour/ Action Tendencies
		Thinks other person acted badly but doesn't think that they don't care		
		Doesn't think of self as alone or uncaring		
		Doesn't dwell on past hurts		
		Doesn't wait for other person to make first move		
Jealousy (unhealthy)	Threat to relationship with partner from another person	Has rigid and extreme attitudes	Looks for sexual/ romantic connotations in partner's conversations with others	Seeks constant reassurance that partner is faithful and loving
		Overestimates visual threat to the relationship	Creates images of partner being unfaithful	Monitors and/ or restricts partner's movements and actions
		Thinks partner is always on verge of leaving for another	Looks for evidence that partner is having an affair	Retaliates for partner's imagined infidelity
		Thinks partner will leave for another person who he has admitted to finding attractive		Sets tests/ traps for partner

Emotion	Theme	Thoughts	Attention Focus	Behaviour/ Action Tendencies
				Sulks
Concern for relationship (healthy)	Threat to relationship with partner from another person	Has flexible and preferential attitudes	Doesn't look for evidence that partner is having an affair	Allows partner to express love without needing excessive reassurance
		Is realistic about degree of threat to relationship	Doesn't create images of partner being unfaithful	Allows partner freedom without monitoring them
		Thinks partner finding others attractive is normal	Views partner's conversation with others as normal	Allows partner to express natural interest in opposite sex without imagining infidelity
Unhealthy envy (unhealthy)	Another person possesses something desirable (self lacks desired thing)	Has rigid and extreme attitudes	Focuses on how to get the desired possession without regard for any consequences	Criticises the person with desired possession
		Thinks about the desired possession in a negative way to try and reduce its desirability	Focuses on how to deprive other person of the desired possession	Criticises the desired possession
		Pretends to self that one is happy without desired possession even though this is untrue		Attempts to steal/destroy the desired possession in order to deprive others

(continued)

Book III

Cognitive Behavioural Therapy

Table 2-1 *(continued)*

Emotion	*Theme*	*Thoughts*	*Attention Focus*	*Behaviour/ Action Tendencies*
Guilt (unhealthy)	Broken moral code (by failing to do something or by committing a sin), hurting or offending significant other	Has rigid and extreme attitudes	Looks for evidence of others blaming one for the sin	Desires to escape from guilt feelings in self-defeating ways
		Thinks one has definitely sinned	Looks for evidence of punishment or retribution	Begs for forgiveness
		Thinks that one deserves punishment		Promises that a sin will never be committed again
		Ignores mitigating factors		Punishes self either physically or through deprivation
		Ignores other people's potential responsibility for sin		Attempts to disclaim any legitimate responsibility for the wrongdoing as an attempt to alleviate feelings of guilt
Remorse (healthy)	Broken moral code (by failing to do something or by committing a sin), hurting or offending significant other	Has flexible and preferential attitudes	Doesn't look for evidence of others blaming oneself for the sin	Faces up to healthy pain that comes with knowing that one has sinned

(continued)

Emotion	Theme	Thoughts	Attention Focus	Behaviour/ Action Tendencies
		Considers actions in context and with understanding before making a judgement about whether one has sinned	Doesn't look for evidence of punish-ment or retribution	Asks for forgiveness
		Takes appro-priate level of responsibility for the sin		Atones for the sin by taking a penalty and/or make appropri-ate amends
		Considers miti-gating factors		Doesn't have tendency to be defensive or to make excuses for the poor behaviour
		Doesn't believe that punishment is deserved and/or imminent		

Book III

Cognitive
Behavioural
Therapy

Defining and rating your emotional problems

The aim of CBT is to help you overcome your emotional problems and move you towards your goals. As with all kinds of problem-solving, *defining* your emotional problems is the first step in solving those problems.

Making a statement

Writing down a problem statement has three main components – the emo-tion, the theme or event (what you feel your emotion about), and what you do in response to that emotion. You can effectively describe an emotional problem by filling in the blanks of the following statement:

Feeling_____ (emotion) about _____
(theme or event), leading me
to_____(response).

For example:

> Feeling *anxious* about *my face turning red in social situations*, leading me
> to *avoid going out to bars and clubs and to splash my face with water if I
> feel hot.*

> Feeling *depressed* about *the end of my relationship with my girlfriend*, lead-
> ing me to *spend too much time in bed, avoid seeing people, and take less
> care of myself.*

Rating your emotional problem

Human nature leads you to focus on how bad you feel, rather than how much
better you feel. As you reduce the intensity of any emotional disturbance,
you can find motivation in being able to see a difference. After you describe a
problematic emotion, rate it on a scale of 0–10, based on how much distress
the emotion causes you and how much it interferes with your life.

As you work on resolving your emotional problem by making changes to your
thinking and behaviour, continue to rate the distress and interference it is
causing you. Your ratings are likely to go down over time as you make efforts
to overcome your unhealthy negative emotions. Review your ratings regularly, once a week or so. Doing this review helps remind you of your progress
and replenishes your motivation to keep up the good work!

Getting rid of guilt

Guilt is an unhealthy negative emotion that's particularly notorious for blocking positive change. You may be telling yourself guilt-provoking things like
the following:

- ✔ 'I'm causing my family a lot of bother through my problems.'
- ✔ 'Other people in the world are so much worse off than me. I've no right
  to feel depressed.'
- ✔ 'I should be more productive. Instead, I'm just a waste of space.'

Guilt sabotages your chances of taking positive action. Guilty thoughts, such
as the preceding examples, can lead you to put yourself down further,
thereby making yourself more depressed. Your depression leads you to see
the future as hopeless and saps your motivation.

Even if the thoughts that are making you feel guilty about your depression, anxiety, or other emotional problem hold some truth, try to accept yourself as someone who's *unwell*. For example, your diminished ability to be productive is a side effect of depression, not an indication that you're a bad or selfish person.

Shame and guilt grow in the dark. Hiding your problems, and your feelings *about* your problems, from other people tends to make things worse over time. Talking about your obsessions, depression, addiction, or other problems gives you the chance to share your fears and discomfort with someone else, who may be far more understanding than you imagine.

Adopting Positive Principles That Promote Progress

Some of the attitudes you hold probably aren't going to do you any favours as you try to overcome your emotional problems. Fortunately, you can swap your unhelpful attitudes for alternative beliefs that can give you a leg-up on the ladder to better emotional health.

Book III

Cognitive Behavioural Therapy

Understanding that simple doesn't mean easy

Most of the steps to overcoming psychological problems with CBT are relatively simple. CBT isn't rocket science – in fact, many of the principles and recommendations may seem like common sense. However, CBT may be sense, but it ain't that common – if it was, fewer people would be suffering with emotional problems.

Even if CBT is as simple as ABC, the actual application of CBT principles is far from easy. Using CBT to help yourself requires a lot of personal *effort*, *diligence*, *repetition* and *determination*.

Because CBT seems so simple, some people get frustrated when they discover that they're not getting well fast or easily enough for their liking. If you want to make CBT work for *you*, take the attitude that getting better doesn't have to be easy. Your health is worth working for.

Being optimistic about getting better

One of the biggest blocks that prevent you from getting better is when you refuse to believe that change is possible. Be on the lookout for negative predictions that you may be making about your ability to get better. Challenge any thoughts you have, like the following:

- ✔ 'Other people get better, but they're not as messed up as me.'
- ✔ 'I'll never change – I've been like this for too long.'
- ✔ 'This CBT stuff will never work for someone as useless as me.'

If these thoughts sound familiar, check out the section that covers how to try to be a little kinder to yourself earlier in this chapter. Would you encourage a friend to believe such thoughts, or would you urge your friend to challenge their thinking? Try to give yourself the kind of good advice that you'd give another person with your type of problem.

Look for evidence that you *can* make changes. Remind yourself of other things you've done in the past that were difficult and required lots of your effort to overcome. If you don't give a new treatment method a fair shot, then how can you possibly *know* it can't work?

Staying focused on your goals

If you want to continue making healthy progress, occasionally you need to renew your commitment to your goals. You may find that you stop dead in your tracks because you've forgotten what the point is. Or perhaps you find yourself feeling ambivalent about getting over your problems. After all, staying anxious, depressed, or angry may seem easier than changing.

Remind yourself regularly of your goals and the benefits of striving to achieve these goals. You can use the cost–benefit analysis (CBA) form to reaffirm the benefits of making goal-directed changes.

Always try to set goals that are within your grasp, and you can establish shorter-term goals along the way. For example, if your goal is to move from being largely housebound to being able to travel freely, set a goal of being able to go to a particular shop to buy something specific. You can then concentrate on the steps needed to reach that particular smaller goal, before moving on to tackle larger goals.

Understanding the Nature of Anxiety

Anxiety is a bully. And like most bullies, the more you let it shove you around, the pushier it gets. This section helps you get to know the nature of anxiety and to identify the ways in which it pushes you about. Fundamentally, you can beat anxiety, like any bully, by standing up to it.

Acquiring anti-anxiety attitudes

Your thoughts are what count, because your feelings are influenced greatly by how you think. Feeling anxious increases the chance of you experiencing anxiety-provoking thoughts. Anxious thoughts can increase anxious feelings, and so a vicious circle can develop. You can help yourself to face your fears by adopting the attitudes we outline in this section.

Avoiding extreme thinking

Telling yourself that things are 'awful', 'horrible', 'terrible', or 'the end of the world' only turns up the anxiety heat. Remind yourself that few things are really that dreadful, and instead rate events more accurately as 'bad', 'unfortunate', or 'unpleasant but not the end of the world'.

Extreme thinking leads to extreme emotional reactions. When you mislabel a negative event as 'horrible', you make yourself overly anxious about unpleasant but relatively non-extreme events, such as minor public embarrassment.

Book III

Cognitive
Behavioural
Therapy

Taking the fear out of fear

When people say things like 'Don't worry, it's *just* anxiety', the word 'just' implies – wrongly – that anxiety's a mild experience. Anxiety can, in fact, be a very profound experience, with strong bodily and mental sensations. Some anxious people misinterpret these intense physical symptoms as dangerous or as signs of impending peril. Common misreadings include, assuming that a nauseous feeling means that you're about to be sick, or thinking that you're going crazy because your surroundings feel 'unreal'.

If you have concerns about your physical sensations you may consider seeing your family doctor prior to deliberately confronting your fears. Your doctor may then be able to advise you as to whether deliberately increasing your anxiety in the short-term, in order to be free of it in the long-term, is safe enough for you. It is rare for people to be advised against facing their fears.

Understanding and accepting common sensations of anxiety can help you stop adding to your anxiety by misinterpreting normal sensations as dangerous. Figure 2-2 outlines some of the more common physical aspects of anxiety.

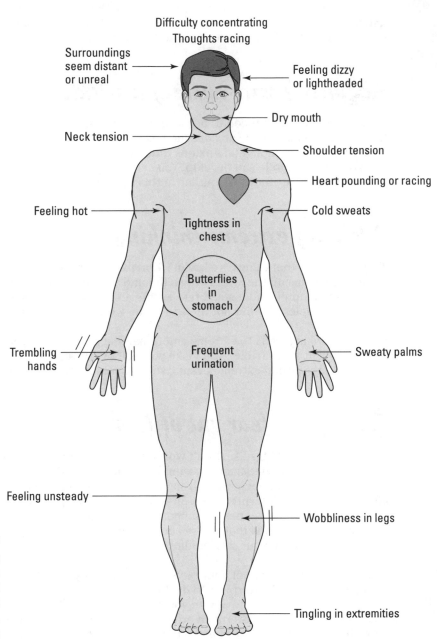

Difficulty concentrating
Thoughts racing

Surroundings seem distant or unreal

Feeling dizzy or lightheaded

Dry mouth

Neck tension

Shoulder tension

Heart pounding or racing

Feeling hot

Cold sweats

Tightness in chest

Butterflies in stomach

Trembling hands

Frequent urination

Sweaty palms

Feeling unsteady

Wobbliness in legs

Tingling in extremities

Figure 2-2:
Common physical sensations of anxiety.

Undoubtedly, anxiety is an unpleasant, sometimes extremely disturbing experience. However, evaluating your anxiety as 'unbearable' or saying 'I can't stand it' only turns up the emotional heat. Remind yourself that anxiety is hard to bear but not unbearable.

Defeating fear with FEAR

Perhaps the most reliable way of overcoming anxiety is the following maxim: FEAR – Face Everything And Recover. Supported by numerous clinical trials, and used daily all over the world, the principle of facing to your fears until your anxiety reduces is one of the cornerstones of CBT.

The process of deliberately confronting your fear and staying within the feared situation until your anxiety subsides is known as *exposure* or *desensitisation*. The process of getting used to something, like cold water in a swimming pool, is called *habituation*. The principle is to wait until your anxiety reduces by at least half before ending your session of exposure – usually between twenty minutes and one hour, but sometimes more.

As Figure 2-3 shows that if you deliberately confront your fears, your anxiety becomes less severe and reduces more quickly with each exposure. The more exposures you experience, the better. When you first confront your fears, aim to repeat your exposures at least daily.

Book III

Cognitive Behavioural Therapy

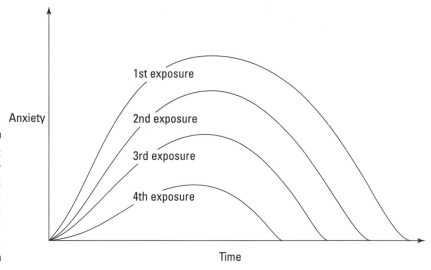

Figure 2-3:
Your anxiety
reduces
with each
exposure to
a feared
trigger.

When confronting your fears, aim for *manageable exposure*, so that you can successfully experience facing your fears and mastering them. If your exposures are overwhelming, you may end up resorting to escape, avoidance, or safety behaviours. The flipside of choosing overwhelming exposures is taking things too gently, which can make your progress slow and demoralising. Strive to strike a balance between the two extremes.

If you set yourself only easy, gentle exposures, you risk reinforcing the erroneous idea that anxiety is unbearable and must be avoided. The point of exposure work is to prove to yourself that you *can* bear the discomfort associated with anxious feelings.

Overriding common anxieties

To wage war on your excessive worry, resist the temptation to try to solve every problem in advance of it happening. Try to live with doubt and realise that the most important thing is not what you specifically worry about but *how* you manage your worrying thoughts. Overcoming worry is the art of allowing thoughts to enter your mind without trying to 'sort them out' or push them away.

Pounding on panic

Panic attacks are intense bursts of anxiety in the absence of real danger, and can often seem to come out the blue. Panic attacks often have very strong physical sensations such as nausea, heart palpitations, a feeling of shortness of breath, choking, dizziness, and hot sweats. Panic sets in when people mistake these physical sensations as dangerous and get into a vicious circle because these misinterpretations lead to more anxiety, leading to more physical sensations.

Put panic out of your life by deliberately triggering off panic sensations. Enter situations you've been avoiding and resist using safety behaviours. Realise, for example, that feeling dizzy does not cause you to collapse, so you don't need to sit down, and that other uncomfortable sensations of anxiety will pass without harming you. Carry out a behavioural experiment to specifically test out whether your own feared catastrophes come true as a consequence of a panic attack.

Assaulting agoraphobia

Georgina was afraid to travel far from her home or from familiar places she felt safe in, which are common characteristics of *agoraphobia*. She feared losing control of her bowels and soiling herself. She had become virtually housebound and relied heavily on her husband to drive her around. She learned about the nature of anxiety and developed the theory that although she may *feel* like she was going to soil herself, her sensations were due largely to anxiety and she would be able to 'hold on'.

To gain confidence and overcome agoraphobia, develop a hierarchy of your avoided situations and begin to face them, and stay in them until your anxiety reduces. This may include driving progressively longer distances alone, using public transport, and walking around in unfamiliar places. At the same time, work hard to drop your safety behaviours so you can discover that nothing terrible happens if you do become anxious or panicky, and ride it out.

Dealing with post-traumatic stress disorder

Post-traumatic stress disorder (PTSD) can develop after being involved in (or witnessing) an accident, assault, or other extremely threatening or distressing event. The symptoms of PTSD include being easily startled, feeling irritable and anxious, memories of the event intruding into your waking day, nightmares about the event, or feeling emotionally numb. If you have PTSD you may be sustaining your distress by misunderstanding your normal feelings of distress in response to the event, trying to avoid triggers that activate memories of the event, or trying too hard to keep yourself safe.

To combat PTSD, remind yourself that memories of a traumatic event intruding into your mind, and feelings of distress are normal reactions to trauma. Allowing memories to enter your mind and spending time thinking about them is part of processing traumatic events, and a crucial part of recovery. Many people find that deliberately confronting triggers or writing out a detailed first person account can be helpful. At the same time it's important to reduce any excessive safety precautions you may have begun to take.

Book III

Cognitive Behavioural Therapy

Hitting back at fear of heights

Begin to attack a fear of heights by carrying out a survey among your friends about the kinds of feelings that they have when standing at the edge of a cliff or at the top of a tall building. You'll probably discover that your sensation of being unwillingly drawn over the edge is very common. Most people, however, just interpret this feeling as a normal reaction.

Put this new understanding into action to gain more confidence about being in high places. Work through a hierarchy of entering increasingly tall buildings, looking over bridges, and climbing to the top of high cliffs.

Wending your way out of worry

One of the dilemmas faced by people who worry too much is how to reduce that worry. Some degree of worry is entirely normal – of course problems and responsibilities will cross your mind from time to time. Yet, you may be someone who worries all of the time. Being a true worrywart is intensely uncomfortable. Understandably, you may want to stop worrying quite so much.

Two reasons may account for your excessive worrying:

- ✔ You may think that by worrying about unpleasant events, you can prevent those events from happening. Or, you may believe that your worry can give you clues as to how to prevent negative events from coming to fruition.

- ✔ You may think that worry protects you by preparing you for negative events. You may believe that if you worry about bad things enough, they won't catch you off guard and you'll be better fixed to deal with them.

If you can convince yourself that excessive worry really doesn't prevent feared events from happening or prepare you for dealing with bad things, you may be in a better position to interrupt your repetitive cycle of worries.

Ironically, many people worry about things in a vain attempt to get all possible worries out of the way so they can then relax. Of course, this never happens – worry's a moveable feast, and something else always comes along for you to worry about.

If you worry excessively about everyday events, you may try to solve every possible upcoming problem in advance of it happening. You may hope that your worry will solve potential problems, and thus you won't have to worry about them any more.

Unfortunately, trying too hard to put your mind at rest can lead to increased mental activity and yet more worry. All too often, people then worry that worrying so much is harmful, and they end up worrying about worrying!

Try to see your worrying as a bad habit. Instead of focusing on the content of your worries, try to interrupt the worry process by engaging your mind and body in activities outside of yourself.

Understanding the Nature of Depression

Statistics show that as many as one in two people are estimated to experience depression at some point in their lives. Luckily, the problem is well-recognised and treatable.

Specifically, depression has the following symptoms, usually lasting for at least two weeks:

- ✔ Appetite variation, such as eating far less or more ('comfort eating') than usual

- ✔ Sleep disturbance, including having difficulty sleeping, wanting to sleep too much, or experiencing early-morning wakefulness

✔ Lack of concentration and poor memory

✔ Irritability

✔ Loss of libido

✔ Loss of interest in activities previously enjoyed. Engaging in these activities no longer produces pleasure

✔ Social isolation and withdrawal from others

✔ Self-neglect with respect to feeding or grooming

✔ Neglecting to take care of your living environment

✔ Decreased motivation and activity levels, often described as a feeling of lethargy

✔ Feelings of hopelessness about the future and thinking bleak thoughts, such as 'What's the point?'

✔ Strong and enduring negative thoughts about yourself

✔ Feelings of guilt

✔ Inability to experience feelings of love, often described as a flattening of emotions or feeling numb

✔ Suicidal thoughts, such as feeling that you no longer care whether you live or die

Unfortunately, certain things that you do, in an attempt to alleviate your feelings of depression, may actually be making your symptoms worse. When people are depressed, they often make the mistake of doing what their mood dictates.

CBT helps depressed individuals learn to override their depressed mood and to do the *opposite* of what their depression makes them *feel like doing*. Here are some of the main actions and thoughts that actually stoke depression:

✔ **Rumination:** Getting hooked into a repetitive, cyclical process of negative thinking, repeatedly going over problems in the past, or asking yourself unanswerable questions. (We discuss rumination in detail in the next section.)

✔ **Negative thinking:** In depression, your negative thoughts about yourself are often based on beliefs that you're helpless and worthless. Thoughts about the world being an unsafe and undesirable place to live in are also a common feature of depression.

✔ **Inactivity:** Feeling that you can't be bothered to do day-to-day tasks, not participating in activities that previously you enjoyed, and staying in bed because you don't believe you can face the day.

Book III

Cognitive Behavioural Therapy

✓ **Social withdrawal:** Avoiding seeing other people and not interacting with the people around you.

✓ **Procrastination:** Avoiding specific tasks, such as paying bills, booking appointments, and making phone calls, because you think they're too difficult or scary to confront.

✓ **Shame:** Feeling ashamed about your depression, and telling yourself that other people would judge you harshly if they knew how much your effectiveness and productivity had decreased.

✓ **Guilt:** Feeling guilty about your depression, and overestimating the degree to which your low mood causes inconvenience and suffering to your loved ones.

✓ **Hopelessness:** Thinking that you'll never feel better or that your situation will never improve.

Doing only what you feel like doing when you are depressed is likely to maintain or worsen your symptoms. Instead, try doing the opposite of what your depression directs you towards doing. For example, if you feel depressed and want to stay in bed all day avoiding phone calls and seeing friends, do the opposite. Try to make the colossal effort (and it can really feel colossal!) of getting up and dressed, answering the phone, and going out of the house to meet friends. Doing this limits you ruminating on your bad feelings and thoughts, and forces your attention onto external things, such as other people and your environment.

Going round and round in your head: Ruminative thinking

Rumination is an integral process in maintaining your depression. Most people with depression are likely to engage in some rumination, even if they're not aware that they do.

Rumination is a circular thought process in which you go over the same things again and again. Often, the focus is on how bad you feel or doubting that you can ever feel differently or better. Your rumination may also focus on trying to work out the root cause of your depression, or on the events that have contributed to you being depressed.

Several different tricks can help you stop the rumination process. Try some of the following:

✔ **Get busy.** Perhaps one of the most effective strategies you can adopt is to make your body and mind busy with something outside yourself. If you're vitally absorbed in an activity, you may find it harder to engage in rumination. These types of activities may include doing the housework with the radio on to hold your attention away from your internal thoughts, making a phone call, surfing the Internet, running errands, taking the dogs for a walk, and so on.

✔ **Work out.** Hard aerobic exercise can exorcise those toxic thought processes. Be sure to exercise during the day or in the early morning, because exercising too near bedtime can disturb your sleep.

✔ **Get up and out.** Rumination's more difficult when you're outside of your home or in the company of others. If you know that you're most vulnerable to ruminating at certain hours of the day, make sure that you schedule activities for these times.

✔ **Let your thoughts go.** Practice letting your negative thoughts pass by and simply observe them like pictures across a television screen. Don't engage with your negative thoughts, judge them, or try to answer any questions – just accept their existence and let them slip by.

✔ **Get good at redirecting your attention.** You can strengthen your attention muscles and deliberately focus on less depressing things. Try using *task concentration training*, a method of attending to external aspects of your environment, as it can successfully interrupt rumination.

✔ **Be sceptical.** Your depressed thoughts are a symptom of your depression, so try to take them with a sizable pinch of salt. You can resist the urge to ruminate about your depressed thoughts by deciding that they're neither true nor important.

Book III

Cognitive Behavioural Therapy

Keeping busy is a great technique for interrupting ruminative thinking. However, you can still end up ruminating while you're engaged in an activity. Be aware of paying attention to whatever you're doing. Be mindful of your actions when you're ironing, cleaning, stringing beads, weeding the garden, or whatever. Rumination can take hold during activities if you're acting *mindlessly* rather than *mindfully*.

Catching yourself in the act

Rumination is all-consuming. It will typically absorb you quite totally. You may look like you're simply staring blankly into space, but in your head your thoughts are going ten to the dozen. The key is to knowing when you're going *into* rumination, so you can take steps towards *getting out* of rumination.

Early warning signs of rumination taking hold include the following:

- ✔ **Getting stuck.** You may be in the middle of doing something and find that you've stopped moving and are deep in thought. For example, you may be perching on the side of the bed for several minutes (or even much longer!) when actually you intended going for a shower.

- ✔ **Feeling low.** Beware of times when your mood's at its lowest ebb: This is when you're most likely to engage in rumination. Most people ruminate at particular times of the day, more often than other times (although rumination can happen at any time).

- ✔ **Slowing down.** You may be doing something and then start to move more slowly, like pausing in the aisle at the supermarket. You start to slow down because your concentration's heading elsewhere.

- ✔ **Getting repetitive.** The same old thoughts and questions drift into your head, time and time again. You get a familiar niggling feeling that these vague questions must be answered.

The content of your ruminations is not the problem – the process of rumination itself is. You don't need to do anything with your thoughts other than disengage from them.

Tackling inactivity

One of the best ways of starting to overcome depression is to gradually become more active, to steadily re-engage with other people, and to start tackling daily chores and other problems.

Use the activity schedule in Table 2-2 to start to plan each day with a realistic balance of activities and rest. Build up your activities gradually. If you've been in bed for days, getting out of the bedroom and sitting in a chair is a big move in the right direction. Remember: Take it step by step. Using the activity is incredibly simple; it merely involves allocating a specific time to do a specific activity. You can photocopy the blank schedule in Table 2-2 and fill it in.

Don't overload your activity schedule, otherwise you may feel overwhelmed, sink back into inactivity, and probably berate yourself for being ineffective. It's crucial to *realistically* plan a gradual increase in activities, starting from where you are *now*, not from where you think you *should* be.

Table 2-2	Activity Schedule						
	Mon-day	Tues-day	Wednes-day	Thurs-day	Fri-day	Satur-day	Sun-day
6–8 a.m.							
8–10							
10–12							
12–2							
2–4							
4–6							
6–8							
8–10 p.m.							

Book III

Cognitive Behavioural Therapy

Dealing with the here and now: Solving problems

As with other aspects of your daily or weekly activities, you need to be steady and systematic in your attempts to deal with practical problems, such as paying bills, writing letters, and completing other tasks that can pile up when you're less active.

To get started, set aside a specific amount of time each day for dealing with neglected chores. Allocating your time can help things seem more manageable. Try the following problem-solving process:

1. **Define your problem.**

   At the top of a sheet of paper, write down the problems you're struggling with. For example, you might consider problems with the following:

   - Relationships
   - Isolation

- Interests and hobbies

- Employment and education

- Financial issues

- Legal issues

- Housing

- Health

Apply the following steps to each of your identified problems. You may need to do Steps 2 through 5 on each of your different problems.

2. Brainstorm solutions to your problem.

Write down all the possible solutions you can think of. Consider the following questions to help you generate some solutions:

- How did you deal with similar problems in the past?

- How have other people coped with similar problems?

- How do you imagine you'd tackle the problem if you weren't feeling depressed?

- How do you think someone else would approach the problem?

- What resources (such as professionals and voluntary services) can you access for help with your problems?

3. Evaluate your solutions.

Review your 'brainstormed' list. Select some of your most realistic seeming solutions, and list the pros and cons of each.

4. Try out a solution.

On the basis of your evaluation of pros and cons, choose a solution to try out.

You can easily feel overwhelmed when your mood is low. Even the best of solutions can seem too difficult. To deal with this, break down your solution into a series of smaller, more manageable steps. For example, if you're dealing with financial problems, your first step may be to ask friends for a recommended accountant, or to visit a financial consultant in your area. A second step may be to get your tax returns, proof of income, and so on, together. A third step may be selecting an accountant, and contacting them for information about their fees and the services they provide.

5. Review.

After trying out a solution, review how much it has helped you to resolve your problem. Consider whether you need to take further steps, to try another solution, or move on to tackling another problem.

Taking care of yourself and your environment

One of the hallmarks of depression is neglecting yourself and your living environment, which in turn leaves you feeling more depressed.

Instead of allowing your depression to be mirrored in your appearance and your home, make an extra effort to spruce things up. Your environment can have an astounding affect on your mood, both positive and negative.

Include bathing, laundry, tidying, and cleaning as part of your weekly activity schedule.

Getting a good night's sleep

Good night, sleep tight, and don't let the bedbugs bite!

Sleep disturbance, in one form or another, can often accompany depression. Here are some tips you can use to improve your chances of greeting the sandman.

Book III

Cognitive Behavioural Therapy

- ✔ **Get some exercise.** We cannot overstate the benefits of taking regular exercise. Exercise is good for your mood and good for your sleeping. You can take vigorous exercise during the day or even first thing in the morning to get your *endorphins* ('feel good' chemicals in your brain) charging. If you want to take some exercise in the evenings to help you wind down and de-stress, keep it gentle and not too close to your bedtime. A stroll, or an easy cycle ride, is an ideal choice.

- ✔ **Establish a schedule.** Getting up at the same time every day and avoiding daytime naps can help you get your sleeping back on track. Catnapping may be very tempting, but ultimately it interferes with your bedtime and can actually lower your mood. If you know that you get the urge for a siesta around the same time every day, make plans to be out of the house at this time. Make yourself busy to keep yourself awake.

- ✔ **Avoid lying in bed awake.** If you find dropping off to sleep difficult, don't lie in bed tossing and turning. Get out of bed and do something – ideally, something boring like sorting laundry or reading a book on something you find dull, drinking something warm and low-in-caffeine, such as milk or cocoa – until you feel ready for sleep. Try to stay up until your eyelids start to feel heavy. The same applies if you wake in the middle of the night and can't get back to sleep easily. Don't stay in bed for longer than ten minutes trying to get back to sleep. Get up and do something like the above ideas, then get back into bed only when you feel sleepy.

✔ **Watch your caffeine and stimulant intake.** Avoid caffeinated drinks from mid- to late-afternoon. Caffeine can stay in your system for a long time. Remember that as well as tea and coffee, many soft drinks, chocolate (although not so much), and various energy drinks contain caffeine. Even some herbal teas contain stimulants, such as matte and guarana.

✔ **Establish a bedtime routine.** Going through the same pre-bedtime procedures each night can help your mind realise that it's getting near to shutdown time. Your routine may include having a warm bath, listening to a soothing radio programme, having a warm, milky drink, or whatever works for you. Sometimes, having a very light, easily digestible snack before bedtime is a good idea to prevent sleep disturbance associated with going to bed hungry.

Setting realistic sleep expectations

During the day and while you try to fall asleep, you may well have thoughts like 'I'll never be able to get to sleep', or 'I'm in for another night of waking up every two hours'. Understandably, you may have these expectations if your sleep has been disturbed for some time, but such thinking is likely to perpetuate your sleep disturbance. Be aware of your worrying thoughts about sleep problems, such as 'I'll never be able to cope on such little sleep', or 'I've got to get some sleep tonight'. Trying to force yourself to go to sleep is rarely successful, and doing so contradicts the concept of *relaxation*, because you're making an *effort* to sleep.

Although it may sound like a tall order, try to take the attitude that you *can* cope with very little, or poor-quality, sleep. Also, answer back your sleep expectations by briefly telling yourself that you don't know for definite how you may sleep tonight and that you're just going to see how it goes.

Chapter 3

Putting CBT into Action

*D*isturbing feelings, such as depression, anxiety, shame, guilt, anger, envy, and jealousy, are often rooted in low self-opinion. If you're prone to experiencing these feelings, then you may well have a problem with your self-esteem. You may assume that you're only as worthwhile as your achievements, love life, social status, attractiveness, or financial prowess. If you link your worth to these *temporary conditions* and for some reason they diminish, your self-esteem can plummet too. Alternatively, you may take a long-standing dim view of yourself: However favourable the conditions mentioned above, your self-esteem may be chronically low. Whatever the case, you can follow the philosophy of self-acceptance that we outline in this chapter, which can significantly improve the attitude you hold towards yourself.

Identifying Issues of Self-Esteem

Implicit in the concept of self-esteem is the notion of *estimating*, or rating and measuring, your worth. If you have high self-esteem, then your measure of your value or worth is high. Conversely, if you have low self-esteem, your estimate of your value is low.

Condemning yourself globally is a form of overgeneralising, known as *labelling* or *self-downing*. This thinking error creates low self-esteem. Labelling yourself makes you feel worse and can lead to counterproductive actions, such as avoidance, isolation, rituals, procrastination, and perfectionism, to name but a few.

Examples of labelling or self-downing include statements, such as the following:

I'm disgusting	I'm a failure	I'm stupid
I'm inferior	I'm useless	I'm less worthwhile
I'm inadequate	I'm not good enough	I'm bad
I'm unlovable	I'm worthless	I'm defective
I'm incompetent	I don't matter	I'm pathetic
I'm weak	I'm no good	I'm a loser

When you measure your worth on the basis of one or more external factors, you're likely to go up and down like a yo-yo in both mood and self-concept because life is changeable.

Developing Self-Acceptance

One approach to tackling your low self-esteem is to boost the estimate you have of your worth. The underlying problem, however, still remains; and like an investment, your self-esteem can go down, as well as up.

Self-acceptance is an alternative to boosting self-esteem and tackles the problem by removing self-rating. If you don't have a sturdy belief that your value is *intrinsic*, or built-in, you may have difficulty concluding that you have any worth at all when things go wrong for you.

Unconditional self-acceptance means untangling your self-worth from external 'measures' or 'ratings' of your value as a person. Eventually, you can become less likely to consider yourself defective or inadequate on the basis of failures or disapproval, because you view yourself as a *fallible human being*, whose worth remains more or less constant.

Self-acceptance involves making the following assertions:

- ✔ As a human being, you're a unique, multifaceted individual.
- ✔ You're ever-changing and developing.
- ✔ You may be able, to some degree, to measure specific aspects of yourself (such as, how tall you are), but you'll never manage to rate the whole of yourself because you are too complex and continuously changing.
- ✔ Humans, by their very nature, are fallible and imperfect.
- ✔ By extension, because you're a complex, unique, ever-changing individual, you cannot legitimately be rated or measured as a whole person.

The following are the principles of self-acceptance. Read them, re-read them, think them over, and put them into practice in your daily life to significantly enhance your self-acceptance. The principles are good sense, but we're leaving it up to you to decide how 'common' this kind of sense is. The principles are derived from the rational (self-helping) thinking methods developed by Albert Ellis and Windy Dryden.

Understanding that you have worth because you're human

Albert Ellis, founder of rational emotive behaviour therapy – one of the very earliest approaches to CBT – states that *all human beings* have *extrinsic* value to others and *intrinsic* value to themselves. But we humans gamely confuse the two and classify ourselves as 'worthy' or 'good' on the basis of assumed value to others. We humans too easily allow our self-worth to be contingent upon the opinions and value judgements of others. Many cognitive behaviour therapists (and indeed other kinds of psychotherapists) hold the implicit value of a human being at the very heart of their perspective.

Imagine how much easier your life will be, and how much more stable your self-esteem will be, if you realise that you have worth as a person *independently* of how much other people value you. You can appreciate being liked, admired, or respected without it being a dire necessity to get it, or living in fear of losing it.

Book III

Cognitive Behavioural Therapy

Appreciating that you're too complex to globally measure or rate

You may mistakenly define your whole worth – or even your entire self – on the basis of your individual parts. This is pointless, because humans are ever-changing, dynamic, fallible, and complex creatures.

Humans have the capacity to work on correcting less desirable behaviours and maximising more desirable behaviours. You have the distinctive ability to strive for self-improvement, to maximise your potential, and to learn from your and others' histories, mistakes, and accomplishments. In short, you have the ability to develop the ability to accept yourself as you are, while still endeavouring to improve yourself if you so choose.

Consider a bowl of fresh, hand-picked fruit, beautiful in almost every respect. Now imagine that one of the apples in the fruit bowl is bruised. Do you consider the whole bowl of fruit to be worthless? Of course not! It's a great bowl of fruit, with a single bruised apple. Avoid overgeneralising by seeing that your imperfections are simply *facets* of yourself and do not define the whole of you.

Letting go of labelling

Self-acceptance means deciding to resist labelling yourself at all and rather to entertain the idea that ratings are inappropriate to the human condition. For example:

- ✔ You lied to a friend once. Does that make you a liar forever and for all time?

- ✔ You used to smoke cigarettes but then you decided to give them up. Are you still a smoker because you once smoked?

- ✔ You failed at one or more tasks that were important to you. Can you legitimately conclude that you are an utter failure?

- ✔ By the same token, if you succeeded at one important task, are you now a thoroughgoing success?

As you can see by reviewing these examples, basing your self-esteem on one incident, one action, or one experience is a gross overgeneralisation.

Believing you're more than the sum of your parts

Take a look at Figure 3-1. The big *I* is comprised of dozens of little *i*s. So, what's the point of the figure? When you evaluate yourself *totally* on the basis of one characteristic, thought, action, or intention, you're making the thinking error that a single part (the little i) equals to the whole (the big I).

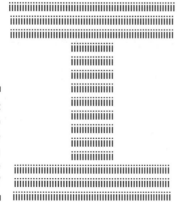

Figure 3-1:
Which do you see first: the big *I* or all the little *i*s?

Along similar lines, consider a finely woven tapestry comprised of countless variations of textures, colours, and patterns. Within this tapestry, you may find one or more flaws, where the colours fail to meet or the patterns are slightly out of sync. The flaws in the tiny details don't cancel out the beauty or value of the overall piece. And what about the *Venus de Milo*? Over the years, she's lost a limb or two, but the officials at the Louvre don't say, 'Um, sorry, she's flawed: Put her in the bin!' The fact that the statue is damaged does not diminish or *define* its overall worth. The statue is valued *as it is*, and the absence of arms does not negate the impact it has on our understanding of the evolution of art.

If your child, sibling, or nephew failed a spelling test, would you judge them a total loser? Would you encourage them to think of themselves as a global failure, based entirely on one action? If not, why are you doing this to yourself?

Start acting in accordance with the belief that your parts do not define your wholeness. If you truly believe this idea, what do you do when you fail at doing something, behave badly or wickedly, or notice that you have a physical imperfection or character flaw? How do you expect to feel when endorsing this belief?

Take a pack of self-adhesive notes and a large, flat surface. A wall or a door works well – or try a mate if he has a few spare minutes. Write down on one of the notes a characteristic that you, as a whole person, possess; then stick the note on the wall, door, or volunteer. Keep doing this, writing down all the aspects of yourself that you can think of until you run out of characteristics, or sticky notes. Now step back and admire your illustration of your complexity as a human being. Appreciate the fact that you cannot legitimately be rated globally.

Book III

Cognitive Behavioural Therapy

Acknowledging your ever-changing nature

As a human being, your nature is to be an ever-changing person. Even if you measure all your personal characteristics today and come up with a global rating for yourself, it'll be wrong tomorrow. Why? Because each day, you change a little, age very slightly, and gather a few new experiences.

Consider yourself as work-in-progress and try holding a *flexible* attitude towards yourself. Every skill you acquire or interest you develop effectively produces a change within you. Every hardship you weather, every joyous event that visits you, and every mundane occurrence you endure causes you to develop, adapt, and grow.

Forgiving flaws in yourself and others

Interestingly, you may overlook some imperfections in yourself while condemning the same shortcomings in others, or vice versa. To some degree, this relates to what you consider important, your flexibility, and your level of self-acceptance. Consider the following scenarios:

✔ Julian works in a computer shop. Whenever he's about to close a sale, he gets excited and trips over some of his words. He feels a bit foolish about this, although none of his customers has ever mentioned it.

✔ Margarita has a poor sense of direction. Sometimes she forgets which way is left and which is right. When she's driving, Margarita has difficulty following directions and frequently finds herself lost.

✔ Carlos is a good student, but has difficulty in exam situations. He studies earnestly, but come the day of the test, he forgets what he's read and performs poorly.

You can't always change things about yourself. Sometimes you can improve a bit, but sometimes you can't change at all. If you're a fully developed adult and five-foot tall, you're unlikely to be able to make yourself grow to six foot through sheer determination. The trick is to begin to recognise where you can make changes and where you can't. Living happily is about accepting your limitations without putting yourself down for them and capitalising on your strengths. So, taking the three examples above:

✔ Julian may be able to make himself less anxious about a potential sale; therefore,

he may speak more coherently. By accepting that he mangles his words sometimes, but not condemning himself for it, he may come some way towards overcoming this aspect of his behaviour.

✔ Margarita may simply be someone who's not particularly good at navigation. She may improve with practice, but she may also do well to accept that she's the person who turns up late for parties two streets away from her home.

✔ Carlos can look at his studying habits and see whether he can study more effectively. However, he may simply be someone who does better on practical assignments rather than tests.

Overall, Julian, Carlos, and Margarita can choose to accept themselves as fallible human beings and work to improve in the areas described, while also accepting their personal limitations. They can choose to embrace their inherent fallibility as part of the experience of being a human, and understand that their 'less good' traits are part of their individual composition as much as their 'good' traits.

Alternatively, they can choose to evaluate themselves on the basis of their 'less good' traits and judge themselves as worthless, or less than worthy. But where, oh where, do you go from there?

Ellis theorises that your essential value or worth cannot be measured accurately because your *being* includes your *becoming*. Ellis suggests that each human is a *process* with an ever-changing present and future. Hence, you cannot conclusively evaluate yourself while you're still living and developing.

Accepting your fallible nature

Sorry if we're the ones to break it to you, but human beings are flawed and imperfect. You may be the pretty impressive product of evolution, but essentially you're just the smartest animal on the planet. Even if you believe you're the creation of a divine entity, do you really think the design brief was perfection? Maybe being complex, different, and with an in-built tendency to make mistakes are all part of the plan. When people say 'You're only human,' they have a point: Never, ever, can you be flawless or stop making mistakes. And neither can anyone else. It's just how we're built.

During the process of accepting yourself, you may experience sadness, disappointment, or remorse for your blunders. These healthy negative emotions may be uncomfortable, but usually they can lead to self-helping, corrective, and 'adaptive' behaviours. Self-condemnation or self-depreciation, on the other hand, are likely to lead to far more intense, unhealthy negative emotions, such as depression, hurt, guilt, and shame. So, you're more likely to adopt self-defeating, 'maladaptive' behaviours, such as avoidance or giving up.

Why self-acceptance beliefs work

At first glance, self-acceptance and self-acceptance beliefs may seem like a tall order or 'not what people think'. However, incorporating self-accepting beliefs into your life can really make a difference in your life, and we recommend it for the following reasons:

✔ **Self-acceptance beliefs are helpful.** You're inspired to correct your poor behaviour or address your shortcomings on the basis that you give yourself permission to be flawed. You allow yourself a margin for error. When problems occur or you behave poorly, you can experience appropriate and proportionate negative emotions and then move on. People are generally more effective problem-solvers when they're not severely emotionally distressed.

✔ **Self-acceptance beliefs are consistent with reality.** Do you know anyone who's entirely flawless? If you have only conditional self-acceptance, you're subscribing to a belief that you cease to be acceptable, or worthwhile, when you fall short of those conditions or ideals. Basically, you're telling yourself that you must succeed at any given task. Because you can (and do) both fail and succeed, the evidence suggests that your demand to always succeed is erroneous.

✔ **Self-acceptance beliefs are logical.** Just because you *prefer* to behave in a certain way, doesn't mean that you *must* behave in a certain way. Nor, does your failing to act in that manner logically render you a failure in all respects. Rather, this 'failure' supports the premise that you're a fallible human capable of behaving in differing ways at various times. To broaden the point, this 'failure' highlights your humanness and your inherent capacity to do both 'well' and 'less well'.

Book III

Cognitive Behavioural Therapy

Valuing your uniqueness

Who else do you know who's exactly – and yes, we do mean *exactly* – like you? The correct answer is no one, because the human cloning thing hasn't really taken off yet. So, you are, in fact, quite unique – just like everyone else!

You alone are possessor of your own little idiosyncrasies. So learn to laugh it up, because the mistakes and foot-in-mouth moments will just keep on coming, whether you like it or not.

Taking yourself overly seriously is not a successful path to obtaining good mental health. Your individual human fallibility can be both amusing and illuminating. Think about comedy programmes and films. Much of what makes these shows funny is the way the characters *behave*, the mistakes they make, their social blunders, their physicality, their personal peculiarities, and so on. When you laugh at these characters, you aren't being malicious – you just recognise echoes of yourself and of the entire human experience in them. Furthermore, you're unlikely to put down these characters on the basis of their errors. Give yourself a similar benefit of the doubt. Accepting the existence of personal shortcomings can help you to understand your own limitations and identify areas that you may wish to target for change.

For example, we have a couple of our own quirks that we try to accept, and even celebrate, as unique. Rob does this weird little twitch every now again when he's tired. The twitch is a bit disconcerting when he's driving, but most of the time it's just something that Rob does. Rhena tends to fiddle with her jewellery when she's thinking or just idle – irritating to some, endearing to others.

You're unique because no one is a facsimile of you. At the same time, you're also not special or unique in any way, because *everyone* is an individual and, hence, unreplicable. Your uniqueness means that you're *different* from all others and paradoxically that you're the *same* as all others.

Using self-acceptance to aid self-improvement

As we touch upon in the nearby sidebar, which covers accepting flaws in others and yourself, self-acceptance can lead to healthy and *appropriate* negative emotional responses to adverse experiences. This type of emotional response tends to lead to functional or *adaptive* behaviours. Self-denigration, on the other hand, leads to unhealthy, *inappropriate* emotional responses, which in turn tend to produce unhelpful or *destructive* behaviours. Look at the following situation:

Wendy's been a full-time mum for the past ten years. Before she had her children, she worked as a legal secretary. Now that her children are older, she wants to return to work. Wendy attends a job interview. During the interview, she becomes very nervous and is unable to answer some of the questions adequately. She notices that she's becoming flustered and hot. It also becomes clear to her that secretarial work has evolved in the past ten years and that she lacks the computer skills necessary for the post. Unfortunately, she doesn't get the job.

Now consider two very different responses to the interview:

> **Response A:** Wendy leaves the interview, ruminating on her poor performance all the way back home. 'I looked such an idiot,' she tells herself. 'They must have thought me a real amateur, blushing and stuttering like that. I'm such a failure. Who'd want to hire someone as lacking in skills as me? I don't know what made me think I'd be able to get into work again anyway. I'm clearly not up to standard at all.' Wendy feels depressed and hopeless. She mopes around the house and continues to think about what a failure she is. She feels so ashamed about failing the interview that she avoids talking about it to her friends, thus denying herself the opportunity to receive feedback, which may be useful or help her feel more balanced. Wendy stops looking in the employment pages.

> **Response B:** Wendy leaves the interview and thinks: 'I really didn't present very well in there. I wish I hadn't been so obviously nervous. Clearly, I need to get some computer skills before I'm likely to get a job offer.' Wendy feels very disappointed about not getting the job, but she doesn't conclude that failing one important task makes her a failure. She feels regretful, but not ashamed, about her performance and talks to a few friends about it. Her friends give her some encouragement. Wendy then enrols on an IT course at her local college. She continues to look through the job ads in the paper.

In response B, Wendy is understandably disappointed with how the interview turned out. She's able to recognise her skills' deficit. Because she accepts herself with this *specific deficit*, she takes concrete steps towards increasing her skills base.

In response A, Wendy is not thinking about how to do better at the next interview. She's thinking about how she'd like to crawl under the carpet and spend the rest of her days there. A bit of an extreme reaction considering the circumstances, but Wendy isn't considering the circumstances. She has decided that messing up an interview equals total failure, and she's feeling far too depressed and ashamed to start problem-solving.

Generally, your failures and errors are not as important or calamitous as you think they are. Most of the time, your failures mean a lot more to you than they do to other people.

Understanding that acceptance doesn't mean giving up

In the example of Wendy, we don't suggest that she must resign herself to a life of unemployment simply because she lacks computer skills. Why should she? Clearly, she can do things to ensure that she stands a good chance of getting back into the job market.

In Wendy's case, self-acceptance means that she can view herself as worthwhile, while getting on with self-improvement in specific areas of her life. By contrast, if Wendy refuses to accept herself and puts herself down, she's far more likely to resign – perhaps even condemn – herself to her current state of unemployment.

Resignation requires little or no effort, but self-acceptance can involve a lot of personal effort.

- **High frustration tolerance** (HFT) is the ability to tolerate discomfort and hard work in the *short term*, en route to achieving an identified *long-term* goal. In response B in the job-interview example, Wendy accepts herself and holds an HFT attitude. She is prepared to do the work necessary to reach her goal of getting a job.

- **Low frustration tolerance** (LFT) is unwillingness to tolerate *short-term* pain for *long-term* gain. An LFT attitude is present in statements, such as 'It's too difficult to change – this is just the way I am', and 'I may as well just give up'. Resignation and LFT go hand in hand. In Wendy's response A, she refuses to accept herself in view of her recent experience and resigns herself to unemployment.

Resignation may seem like an easier option than self-acceptance because it means that you have to *do* less. However, people tend to feel pretty miserable when they resign and condemn themselves, refusing to put effort into improving their situation.

Being Inspired to Change

You may think that self-acceptance is all fine and well when talking about human error, social gaffes, and minor character flaws, but the dice are more loaded in instances where you've transgressed your personal moral code.

If you've behaved in an antisocial, illegal, or immoral manner, you may have more difficulty accepting yourself. But you can! Accepting *yourself* does not mean accepting the negative behaviour and continuing to do it. On the contrary, accepting yourself involves recognising that you – an acceptable human being – have engaged in a poor, or unacceptable, behaviour. Accepting yourself makes you more likely to learn from your mistakes and act more constructively – which is in both your interest and in the interest of those around you.

Consider the following two scenarios:

- ✔ Malcolm has an anger problem. He puts unreasonable demands on his wife and children to never get on his nerves. He has a bad day at work and comes home to find no dinner on the table and his two young children playing noisily in the sitting room. Malcolm shouts at his wife and slaps her. He calls his children names and hits them. His family is afraid and upset. This happens on a regular basis.

- ✔ Fiona works in a shoe shop. She's been stealing money from the till to buy alcohol and codeine-based painkillers. Usually, she takes the tablets throughout the day and drinks heavily in the evenings, until she passes out. Lately, she has called in sick to work more often because she has terrible hangovers and feels very depressed. Fiona often calls herself a 'useless drunk' and 'a low-life thief', and then drinks more to stop herself thinking. She works hard to hide her drinking and stealing, and feels ashamed of herself most of the time.

Are Malcolm and Fiona bad people, or are they just currently exhibiting bad behaviours? If you condemn Malcolm or Fiona – or, indeed, yourself – as a 'bad person' on the basis of bad behaviour, you're missing the point that a person is more complex than a single act.

In order to overcome destructive or socially unacceptable behaviours, you need to do the following:

- ✔ **Take personal responsibility for your bad behaviour.** Rather than deciding you're just a bad person who has no control or responsibility for your actions, accept that you're doing bad things.

   In the example above, Malcolm's doing very bad things when he takes out his anger on his family. But, if he decides that he's a bad person

Book III

Cognitive Behavioural Therapy

overall, he relinquishes his responsibility to change. Basically, he's saying: 'I beat my family because I'm a bad person through and through and therefore I can't change.' He's also more likely to attribute his violence to external factors rather than to his own unreasonable demands: 'They know what I'm like and they should bloody-well stay out of my way when I come in from work.'

✔ **Identify clearly what you're doing that's wrong or unacceptable.** You must be specific when pinpointing bad behaviours.

For example, Fiona has two definite serious problems or 'bad' behaviours. First, she has an addiction; second, she's stealing to support that addiction. Fiona's shame and self-condemnation are very likely going to get in the way of her overcoming her problems. She cannot put in the hard work needed to recover from her addiction (which includes seeking professional help) if she can't accept herself as worth the effort.

To move on in life in a way that contributes to the kind of world you'd like to live in, assume personal responsibility and keep working on your self-acceptance.

Actioning Self-Acceptance

Just like virtually all skills worth acquiring, you're going to have to work hard and practice in order to achieve successful self-acceptance skills. This section focuses on ways to start integrating self-acceptance into your daily life.

Self-talking your way to self-acceptance

What's in a name? Rather a lot, actually. Most people largely *feel* the way they *think*. In other words, the meanings you assign to events have a great deal to do with how you ultimately feel about those events.

Similarly, meaning is attached to the names your call yourself. If you use abusive, harshly critical, or profane terminology to give utterance to your behaviours or traits, then you're heading towards emotional disturbance.

The notion that you may start to believe something if you tell yourself it enough times, is partly true. Fortunately, you can *choose* what messages you give yourself and, therefore, choose how you think and feel about yourself.

How you talk to yourself impacts immediately, or obliquely, on your self-concept. Try the following self-talk strategies to make the best impact on yourself:

✔ **Desist with global labels.** Humans often call themselves losers, idiots, failures, stupid, or unlovable because of certain events or actions they've been involved in or done. You may use even worse language on yourself in the privacy of your own head. Why? Because, you're caving in to the temptation to rate your entire selfhood on the evidence of one, or more, isolated incidents.

✔ **Be specific with your self-assessments.** Before you classify yourself as a failure, ask yourself the following questions: 'In what specific way have I failed?' 'In what specific way have I acted stupidly?' It's far less easy to fall into global self-rating when you force yourself to be specific.

✔ **Say what you mean and mean what you say.** You may be saying to yourself right now: 'Oh, but I don't *mean* it when I call myself those bad names.' No? Then don't say them! Get into the practice of using language that describes accurately your behaviour and is in keeping with self-acceptance beliefs. Instead of muttering 'I'm such an idiot for missing that deadline,' try saying: 'Missing that deadline was a really bad move. I'm really disappointed about it.'

Resisting self-abusive language cuts two ways. This chapter focuses on self-acceptance, but much of the advice applies to acceptance of others, too. Generally, people are nicer and more forgiving to their mates than they are to themselves. But, people are still capable of damning others and calling them ugly names. Start exercising a different type of consistency: Stop name-calling, full stop. When you do put a halt on name-calling, it can lead you to feel less intense anger and hurt when others behave poorly, which helps to reinforce your self-acceptance beliefs. If you're practicing not globally rating others, then you're also minimising the tendency to globally rate yourself.

Book III

Cognitive Behavioural Therapy

Following the best-friend argument

Out of habit, most humans employ double standards: You judge your friends by an entirely different, often more accepting, standard than you use on yourself.

Try to take the same attitude of acceptance towards yourself that you take towards your friends and family. Consider the following:

✔ **Act like your best friend by judging your behaviour but not judging yourself.** Eustace has been having difficulties in his marriage. He has been staying out late, drinking with his mates, before going home and being verbally abusive to his wife. His best mate, Lucian, has highlighted Eustace's poor behaviour in their conversations but he has maintained an understanding attitude towards his friend's unhappiness. Lucian is not about to define Eustace as a total rotter on the strength of his recent, excessive drinking and arguments with his wife.

✔ **Accept your failings as you would those of a dear friend.** Laura just failed her driving test for the fourth time. She feels very down about it. Her best friend Maggie tells her to try again and to be less hard on herself. Maggie wants Laura to do the driving test again. She doesn't view Laura as a total failure based simply on her difficulty in passing a test. Even if Laura never drives, Maggie will likely remain her friend because of other things she likes and appreciates about Laura.

✔ **View your behaviour within the context of your circumstances, and above all, be compassionate.** Rivka had an abortion following a short affair. She feels very guilty and can't imagine putting the event behind her. Rivka's close friend, Carla, reminds her of the unfortunate circumstances she found herself in at the time, and tells her that she's still someone that she likes and respects very much. Carla can see that Rivka has made a difficult decision. She compassionately considers that Rivka has acted out of a degree of desperation. Rivka may have been unlucky, or a bit careless, with respect to birth control, but Carla does not judge her on the basis of the abortion.

Ask yourself whether the punishment fits the crime. Are you being fair on yourself? What punishment would you dole out to your best friend for the same behaviour? Be aware that you may be making yourself feel extremely guilty, or ashamed, inappropriately. If you wouldn't like to see anyone else feeling such extreme emotions in response to the same transgression you've committed, then you're applying a double standard that's loaded against you.

Are you created so differently that you must subscribe to an exceptional code of conduct? (Consider this an inverted inferiority complex.) Having some exceptional code of conduct implies that you, and you alone, are somehow designed exclusively to transcend the ubiquitous human essence of fallibility. However, you are human. You don't fail any more extravagantly than any of your peers – nor do you succeed more dramatically than they do. If you're going to exercise compassion towards your friends' failures and wobbles, you need to consistently apply the same rules of compassion and understanding towards yourself.

Dealing with doubts and reservations

Many people feel that by accepting themselves, they're simply letting themselves off the hook. But, self-acceptance is about taking personal responsibility for your less good traits, actions, and habits. Self-acceptance is about target-ing areas that you both *can* and *wish to* change and then taking the appropri-ate steps towards change. Self-acceptance is not saying: 'Hey, I'm human and fallible! Therefore, I just am the way I am and I don't need to think about changing anything.'

You are, at baseline, worthy and acceptable, but some of your behaviours and attitudes may be simultaneously unacceptable.

Another common fear is that by accepting yourself, you're actually condon-ing undesirable aspects of yourself: 'Hey, I'm an acceptable human being and, therefore, all I think and do is acceptable.' Not so.

Work on accepting your overall self on the basis of your intrinsic human falli-bility, and be prepared to judge *specific aspects* of yourself. You can both condone your personhood and also condemn, or reject, certain things that you do.

Selecting the Self-Help Journey to Self-Acceptance

A common reason for people persistently putting themselves down, is that they hope to become better by calling attention to their mistakes, flaws, and failings. Unfortunately, this process frequently includes feeling depressed or anxious, which may well already be underpinned by low self-esteem.

Trying to solve an emotional problem at the same time as calling yourself useless, worthless, and pathetic is much like trying to learn a foreign lan-guage while hitting yourself over the head with a textbook – your actions are likely to make both jobs much harder.

Book III

Cognitive Behavioural Therapy

Imperfect self-acceptance

As you're a fallible human, you won't be perfect at self-acceptance either. You'll very probably slip into putting yourself down from time to time, as everyone does – us included. The aim is to accept yourself more often and to accept your-self again more quickly, if you notice that you're putting yourself down. Such acceptance defi-nitely gets easier and more consistent with practice.

Broadly speaking, you may be using one of two common strategies to manage low self-esteem: Avoiding doing things, or doing things exces-sively. For example, a person who believes they're worthless unless they're liked by every-body may try extra hard to avoid rejection or to win people's approval, while a person who regards themselves as a 'failure' may try to avoid situations in which they might fail.

Accepting yourself has two interesting implications for overcoming emotional problems and personal development. First, you're equal in worth to other human beings just as you are, which helps to reduce emotional pain. Second, because you're not distracted by beating yourself up, you can focus better on coping with adversity, reducing disturbance, and self-improvement.

Cooling Down Your Anger

Anger's a pretty common emotion. However, anger is also increasingly recognised as an important emotional problem. Anger can be bad for your relationships, your health, and your self-esteem.

In the bad old days of psychological treatment for anger, people were encouraged simply to 'get it out', often by beating pillows to vent their fury. The result? Just like anything you practise, these people got better at being angry. The notion that expressing your rage can 'get it out of your system' is something of a myth. More often you wind yourself up further, generating even more anger. A better solution is to get to grips with managing your angry feelings responsibly, and to master skills that can help you to feel less angry, less often.

CBT offers clear and effective management of anger, by tackling the thinking that underpins your anger and helping you express that anger in a healthy manner. This chapter focuses on CBT techniques that can help you deal directly with your feelings of anger.

Discerning the difference between healthy and unhealthy anger

Essentially, two different types of anger exist – healthy and unhealthy:

- ✔ **Healthy anger is helpful annoyance and irritation.** This is the kind of anger that spurs you on to assert your rights when it is important that you do so.

- ✔ **Unhealthy anger is unhelpful rage, and hate.** This type of anger leads you to behave aggressively or violently even in response to mild or unimportant provocation.

All emotions have *themes* – that is, sets of circumstances or triggers from which they arise. Themes for anger include someone breaking one of your personal rules, or threatening your self-esteem through word or deed.

Another anger theme is frustration, when someone or something gets in the way of you reaching a goal.

The triggers for healthy and unhealthy anger are the same, but the behavioural responses they typically produce are very different. Both anger types are also associated with different ways of thinking and attention focus.

Key characteristics of unhealthy anger

Unhealthy anger is far more likely than healthy anger to cause fractures in your personal relationships, create trouble in your workplace, or land you in prison. You're also likely to feel more physically and emotionally uncomfortable when you're unhealthily angry.

Several ways of thinking typically underpin unhealthy anger:

- Holding rigid demands and rules about the way other people must or must not behave

- Insisting that other people do not insult or ridicule you

- Demanding that life conditions and other people don't get in the way of you getting what you want

- Overestimating the degree to which people deliberately act in undesirable ways towards you

- Assuming automatically that you're right and the other person's wrong

- Refusing to consider another person's point of view

Common behavioural characteristics associated with unhealthy anger include the following:

- Attacking or wanting to attack another person physically or verbally

- Attacking another person in an indirect – also known as *passive-aggressive* – way, for example trying to make someone else's job difficult

- Taking out your anger on innocent parties, such as another person, an animal, or an object

- Plotting revenge

- Attempting to turn others against the person you believe has behaved undesirably

- Sulking

- Looking for evidence that someone has acted with malicious intent

Book III

Cognitive Behavioural Therapy

✔ Searching for signs of an offence being repeated

✔ Being overvigilant for people breaking your personal rules or acting disrespectfully towards you

Common physical signs of unhealthy anger include the following:

✔ Clenched fists

✔ Muscular tension, especially in the neck and shoulder muscles

✔ Clenched jaw

✔ Trembling or shaking

✔ Raised heart rate

✔ Feeling hot

For many people, anger can come on hot and fast. Familiarising yourself with your own early warning signs of anger can help you to intervene earlier.

Hallmarks of healthy anger

In general, people experience healthy anger as intense but not overwhelming experience. You can feel intensely angry in a healthy way without experiencing a loss of control. Healthy anger does not lead you to behave in antisocial, violent, or intimidating ways.

In addition, healthy anger is typically underpinned by the following ways of thinking:

✔ Holding strong preferences rather than rigid demands about how people should act

✔ Having flexibility in the rules you expect people to abide by

✔ Strongly preferring that others don't insult or ridicule you

✔ Desiring that other people and life conditions don't get in the way of you getting what you want

✔ Thinking realistically about whether other people have deliberately acted undesirably towards you

✔ Considering that both you *and* the other person may be right *and* wrong to a degree

✔ Trying to see the other person's point of view

Behavioural characteristics typical of health anger include:

- ✔ Asserting yourself with the other person

- ✔ Staying in the situation with the intent of resolving any disagreement

- ✔ Requesting the other person to modify her behaviour – and respecting her right to disagree with you

- ✔ Looking for evidence that the other person may not have behaved with malicious intent

Understanding attitudes that underpin anger

If you're serious about overcoming your unhealthy anger, you have to take a long hard look at some of the attitudes you hold. This involves honestly looking at the way you believe that other people and the world at large *must* treat you. You may hold some common toxic beliefs that frequently lead to unhealthy anger in people. Some of these toxic thoughts include:

- ✔ No one must ever treat me poorly or disrespectfully.

- ✔ The world must not be unjust or unfair and *especially* not to me!

- ✔ I must get what I want when I want it and nothing should get in my way.

- ✔ I must never be led into feeling guilty, inadequate, embarrassed, or ashamed by other people or life events.

- ✔ No one and nothing must ever expose my weaknesses or errors.

Having looked long and hard at your attitudes, you need to make your toxic attitudes more helpful and realistic. Yes! Once again, positive emotional change comes from changing the way you think about yourself, about other people, and the world in general. If you want to be emotionally healthy and high-functioning, you need to start developing flexible, tolerant, and accepting attitudes. High-functioning individuals experience fewer disturbing emotional responses, they are able to enjoy life, and they bounce back fairly readily from everyday hassles and annoyances. It's all in the way you look at life and the kind of attitude you take toward life's ups and downs (particularly with regard to anger).

We can explain the types of attitude that are likely to help you overcome unhealthy anger. However, *you* must decide to agree with these attitudes and ultimately *act in accordance with them* if you want to see a change in the amount of anger you experience.

Book III

Cognitive Behavioural Therapy

The following sections describe the healthy attitudes that you need to take in order to overcome your unhealthy anger.

Putting up with other people and being flexible

Other people exist in the same universe as you. Sometimes, this can be a rather pleasant state of affairs, but on occasions you may find that these other people are a damnable inconvenience. Whether you like it or not, other people can exist, do exist, and will continue to exist in your universe for the foreseeable future. Accepting that these other people have as much right as you to inhabit the planet just makes sense. And while cohabitating, you may as well accept the reality that sometimes other people may get on your nerves. As you're not in charge of the universe, you'd better accept that other people are *allowed* to act according to their rules and values – not yours.

You've probably noticed that humans come in a variety of shapes, sizes, and colours. No doubt you've seen that not all people share the same religion, culture, political opinions, moral codes, or rules of social conduct. Now, without going into a long-winded speech about the value of diversity, accepting individual difference is terribly important. Acknowledging that other people have a right to their own ideas about how to live their lives – even when you flatly disagree with their ideas – can save you a lot of emotional upset. People will continue to exercise these rights, whatever your opinion.

Accepting others can save you a world of unhealthy anger. Consider this: Every morning Jill and Tim travel to work together by bus. Every time she boards the bus, Jill says a pleasant 'Good morning!' to the driver, who always ignores her completely. One day, Tim asks Jill why she persists in greeting the driver, even though he never acknowledges her. Jill says: 'Because I choose to behave in line with my standard of politeness rather than to respond to his standard of rudeness.'

Jill's high tolerance to rudeness from the bus driver means that she can avoid making herself unhealthily angry. She does this by:

- Accepting that the driver has the right to be rude. No law exists against responding (or not) to another person's greeting.

- Not taking the driver's rudeness over-personally. The driver doesn't know Jill, so it is highly unlikely that he is actually 'out to get her' specifically. He's probably foul-tempered to many people in addition to Jill.

- Exercising her right to behave according to her own standard of politeness, even in the face of another person's rudeness. Although the bus driver is rude to Jill, she chooses not to respond in the same way. She can carry on being a generally polite person even in the face of another person's rudeness if she so chooses.

Wanting others to treat you well and with respect makes sense. Similarly, you probably want other people to do their jobs well and to help you to get what you want. You're likely to want life to roll your way and for world events to gel with your personal plans.

However, expecting and demanding these conditions to be met all the time doesn't make sense!

Keeping your attitudes flexible and based on *preferences*, rather than demands or expectations, can keep your anger in the healthy camp. Rigid and demanding attitudes can land you in unhealthy destructive anger, time and time again.

Consider the relationship of Ade and Franco: Ade holds rigid beliefs about other people showing him respect and courtesy. Franco holds the same principal attitudes, but flexibly. Ade and Franco go for lunch together and sit near a table of young men, who drink a bit too much and end up talking very loudly and rudely. Franco and Ade can't hear each other and their lunch is being ruined by the behaviour of these young men. Franco suggests that he and Ade move to another table, where they won't be disturbed by the men's anti-social behaviour. Ade, however, gets up and shouts at the men, ending up in a brawl outside the cafe. He's lucky not to be hurt more seriously than he is.

Ade's rigid attitudes about the situation are:

> 'How dare these idiots treat me this way?'
>
> 'I won't tolerate being disrespected like this.'
>
> 'I've got to show these idiots who's the boss.'

Franco's more flexible attitudes about the situation are:

> 'These guys are behaving like idiots.'
>
> 'These guys are really annoying me with their disrespectful behaviour.'
>
> 'I don't want to put up with this, so I think I'll get away from these guys.'

Flexible preferences for things like respect allow for the possibility of you being treated disrespectfully. Rigid demands don't allow for the possibility of life and other people treating you in ways that you think they shouldn't. Inevitably, you can end up feeling outraged if you always demand that others behave in a specific way. People behave according to how *they* want to behave – not how *you* want them to behave.

When you angrily condemn another person as 'useless', 'no good', or 'idiotic', you make a gross overgeneralisation. The other person isn't a thoroughgoing idiot just because she's acting idiotically – she surely acts in different ways in other situations, just like you do.

The critical point here is also a practical point: Putting down other people makes respecting others difficult. You need to sustain a level of respect for others in order to be able to consider behaviours objectively and act appropriately assertive.

The alternative to putting down others is to accept them as FHBs – fallible human beings – who may act in objectionable ways (to you). When you consider others as FHBs, you can appropriately condemn the behaviour but not the person. This acceptance is critical in helping you to keep a level head and master your angry feelings.

Accepting other people is the other side of the coin to accepting yourself. You can eventually accept yourself because you're essentially applying the same philosophy to everyone.

Sometimes, people default to unhealthy anger because they have a fragile sense of their own worth. If someone treats you poorly, insults you, or seems to hold a negative opinion of you, you may be reminded of how low an opinion you have of yourself. In order to protect your self-worth, you may attack the other person. Think of the rationale as 'If I can put you down, then I can avoid putting myself down.'

By believing that you're an unrateable, complex, ever-changing, fallible human, you may see that you can never be less worthwhile, even when people treat you poorly.

Developing high frustration tolerance

Frustration occurs most often when something or someone gets in the way of you achieving your specific goals and aims. The more important your goal is to you, the more angry or annoyed you're likely to feel when something blocks your attempts to reach that goal.

People who frequently experience unhealthy anger tend to have a low tolerance for frustration. Their low threshold for tolerating hassle, mishaps, or obstruction from others is echoed in statements like these:

> 'I can't stand it!'
>
> 'It's intolerable!'
>
> 'I just can't take it anymore!'

Increasing your tolerance for frustration helps you to experience appropriate levels of healthy annoyance in response to goal obstruction. Having a *high frustration tolerance* (HFT) makes you more effective at solving problems. So, your anger doesn't get in the way of you seeing possible solutions to every-day hassles and setbacks. High frustration tolerance is present in statements such as:

'This is an uncomfortable situation but I can stand the discomfort!'

'This event is hard to bear but I can bear it – some difficult things are worth tolerating.'

'Even if I *feel* like I can't take it anymore, chances are that I can.'

To increase your tolerance for frustration, ask yourself these kinds of questions when life pulls a fast one on you:

'Is this situation really terrible or is it just highly inconvenient?'

'Is it true that I can't stand this situation or it is it more true that I don't like this situation?'

'Is this situation truly unbearable or is it really just very difficult to bear?'

Being less extreme in your judgement of negative events can help you to have less extreme emotional responses, such as unhealthy anger.

REMEMBER

Most of what you think is intolerable isn't as bad as it seems. Many things are difficult to tolerate but are tolerable, hard to bear but bearable, unpleasant and inconvenient – but you *can* stand them!

To underscore the point, imagine getting stuck in traffic on your way to the airport and then missing your flight. Deeply annoying! However, by you get-ting angry and screaming at the traffic, isn't going to make the cars move any faster. Of course, becoming healthily annoyed about the traffic doesn't change the situation either. But your healthy anger is less likely to cause you such extreme discomfort and is more likely to help you create a contingency plan. Rather than using up your energy swearing and bashing your mobile against the dashboard, you can focus your efforts on phoning the airline and trying to get yourself bumped on to the next available flight.

Book III

Cognitive Behavioural Therapy

Doing your ABCs

Practise writing down your unhealthy angry thoughts on paper and replacing them with healthier thoughts. Refer to Chapter 1 to see how to use an ABC form to tackle toxic thoughts and replace them with realistic ren-derings, pertinent preferences, additional acceptances, self-acceptance, and high frus-tration tolerance.

Pondering the pros and cons of your temper

Believe that you're *right* to be angry and steadfastly stick to this perception, is one of the more common obstacles to conquering unhealthy anger.

You certainly have the *right* to feel angry. You may even *be right* to be angry, in the sense of objecting to something you don't like. However, you may feel better and behave more constructively if you have *healthy* anger rather than *unhealthy* anger.

Asserting yourself effectively

Expressing your feelings readily when they occur can be a good antidote to bouts of unhealthy anger. On the other hand, bottling up your feelings can mean that you fester on your emotions until they bubble up to the surface and you explode.

People who talk openly and appropriately about their emotional responses to events are less prone to unhealthy feelings like anger and depression. The following sections offer tips and techniques to improve your communication skills and to deal with dissatisfaction in a healthy manner.

Assertion involves standing up for yourself, voicing your opinions and feelings, and firmly ensuring that your basic rights are considered. Assertion differs from aggression, in that it does not involve violence, intimidation, or disregard for the rights of others.

Using assertion rather than aggression is more effective in getting you what you want. When you're being assertive, you're still in control of your behaviour, but when you're unhealthily enraged much of your behaviour is impulsive.

People are likely to respond to your wishes when you're being assertive simply because you're making yourself clear – not because they're afraid of your anger.

Often, your aggression is about winning an argument and getting the other person to back down and agree that you're right. Assertion is not about winning per se. Rather, assertion is about getting your point across but not insisting that the other person agrees with you or backs down.

If you have a tendency to become angry, and get verbally or physically aggressive quickly, give yourself time out and go and count to ten (or as high as you need to feel calmer). You can then consider your next thinking and behavioural steps.

Assertion is a skill that you can practice. Many people with anger problems benefit from breaking down assertion into the following steps:

1. **Get the other person's attention.** For example, if you want to make a complaint in a shop, wait until you have the shop assistant's attention rather than shouting at them when they are busy with another task. If you want to talk to your partner about a specific issue, ask for some of her time.

2. **Be in the right place.** The best time to assert yourself may depend on where you are when you get irked. If your boss makes a comment that undermines you during a board meeting, you're probably best to bring it up with her a bit later in less public surroundings.

3. **Be clear in your head about what you want to say.** If you're new to assertion, but more familiar with the shouting and screaming thing, give yourself time to really think about what you want to get across.

4. **Stick to your point and be respectful.** Don't resort to name-calling or hurling insults.

5. **Take responsibility for your feelings of annoyance.** Don't blame the other person for *making* you feel angry. Use statements like 'I feel angry when you turn up an hour late for our appointments', or 'I felt let down and angry that you didn't invite me to your wedding reception'.

Book III

Cognitive Behavioural Therapy

Assertion doesn't always work. Simply because you make the superlative effort to stop yelling your lungs out and to stop battering other people about the head and ears, doesn't mean that you're always going to get what you want. Oh, no, siree Bob! In fact, some people may even meet your assertion with their own aggression. So, strive to maintain your healthy anger and to behave assertively, even when other people don't. Remind yourself that other people have the right to choose to behave badly and that you have the right to remove yourself from them rather than responding in kind.

Before you assert yourself, decide whether the situation's really worth your time and energy. Ask yourself whether the problem merits you being assertive. Is the issue more trouble than it's worth? If you're a former unhealthy anger junkie, you're probably not used to just letting things go. You can practise deciding when asserting yourself is in your best interests and when you're wiser to simply not respond at all.

Coping with criticism

Criticism isn't always intended to anger or undermine the receiver. Well-delivered specific criticism can provide useful information and need not cause offence. Most people like to hear positive feedback – it's the negative stuff that really gets under your skin.

People who demand perfection from themselves, or expect approval from significant others, can often take criticism badly. They tend to take criticism overly seriously and personally. They often assume that any form of negative comment means that they're less than worthy. If you're this sort of person, a comment from your boss such as 'I'm not entirely happy with this report you've written' gets translated in your head something like this:

> *My boss thinks my report is rubbish = All my reports are rubbish = I'm rubbish at my job = I'm rubbish*

You may even become unhealthily angry in an attempt to defend your self-worth, and launch a counteroffensive on the person you feel has attacked you.

You can take the sting out of criticism by keeping these points in mind:

- ✔ Criticism can help you to improve your work performance and your relationships.

- ✔ You can assess criticism, decide how much of it you agree with, and reject the rest.

- ✔ Criticism is something pretty much everyone experiences from time to time. You cannot reasonably expect to always avoid being criticised.

If someone criticises you in a global way – for example, your sister calls you an incompetent loser – try asking her to be more specific: 'In what specific ways am I an incompetent loser?' Asking questions can make the criticism more useful to you. Or, if the person cannot be more specific, your question can disarm her. The following section discusses disarming in greater detail.

Using the disarming technique

Okay, not all the criticism that you get is well-intended. Sometimes, another person may bombard you with a load of negative remarks or insults. What are your options? You *can* get unhealthily angry and shout at or otherwise attack your antagonist. Or, you can keep your annoyance in the healthy camp and try non-defensively disarming your critic. The disarming technique works on the following principles:

- ✔ Look for a grain of truth in what the other person is saying and agreeing with her on that specific point.

- ✔ Show your critic some empathy

- ✔ Ask your critic for more information about her point of criticism

- ✔ Express your own point of view as 'I feel' statements

For example, Hilda's friend criticises her for being late to meet her for coffee. Hilda's friend says angrily: 'You're always late. You're just so disorganised!' Hilda would usually be defensive and hostile about criticism, resulting in many past arguments. Instead, this time Hilda uses the disarming technique and replies, 'You're right! I'm not the most organised person in the world' (partial agreement). 'Are you feeling really annoyed?' (empathy/asking for more information). This takes the heat from her friend's anger, who then goes on to say how frustrated she's feeling in general.

Using the disarming technique, you come out on top by keeping your cool. You also gain the satisfaction of having managed a critical comment well. Who knows – you may even *improve* your relationship with your critic.

Dealing with difficulties in overcoming anger

Even if you know that your anger responses are causing you problems in your life, you may still be reluctant to let go of your anger. Sometimes, people are reluctant to break free from unhealthy anger and related behaviours because they can't see an alternative, and think that they may end up being passive or getting walked over instead.

However, if you develop your assertion skills, you may well be more inclined to let go of your anger. Nevertheless, here are some common obstacles to getting rid of unhealthy anger and some suggestions to help you take on healthy anger instead:

Book III

Cognitive Behavioural Therapy

- ✔ **You lack empathy and understanding of the impact your unhealthy anger responses have on those near to you.** When you're not angry, ask your loved ones how they feel about your anger. Try to remember times when you've been on the receiving end of aggressive or intimidating behaviour and how it affected you. Use feedback about your anger, and your own experiences of aggression from others, to help you change how you express feelings of annoyance in the future.

- ✔ **Letting go of your anger means that you're weak.** You may consider yourself an angry person, and you may like it that way. You may think that if you don't continue to be angry, other people may discover that you're weak, a pushover, someone they can mess with. Work to realise that people who're assertive – firm but fair – tend to earn respect. You don't need to be angry to be strong.

- ✔ **You think that your unhealthy anger helps you to control other people and encourages them to respect you.** If you're very aggressive, people who are important in your life, such as your children or your partner, may go out of their way to avoid incurring your wrath. Don't mistake fear and dislike for respect. You may control the people in your life by your anger, but their compliance is likely born of fear and loathing, not from genuine regard for you. When you behave respectfully and assertively, people are likely to respond out of a genuine regard for your feelings rather than out of fear.

✔ **Your unhealthy anger makes you feel powerful.** Although some people find the intensity of their unhealthy anger pretty uncomfortable and even scary, others feel invigorated by the rush of their fury. Unhealthy anger is based on putting down another person. Unhealthy anger often means that you are stepping on another person's rights, or abusing, or intimidating somebody else. If you enjoy these aspects of your anger, you probably hold a low opinion of yourself generally. Look for other ways to experience your personal power without undermining those around you.

✔ **Your anger is self-righteous.** You may be clinging stubbornly to your anger because you think it's justified. You may be refusing to admit that you could be wrong or that the other person could be right. Rarely are confrontations as cut and dry as one party being utterly in the right and the other utterly in the wrong. Remind yourself that it is okay to be wrong. It is not a sign of weakness or inferiority. Allow yourself to admit that you may be wrong and that the other person may have a good point.

Feeling a bit sceptical? Test out your predictions about adopting healthy anger and behaving in an assertive rather than an aggressive manner.

Body benefits for bridling your anger

Being angry, especially feeling frequently hostile towards other people and the world, is bad for you. Scientific research shows an association between hostility and raised blood pressure, which can lead to heart problems. Take the pressure off your mind, your interactions with other people, and your heart by controlling — rather than being controlled by — your anger.

Chapter 4

Taking a Fresh Look at Your Past

. . . .

In This Chapter

▶ Putting your current problems into context

▶ Identifying your core beliefs

▶ Strengthening your beliefs

▶ Acting in accordance to your new beliefs

▶ Developing alternative beliefs

. . . .

*Y*our past experiences have an effect on how you think and function now. Sometimes, you may endure bad experiences and be able to make some good things happen from them. At other times, you may be wounded by unpleasant events and carry that injury with you into your present and future.

This chapter encourages you to examine openly whether your past experiences have led you to develop *core beliefs* that may be causing your current emotional difficulties.

People are sometimes surprised to find out that CBT considers the past an important aspect of understanding one's problems. Unlike traditional Freudian psychoanalysis, which focuses intensively on childhood relationships and experiences, CBT specifically investigates past experiences in order to see how these early events may still be affecting people in their *present* lives.

Exploring How Your Past Can Influence Your Present

We don't know what your childhood and early adulthood were like, but many people share relatively common past experiences. The following examples highlight various aspects of past experience that may resonate with your life history. Rather than focusing on the differences between these examples and your own experiences, use the examples to identify similar things that have happened to you in your own life.

✔ Sybil grew up with parents who fought a lot. She learnt to be very quiet and to keep out of the way so that her parents' anger would not be directed at her. She always tried to be a very good girl and no trouble to anyone.

✔ Rashid had critical parents. The demands Rashid's parents made on him to be a 'high achiever' made it clear to him that he would get their love and approval only when he did well in sports and at school.

✔ Beth had a violent father who would frequently beat her and other family members when he was in a bad mood. At other times, her father was very loving and funny. Beth could never predict accurately what mood her father would be in when he came through the front door.

✔ Milo's relationships have never lasted for very long. Most of the women he's dated have been unfaithful to him. Milo's partners often complain that he is too insecure and suspicious of their friendships with members of the opposite sex.

✔ Mahesh lost the family business and his oldest son in a fire five years ago. His wife has been depressed since the fire, and their marriage seems to be falling apart. Recently, his teenage daughter has been in trouble with the police. No one seems to offer Mahesh support. He feels dogged by bad luck.

Many other different kinds of difficult experiences can contribute to the development of negative core beliefs:

✔ Death of loved ones

✔ Growing up with neglectful, critical, or abusive parents or siblings

✔ Divorce

✔ Being bullied at school

✔ Being abandoned by a parent or significant other

✔ Undergoing a trauma, such as rape, life-threatening illness, accidents, or witnessing violent attacks on other people

These are just some examples of the types of events that can have a profound effect on mental health generally. Negative events that contribute to the way you think about yourself, other people, and the world often occur in childhood or early adult life. However, events occurring at any stage of your life can have a significant impact on the way you think about the world.

Identifying Your Core Beliefs

Your *core beliefs* are ideas or philosophies that you hold very strongly and very deeply. These ideas are usually developed in childhood or early in adult life. Core beliefs are not always negative. Good experiences of life and of other people, generally lead to the development of healthy ideas about yourself, other people, and the world. In this chapter we deal with negative core beliefs because these are the types of beliefs that cause people's emotional problems.

Sometimes, the negative core beliefs that are formed during childhood can be reinforced by later experiences, which seem to confirm their validity.

For example, one of Beth's core beliefs is 'I'm bad'. She develops this belief to make sense of her father beating her without any real or obvious reason. Later, Beth has a few experiences of being punished unreasonably by teachers at school, which reinforces her belief in her 'badness'.

Core beliefs are characteristically global and are absolute, like Beth's 'I'm bad'. People hold core beliefs to be 100 per cent true under all conditions. You often form your core beliefs when you're a child to help you make sense of your childhood experiences, and so you may never evaluate whether your core beliefs are the best way to make sense of your adult experiences. As an adult, you may continue to act, think, and feel as though the core beliefs of your childhood are still 100 per cent true.

Your core beliefs are called 'core' because they're your deeply held ideas and they're at the very centre of your belief system. Core beliefs give rise to rules, demands, or assumptions, which in turn produce *automatic thoughts* (thoughts that just pop into your head when you are confronted with a situation). You can think of these three layers of beliefs as a dartboard with core beliefs as the bull's-eye. Figure 4-1 shows the interrelationship between the three layers, and shows the assumptions and automatic thoughts that surround Beth's core belief that she's bad.

Another way of describing a core belief is as a lens or filter, through which you interpret all the information you receive from other people and the world around you.

Book III

Cognitive Behavioural Therapy

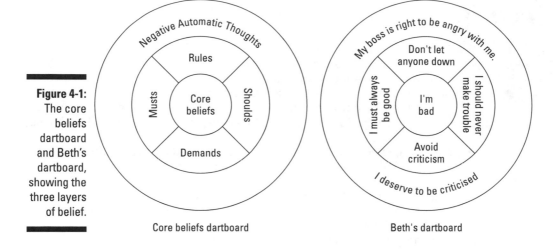

Figure 4-1:
The core
beliefs
dartboard
and Beth's
dartboard,
showing the
three layers
of belief.

Core beliefs dartboard   Beth's dartboard

Seeing how your core beliefs interact

Identifying core beliefs about yourself can help you to understand why you keep having the same problems. However, if you can also get to know your fundamental beliefs about other people and the world, you can build a fuller picture of why some situations distress you. For example, Beth may find being yelled at by her boss depressing because it fits with her core belief 'I'm bad', but the experience also seems to confirm her belief that people are unpredictable and aggressive.

Like many people, you may hold core beliefs that you're unlovable, unworthy, or inadequate – these beliefs are about your basic worth, goodness, or value. Or perhaps you hold beliefs about your capability to look after yourself or to cope with adversity – these beliefs are about how helpless or powerful you are in relation to other people and the world.

Mahesh, for example, may believe 'I'm helpless' because he has experienced tragedy and a lot of bad luck. He may also hold beliefs that 'the world is against me' and 'other people are uncaring'. Looking at these three beliefs together, you can see why Mahesh is feeling depressed.

Understanding the impact of core beliefs

Core beliefs are your fundamental and enduring ways of perceiving and making sense of yourself, the world, and other people. Your core beliefs have been around since early in your life. These core beliefs are so typically engrained and unconscious that you're probably not aware of their impact on your emotions and behaviours.

Spotting when you are acting according to old rules and beliefs

People tend to behave according to the beliefs they hold about themselves, others, and the world. To evaluate whether your core beliefs are unhealthy, you need to pay attention to your corresponding behaviours. Unhealthy core beliefs typically lead to problematic behaviours.

For example, Milo believes that he's unlovable and that other people cannot be trusted. Therefore, he tends to be passive with his girlfriends, to seek reassurance that they're not about to leave him, and to become suspicious and jealous of their interactions with other men. Often, Milo's girlfriends get fed up with his jealousy and insecurity and end the relationship.

Because Milo operates according to his core belief about being unlovable, he behaves in ways that actually tend to drive his partners away from him. Milo doesn't yet see that his core belief, and corresponding insecurity, is what causes problems in his relationships. Instead, Milo thinks that each time a partner leaves him for someone else, it is further evidence that his core belief of 'I'm unlovable' is true.

Sybil believes that she mustn't draw attention to herself because one of her core beliefs is 'other people are likely to turn on me'. Therefore, she's quiet in social situations and is reluctant to assert herself. Her avoidant, self-effacing behaviour means that she doesn't often get what she wants, which feeds her core belief 'I'm unimportant'.

Sybil acts in accordance with her core belief that other people are likely to turn on her and, subsequently deprives herself of the opportunity to see that this is not always going to happen. If Sybil and Milo identify their negative core beliefs, they can begin to develop healthier new beliefs and behaviours that can yield better results. We look more closely at how to develop new, more positive core beliefs later in this chapter.

Book III

Cognitive Behavioural Therapy

Understanding that unhealthy core beliefs make you prejudiced

When you begin to examine your core beliefs, it may seem to you that everything in your life is conspiring to make your unhealthy core belief ring true. More than likely, your core belief is leading you to take a prejudiced view of all your experiences. Unhealthy beliefs, such as 'I'm unlovable' and 'other people are dangerous', distort the way in which you process information. Negative information that supports your unhealthy belief is let in. Positive information that contradicts the negative stuff is either rejected, or twisted to mean something negative in keeping with your unhealthy belief.

The prejudice model in Figure 4-2 shows you how your unhealthy core beliefs can reject positive events that may *contradict* them. At the same time, your core beliefs can collect negative events that may *support* their validity. Your unhealthy core beliefs can also lead you to distort positive events into negative events so that they continue to make your beliefs seem true.

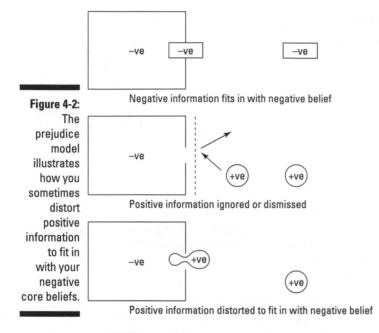

Figure 4-2:
The prejudice model illustrates how you sometimes distort positive information to fit in with your negative core beliefs.

Negative information fits in with negative belief

Positive information ignored or dismissed

Positive information distorted to fit in with negative belief

For example, here's how Beth's core belief 'I'm bad' causes her to prejudice her experiences:

- ✔ **Negative experience:** Beth's boss is angry about a missed deadline, affirming her belief that 'I'm bad'.

- ✔ **Positive experience:** Beth's boss is happy about the quality of her report, which Beth distorts as 'he's happy about this report only because all my other work is such rubbish', further affirming her belief that 'I'm bad'.

Beth also ignores smaller *positive* events that don't support her belief that she's bad, such as:

- ✔ People seem to like her at work.

- ✔ Co-workers tell her that she's conscientious at work.

- ✔ Her friends telephone her and invite her out.

However, Beth is quick to take notice of smaller *negative* events that do seem to match up with her belief that she's bad, for example:

- ✔ Someone pushes her rudely on a busy train.

- ✔ Her boyfriend shouts at her during an argument.

- ✔ A work colleague doesn't smile at her when she enters the office.

Beth's core belief of 'I'm bad' acts as a filter through which all her experiences are interpreted. It basically stops her from re-evaluating herself as anything other than bad; it makes her prejudiced against herself. This is why identifying negative core beliefs and targeting them for change is so important!

Limiting the damage and developing alternatives

To reduce the negative impact of your unhelpful core beliefs, try to get better at spotting the beliefs being activated. Step back and consider a more unbiased explanation for events rather than getting swept along by the beliefs.

One way of improving your awareness of your core beliefs is to develop a *core belief flashcard*. This written-down statement includes the following:

- ✔ What your core belief is.
- ✔ How your core belief affects the way you interpret events.
- ✔ How you tend to act when the core belief is triggered.
- ✔ What a more unbiased interpretation of events is likely to be.
- ✔ What alternative behaviour may be more productive.

For example, Sybil wrote the following core belief flashcard:

> *When my core belief of 'I'm unimportant' is triggered, I'm probably taking something personally and wanting to withdraw. Instead, I can remember that most people don't hold this view of me, and then I can stay engaged in the social situation.*

Carry your flashcard around with you and it review it often, even several times a day. Use your flashcard, especially when you notice that your core belief has *been* triggered, or just before you enter a situation where you know that your old core belief is *likely* to be triggered.

When you've put your finger on your core beliefs and identified those that are negative and unhealthy, you're in a position to develop healthier alternative beliefs.

Your new core belief doesn't need to be the extreme opposite of your old belief. Changing an extreme belief, such as 'I'm unlovable' to 'I'm lovable', may be too difficult when you're just starting out. Instead, cut yourself some slack and realise that simply by beginning to understand that an unhealthy core belief is not 100 per cent true all the time is enough. Here are some examples:

Book III

Cognitive Behavioural Therapy

Shaping your world

When you start to adopt healthy core beliefs, it can feel as if you're going against the grain because in fact that is what you are trying to do. Your old, negative core beliefs are familiar, deeply entrenched, and 'feel' like they must be true. New, healthy beliefs can 'feel' false and unnatural at first. Remind yourself that just because you've believed something for a long time doesn't make it true. People believed the earth was flat for a long time but that old belief doesn't change the fact that the world is round!

Some things are true, regardless of whether you believe them. Other things will never be true, no matter how fervently you believe them.

✔ Beth's alternative to her unhealthy belief 'I'm bad' is 'there are good things about me'.

✔ Rashid replaces his unhealthy belief 'I'm a failure' with 'I succeed at some things'.

✔ Mahesh chooses the alternative 'good things do happen in the world' to replace his old belief 'the world's against me'.

✔ Sybil replaces her belief 'other people will turn against me' with the healthier belief 'many people can be kind'.

✔ Milo substitutes his old core belief 'I'm unlovable' with the more accurate belief 'some people do like me, and some people will love me'.

Generating alternatives for your unhealthy and absolute core beliefs is not about positive thinking or platitudes, but is about generating less absolute, more accurate, more realistic opinions about yourself, other people, and the world around you.

Revisiting history

Many people can look back over their lives and get a fairly clear picture of where their core beliefs have come from. Sometimes, though, the source of core beliefs is not so clear.

Although most core beliefs arise from your early experiences, you can still form deep entrenched ideas about yourself, life, and other people when you're older. For example, Mahesh develops his core beliefs about the world being against him following a string of bad luck and tragic events during his adult years.

Revisit your history with a view to come up with some reasons behind the ways that you think and behave in the present. Be compassionate with yourself, but recognise that you're the only one who can retrain your brain into updated and healthier ways of understanding your experiences.

Replacing old meanings with new meanings

Experiences that you had earlier on in life were given a meaning by you at the time. As an adult, you're in the fortunate position of being able to reassess the meanings you originally gave certain events and to assign more sophisticated meanings where appropriate.

For example, Beth forms the belief 'I'm bad' based on the information she had when her father was abusing her. She was young and worked on various assumptions, including:

- ✔ Daddy tells me that I've been bad, and this must be true.

- ✔ You get punished when you're bad.

- ✔ I must've done something bad to deserve this treatment.

Now that she's no longer a child and recognises that she has this core belief, Beth can choose to look at her father's abuse and assign different meanings to his treatment of her:

- ✔ My father had an anger problem that had nothing to do with me.

- ✔ No child should be punished so severely, no matter how disobedient they've been.

- ✔ My father was wrong to beat me, and I didn't deserve to be beaten.

- ✔ My father did a bad thing by beating me and his bad behaviour doesn't mean that I am bad.

Book III

Cognitive Behavioural Therapy

Use the three-column old meaning/new meaning worksheet in the appendix to review past events that contributed to the development of your core beliefs and reinterpret them now as an older, wiser person.

The sheet has three headings. Fill them in as follows:

1. **In the first column, 'Event', record what actually happened.**

2. **Under 'Old Meaning' in the second column, record what you believe the event means about you.**

   This is your unhealthy core belief.

3. **In the 'New Meaning' third column, record a healthier and more accurate meaning for the event.**

   This is the new belief that you want to strengthen.

Table 4-1 shows an example of Beth's worksheet.

Table 4-1	Beth's Old Meaning–New Meaning Worksheet	
Event	*Old Meaning*	*New Meaning*
My Dad yelling, telling me I was bad when I was little.	I must be bad for him to say this so often.	I was much too young and afraid to be 'bad'. It was my father's anger that was the problem.

Incorporating new beliefs into your life

Constructing newer, healthier, more accurate core beliefs is one thing, but beginning to live by them is another. Before your new beliefs are really stuck in your head and heart, you need to act *as if* they're already there. For Beth, this may mean her forcing herself to face up to criticism from her boss and making appropriate adjustments to her work without berating herself. In short, she needs to act *as if* she truly believes that there are good things about herself, even in the face of negative feedback. She needs to operate under the assumption that her boss's anger is a reasonable (or possibly an unreasonable) response to an aspect of her work, rather than proof of her intrinsic badness.

Starting from scratch

We won't tell you that changing your core beliefs is easy, because that simply isn't true. In fact, erasing your old belief systems is so difficult that we think the best way of dealing with them is to make alternative healthy beliefs stronger so that they can do battle with your unhealthy beliefs.

Think of your old beliefs as well-trodden paths through an overgrown field. You can walk quickly and easily down these paths, as they've been worn down from years of use. Developing new alternative beliefs is like making new paths through the field. At first, the new paths are awkward and uncomfortable to walk on, because you need to break down the undergrowth.

You may be tempted to walk along the old paths because they're easier and more well-known, but with practice, your new paths can become familiar and natural to walk along. Similarly, with regular practice, thinking and acting along the lines of your alternative beliefs can become stronger and more automatic, even when the going gets tough!

Thinking about what you'd teach a child

When you're challenging your negative core beliefs, try to think about what you'd tell a child. Act as your own parent by reinstructing yourself to endorse healthy ways of viewing others, yourself, and the world.

Ask yourself what types of belief you'd teach a child. Would you encourage him to grab hold of the negative core beliefs that you may hold about yourself, or would you want him to think of himself in a more positive and accepting way? Would you wish for him to think of other people as evil, mistrustful, dangerous, and more powerful than himself? Or would you rather he had a more balanced view of people, such as variable but basically okay, generally trustworthy, and reliable? Would you want him to believe that he can stand up for himself?

Considering what you'd want a friend to believe

When challenging your core beliefs, think about having a friend like Mahesh, Beth, Rashid, Milo, or Sybil. What advice would you give them? Would you say 'Yes, Rashid, you're a failure'? 'I agree, Mahesh – life's against you'? 'Beth, you're bad'? 'Sybil, no one ever thought you were important anyway'?

Or would you be quietly horrified to spout these unhealthy and damaging beliefs? We assume the latter.

If you wouldn't want your dear friends to believe such things, why believe them yourself? Talk to yourself like you would to your best friend when your negative core beliefs are activated.

Defining the Beliefs You Want to Strengthen

After you've identified your unhelpful patterns of thinking and developed more helpful attitudes, you need to reinforce your new thoughts and beliefs. The process of reinforcing new beliefs is like trying to give up a bad habit and develop a good habit in its place. You need to work at making your new, healthy ways of thinking second nature, at the same time as eroding your old ways of thinking.

In many ways, *integrating* your new method of thinking with your mind, emotions, and actions is *the* critical process in CBT. A parrot can repeat rational philosophies, but the parrot doesn't understand or *believe* what it's asaying. The real work in CBT is turning intellectual understanding into something you that know in your gut to be true.

Many people who work at changing their attitudes and beliefs complain: 'I know what I *should* think, but I don't believe it!' When you begin to adopt a new way of thinking, you may *know* that something makes sense but you may not *feel* that the new belief is true.

When you're in a state of *cognitive dissonance* you know that your old way of thinking isn't 100 per cent right, but you aren't yet convinced of the alternative. Being in a state of cognitive dissonance can be uncomfortable because things don't feel quite right. However, this feeling is a good sign that things are changing.

In CBT, we often call this disconnection between thinking and truly believing the *head-to-heart problem*. Basically, you know that an argument is true in your head, but you don't feel it in your heart. For example, if you've spent many years believing that you're less worthy than others or that you need the approval of other people in order to approve of yourself, you may have great difficulty *internalising* (believing in your gut) an alternative belief. You may find that the idea that you have as much basic human worth as the next person, or that approval from others is a bonus but not a necessity, difficult to buy.

Your alternative beliefs are likely to be about three key areas:

- ✔ Yourself
- ✔ Other people
- ✔ The world

Alternative beliefs may take the following formats:

- ✔ A *flexible preference*, instead of a rigid demand or rule, such as 'I'd very much prefer to be loved by my parents, but there's no reason they absolutely *have* to love me.'
- ✔ An *alternative assumption*, which is basically an if/then statement, such as '*If* I don't get an A in my test, *then* that won't be the end of the world. I can still move on in my academic career.'
- ✔ A *global belief,* which expresses a positive healthy general truth, such as 'I'm basically okay' rather than 'I'm worthless', or 'The world's a place with some safe and some dangerous parts' instead of 'The world's a dangerous place'.

When you do experience the head-to-heart problem, we recommend acting *as if* you really do hold the new belief to be true – we explain how to do this in the following section.

One of your main aims in CBT, after you've developed a more helpful alternative belief, is to increase how strongly you endorse your new belief or raise your *strength of conviction* (SOC). You can rate how much you believe in an alternative healthy philosophy on a 0–100 percentage scale, 0 represents a total lack of conviction and 100 represents an absolute conviction.

Acting As If You Already Believe

You don't need to believe your new philosophy entirely in order to start changing your behaviour. Starting out, it's enough to *know* in your head that your new belief makes sense and then *act* according to your new belief or philosophy. If you consistently do the 'acting as if' technique, which we explain here, your conviction in your new way of thinking is likely to grow over time.

You can use the 'acting as if' technique to consolidate any new way of thinking, in pretty much any situation. Ask yourself the following questions:

- ✔ How would I behave if I truly considered my new belief to be true?

- ✔ How would I overcome situational challenges to my new belief if I truly considered it to be true and helpful?

- ✔ What sort of behaviour would I expect to see in other people who truly endorse this new belief?

You can make a list of your answers to the above questions and refer to it before, after, and even during an experience of using the 'acting as if' technique. For example, if you're dealing with social anxiety and trying to get to grips with self-acceptance beliefs, use the 'acting as if' techniques that follow, and ask yourself similar kinds of questions, such as:

- ✔ **Act consistently with the new belief:** If I truly believed that I was as worthy as anyone else, how would I behave in a social situation?

  Be specific about how you'd enter a room, the conversation you may initiate, and what your body language would be like.

- ✔ **Troubleshoot for challenges to your new belief:** If I truly believed that I was as worthy as anyone else, how would I react to any social hiccups?

  Again, be specific about how you may handle lulls in conversation and moments of social awkwardness.

- ✔ **Observe other people:** Does anyone else in the social situation seem to be acting as if they truly endorse the belief that I am trying to adopt?

  If so, note how the person acts and how they handle awkward silences and normal breaks in conversation. Imitate their behaviour.

When you act in accordance with a new way of thinking or a specific belief, you reinforce the truth of that belief. The more you experience a belief *in action*, the more you can appreciate its beneficial effects on your emotions. In essence, you are rewiring your brain to think in a more helpful and realistic

Book III

Cognitive Behavioural Therapy

way. Give this technique a try, even if you think that it's wishful thinking or seems silly. Actions do speak louder than words. So if a new belief makes sense to you, follow it up with action.

Building a portfolio of arguments

When an old belief rears its ugly head, try to have on hand some strong arguments to support your new belief. Your old beliefs or thinking habits have probably been with you a long time, and they can be tough to shift. You can expect to argue with yourself about the truth and benefit of your new thinking several times, before the new stuff well and truly replaces the old.

Your portfolio of arguments can consist of a collection of several arguments against your old way of thinking and several arguments in support of your new way of thinking. You can refer to your portfolio anytime that you feel conviction in your new belief is beginning to wane. Get yourself a small notebook to use as your portfolio of arguments. The following sections help to guide you towards developing sound rationales in support of helpful beliefs and in contradiction of unhelpful beliefs.

Generating arguments against an unhelpful belief

To successfully combat unhealthy beliefs, try the following exercise. At the top of a sheet of paper, write down an old, unhelpful belief you want to weaken. For example, you may write: 'I have to get approval from significant others, such as my boss. Without approval, I'm worthless.' Then, consider the following questions to highlight the unhelpful nature of your belief:

- ✔ **Is the belief untrue or inconsistent with reality?** Try to find evidence that your belief isn't factually accurate (or at least not 100 per cent accurate for 100 per cent of all of the time). For example, you don't *have* to get approval from your boss: The universe permits otherwise, and you can survive without such approval. Furthermore, you cannot be defined as worthless on the strength of this experience, because you're much too complex to be defined.

Considering why a certain belief is *understandable* can help you to explain why you hold a particular belief to be true. For example, 'It's understandable that I think I'm stupid because my father often told me I was when I was young, but that was really due to his impatience and his own difficult childhood. So, it follows that I believe myself to be stupid because of my childhood experiences, and not because there is any real truth in the idea that I am stupid. Therefore, the belief that I am stupid is consistent with my upbringing but inconsistent with reality.'

- ✔ **Is the belief rigid?** Consider whether your belief is flexible enough to allow you to adapt to reality. For example, the idea that you *must* get approval or that you *need* approval in order to think well of yourself, is overly rigid. It is entirely possible that you will fail to get approval from significant others at some stage in your life. Unless you have a flexible belief about getting approval, you are destined to think badly of yourself whenever approval is not forthcoming. Replace the word *must* with *prefer* in this instance, and turn your demand for approval into a flexible preference for approval.

✔ **Is the belief extreme?** Consider whether your unhelpful belief is extreme. For example, equating being disliked by one person with worthlessness is an extreme conclusion. It is rather like concluding that being late for one appointment means that you will always be late for every appointment you have for the rest of your life. The conclusion that you draw from one or more experiences is far too extreme to accurately reflect reality.

✔ **Is the belief illogical?** Consider whether your belief actually makes sense. You may want approval from your boss, but logically she doesn't *have* to approve of you. Not getting approval from someone significant doesn't logically lead to you being less worthy. Rather, not getting approval shows that you've failed to get approval on this occasion, from this specific person.

✔ **Is the belief unhelpful?** Consider how your belief may or may not be helping you. For example, if you worry about whether your boss is approving of you, you'll probably be anxious at work much of the time. You may feel depressed if your boss treats you with indifference or visibly disapproves of your work. You're less likely to say no to unreasonable requests or to put your opinions forward. You may actually be less effective at work because you're so focused on making a good impression. You may even assume that your boss is disapproving of you when actually this isn't the case. So, is worrying about your boss's approval helpful? Clearly not!

Running through the preceding list of questions is definitely an exercise that involves putting pen to paper or fingertips to keyboard. Try to pick out your unhelpful beliefs and to formulate helpful alternatives, then generate as many watertight arguments against your old belief and in support of your new belief as you can. Try to fill up one side of A4 paper for each belief you target.

You can include in your portfolio evidence gathered from other CBT techniques you use to tackle your problems, such as ABC forms and behavioural experiments. You can use any positive results observed from living according to new healthy beliefs as arguments to support the truth and benefits of these new beliefs.

Generating arguments to support your helpful alternative belief

The guidelines for generating sound arguments to support alternative, more helpful ways of thinking about yourself, other people, and the world, are similar to those suggested in the preceding section, 'Generating arguments against an unhelpful belief'.

Book III

Cognitive Behavioural Therapy

On a sheet of paper, write down a helpful alternative belief that you want to use to replace a negative, unhealthy view you hold. For example, a helpful alternative belief regarding approval at work may be: 'I want approval from significant others, such as my boss, but I don't *need* it. If I don't get approval, I still have worth as a person.'

Next, develop arguments to support your alternative belief. Ask yourself the following questions to ensure that your helpful alternative belief is strong and effective:

- **Is the belief true and consistent with reality?** For example, you really can want approval and fail to get it sometimes. Just because you want something very much doesn't mean to say you'll get it. Lots of people don't get approval from their bosses, but it doesn't mean they're lesser people.

- **Is the belief flexible?** Consider whether your belief allows you to adapt to reality. For example, the idea that you *prefer* to get approval but that it isn't a dire necessity for either survival or self-esteem, allows for the possibility of not getting approval from time to time. You don't have to form any extreme conclusions about your overall worth in the face of occasions of disapproval.

- **Is the belief balanced?** Consider whether your helpful belief is balanced and non-extreme. For example, 'Not being liked by my boss is unfortunate but it's not proof of whether I'm worthwhile as a person.' This balanced and flexible belief recognises that disapproval from your boss is undesirable and may mean that you need to reassess your work performance. However, this recognition does not hurl you into depression based on the unbalanced belief that you're unworthy for failing to please your boss on this occasion.

- **Is the belief logical and sensible?** Show how your alternative belief follows logically from the facts, or from your preferences. It follows logically that your boss's disapproval about one aspect of your work is undesirable and may mean that you need to work harder or differently. It does not follow logically that because of his disapproval you are an overall bad or worthless person.

- **Is the belief helpful?** When you accept that you want approval from your boss but that you don't *have* to get it, you can be less anxious about the possibility of incurring your boss's disapproval or failing to make a particular impression. You also stand a better chance of making a good impression at work when you prefer, but are not desperate for, approval. You can be more focused on the job that you're doing and less preoccupied by what your boss may be thinking about you.

Imagine you're about to go into court to present to the jury arguments in defence of your new belief. Develop as many good arguments that support your new belief as you can. Most people find that listing lots of ways in which the new belief is helpful makes the most impact. Try to generate enough arguments to fill one side of A4 paper for each individual belief.

Review your rational portfolio regularly, not just when your unhealthy belief is triggered. Doing so helps you reaffirm your commitment to thinking in healthy ways.

Understanding that practice makes imperfect

Despite your best efforts, you may continue to think in rigid and extreme ways and experience unhealthy emotions from time to time. Why? Well, – oh yes, we say it again – you're only human.

Practicing your new, healthy ways of thinking and putting them to regular use minimises your chances of relapse. However, you're never going to become a perfectly healthy thinker – human beings seem to have a tendency to develop thinking errors and you need a high degree of diligence to resist unhelpful and unhealthy thinking.

Be wary of having a perfectionist attitude about your thinking. You're setting yourself up to fail if you expect that you can always be healthy in thought, emotion, and behaviour. Give yourself permission to make mistakes with your new thinking, and use any setbacks as opportunities to discover more about your beliefs.

Book III

Cognitive Behavioural Therapy

Dealing with your doubts and reservations

You must give full range to your scepticism when you're changing your beliefs. If you try to sweep your doubts under the carpet, those doubts can re-emerge when you least expect it – usually when you're in a stressful situation. Consider Sylvester's experience:

> Sylvester, or Sly for short, believes that other people must like him and goes out of his way to put people at ease in social situations. Sly takes great care to never hurt anyone's feelings and puts pressure on himself to be a good host. Not surprisingly, Sly's often worn out by his efforts. Because Sly's work involves managing other staff, he also feels anxious much of the time. Sly also worries about confrontation and what his staff members think of him when he disciplines them.

After having some CBT, Sly concludes that his beliefs need to change if he's ever going to overcome his anxiety and feelings of panic at work. Sly formulates a healthy alternative belief: 'I want to be liked by others, but I don't always *have* to be liked. Being disliked is tolerable and doesn't mean I'm an unlikeable person.'

Sly can see how this new belief makes good sense and can help him feel less anxious about confronting staff members or being not-so-super-entertaining in social situations. But deep inside, Sly feels stirrings of doubt. Still, Sly denies his reservations about the new belief and ignores niggling uncertainty. One day, when Sly's confronting a staff member about persistent lateness, his underlying doubts rear up. Sly resorts to his old belief because he hasn't dealt with his doubts effectively. Sly ends up letting his worker off the hook and feeling angry with himself for not dealing with the matter properly.

Had Sly faced up to his misgivings about allowing himself to be disliked, he may have given himself a chance to resolve his feeling. Sly may then have been more prepared to deal with the stressful situation without resorting to his old belief and avoidant behaviour.

Zigging and zagging through the zigzag technique

Use the zigzag technique to strengthen your belief in a new healthy alternative belief or attitude. The zigzag technique involves playing devil's advocate with yourself. The more you argue the case in favour of a healthy belief and challenge your own attacks on it, the more deeply you can come to believe in it. Figure 4-3 shows a completed zigzag form example.

To go through the zigzag technique, do the following steps:

1. **Write down in the top left-hand box of the zigzag form a belief that you want to strengthen.**

   On the form, rate how strongly you endorse this belief, from 0 to 100 per cent conviction.

   Be sure that the belief's consistent with reality or true, logical, and helpful to you. Refer to the section that covers generating arguments to support your helpful alternative beliefs, for more on testing your healthy belief.

2. **In the next box down, write your doubts, reservations, or challenges about the healthy belief.**

   Really let yourself attack the belief, using all the unhealthy arguments that come to mind.

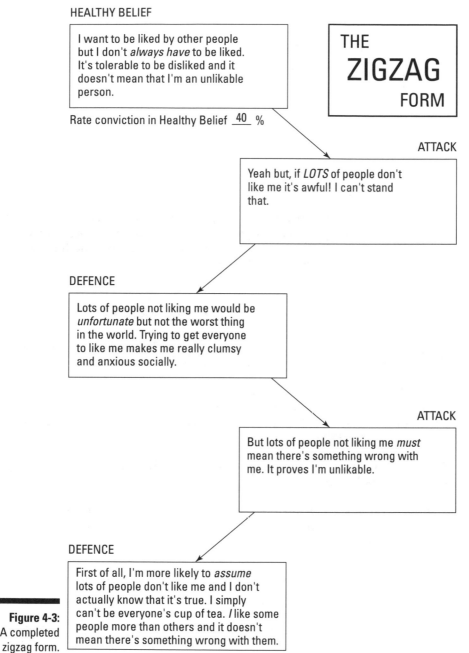

HEALTHY BELIEF

I want to be liked by other people but I don't *always have* to be liked. It's tolerable to be disliked and it doesn't mean that I'm an unlikable person.

Rate conviction in Healthy Belief __40__ %

THE
ZIGZAG
FORM

ATTACK

Yeah but, if *LOTS* of people don't like me it's awful! I can't stand that.

DEFENCE

Lots of people not liking me would be *unfortunate* but not the worst thing in the world. Trying to get everyone to like me makes me really clumsy and anxious socially.

ATTACK

But lots of people not liking me *must* mean there's something wrong with me. It proves I'm unlikable.

DEFENCE

First of all, I'm more likely to *assume* lots of people don't like me and I don't actually know that it's true. I simply can't be everyone's cup of tea. *I* like some people more than others and it doesn't mean there's something wrong with them.

Rate conviction in Healthy Belief __75__ %

Figure 4-3:
A completed zigzag form.

Book III

Cognitive Behavioural Therapy

3. **In the next box, dispute your attack and redefend the healthy belief.**

   Focus on defending the healthy belief. Don't become sidetracked by any points raised in your attack from Step 2.

4. **Repeat Steps 2 and 3 until you exhaust all your attacks on the healthy belief.**

   Be sure to use up all your doubts and reservations about choosing to really go for the new, healthy alternative way of thinking. Use as many forms as you need and be sure to stop on a defence of the belief you want to establish rather than on an attack.

5. **Re-rate, from 0 to 100 per cent, how strongly you endorse the healthy belief after going through all your doubts.**

If your conviction in the healthy belief hasn't increased or has increased only slightly, revisit the previous instructions on how to use the zigzag form. Or, if you have a CBT therapist, discuss the form with her and see whether she can spot where you zigged when you should have zagged.

Putting your new beliefs to the test

Doing pen-and-paper exercises is great – they really can help you to move your new beliefs from your head to your heart.

However, the best way to make your new ways of thinking more automatic is to put them to the test. Putting them to the test means going into familiar situations where your old attitudes are typically triggered, and acting according to your new way of thinking.

So, our friend Sly from earlier in the chapter may choose to do the following to test his new beliefs:

- ✔ Sly confronts his member of staff about her lateness in a forthright manner. Sly bears the discomfort of upsetting her and remembers that being disliked by one worker doesn't prove that he's an unlikeable person.

- ✔ Sly throws a party and resists the urge to make himself busy entertaining everyone and playing the host.

- ✔ Sly works less hard in work and social situations at putting everyone at ease and trying to be super-likeable mister nice guy.

If you're really, really serious about making your new beliefs stick, you can *seek out* situations in which to test them. On top of using your new beliefs and their knock-on new behaviours in everyday situations, try setting difficult tests for yourself. Sit down and think about it: If you were still operating under your old beliefs, what situations would really freak you out? Go there. Doing this will 'up the ante' with regard to endorsing your new beliefs.

Coping with everyday situations, such as Sly's previous example, is very useful, and is often enough to move your new belief from your head to your heart. But if you really want to put your new beliefs under strain, with a view to making them even stronger, put yourself into out-of-the-ordinary situations. For example, try deliberately doing something ridiculous in public or being purposefully rude and aloof. See if you can remain resolute in your new belief such as 'disapproval does not mean unworthiness' in the face of your most feared outcomes. We think you can! This is a tried and tested CBT tool for overcoming all sorts of problems, such as social anxiety.

Here are some tests that Sly (or we could now call him 'Braveheart') may set up for himself:

- Go into shops and deliberately be impolite by not saying 'thank you' and not smiling at the shop assistant. This test requires Sly to bear the discomfort of possibly leaving the shop assistant unhappy after making a poor impression.

- Say good morning to staff without smiling and allow them to form the impression that he was 'in a bad mood'.

- Mooch about, deliberately trying to look moody and aloof in a social setting.

- Make a complaint about faulty goods he's purchased from a local shop where the staff know him.

- Bump into someone on public transport and do not apologise.

You may think that Sly's setting himself up to be utterly friendless as a result of this wretched belief change lark. *Au contraire, nos chere!* Sly has friends. Sly still has a reputation of being a generally kind and affable bloke. What Sly doesn't have now is a debilitating belief that he has to please all the people all the time. Rather, Sly can come to truly believe that he can tolerate the discomfort of upsetting people occasionally and that being disliked by one or more people is part of being human. That's life. That's the way it goes sometimes. Sly can believe in his heart that he's a fallible human being, just like everyone else, that he's capable of being liked and disliked but basically he's okay.

Book III

Cognitive Behavioural Therapy

Nurturing Your New Beliefs

As you continue to live with your alternative helpful beliefs, gather evidence that supports your new beliefs. Becoming more aware of evidence from yourself, other people, and the world around you that supports your new, more helpful way of thinking, is one of the keys to strengthening your beliefs and keeping them strong.

A *positive data log* is a record of evidence you collect that shows the benefits of holding your new belief. The positive data log helps you overcome the biased, prejudiced way in which you keep unhelpful beliefs well-fed, by soaking up evidence that fits with them and discounting or distorting evidence that doesn't fit. Using a positive data log boosts the available data that fit your new belief and helps you to retrain yourself to take in the positive.

Your positive data log is simply a record of positive results arising from acting in accordance with a healthy new belief and evidence that contradicts your old unhealthy belief. You can use any type of notebook to record your evidence. Follow these steps:

1. **Write your new belief at the top of a page.**

2. **Record evidence that your new belief is helpful to you; include changes in your emotions and behaviour.**

3. **Record positive reactions that you get from others when you act in accordance with new beliefs.**

4. **Record any experiences that contradict your old belief.**

   Be specific and include even the smallest details that encourage you to doubt your old way of thinking. For example, even a newspaper vendor making small talk when you buy your paper can be used as evidence against a belief that you are unlikeable.

5. **Make sure that you record every bit of information in support of your new belief and in contradiction to your old belief.**

   Fill up the whole notebook if you can.

If you still have trouble believing that an old, unhelpful belief is true, start by collecting evidence on a daily basis that your old belief isn't 100 per cent true, 100 per cent all of the time. Collecting this sort of evidence can help you steadily erode how true the belief seems.

In your positive data log, you can list the benefits of operating under your new belief, including all the ways in which your fears about doing so have been disproved.

For example, Sly might record the following observations:

> ✔ His staff members still seem to generally like being managed by him, despite the fact that he disciplines them when needed.
>
> ✔ Being less gregarious at parties doesn't stop others from having a good time or from engaging with him.
>
> ✔ His anxiety and panic about the possibility of being disliked have reduced in response to his belief change.

Your positive data log can not only remind you of the good results you have reaped from changing your unhealthy beliefs to healthy ones, but also help you be *compassionate* with yourself when you relapse to your unhealthy beliefs and corresponding behaviours. Use your positive data log to chart your progress, so when you *do* fall back you can assure yourself that your setback need be only temporary. After all, practice makes imperfect.

Many people add to their positive data log for months or even years. Keeping the log provides them with a useful antidote to the natural tendency to be overly self-critical.

Be sure to refer to your positive data log often, even daily, or several times each day when you are bedding down new beliefs. Keep it in your desk or handbag or wherever you are most likely to be able to access it during the day. As a general rule, you can't look at your positive data log too often!

Book III

Cognitive Behavioural Therapy

Chapter 5

Setting Your Sights on Goals

· ·

In This Chapter

▶ Defining your goals for emotional and behavioural change

▶ Living a healthy lifestyle

▶ Filling your time constructively

▶ Looking after the positive changes you've made

· ·

*I*f we had to define the purpose of therapy, its purpose would *not* be to make you a straighter-thinking, more rational person. Rather, the purpose of therapy is to help you achieve your goals. Thinking differently is one way of achieving those goals. CBT can help you change the way you feel and behave. This chapter helps you define your goals and suggests some sources of inspiration for change.

Setting Your Sights on Goals

Aaron Beck, founder of cognitive therapy, says that CBT is whatever helps you move from your problems to your goals. This definition emphasises the pragmatic and flexible nature of CBT, and encourages clients and therapists to select from a wide range of psychological techniques to help achieve goals in therapy. The crucial message though, is that effective therapy is a constructive process, helping you to achieve your goals.

Putting SPORT into your goals

Many people struggle to overcome their problems because their goals are too vague. To help you develop goals that are clearer and easier to set your sights on, we developed the acronym SPORT, which stands for:

  ✔ **Specific:** Be precise about where, when, and/or with whom you want to feel or behave differently. For example, you may want to feel concerned rather than anxious about making a presentation at work, and during the presentation you may want to concentrate on the audience rather than on yourself.

✔ **Positive:** State your goals in positive terms, encouraging yourself to develop more, rather than less, of something. For example, you may want to gain more confidence (rather than become less anxious) or to hone a skill (rather than make fewer mistakes).

Think of therapy as a journey. You're more likely to end up where you want to be if you focus on getting to your destination rather than on what you're trying to get away from.

✔ **Observable:** Try to include in your goal a description of a behavioural change that you can observe. Then, you can tell when you've achieved your goal because you can see a specific change.

If you're finding it hard to describe an observable change, think to yourself: 'How would the Martians, looking down from Mars, know I felt better simply by watching me?'

✔ **Realistic:** Make your goals clear, concrete, realistic, and achievable. Focus on goals that are within your reach, and that depend on change from you rather than from other people. Try to visualise yourself achieving your goals. Realistic goals help you to stay motivated and focused.

✔ **Time:** Set a timeframe to keep you focused and efficient in your pursuit of a goal. For example, if you've been avoiding something for a while, decide when you plan to tackle it. Specify how long and how often you wish to carry out a new behaviour, such as going to the gym three times a week for an hour at a time.

Some goals, such as recovering from severe depression, can vary a lot in terms of how long they take to achieve. Setting schedules too rigidly can lead you to become depressed or angry at your lack of progress. So, set your deadlines firmly but flexibly, accept yourself if you don't achieve them on time, and persevere!

Homing in on how you want to be different

Defining your goals and writing them down on paper forms the foundation of your CBT programme. This section helps you identify how you may want to feel and act differently.

Setting goals in relation to your current problems

To set a goal concerned with overcoming an emotional problem, you first need to define the problem, which we talk about in Chapter 2 (where we explore unhealthy emotions and behaviours and their healthy counterparts).

A *problem statement* contains the following components:

- ✔ Feelings/emotions
- ✔ A situation or theme that triggered your emotion
- ✔ The way you tend to act in the situation when you feel your problem emotion

Defining how you want to feel as an alternative

CBT can help you attain changes in the way you feel emotionally. For example, you may decide that you want to feel sad and disappointed, rather than depressed and hurt, about the end of your marriage.

Aiming to feel 'okay', 'fine', or 'relaxed' may not fit the bill if you're dealing with a tough situation. Feeling negative emotions about negative events is realistic and appropriate. Keep your goals realistic and helpful by aiming to have healthy emotions, and try to maintain an appropriate level of intensity of your emotions when faced with difficult events (take a look at Chapter 2 for more on healthy emotions).

Defining how you want to act

The second area of change that CBT can help you with is your behaviour. For example, after going through a divorce, you may decide that you want to begin seeing your friends and return to work, instead of staying in bed and watching TV all day.

You can also include changes to your mental activities within your goal, such as refocusing your attention on the outside world or allowing *catastrophic* (upsetting or worst-case scenario) thoughts to pass through your mind.

Maximising your motivation

Motivation has a funny way of waxing and waning, just like the moon. Luckily, you don't necessarily have to feel motivated about changing before you can take steps forward. Motivation often follows rather than precedes positive action – often people find they 'get into' something once they've started. This section suggests some ways to generate motivation and encourages you to carry on working towards goals in the temporary absence of motivation.

Lots of people find change difficult. Your motivation may flag sometimes, or you may not ever be able to imagine overcoming your difficulties. If either of these situations sounds familiar to you, you're in good company. Many people draw on sources of inspiration when starting with, and persevering through, the process of overcoming emotional problems. Sources of encouragement worth considering include the following:

Book III

Cognitive Behavioural Therapy

- ✔ **Role models who have characteristics you aspire to adopt yourself.** For example, you may know someone who stays calm, expresses feelings to others, is open-minded to new experiences, or is assertive and determined. Whether real-life or fictional, alive or dead, known to you or someone you've never met, choose someone who inspires you and can give you a model for a new way of being.

- ✔ **Inspirational stories of people overcoming adversity.** Ordinary people regularly survive the most extraordinary experiences. Stories of their personal experiences can lead you to make powerful personal changes.

Focus on taking a leaf out of an inspirational individual's book, not on comparing yourself negatively with someone's 'superior' coping skills.

- ✔ **Images and metaphors.** Thinking of yourself as, for example, a sturdy tree withstanding a strong wind blowing against you, which can be an inspiring metaphor to represent you withstanding unreasonable criticism.

- ✔ **Proverbs, quotes, and icons.** Use ideas you've heard expressed in novels, religious literature, films, songs, or quotes from well-respected people, to keep you reaching for your goals.

Completing a cost–benefit analysis

Carrying out a *cost–benefit analysis* (CBA) to examine the pros and cons of something can help galvanise your commitment to change. You can use a CBA to examine the advantages and disadvantages of a number of things, such as:

- ✔ **Behaviours:** How helpful is this action to you? Does it bring short-term or long-term benefits?

- ✔ **Emotions:** How helpful is this feeling? For example, does feeling guilty or angry really help you?

- ✔ **Thoughts, attitudes, or beliefs:** Where does thinking this way get you? How does this belief help you?

- ✔ **Options for solving a practical problem:** How can this solution work out? Is this really the best possible answer to the problem?

When using a CBA form similar to the one shown in Table 5-1, remember to evaluate the pros and cons:

- ✔ In the short-term
- ✔ In the long-term
- ✔ For yourself
- ✔ For other people

Table 5-1	The Cost–Benefit Analysis Form
Costs and Benefits of:	
Costs (Disadvantages)	*Benefits (Advantages)*

Try to write CBA statements in pairs, particularly when you're considering changing the way you feel, act, or think. What are the *advantages* of feeling anxiety? And the *disadvantages*? Write down pairs of statements for what you feel, do, or think *currently,* and for other, healthier alternatives. Tables 5-2 and 5-3 show completed CBA forms.

Table 5-2   Cost–Benefit Analysis: 'Costs and Benefits of Saying What Comes Into My Mind and Paying Attention to the Conversation'

Costs	*Benefits*
I may end up saying something stupid.	I won't have to think so much and I might be able to relax.
I may not come up with the best thing to say.	I can be more spontaneous.
I may end up running off at the mouth and people might not like me.	I'll be able to concentrate on what's being said and I won't seem so distracted.

Book III

Cognitive Behavioural Therapy

Table 5-3   Second Cost–Benefit Analysis: 'Costs and Benefits of Preparing in My Head What I'm Going to Say Before Speaking'

Costs	*Benefits*
I end up feeling very tired after going out.	I can make sure I don't say something foolish.
I can't relax into the conversation.	I may think of something funny or entertaining to say.
Sometimes, I feel like the conversation moves on before I've had the chance to think of the right thing to say.	I can take more care not to offend people.

After you've done a CBA, review it with a critical eye on the 'benefits' of staying the same and the 'costs' of change. You may decide that these costs and benefits are not strictly accurate. The more you can boost your sense that change can benefit you, the more motivated you can feel in working towards your goals.

Write out a motivational flashcard that states the *benefits of change* and *costs of staying the same*, drawn from your cost–benefit analysis. You can then refer to this to give yourself a motivational boost when you need it.

A large aspect of achieving a goal, whether learning to play the guitar or building up a business, is about accepting temporary discomfort in order to bring long-term benefit.

Recording your progress

Keeping records of your progress can help you stay motivated. If your motivation flags, spur yourself on towards your goal by reviewing how far you've come. Use a problem-and-goal sheet like that in Figure 5-1, to specify your problem and rate its intensity. Then define your goal, and rate your progress towards achieving it. Do this at regular intervals, such as every one or two weeks.

1. **Identify the problem you're tackling.** Include information about the emotions and behaviours related to a specific event. Remember, you're feeling an *emotion* about a *situation*, leading you to *behave* in a certain way.

2. **At regular intervals, evaluate the intensity of your emotional problem and how much it interferes with your life.** 0 equals no emotional distress, and no interference in your life, and 10 equals maximum possible emotional distress, at great frequency, with great interference in your life.

3. **Fill in the goal section, keeping the theme or situation the same, but specifying how you wish to feel and act differently.**

4. **Rate how close you are to achieving your goal.** 0 equals no progress whatsoever, at any time, and 10 means that the change in your emotion and behaviour is completely and consistently achieved.

Change doesn't happen overnight, so don't rate your progress any more frequently than weekly. Look for *overall* changes in the *frequency*, *intensity*, and *duration* of your problematic feelings and behaviours.

Figure 5-1:
The
Problem-
and-Goal
Sheet.

Using the form below, identify one of the main problems you wish to work on in therapy. A problem statement includes information about the emotions and behaviour related to a specific situation or event. For example: *'Feeling depressed about the end of my marriage leading me to become withdrawn and spend until around 6pm each day in bed'.* or *'Feeling anxious about social situations leading me to avoid going to pubs, restaurants, and meetings, or to be extremely careful about what I say if I do socialise'.* Think of writing your problem statement as filling in blanks: Feeling _____ (emotion) about _____ (situation), leading me to _____ (behaviour). Use the same format to identify the goal you would like to achieve, but this time specify how you would like things to be different in terms of your emotions and behaviour.

PROBLEM No. ☐

DATE:	DATE:	DATE:	DATE:
RATING:	RATING:	RATING:	RATING:
DATE:	DATE:	DATE:	DATE:
RATING:	RATING:	RATING:	RATING:

Rate the severity of your emotional problem 0 - 10. **0 = No distress/No impairment in ability to function 10 = Extreme distress/Virtuality unable to function in any area of life**

GOAL RELATED TO PROBLEM

DATE:	DATE:	DATE:	DATE:
RATING:	RATING:	RATING:	RATING:
DATE:	DATE:	DATE:	DATE:
RATING:	RATING:	RATING:	RATING:

Rate how close you are to achieving your goal. **0 = No progress whatsoever 10 = Goal achieved and sustained consistently**

Mercurial desires

People often find that they want to change their goals on a whim or a fancy. For example, you may have a goal of being more productive and advancing your position at work. Then, after going to a Summer Solstice rave, you decide that really your goal is to be free and to travel the world, communing with the essence of life. What you choose as your definitive goal is up to you. But be wary of being influenced too easily by whatever's foremost in your mind. Constantly abandoning former goals and adopting new ones can be a mask for avoidance and procrastination. Use the SPORT acronym, as described at the start of this chapter, to assess the durability and functionality of each of your chosen goals.

Heading for a Healthier and Happier Life

The way that you think influences the way that you feel and behave. How you behave also influences the way you end up feeling and thinking . . . and round and round the cycle goes.

So, how you *live* from day to day has an effect on your overall mood. In this chapter, we look at what makes a lifestyle *healthy*. Developing a healthy lifestyle can contribute enormously to keeping you in tiptop physical and psychological condition.

We use the term 'healthy' to mean looking after your physical self, which includes exercise, sleep, sex, your eating habits, and keeping your living environment a pleasant place to be. Psychological health is about doing things that give you a sense of enjoyment and achievement, holding helpful and balanced attitudes toward life, and building satisfying relationships.

Make looking after yourself a priority rather than an afterthought. An ounce of prevention really is worth a pound of cure.

Planning to Prevent Relapse

Once you start to recover from your problems, your next step is to devise a plan to prevent a resurgence of symptoms – to ensure that you don't suffer a *relapse*. A relapse basically means that you return to your original state of mind. An important part of your relapse prevention plan is nurturing yourself and guarding against falling back into old, unhelpful lifestyle habits, such as working too late, eating unhealthily, drinking too much caffeine and alcohol, or isolating yourself. The last part of this chapter deals with relapse prevention in depth. The following sections provide some pointers on how you can make your life fuller and how to take care of yourself.

Filling In the Gaps

When you start to recover from some types of emotional problems, such as depression, anxiety, or obsessions, you may find that you have a considerable amount of spare time available to you, which previously your symptoms took up. Indeed, you may be astounded to find out just how much energy, attention, and time, common psychological difficulties can actually consume.

Finding constructive and enjoyable things to do to fill in the gaps where your symptoms once were is important. Keeping yourself occupied with pursuits that are meaningful to you gives you a sense of well-being and leaves less opportunity for your symptoms to re-emerge.

Choosing absorbing activities

Activities that you used to enjoy may take a back seat while you wrestle with your problems. However, maybe you can think of some new activities that interest you and that you may like to try. The following are a few pointers to help you generate ideas about what activities and hobbies you can begin building into your life:

Book III

Cognitive Behavioural Therapy

- Make a list of things you used to do and would like to start doing again.

- Make a separate list of new activities that you'd like to try.

- Try to create a balance between activities that do and don't involve physical exercise.

- Include everyday activities like cooking, reading, DIY, and keeping up social contacts. These activities are often neglected when you're overwhelmed by symptoms.

- Choose to focus on around five activities to revive or pursue, depending on how full your life is with work and family commitments.

In case you're still at a loss as to what you want to do, here's some ideas – but remember that this list is by no means exhaustive: Antiques, art appreciation, astronomy, baking, chess, dance, drama, dressmaking, enamelling, fishing, football, gardening, golf, interior decorating, kick boxing, languages, motoring, painting, pets (Rhena has a cat called Jack, he has transformed her life!), quizzes, tennis, voluntary work, wine-tasting, writing . . . the list goes on!

Don't just think about it! Decide *when* you're going to begin doing your chosen activities. If you don't give yourself a concrete start date, forgetting about things or putting them off can be all too easy.

Matchmaking your pursuits

You know yourself better than anyone else, so you're the best person to judge which hobbies can bring you the most satisfaction. Try to match your recreational pursuits to your character. If you know that you love paying attention to detail, you may enjoy needlework or making jewellery. Extreme sports may appeal to you if you've always been good at physical activities and like adrenalin rushes. Conversely, if you've never been very musical, taking up an instrument may not be the best choice for you.

We recommend that you stretch yourself by trying things that you haven't done before. Who knows – you may end up really liking the new activities. However, if you choose pursuits that are too far removed from your fundamental personality or natural abilities, you might lose heart and abandon them.

Putting personal pampering into practice

Oh, the joys of a good massage, a hot foamy bath, or a trip to the opera (okay, we understand that not everyone feels the same about opera). You can't overcome your problems without a significant degree of personal effort. Congratulate yourself for your hard work, and treat yourself to a few nice things.

Take care of yourself on a day-to-day basis, and look out for times when you deserve a few extra special treats. Friday nights are a good time to regularly treat yourself after a long week at work.

Your treats don't have to be expensive. You can do many small things – such as putting some cut flowers in a vase, making your living space smell nice, playing pleasant music, watching a favourite film or television programme – which are free or inexpensive.

Consider pampering yourself as part of your *relapse-prevention plan* (see the last few sections of this chapter for more on relapse prevention). Even doing little things like using nice bath oils or eating a special meal once a week can remind you to value yourself and to treat yourself with loving care.

Overhauling Your Lifestyle

We suggest that you take a close look at the way you currently live and decide on the things that are good, and the things that are not so good for you. Be sure to consider the following key areas:

✔ **Regular and healthy eating.** The principle is relatively simple: Have three meals and a couple of healthy snacks a day, with plenty of fruit, vegetables, and wholegrain foods. Minimise your consumption of sugar and simple carbohydrates, like white bread, and don't overdo the saturated fat. Have what you fancy in moderation. If you think you need extra help with healthy eating, talk to your doctor, who can refer you to a dietician.

Try keeping a record of everything you eat, for a week. Identify where you can make positive changes towards eating more regularly and more healthily.

✔ **Regular exercise.** Ample evidence suggests that exercise is very beneficial for both your mental health and your physical health. Aim for at least three sessions of physical exercise, lasting 20-30 minutes each, per week. Consult your doctor if you haven't exercised regularly for some time.

✔ **Leisure pursuits.** Include activities that bring you pleasure or satisfaction and aren't attached to your job or home life. Remind yourself of what you used to do and of what you've been meaning to do, when choosing activities and hobbies.

✔ **Social contact.** Get to know new people or reinvigorate your existing relationships. Sometimes relationships suffer as a result of psychological illness; read more about getting intimate further on in this chapter, which address issues of intimacy and communication.

✔ **Vitally-absorbing interests.** Get involved with causes you feel are important, such as recycling or animal rights campaigns.

✔ **Resource management.** This catch-all may involve you doing a budget, getting an accountant, developing a system to deal with your household bills efficiently, renegotiating your working hours, or hiring a cleaner.

Ideally, you can create a nice balance between the different aspects of your life so that none is neglected.

Look at the things you do on a daily or weekly basis, and decide what you're doing *too much of*, such as drinking in the pub, working late, or eating fast food. Try to replace some of these activities with others that you're doing too little of, such as getting exercise, spending time with your family, or studying.

Walking the walk

The best-laid plans of mice and men are apt to go astray. And how.

You're really serious about making positive changes to your lifestyle; however, just thinking about it and setting out plans aren't enough – although they *are* a great first step. The next step is to *do it*! Actions speak louder than words, so act on your intentions sooner, rather than later.

Book III

Cognitive Behavioural Therapy

We cannot emphasise enough about the multiple benefits of you taking regular exercise. It's so darn good for you, in so darn many ways. If you don't believe us, try it out! Exercise a few times each week and see if you don't end up feeling better – we defy you to contradict us.

You can exercise in ways that don't involve going to the gym. Gardening, walking, cycling, dancing, and housework, all give your body a workout. Find out which activities suit you, your interests, your schedule, and your current level of fitness – *and do them!*

Using your head

Perhaps your emotional problems get in the way of your work or study. Maybe your difficulties interfere with you making progress in your career or changing jobs – after all, many people with psychological problems also experience work and education difficulties.

Start to set goals for how you'd like your work or academic life to develop. Build a realistic plan of action for reaching your professional or educational goals by following these steps:

1. **Start your plan by considering where you'd like to be and what you need to do in terms of study and training to get there.**

2. **Break your ultimate goal down into smaller, bite-sized chunks.** You may need to gather references, build a portfolio, write a CV, or apply for a loan or grant to fund your studies.

3. **Investigate facilities for learning.** Use the Internet to look for specific courses, contact universities and colleges for a prospectus, see a careers advisor, or visit an employment agency.

4. **Build your study or training plan into your life with a view to keeping a balance between study, work, social, and leisure activities.**

5. **Set a realistic time frame to achieve your goal.** Pushing yourself to get there too fast is likely to cause you stress, impair your enjoyment of the journey to your goal, or even lead you to abandon your goal altogether.

Go out and study just for the sake of it. Developing a new skill or exploring a new subject area can be highly rewarding for you, whether or not the studying is applicable directly to your work. Adult education classes and intensive workshops can be a great way for you to explore new topics – and for you to meet new people, which can be beneficial if your social life has suffered during your illness.

Talking the talk

Emotional problems can have a detrimental effect on your personal relationships. Sometimes, your symptoms can be so all-consuming that you have little space to show interest in what others around you are feeling and doing. Therefore, you may need to do some work to rebuild your existing relationships when you feel better.

When your symptoms subside, you may want to give more of your attention to the other people in your life. This may involve playing with your kids, talking to your partner about how your problems have affected your relationship (without blaming yourself, of course), or renewing contact with friends and extended family.

People in your life are likely to be aware of how troubled you've been and they may notice recent positive changes in you. Let them talk about the changes they've noticed within you. Listening to other people's experiences of your problems can help to reinforce the idea that the other people in your life care about you. Improving your relationships and simply spending time in the company of other people can help you keep your symptoms at bay. You can also involve others in your relapse-prevention plan, if appropriate.

A supportive relationship with a significant other can help you to stay healthy. This relationship doesn't need to be a romantic relationship – platonic relationships are important as well. Research has shown that having a network of social contacts, as well as having someone you're able to confide in, helps to reduce your emotional problems in general.

It's never too late for you to make friends. Even if your problems have led you to isolate yourself, now's the time to go out and meet people. Be patient and give yourself the time and opportunity to start forming good relationships. Go to where the people are! Join some clubs or classes.

Getting intimate

Your specific problems may lead you to avoid intimate relationships with other people. You may have been too preoccupied by your problems to be able to form or maintain intimate relationships. If you want to be close to others, you've got to get your head round the concept of letting others into your life. Allowing yourself to trust others enough to share at least some of your personal history can make you feel closer to your listeners. Intimacy is a give-and-take affair – ideally, the balance is roughly equal.

If you think you're incapable of getting truly close to someone else, you're probably wrong. Give other people – and yourself – a chance to be honest with one another. Reciprocally enhancing relationships usually evolve naturally, but

Book III

Cognitive Behavioural Therapy

you need to be open to the possibilities of intimate relationships for this evolution to happen.

Sex and other animals

Your interest in sex, regardless of your age or gender, may diminish as a result of your emotional disturbance. Many people dealing with emotional problems can lose interest in sex. When you begin to feel better, getting your sex life back on track may take some time.

Sex drive is a bit like appetite: You don't always realise you're hungry until you start eating.

Sometimes, couples stop having sex regularly but don't ever discuss the change. Often, both partners get into a routine of not being sexually intimate and try to ignore the problem. Some people are too shy to talk about sex or feel guilty for having lost their interest in sex. Additionally, many people are afraid of discussing their loss of sex drive with their doctors, or friends, for fear of embarrassment.

Taking the plunge and talking about changes in your sex drive with your therapist or doctor can be very worthwhile. Your therapist or doctor may offer you useful suggestions and may even tell you that certain medications you've been taking may contribute to your decreased interest in sex.

Loss of interest in sexual activities is a normal side effect of certain experiences. Many psychological disorders, such as depression, post-traumatic stress disorder, obsessional problems, health anxiety, postnatal depression, and low self-esteem, can impact on your ability to feel aroused. Bereavement, physical illness, and stress can also put your sexual desires on the backburner. Fortunately, decreased libido is often temporary.

Talking about sex

'Birds do it, bees do it, even educated fleas do it', but sometimes the issue of sex is like an elephant in a tutu doing the dance of the seven veils in the middle of your bedroom. Both you and your partner can end up studiously ignoring its presence, even though it's right there, begging for your attention.

If you can't bring yourself to broach the topic of sex with your partner as you begin to recover, you can do a few things to help rekindle the flames of desire. Try some of the following:

✔ **Resume non-sexual physical contact.** Hold hands, stroke your partner's arm or back as you chat, sit closer to each other on the sofa, and reintroduce cuddling. Non-sexual contact can help you to get comfortable with touching one another again, and set the scene for a revival of more intimate contact.

✔ **Kiss.** If you've got into the habit of a quick kiss on the cheek as you leave the house, aim for the mouth instead. Kissing is a powerful form of communication. It also can be highly sensual and enjoyable.

✔ **Create opportunities.** Getting into bed at the same time before you're both bone tired, and then snuggling up, can create a non-threatening reintroduction to sexual relations.

✔ **Take the pressure off.** If you tell yourself that you've *got* to get aroused or you've *got* to have sex tonight, you can work yourself into such a state that all spontaneity is quashed. Try to take the attitude that if it happens, it happens.

✔ **Give yourself a chance to get in the mood.** You don't have to feel very aroused to start getting intimate. Sometimes you may need to have a lot of low-level sexual contact like stroking, petting, and kissing before you're ready to go further. Be patient with yourself and try to talk to your partner about how you're feeling. Sometimes, just talking about sex is enough to relax you to let nature take its course.

✔ **Take the onus off orgasm.** Any sexual or close physical contact can be fulfilling. You may not be able to achieve orgasm for some time, so instead enjoy foreplay like you may have done in the early stages of your relationship. For example, kissing is a very powerful form of expression. You can really get your sex life back on track, and you may even be able to make it better than it was before, if you give a lot of attention to the preliminaries.

Whatever turns you on is worth exploring further. Talk to your partner: You may be able to find things that can help you both get more in the mood for lovemaking. Try to be open-minded about your sex life. Just be careful to set your own personal boundaries about what turns you on and what has the opposite effect.

Book III

Cognitive Behavioural Therapy

Psychological Gardening: Maintaining Your CBT Gains

Looking after the positive changes you've made is a major part of helping you stay emotionally healthy. You can nurture your belief and behaviour changes everyday. The process is a bit like watering a plant to keep it thriving. The more care you take of yourself both generally and specifically – for example, by practising your new ways of thinking and acting – the more you reduce the chances of returning to your old problematic ways.

Six steps for talking and listening

Good relationships are sustained by thoughtfulness, effort, and time. Many of the changes in your relationships may occur naturally because as you become less preoccupied with your problems you are more able to focus on the world around you.

Effective communication is the cornerstone of good relationships. Bear in mind that you can communicate not only with what you say, but also with how you *listen*. Your body language can also convey a message to others. Things like eye contact and physical contact are also means of getting the message across. A simple hug can really mean a lot.

Try the following six steps to improve your communication skills:

1. When you have something important to discuss with someone, find a mutually good time to do so. Make sure that you both have ample time to talk and listen to each other.

2. Use 'I feel' statements, such as '*I feel* disappointed that you came home late', rather than blaming language, such as '*You* made me so angry'.

3. If you want to give negative feedback to someone about his behaviour, keep it clear, brief, and specific. Remember to also give positive feedback about the behaviour you want to reinforce, for example thank your partner for calling to say he'll be late.

4. After you've given positive or negative feedback, ask the person how he feels and what he thinks about what you've said.

5. Don't fall into the trap of thinking that a right or true way of doing things exists. Accept that different people value different things. Seek compromises when appropriate. Listen to the other person's point of view.

6. Be prepared to accept negative feedback and criticism from others. Look for points that you agree with in what the other person is saying. Give the other person a chance to air his views before you get defensive or counteractive. Give yourself time to assess the feedback you receive.

Knowing your weeds from your flowers

Think of your life as a garden. Unhealthy, rigid ways of thinking and corresponding behaviours like avoidance, rituals, safety strategies, perfectionism, and trying too hard to please (to name but a few) are the weeds in your garden. The flowers consist of your healthy flexible thinking, such as acceptance of self and others, acceptance of uncertainty, and allowing yourself to be fallible, and your healthy behaviours, such as assertion, communication, problem-solving, and exposure.

No garden's ever weed-free. Planting desirable plants isn't enough. You need to continuously water and feed the flowers, and uproot the weeds to keep your garden healthy. If you tend your garden regularly, the weeds don't get a chance to take hold because there you are with your trowel, digging 'em out at the first sign of sprouting. Depending on the virulence of your weeds, you may need to use some weedkiller from time to time in the form of appropriately prescribed medication. So, *know thy garden*.

After you've identified your unhealthy behaviours and thinking tendencies, and bedded down some healthy alternatives, you can keep a better look out for emerging weeds and keep an eye on the health of your flowers.

Ask yourself the following questions, which can help you to know your weeds from your flowers:

- ✔ **What areas do I most need to keep working at in order to maintain my CBT gains?** The areas you identify are those where weeds are most likely to first take root.

- ✔ **What CBT strategies aid me most in overcoming my emotional problems?** Think about the new attitudes you've adopted towards yourself, the world, and other people. These areas are your tender, new flowers – their delicate shoots need your attention.

- ✔ **What are the most useful techniques that I've applied to overcoming my emotional problems?** Think about the new ways of behaving that you've adopted (daffodils) and the old ways of behaving that you've dropped (thistles). Stick to your new healthy behaviours and be aware of slipping back into your former unhealthy patterns of behaviour. Use an activity schedule to help you carry out beneficial routines and behaviours.

Write down the answers to the preceding questions so that you can look at them often to remind yourself of where to put in the hoe.

Working on weeds

This section deals with weed-related topics and offers you some suggestions on how to stop weeds from taking over your garden, anticipating where weeds are likely to grow, and how to manage the weeds that keep coming back.

Out of the corner of your eye, you see a weed sticking up its insidious little head. You may be tempted to ignore the weed. Maybe it'll go away or whither and die on its own. Unfortunately, weeds seldom eliminate themselves. Assume that any weed you identify needs killing.

A common reason for ignoring resurging problems is shame. If you feel ashamed that your problems are recurring, you may try to deny the problems, and you may avoid seeking help from professionals, or support from friends or family. You may be less likely to make a personal effort to whack down the problems in the way you did the first time.

Book III

Cognitive Behavioural Therapy

Setbacks are a normal part of development. Human beings have emotional and psychological problems just as readily as physical problems. You don't have to be ashamed of your psychological problems, any more than you should be ashamed of an allergy or a heart condition.

Another common reason for people ignoring the reappearance of psychological problems is *catastrophising* or assuming the worst (head to Chapter 1 for more info on thinking errors). Many people jump to the conclusion that a setback equals a return to square one – but this certainly doesn't have to be the case. You can take the view that a problem you conquered once is at a fundamental disadvantage when it tries to take hold again. This is because you know your enemy. Use what you already know about recognising and arresting your old thinking and behaviour to help you pluck that weed before it gets too far above the ground.

Some emotional and psychological problems are more tenacious than others, for example bipolar disorder, obsessive-compulsive disorder (OCD), and eating disorders. Just because a problem's tenacious, it doesn't mean that it has to take over your life, or even cause you too much interference in your life. However, you can expect to meet tenacious problems again. Keep up with treatment strategies even when your original problems are no longer in evidence; doing so will help prevent a relapse.

For example, if you have a history of depression, you may notice that weeds are popping up when you do some of the following:

- ✔ Begin to think in a pessimistic way about your future and your ability to cope with daily hassles.

- ✔ Ruminate on past failures and on how poor your mood is.

- ✔ Lose interest in seeing your family and friends.

- ✔ Have difficulty getting out of bed in the morning, and you want to sleep more during the day instead of doing chores or taking exercise.

If you spot these stinging nettles making their way into your otherwise floral existence, try some of these techniques:

- ✔ Challenge your pessimistic thinking bias, and remind yourself that your thoughts are not accurate descriptions of reality but symptoms of your depression. (See Chapter 1 for more on thinking errors.)

- ✔ Interrupt the rumination process by using task-concentration and mindfulness techniques. (We also explain these in Chapter 1.)

- ✔ Continue to meet with family and friends, despite your decreased interest, on the basis that doing so makes you feel better rather than worse.

- ✔ Force yourself out of bed in the morning and keep an activity schedule. (Have a read of Chapter 2 for more on activity schedules.)

Whatever your specific problems, follow the preceding example: Write down your descriptions of anticipated weeds and some specific weed-killing solutions to have at hand.

Don't ignore signs that your problems are trying to get their roots down. Be vigilant. But also be confident in your ability to use the strategies that worked before and in your ability to use them time and again, whenever you need to.

Spotting where weeds may grow

To prevent relapse, become aware of where your weeds are most likely to take root.

Most people, regardless of their specific psychological problems, find themselves most vulnerable to setbacks when they're run down or under stress. If you're overtired and under a lot of environmental stress, such as with work deadlines, financial worries, bereavement, or family/relationship difficulties, you can tend to be more prone to physical maladies, such as colds, 'flu, and episodes of eczema. Psychological problems are no different from physical ones in this regard: They get you when you're depleted and at alow ebb.

You may notice that some problems, like OCD, anxiety, and depression, are more evident when you're recovering from a physical illness. Recognising this common human experience can help you to combat any shame that you may feel, and to de-catastrophise a return of your symptoms.

Compile a list of situations and environmental factors that are likely to give your weeds scope to take on triffid-like power. For example, you may be able to pinpoint *environment triggers* for your depression, such as the following:

- Seasonal change, especially during autumn, when the days get shorter and the weather becomes colder.

- Sleep deprivation, due to work commitments, young children, illness or any other reason.

- Lack of exercise and physical activity.

- Day-to-day hassles piling up at once, such as the boiler breaking down in the same week that the washing machine explodes and a few extra bills arrive.

- Reduced opportunity for positive social interaction with friends and family.

You can also identify *interpersonal* triggers for your depression, such as the following:

- Tired and tetchy partner.

- Disagreements with your partner, children, parents, or extended family.

Book III

Cognitive Behavioural Therapy

✔ Critical or demanding boss.

✔ Disagreeable work colleagues.

Compile a list of high-risk situations for yourself, including situations that are most likely to fire up your unhealthy core beliefs, and situations that put you under strain. Creating such a list helps you to keep a clear idea of when you're most vulnerable to relapse and identify which psychological soil is the most fertile for weed growth.

Tending your flowers

Knowing when you're most prone to the symptoms of your original problems re-sprouting, is one thing. But knowing how to troubleshoot problems and prevent weeds from growing back, is another thing altogether.

The techniques, behavioural exercises, and experiments that helped you to overcome your problems in the first place will probably work again. So, go back to basics. Keep challenging your negative thinking and thinking errors. Keep exposing yourself to your feared situations. If your life is in turmoil due to inevitable things like moving house, work difficulties, or ill health, try to keep to your normal routine as much as possible.

Above all, even when things are going well, water your pansies! *Psychological watering* involves keeping up with your new ways of thinking and behaving, by giving yourself plenty of opportunity to consistently practice and test your new ways of living. Healthy, alternative beliefs take time to become habitual. Be patient with yourself and keep doing healthy things, even when you're symptom-free.

Developing a plan for times of crisis is another good idea. Here are some examples of what you may wish to include in your plan in the event of a potential relapse:

✔ Consider seeing your GP or psychiatrist to determine whether you need to go on medication for a while.

✔ Talk about your feelings to someone you trust. Pick a person who you can rely on to be supportive. Seek the help of a professional if talking to a friend or family member is not enough.

✔ Review your efforts from previous CBT work and re-use the exercises that were most effective.

✔ Keep your lifestyle healthy and active.

Planting new varieties

Digging out a weed (unhealthy belief and behaviour) is important, but you also need to plant a flower (healthy belief and behaviour) in its place. For example, if you notice that an old belief like 'I have to get my boss's approval, otherwise it proves that I'm unworthy' resurging, dispute the belief with arguments about the logic, helpfulness, and truth of the belief. (Chapter 3 has more about disputing unhealthy beliefs.)

You also need to plant a healthy belief, such as 'I want my boss's approval, but I don't have to get approval in order to be a worthwhile person'. You can strengthen the new belief by gathering arguments for the logic, helpfulness, and truth of the alternative healthy belief.

To strengthen new beliefs and behaviours further, you can devise situations that you know are likely to trigger your old unhealthy beliefs, and work at endorsing and acting according to your new beliefs instead. For example, deliberately seek your boss's feedback on a piece of work that you know is not your best. Resist your old behaviours that arise from the unhealthy belief that 'I must get my boss's approval', such as over-apologising or making excuses. Instead accept yourself for producing a less than good piece of work and take note of constructive criticism (refer to Chapter 3 for more about self-acceptance, and head to Chapter 4 for more techniques to strengthen new beliefs).

You can dig out unhealthy behavioural weeds and plant behavioural flowers in their place. For example, you may note that you drink more alcohol in the evenings as your mood lowers with the shortening days. You know that the onset of winter gets you down because you spend more time in the house. You can make the choice to stop drinking more than one glass of wine in the evening and start going to a local dance class or some other activity instead. You can also make a list of activities to do indoors, which will keep you occupied during the winter evenings.

Plant flowers in place of weeds, and tend those flowers to keep them hardy. Your weeds will have greater difficulty growing again where healthy flowers are thriving.

Being a compassionate gardener

What do you do if one of your precious plants isn't doing so well? If you notice that you've got blight on your prize rose, do you deprive it of food and water, or do you try to treat the disease? It's better not to abuse or neglect the plants in your garden for failing to thrive because if you do, they may only wilt further. You probably don't blame the plant for ill-health, so why should you blame yourself when you relapse?

Yes, take responsibility for anything that you may be doing that's self-defeating. And yes, accept responsibility for taking charge of your thinking, and ultimately, for engineering your own recovery. But, also take a compassionate view of yourself and your problems. Some of your unhealthy tendencies may have taken root partly due to childhood and early adulthood experiences.

Others may have some biological underpinnings. Some of your problems may have arisen from a trauma. You're not alone in having emotional problems. You're part of the human race, and there is no reason to expect more of yourself than you do of others with regard to staying emotionally healthy.

If you take a responsible, compassionate view of setbacks, you will be more able to help yourself get well again.

 You know that 'they' say you should talk to your plants to make them grow? Well, it may sound a bit daft, but maybe there's something in it. Try imagining yourself as a little pot plant on your kitchen windowsill. Talk to yourself encouragingly and lovingly when you notice your leaves drooping. Give yourself the types of messages that nurture rather than deplete you.

A happy gardener's checklist

Here are some points to help you prevent and overcome relapse. Use this checklist to stop your marigolds getting choked by bindweed.

- ✓ **Stay calm.** Remember that setbacks are normal. Everyone has ups and downs.

- ✓ **Make use of setbacks.** Your setbacks can show you the things that make you feel worse as well as what you can do to improve your situation. Look for preventive measures that you may have used to get better, but that you may have let slide when your symptoms reduced.

- ✓ **Identify triggers.** A setback can give you extra information about your vulnerable areas. Use this information to plan how to deal with predictable setbacks in the future.

- ✓ **Use what you have learned from CBT.** Sometimes you think that a setback means that you're never going to get fully well, or that CBT hasn't worked for you. But if the stuff you did worked once, then chances are, the same stuff can work again. Stick with it; you've nothing to lose by trying.

- ✓ **Put things into perspective.** Unfortunately, the more you've improved your emotional health, the worse black patches will seem in contrast. Review your improvement and try to see this contrast in a positive way – as evidence of how far you've come.

- ✓ **Be compassionate with yourself.** People often get down on themselves about setbacks. No one is to blame. You can help yourself get back on track by seeing a setback as a problem to overcome, rather than a stick with which to beat yourself.

✔ **Remember your gains.** Nothing can take your gains away from you. Even if your gains seem to have vanished, they can come back. You can take action to make this happen more quickly.

✔ **Face your fears.** Don't let yourself avoid whatever triggered your setback. You can devise further exposure exercises to help you deal with the trigger more effectively next time it happens.

✔ **Set realistic goals.** Occasionally, you may experience a setback because you bite off more than you can chew. Keep your exercises challenging but not overwhelming. Break bigger goals into smaller, mini-goals.

✔ **Hang on!** Even if you aren't able to get over a setback immediately, don't give up hope. With time and effort, you can come out of the setback. Don't hesitate to get appropriate support from friends and professionals if you think you need to. Remind yourself of times in the past when you felt as despairing and hopeless as you do now. Remind yourself of how you got out of the slump – and use the same strategies now.

Happy gardening!

Book III

Cognitive Behavioural Therapy

Book IV
Hypnotherapy

The 5th Wave   By Rich Tennant

"Remember, we're here to cheer him up, but don't be obvious."

In this part . . .

An important point to understand is that hypnosis and hypnotherapy are not the same thing. Hypnosis has been around since humans began to speak and involves going into a trance. Hypnotherapy uses the hypnotic trance to help you achieve a goal, or create a positive change in your thinking, to help solve a problem. Whereas hypnosis is centuries old, hypnotherapy, like other talking therapies, is a relatively recent practice. In many ways hypnotherapy is like counselling, but it is a different approach and much more rapid in producing changes. Hypnotherapy can help people to overcome a surprisingly wide range of habits, emotional problems, and phobias. Hypnotherapy can also dramatically improve performance for students taking exams, athletes wanting to improve their game, and creative artists wishing to deepen their abilities.

Here are the contents of Book IV at a glance:

Chapter 1

Taking a Separate View of Yourself

*Y*our mind is like a complex network of pipes, with each pipe having its own function and route. Some pipes are interconnected, and some pipes run on their own; some pipes are very small, and some pipes are extremely well hidden. In order for the network to run efficiently, all these pipes need to be kept in good working order; occasionally polished, or repaired, or even replaced. Most of the time, you can take care of your own plumbing, ensuring that it flows freely, by giving it a bit of a clean every now and then. Sometimes though, something happens that is beyond your ability to cope, and you need to call in a plumber to prevent the network from collapsing.

Think of your hypnotherapist as that plumber. The hypnotherapist's job is to ensure that your psychological pipework is flowing well, by cleaning and unblocking the pipes; sometimes replacing pipes that have been worn away, or repairing those that are leaking. It may be necessary for the hypnotherapist to go on a search to find a hidden and elusive pipe that is proving to be irksome. You may find that your hypnotherapist has to look at old plans of the pipework with you; or perhaps help you plan a new way to run those pipes. Whatever the job, your hypnotherapist is there to help you return the network to normal or even improve it in some way or other. In order to do this properly, just like any plumber, your hypnotherapist uses an impressive array of tools.

All the techniques we talk about in this chapter comprise only some of the tools available in your hypnotherapist's toolbox. Your hypnotherapist may use some of these tools and not use others. More than likely, you'll find your hypnotherapist using a combination throughout the time you are in therapy, in order to help you achieve your outcome.

Suggesting Solutions

Perhaps the earliest tool created for the hypnotherapist's toolbox is the use of suggestion. In hypnotherapy terms, a *suggestion* is a statement given in trance that something will happen. For example, your hypnotherapist may suggest that your hand is beginning to lose all sensation and become completely numb; or she may suggest that you feel completely relaxed as you think about walking across a bridge.

Simply put, a suggestion is the tool that helps you reprogramme your mind to respond in a healthier way to something. As we write this book, a very pertinent analogy springs to mind: We write what we think is best and submit it to our editors. They may then suggest that such-and-such a paragraph would sound better if it were written in such-and-such a way. We listen to their suggestions, and if we feel that this is sensible and safe, we make the appropriate changes. If we don't agree with what they suggest, we can reject the changes; after all, it's our book, and we're in control. In a similar way, you can view your hypnotherapist as being the editor of your mind. She's there to make suggestions to the way you write paragraphs of your life. You can choose to accept her suggestions, or to reject them if you want; after all, it's your mind and *you* are always in control.

A *post-hypnotic suggestion* is a suggestion given in trance, for you to make something happen when you are not in trance. Someone who has a problem bingeing on chocolate may be given the post-hypnotic suggestion that they enjoy a sense of self-control whenever they see chocolate, and choose not to eat it.

Like every other discipline in psychotherapy, hypnotherapy has developed over the years. As it has done so, the techniques it uses have developed too. This becomes very obvious in looking at the use of suggestions. Originally suggestions were given in a very direct manner, sometimes called *authoritarian*. After Milton Erickson came on the scene, a new approach to suggestions was placed in the hypnotherapist's toolbox: that of *indirect* or *permissive* suggestion. Both approaches are still used effectively in therapy, and both form the most basic tools in any hypnotherapist's collection.

Getting direct suggestions

A *direct* (or *authoritarian*) *suggestion* is one that gives an explicit instruction to do something. It leaves no room for error in what it asks you to do – for example, 'Stop smoking now' or 'You have no desire to eat sickly sweet chocolate cake' – and it really acts as a form of reprogramming.

Generally, your hypnotherapist uses direct suggestions if you are trying to give something up or want to make a specific change to a particular behaviour.

Convention has it that direct suggestions tend to be used with people who are used to taking or giving orders (such as soldiers, teachers, and policemen for example), and with people who have very logical minds (scientists, mathematicians, chessplayers, and so on). However, nowadays this convention seems to have fallen by the wayside, as many therapists use direct suggestion with a broad spectrum of people. It's down to your therapist's judgement as to which type of suggestion (direct or indirect) is most suitable for you.

In ye olden days, direct suggestion was virtually the only approach used in hypnotherapy. Today, most therapists now find only using direct suggestions to be restricting because many other approaches have been developed (as this chapter shows) that complement and enhance their use.

Going the indirect route

An *indirect* (or *permissive*) *suggestion* is one that allows your unconscious mind to explore a variety of possibilities before coming up with a response. For example, 'I wonder how soon it will be before you stop eating sickly sweet chocolate cake, and start to enjoy eating the right kind of healthy food you know will help you to lose weight?' An indirect suggestion induces an expectation of change without explicitly stating it. It also allows your unconscious mind to make that change in a way that fully suits you.

So why choose this approach over direct suggestion? The answer is simple. Some people find the direct approach threatening, and some people don't respond to authority very well, for one reason or another. Also, children are typically more responsive to an indirect approach. Indirect suggestions are seen to be less demanding and seemingly more comfortable to accept.

This indirect approach can be restricting, and many therapists now favour a mix-and-match approach when using suggestions.

Safely Splitting Your Mind with Dissociation

Have you ever been in two minds over something; one part of your mind thinking one thing and another thinking of something else? Have you ever had the experience of slipping into autopilot when you're doing something, hardly aware of what you're doing, because your concentration is focused elsewhere? These represent times when your mind appears to split into several parts, each seemingly operating independently from the whole. These are times when your mind experiences dissociation.

Book IV

Hypnotherapy

Some examples of everyday dissociation:

- Safely ironing whilst being completely engrossed in the television programme you're watching.
- Talking to a friend in a noisy and crowded bar and editing out the surrounding din as you focus on your conversation. (Or perhaps editing out your friend as you tune into someone else's more interesting conversation!)
- Driving your car without having to think about how you do it.
- Daydreaming in class as you tune out the boring drone of the teacher.

Dissociation is a natural phenomenon you experience every day of your life. It helps you to function in the world at large and allows you to cope when things start to get tough. And as your problems form part of your daily existence, it's only natural that dissociation can have a role in the development and maintenance of these, too.

Minding your associations

Your mind is like a computer. All your thoughts and behaviours form part of the computer program that is your life. Like all computer programs, your mind contains many subroutines that have specific functions with regard to running certain behaviours. You can say that when these subroutines are running, functioning independently of the rest of the program, your mind is dissociated.

When you're ironing, a subroutine (or dissociated part of your mind) allows you to carry out all the functions associated with ironing automatically, so that you don't have to consciously spend much time focussing on the ironing actions. Running the subroutine frees up the rest of your mind (the main body of the computer program as it were) to watch TV, or listen to the radio, or compose your shopping list, or plan a project.

As any computer programmer knows, a program doesn't necessarily run smoothly the first time you run it. This is true of the mind, too. When you encounter a regular situation in your life, a subroutine in your mind allows you to cope with it in whatever way is appropriate. Many of these subroutines are written, as you progress through life, to incorporate what you learn and experience. Some run smoothly, whilst others have little glitches in their programming (and some have major glitches!).

Whenever you encounter a new situation, your mind has to create a new subroutine on the spot in order to help you cope with it. Your mind may copy elements from older subroutines, or it may have to write the new one entirely from scratch. However your mind does it, it may or may not get it right straight away, so your life may proceed smoothly, or things may go spectacularly wrong.

Even when it does get it right, the new subroutine can sometimes corrupt older subroutines, or end up completely erasing them. Take the development of a flying phobia. You have comfortably flown many times before. Your mind holds a subroutine that allows you to relax as you are on the plane. Then, on one flight, you experience dreadful turbulence. Your mind has to come up with a new subroutine to allow you to cope in this situation. Part of this new program, rightly or wrongly, causes you to tense your muscles and become fearful. The next time you fly you may find that this new subroutine has either corrupted the old one, or completely overwritten it, and what you now experience is good, old-fashioned fear!

Associating hypnosis and dissociation

As you have probably worked out by now, there is a very close link between hypnosis and dissociation. To put it simply: when you dissociate, you enter into a trance state, and entering a trance state is the basis of hypnosis.

So, the ability to dissociate is very useful for us hypnotherapists, as it provides a means of helping patients into the trance. But it doesn't stop there. Not only can we use it to induce trance, but dissociation can be a very powerful therapeutic tool.

Gaining a more objective point of view

One of the main aspects of dissociation is that it allows you to leave feelings behind. This means that as the mind splits, it can separate you from feelings both good and bad. Okay, so why is this important?

Your feelings colour your experiences in life. How you feel at the time can determine how you respond to a specific situation, which, in turn, can affect how your mind handles that situation. The next time you experience the situation – or even think about it – the feelings you had at the time can come back and once again influence how you experience it this time round. The more this happens, the more likely you are to develop an automatic response to that situation, governed by your unconscious mind. Because your response becomes automatic, you may not understand why you respond the way you do, or be able to control yourself.

Book IV

Hypnotherapy

For example, when you think about, or meet someone you love, your feelings play a role in determining your behaviour – being soppy and childlike with a big grin spreading across your face, and so on. By the same token, when you meet someone you don't like, your feelings once again shape your behaviour – you become tense, use an aggressive tone of voice, show defensive or aggressive posturing, and so on.

Using dissociation hypnotherapy allows you to separate the feelings you experience with regard to the event, from the event itself. In this way you are able to examine the event more objectively, and consequently alter your response to it.

The words *subjective* and *objective* have a variety of meanings, so it's usefu to have an understanding of what they mean when used in hypnotherapy-speak:

- ✔ **Subjective:** Your feelings and emotions intervene and affect the way you assess a situation.

- ✔ **Objective:** Your feelings are put to one side, and you can assess a situation without involving your personal opinions.

Using dissociation in hypnotherapy can help you gain a more objective view of your problem without your emotions affecting your judgement. This separation is important so that you get a clearer picture of what is going on.

Supposing you're very stressed at work. The amount you have to do keeps piling up and you feel completely swamped. When you try to think about ways of managing your workload, those stressful feelings come flooding in and cloud your judgement. You can't see a way round it all and your stress increases. In hypnotherapy, your therapist can use a technique that dissociates you from those feelings, so that you can view that stressful situation as if it were on television. You can see what's going on, but you have none of those awful stressful feelings you had whenever you thought about the situation before. You are now viewing the situation objectively. Because the feelings are no longer interfering with your thoughts, you can see how to prioritise your workload or where you can delegate tasks. You realise that by having some leisure time you can actually work more effectively. The result: your stress levels drop!

Stepping away from yourself in stage dissociation

There are several different ways of working with dissociation in hypnosis. Your hypnotherapist may use it as a method of taking you into trance and as a very powerful therapy tool. One of the most common approaches to using it in either of these ways is an approach that is sometimes called *stage dissociation*. Simply put, *stage dissociation* is imagining seeing yourself – seeing yourself sitting in the chair you are in, seeing yourself enjoying a wonderful holiday, seeing yourself reading this book, and so on.

Dissociation is useful in a variety of hypnotherapy situations:

- ✔ **To take you into trance:** Your hypnotherapist may ask that you imagine stepping or floating out of your body, perhaps taking you on a journey to a favourite place. She may even ask you to imagine that you step out of your body and see yourself enjoying that wonderful holiday you are soon going to be taking. In other words, your therapist encourages you to daydream (and you won't get told off for doing so!).

- ✔ **As a therapy tool:** Your hypnotherapist may ask you to imagine seeing a scene projected onto a screen. For example, she may ask you to see yourself handling a specific situation in a certain way. Because you're dissociated from the image (you're watching it), you can view it more objectively, with few or no unwanted feelings.

This isn't all there is to dissociation. Far from it! Another very powerful use is in *parts therapy*.

Parts Therapy

How often have you said to yourself 'There's a part of me that . . .'; or 'I want to quit (some bad habit), but that rebel inside of me just won't let me do it'; or even 'Something just makes me lash out when . . .'? Whenever you come out with a statement like any of these, you're simply recognising that one aspect of your mind is responsible for a particular behaviour, or for making you feel a certain way, or for stopping you from doing certain things. As hypnotherapists, when we hear one of our patients coming out with a statement like these, we have a very good pointer as to the therapy technique we can use: parts therapy.

In *parts therapy*, the therapist isolates the subroutine that controls a particular behaviour, or emotional response, and does therapy on it. In effect, separating the *part* of the mind responsible for the problem. Why? Because it's the part of your mind that needs corrective action. It's the part of your mind supplying the reason you're going for therapy. It's the part of your mind annoying the heck out of you.

But hang on a moment. You also have a part responsible for your confidence, a part responsible for your ability to focus as you study, a part responsible for your ability to be courageous, and so on. You, or your hypnotherapist, may also want to work with more than one part. For example, you may be going to see your therapist because you have lost confidence when you're driving. Your hypnotherapist may want to help you get in touch with the part of your mind responsible for your confidence and help you to make it stronger; or perhaps just to bring that part back into contact with the rest of your mind so that once again you can enjoy (safely!) getting back behind the wheel.

Communicating and negotiating with a part of you

So, how do you and your therapist work with your different parts? In a nutshell, you isolate the offending part and simply talk to it. The basic process is as follows:

1. **Become aware of the part.**

   Your hypnotherapist may ask you to become aware of the part, perhaps by asking you to float it out of your body, or maybe by asking you to look at the palm of one of your hands and to imagine it resting there.

You may be asked to describe what the part looks like. Don't worry if you imagine it to look like something strange, such as a lump of coal or a cute bunny rabbit. It's your perception that counts!

By imagining the part in this way you are dissociating it – splitting it off from the rest of your mind. In this way, you can remove any unwanted feelings that accompany it.

2. **Find out what the part has been trying to do for you.**

   In hypnotherapy-speak, this is called *eliciting the positive intent*, or finding out what function this part has been serving in your life and why it's there.

   The simplest way of eliciting the positive intent is to ask that part what it has been up to and why it was doing that, and to then listen to what it has to say.

   No, we haven't taken leave of our senses and drifted into the mystical world of the arcane. This is all about helping you to gain insight into what that annoying little part of you is up to. The interesting thing is that once you gain insight, your symptom starts to collapse as you gain a measure of power over it.

3. **Thank the part for what it has been doing for you.**

   'What! Thank it! It's been such a pain for so long why should I do that?' Because it was originally trying to do something of benefit for you. Whatever benefit there may have been is long gone, but it is important that you keep a positive state of mind for the rest of the procedure. Ranting at it will hardly achieve that, will it?

4. **Negotiate with the part so that it is happy to change.**

   Your hypnotherapist may then suggest that you explain to the part that what it was doing for you is no longer needed. After this, you can ask it if it's willing to make a change in what it has been doing for you, so that it can do something that is more acceptable for you both. You may find that it says 'yes' straight away, or it may need some resource to help it.

   If the part needs some help, your hypnotherapist will then ask you to become aware of what resource the part wants (for example, more confidence), and to dissociate the part of your mind responsible for that resource in the same way as in Step 1.

   After you do this, you will be asked to give that resource to the first part you dissociated, perhaps by imagining that resource floating into and merging with it.

5. **Transform the part to serve a useful role.**

The part has finally said 'yes' to making the change and it now has the resources to do that. So now what? Your hypnotherapist will ask you to thank the part for agreeing to make the change – as this maintains the positive state of mind. To further enhance this mindset, your hypnotherapist will also ask you to make the image you have of the part more pleasing to you, perhaps by imagining a smiling face on it, by changing its colour, by changing the way it feels to you, or through some other means.

The part's agreeing to change, and your subsequent altering of its image sets in motion an unconscious process that allows the part to take on a new and more functional role; one that allows you to get on with your life *without* the problem you originally came to see your hypnotherapist about.

6. **Bring the part back home.**

   You're almost done! The final step is to bring that part back home. It is no good thinking 'Oh, I can just chuck this unnecessary part away.' Remember, it is a part of *you!* It may have been unintentionally naughty, disruptive, or whatever, but it has changed its ways and now holds a positive and functional role in your life. Just as the parent of a naughty child, after sending her to her room, gives her a hug and welcomes her back to the family after she has repented, so it is with your errant parts. Welcome them back and let them rejoin the family of your mind.

   To accomplish this, your hypnotherapist may ask you to imagine the new, improved part floating back inside you and once again becoming a fully functioning part of your own inner world. Or maybe she'll ask you to pull the part in with your hands, as you welcome it back inside yourself. However you are asked to do it, it is important that you bring the part back home. The next section explains why.

Bringing it all back together again: The importance of reintegration

So, what will happen if you don't bring that part back in or, as we like to say in hypnotherapy circles, reintegrate it? Remember that your mind has been split wide open, and if you don't reintegrate the split part, you're going to feel a little spaced out, to put it bluntly. After a period of time, you would feel normal again. But in the meantime something just as bad as the part you just got rid of may well take its place. So why risk it? Welcome that changed part back with open arms.

If you do come out of a dissociation technique feeling a little spaced out, let your hypnotherapist know. It may be that another part has dissociated without your being aware of it. That part may simply need to be brought back in; a very simple and straightforward process.

Travelling in Time

You may want to play the theme tune to Doctor Who as you read this section! As with the good Doctor (a television time traveller), time can play an important role in vanquishing your adversaries. Unlike the Doctor, your adversaries do not come in the form of Daleks and Cybermen (although the upcoming section on metaphor may turn that statement on its head). Instead, your foes come in the form of phobias, anxieties, and so on. Oh, and it's worth knowing that hiding behind the sofa won't make them go away either!

Your perception of time plays an important role in both the development and maintenance of your symptoms. How you perceive the past, the future, or even the passing of time, influences the way you handle the problems in your life. And with that in mind, your ever resourceful hypnotherapist has an array of tools to help you alter your perception of time: taking you back into the past, forward into the future, or helping you to alter your perception of the very passing of time.

Going back in time: Age regression techniques

Let's start by dispelling a myth: You do *not* have to be regressed for hypnotherapy to be successful! Despite what you may hear or be told, uncovering the past and dealing with it is not an essential part of getting over your symptom. Regression is simply another tool in the hypnotherapist's toolbox that can be very effective, when used at the right time and in the correct manner.

That little rant over and done with, let's get on with talking about what regression is. Very simply, *regression* is a technique in which your hypnotherapist takes you back in time, in your mind, to an event that actually happened or that happened in your imagination.

Considering the reasons for regression

Why does a hypnotherapist consider using regression? For several reasons, that may include:

✔ **You want to find out about the origin of your symptom.** You've had your symptom for a long while, but can't remember how, why, or when it started and want to.

Your therapist may suggest you find the origin of your symptom, believing the origin may well have an important bearing on helping you to finally remove the symptom.

Several seemingly small events may have compounded together to give you the symptom you're experiencing. And your therapist may suggest that in order to remove your symptom, you need to work through the individual components.

✔ **You want to change the way you perceive an event in your past.** You have experienced an event in the past, and as you think about it in the present, you find it disturbing; perhaps feeling disempowered, lacking in confidence, anxious, and so on. Your hypnotherapist may regress you to that time and allow you to change how you remember that event, or how you responded to it.

For example, you may remember being scared as a child by a particularly grumpy dentist who was nasty to you when you cried as you were being given an injection. The sense of powerlessness you felt then contributed greatly to the dental phobia you have in the present. You can be regressed to that time, but this time, as you remember it, you can be empowered to safely tell the dentist exactly what you think of her. Once you're empowered in the past, that sense of empowerment can be brought back into the present and sort out a major component of your phobia.

✔ **You want to remember an event from your past.** Perhaps you hid a particularly valuable piece of jewellery in a very safe place, so safe in fact that you can't remember where you put it!

You may have prevented yourself from experiencing some emotion connected to an event in your past, such as bereavement. Unfortunately, that emotion got locked away inside you, fuelling your symptom in the present. Your hypnotherapist may use a regression technique to let you re-experience the event and let out that emotion in safety. Because the emotion is no longer locked away, your symptom runs out of fuel and disappears.

✔ **You want to access a good feeling from your past.** Perhaps until recently you have always been very focused when you are playing tennis. However, recently your game has been very poor for one reason or another. Your hypnotherapist can use a regression technique to take you back to a time when you had those important feelings of focus; allowing you once again to get in touch with them, and to bring them back to the present and back into your game.

Book IV

Hypnotherapy

Defining the terms

It's useful to define some of the terms associated with this process of going back in time:

- ✔ **Regression:** Going back in time but viewing past events with your adult eyes. Through regression, it's as if you're watching yourself as the event unfolds. And yes, it's a form of dissociation (see the preceding 'Safely Splitting Your Mind with Dissociation' section).

- ✔ **Revivification:** Going back in time and experiencing an event as if it were happening to you now. Your reference to the present is lost and you act, think, and feel as you did during the event.

- ✔ **Past-life regression:** An interesting one this: Going back in time to a life you experienced before you were born into the one you are living now.

If you read the hypnotherapy literature, you see that the terms *regression* and *revivification* are often used interchangeably. More often than not, authors don't bother with the word 'revivification' and stick to using the word 'regression'. We have often wondered why this is, and apart from it being sheer laziness, have come to the conclusion that it is because 'revivification' is harder to spell than 'regression'!

Regression allows you to gain insight into what has gone before. And with insight comes a measure of control over your symptom. Once you have control, it's a relatively simple step to progress forward to finally ridding yourself of the symptom.

Going through the techniques

The time is right and you have agreed to be regressed. So how will your hypnotherapist do this? There are several ways to go about it:

- ✔ **Counting you back through the years.** Your hypnotherapist may take a formal approach, counting you back through the years as your mind drifts back through time.

   Your hypnotherapist may also use a technique that allows you to scan the years to find those times that contributed to your problem; asking your unconscious mind to lift one of your fingers each time you identify an event. The hypnotherapist may then use one of a variety of approaches to let you visit those times.

- ✔ **Letting your unconscious mind decide where to go.** Your unconscious mind is given the task of taking you back in time to an event that has relevance to the development of your problem.

- ✔ **Asking you to remember a specific time in your past.** This technique is nice and straightforward. If you know when an event happened, and some of what happened at the time, your hypnotherapist may simply ask you to start remembering that time. As you become more involved in that memory, your recall will improve.

✔ **Being creative.** You, or your hypnotherapist, may have a creative streak and take you back by having you, for example, imagine that you're flicking through the pages of a biography of your life. As you reach the chapter detailing the events that led up to the development of your symptom, you may be asked to step into the pages of the book and re-experience what happened.

And for those with a liking for science fiction, you can always imagine that you're travelling back in time in Doctor Who's time machine, the TARDIS!

You do not have to be regressed if you don't want to. However, your hypnotherapist will always make sure that it's safe for you to go back in time, if you do agree to it.

Going forward in time: Age progression techniques

If you can go back in time in your mind, it stands to reason you can go forward, right? You may be thinking that the past has actually happened, and you have memories of the events in your life, and think that the future is yet to occur, and wonder how you can progress into a future that hasn't happened yet.

Well, the truth is, you go forward in time, all the time. Whenever you start thinking longingly about an upcoming event, you travel forward in time in your mind. Whenever you plan an event or make a date, you travel forward in time. Your hypnotherapist can use this ability as part of the package that helps to resolve your symptoms.

Your mind is goal-directed. This means that you consciously, and unconsciously, set yourself up to achieve things – both good and bad!

When you think about an upcoming event, your mind has a habit of playing out various scenes relating to that event, perhaps creating pictures that almost predict how you're going to look or behave. You also create a wide variety of self-statements that describe how you think things are going to be. In effect, you set goals in your mind that influence the way you approach an event, subtly altering your feelings and behaviours.

Self-statements are those little things we say to ourselves that confirm our attitude towards some event, person, or situation. They can be positive; for example, 'I can do this' or 'I'm enjoying this'. Or they can be negative; for example, 'I can't do this' or 'I'm fat'.

For example, if you're scared of giving a talk you have to make in the near future, how you view that future talk affects you in the present. You may see yourself as being nervous, stumbling over your words, and panicking. Because of this vision, you feel anxious in the present, which may influence how you behave – becoming snappy with people around you, for example. Furthermore, you give yourself negative self-statements such as 'I'm going to be dreadful when I give this talk' or 'I'm going to be so nervous when I am up there.' When you finally give the talk, you will more than likely have the same negative experience that you have been visualising: you will have achieved your negative goal.

However, if you think about the talk in a more optimistic way, you create more positive goals. Perhaps you can see yourself confidently stepping up to the lectern and clearly delivering your speech. You give yourself positive self-statements such as 'I am going to do well when I give this talk' or 'I am going to remain confident when I am up there.' You feel good in the present and when you finally give the talk, this time you give it well, because you've been focusing on a positive goal that subtly altered your feelings and behaviours in a positive way.

Your hypnotherapist can take this process of looking into the future and use it in a very beneficial way, helping you to create very clear images of what you want to achieve. As she continues with this process, so you break down the negative goals that you have unconsciously set yourself, which have been keeping your symptom in place. By changing your view of the future in this manner, you change the negative feelings and behaviours that you've been experiencing in the present. Both consciously and unconsciously you start to move towards this positive new goal.

So, how does your hypnotherapist send you into the future? Simple! She uses an age regression technique (outlined in the preceding 'Going back in time: Age regression techniques' section), but takes you in the opposite direction. Instead of counting you back in time, she counts you forward; instead of letting your unconscious mind decide where in the past you should go, she lets it decide where in the future you should be, and so on.

Age progression techniques are often referred to as *pseudo orientation in time* or *hallucinated age progression*.

Altering time: Time distortion techniques

'We're preparing to deploy the Phase Shift Stimulator in order to distort the time/space continuum!' Er, no. This isn't how this works (although it would be fun if it were!). What we're referring to when we talk about time distortion is not altering time itself (that does lie firmly in the realms of science fiction), but how human beings perceive the passing of time.

There are two types of time:

✔ **Clock time:** This is a constant and is not affected by your own point of view or thoughts because it is determined by an instrument such as a clock (unless you have access to a Phase Shift Stimulator!).

✔ **Subjective time:** Your personal perception of passing time, influenced by the way you feel. As such it is variable.

So, why would your hypnotherapist want to help you alter your subjective time? Because subjective time influences how you feel about something, and vice versa.

Sometimes you feel that time seems to fly when you're enjoying something but drags when you're not (and we hope time is zooming past for you as you read this book). Enjoyment and boredom are not the only factors that can affect your perception of passing time; many emotions and feelings – including anxiety, depression, pain, sadness, stress, elation, and interest – and their consequent effects on your perception of passing time, determine how you view situations and events in your life.

If your hypnotherapist decides to use time distortion with you, she will probably do so by reminding you, when you are in trance, of positive times in your past when time seemed to either speed up or slow down. She then associates those experiences to the event you want to change your perception of, by using direct suggestion.

Take the tennis player who feels she never has enough time to accurately serve the ball, and the flying phobic who feels that a one-hour flight seems to last for ten. In both these examples time plays an important role in manipulating feelings. For the tennis player, her perception of passing time causes her to experience anxiety and stress to such an extent that it interferes with her game. For the flying phobic, the experience of time dragging as she sits on a plane serves to heighten her feelings of fear. In hypnotherapy, the tennis player may be given a suggestion that time slows down when she's serving, just as it did when she was waiting to go on that holiday of a lifetime, and that she now has all the time she needs to toss the ball in the air and accurately serve it to her opponent. By altering her perception of time, her feelings change too, and her serve improves. Alternatively, the flying phobic may be given suggestions that time flies by as she sits on a plane, just as it did when she got those wonderful presents on Christmas Day, when she was a child. She's encouraged to experience every minute of the flight as just a second, so that she reaches her destination before she knows it. Contracting her perception of passing time helps break the fear response, allowing her to feel more comfortable as she journeys towards her destination.

Time distortion techniques manipulate your *perception* of events past and future, as well as how you experience the passing of time. You only have memories of what has been, or hopes for what is yet to come. By working with these memories and hopes, you can make positive changes in the way you live your life today.

Book IV

Hypnotherapy

Visualising, Imagining, or Pretending Change

Because change always begins in the mind first, your hypnotherapist may suggest that you 'visualise, imagine, or pretend' that you are enjoying the change you wish to make. If you want to be confident taking an upcoming exam, she may ask you to visualise, imagine, or pretend that you are well rested, thoroughly prepared, and actually eager to get the answers out of your mind and onto the paper! Virtually everyone has the ability to visualise, or to imagine, or to pretend. All are valid modalities of representation to achieve the same goal.

Modality of representation describes how you use your senses to represent things in your mind.

When you think, you don't use just words. Thinking is a creative experience that involves your five basic senses – sight, hearing, touch, taste, and smell. Your mind uses these senses as a means of expanding and enhancing your thinking process. For example:

- **Sight:** As you think you see images in your mind.
- **Hearing:** As you think you hear sounds in your mind.
- **Touch:** As you think you experience feelings in your mind.
- **Taste:** As you think you experience tastes in your mind.
- **Smell:** As you think you experience smells in your mind.

Most people favour one sense (generally sight, hearing, or touch) as their primary modality of representation, and favour the other senses less – their secondary modalities of representation. This doesn't mean that you only ever think in one modality. For example, when asked to imagine a beautiful garden, some people see the garden in their mind very clearly (visual primary modality). However, they may also be able to hear the sounds of the birds and the bees (hearing as a secondary modality). These modalities colour your thoughts and help to give them meaning and vitality.

Try thinking about your best friend:

- How do you know you're thinking about your best friend?
- What comes into your mind that tells you who you're thinking of?

Whatever your answers are, they're proof that you can visualise or imagine! You're representing your best friend in your mind.

In hypnotherapy, this process is used in a variety of ways. It's certainly used in age regression and age progression techniques (see the previous 'Travelling in Time' section) because you need to imagine yourself in your past or future. You may also be asked to visualise and engage in a dialogue with a wise person who has the answers to all the questions you want to ask. You may be asked to pretend that you're digging up weeds in a beautiful garden; where the digging up of the weeds represents digging up and getting rid of your problem.

Using your mind in this way is a powerful tool because it lets you fully represent whatever it is your hypnotherapist is asking you to do. You will find that this technique holds a very important position in your hypnotherapist's toolbox.

Finding Out How to Forget

What were we going to say about forgetting? We can't remember! Okay, we know it's a very tired joke! However, your ability to forget can play an important role in therapy. How you remember things in your past can taint the way you experience similar events in the future.

A person who has to have a regular and painful procedure carried out by her doctor has a memory of the pain she experienced during that procedure in the past. This memory influences the way she thinks about future procedures, predicting that they will be as painful, if not more so, than those she's already had. As a consequence she'll experience the next procedure as a nasty and painful event! However, if she can forget about the previous pain, she won't necessarily set herself up in a negative way, and can experience the procedure with considerably less discomfort.

If your hypnotherapist decides that it would be useful for you to forget something, she will probably do this by using suggestions that you simply forget it. Because you are motivated to do so, your unconscious mind allows it to happen. It's almost as though you push the erase button on that particular part of the memory. In fact, your hypnotherapist may ask you to visualise yourself doing just that.

Book IV

Hypnotherapy

You may have an event in your past that you particularly want to forget. Dealing with the emotions that accompany the memory is much healthier than forgetting it in its entirety. In this way you can recall the memory without feeling pain or discomfort. Even if you consciously forget the event, your emotions about it are still there in your unconscious, festering away and perhaps leading to a whole new batch of symptoms.

Another area where you may experience forgetting is when you awaken from the trance and can't remember what went on during the session. This can be because:

- ✔ It is a natural response of having drifted into one of the deeper levels of trance.
- ✔ Your hypnotherapist has asked that you forget what happened during the trance.

It may seem strange that your hypnotherapist wants you to forget events in trance. You may wonder if she's trying to hide something from you. The answer is no. The reason your therapist will suggest that you forget your trance may be because she feels that you're a very analytical person, and that the moment you are out of trance you'll start analysing everything that went on, and in the process undo all the good that the session has brought you!

Even though you will probably forget whatever it was suggested you forget, the reality is that your memory eventually will return. However, as it returns, you will probably find that your perception of the memory has changed to something much more positive.

You cannot be made to forget anything you don't want to forget. If you are in good rapport with your therapist, you're motivated to forget something because you know that doing so will help you to achieve your required goal from the therapy. The result is that your unconscious mind is much more likely to allow you to forget.

Substituting a Memory

If you can forget something, surely you can fill that gap in memory with something else? This is very true. You have a great capacity to alter the way you remember events from the past.

If you were to ask a group of people to recall an event they had all witnessed, you would get as many different versions of that event as there are people in the group. This is not because they are all inattentive, and can't remember things very well, but because of the way memory works.

When a digital television signal is sent out, only the important parts are transmitted over the airways. When they reach the television set, the set itself fills in the missing pieces, and creates a representation of the original image. Your memory is a bit like digital television signals. Very few people have 100 per cent accurate recall, which means that most of us store only a variety of fragments of a memory. When you retrieve a memory, you pull up only those fragmented parts stored in your brain. Your brain acts a bit like a television set and fills in the missing pieces so that you can have a reasonably accurate recall.

Your hypnotherapist can use this ability of your brain to create components of a memory as part of the process of resolving your problem. By taking the original memory and forgetting specific parts of it, your therapist has an open canvas upon which to help you create a more acceptable memory through a process of suggestion and visualisation. Don't worry, your therapist won't alter your memory to suit herself. She will have discussed the process with you beforehand, and asked you what you would like to remember – this is the picture that she helps you paint onto the canvas.

Exchanging an old memory for an entirely new one is very difficult. This technique works best when an old memory is subtly altered in some way.

A flying phobic, who has developed her phobia because she had one bad experience of turbulence on a flight, may wish to alter the memory of that flight so that she recalls having remained calm, relaxed, and in control as she sat through the experience. This has a knock-on effect into the present, helping her to feel comfortable whenever she flies, because she does not have the negative reference to the original memory to taint her flying experience.

You are likely to retain the original memory after a memory substitution. However, because you have been playing around with it in a positive manner, your perception of that memory will be radically changed.

Memory substitution is carried out only with informed consent from you. You cannot be made to change a memory if you don't want to.

Telling Stories

Perhaps the oldest form of learning is through listening to stories. You teach your children important social and moral truths by reading them fairy tales and various stories found in religious texts. As you grow older, you learn further truths through reading stories in newspapers (hmm! Truths?), magazines, books, television, and films.

Book IV

Hypnotherapy

The psychotherapy community being the resourceful thing it is, recognised that stories offer an indirect learning method and began to use the concept across its various disciplines, including hypnotherapy. As the listener pays attention to a story, its content creates associations with material already stored in her mind; helping to shape and alter self-perceptions and the way she views the world in general, in a positive or negative way, depending on the story. This means that a positive story can be used in therapy to help you resolve your problems.

In psychotherapy, a story representative of something that holds some significance to the listener is called a *metaphor*.

Your hypnotherapist may use a metaphor during the trance session, or may deliver one when you are not in a state of hypnosis. It may come in the form of a story, or it may come as a reminiscence of the way a previous patient dealt with a symptom similar to yours. Your therapist may tell several metaphors at the same time, one embedded in another, in order to make several different points about the way you can resolve your symptom.

Another way your therapist may use a metaphor is to create a metaphorical representation of something. For example, for a person beset with the problems of premature ejaculation, a therapist may use a version of the following metaphor:

> *'As a child you may remember feeling hungry, enjoying an urge to eat. Perhaps you can remember rushing to sit down at the dinner table and wolfing down your food, paying little attention to anything except the instant gratification of your hunger. But now, as an adult, you can appreciate that hunger in a different way. You can take your time arriving at the table, enjoying looking at the feast that is laid out for you, perhaps complimenting the cook, before you take your first mouthful of food. You can slow down in satisfying your hunger by savouring each and every mouthful you take, pausing every so often to appreciate the flavours and aromas that have been so carefully prepared for you. And slowly, gradually, you prolong your enjoyment, and the enjoyment of others around that table, as you learn to appreciate and control, in an adult way, the satisfaction of your hunger.'*

The message contained in this metaphor is to slow down and take your time during sex, as you appreciate your partner more. At the same time there is encouragement to take a more adult approach to making love.

Metaphors can be scattered liberally throughout your hypnotherapy sessions (and they are certainly scattered with gay abandon throughout this book!). They can inspire you by telling stories of how people overcame adversity. They can help you understand something (as we did at the beginning of this chapter where we likened the mind to a network of pipes). They can empower you by getting you to imagine, for example, that your immune system is a Phase Shift Stimulator blasting cancer cells into oblivion. Metaphors can help you overcome a whole variety of difficulties and concerns. However they are used, they provide a very gentle and effective form of therapy.

Chapter 2

Considering How Hypnotherapy Can Help

*W*e all have habits. Some are good, some are not so good and some are downright dangerous to your health. Your habits are part of what makes you who you are. They're a part of your personality; part of those quirky little things that draw some people to you and repel others. On the whole, you happily live with your habits. Happily, that is, until habits go bad! In this chapter, we address the most common bad habits and tell you how hypnotherapy can help you change them.

Breaking Away from Old Habits

The word *habit* has several different meanings, but we use it to refer to any pattern of behaviour you carry out time and time again with little thought or effort.

A habit is not an addiction. Having an addiction means that you depend on some form of drug – such as nicotine, alcohol, or cocaine – to help get you through the day. When you're addicted to a drug, your body *needs* it to be present in your system. If it is not, you tend to feel awful – something known as withdrawal. In order to get back to feeling normal, you have to take some more of whatever it is you are addicted to.

Of course, habits can be part of an addiction. Just look at the smoker who habitually lights up when he talks on the phone, or reaches for his packet of cigarettes, the moment he steps out of his office. His body is addicted to the nicotine and he also has habits that maintain the addiction.

Hypnotherapy is a very effective way of helping you to overcome those annoying bad habits that interfere with your life. Even habits associated with addictions can be effectively treated. However, it is important that you realise that certain habits/addictions can be treated using hypnotherapy – such as smoking – and certain habit/addictions – such as those to do with heroin, cocaine, and alcohol – should be treated by a doctor. Of course, hypnotherapy can play a very important role in helping you stay drug-free, after you successfully beat a serious addiction.

Where do habits come from? In general, you learn them. You start a pattern of behaviour for one reason or another and after a while it becomes so ingrained in your mind that you carry it out almost unconsciously. Aha! *Unconsciously!* This word should give you a pretty hefty clue as to why hypnotherapy can be so effective in treating habits. If habits are stored in your unconscious mind, and hypnotherapy can help make changes to what is stored in the unconscious mind, then it stands to reason that hypnotherapy can help to change habits.

So, why would you want to change your habits? After all, your habits are a part of your personality aren't they? Of course they are, but that doesn't mean to say that you're happy with every aspect of your personality. And by extension, it certainly doesn't mean to say that you're happy with those habits that are harming your health, or making your life less pleasurable to experience.

'Right, I'm unhappy with my habit so I am just going to change it. Simple!' For some people, changing habits can be as straightforward as that. Make the decision and then make the change. But for many other people, changing isn't that simple. The habit has become a part of your life, something you're used to doing on a day-to-day basis. Changing a habit means removing something that has been an integral part of your life.

You may miss your habit. Quite strongly! You may associate certain activities with the habit and feel at a loss when you carry them out. You may erroneously associate the habit with reducing your stress and feel even more anxious when you are under pressure because you can't turn to your habit. In the end you give in to your feelings and suddenly the habit is back with a vengeance.

Quitting smoking

Smoking is bad for you. You know it, and you know what it can do to you in the long-run – make you very ill and kill you. No point in mincing words here. So, why do people do it? Why do people, when they know the consequences, continue to puff on the old coffin nails? Probably because:

✔ **Smoking is addictive.** Nicotine is a drug that causes your body to become addicted to it. This means that after you have been smoking for a while your body gets so used to the nicotine coursing through your veins and invading your nervous system that in its absence your body misses it. Because your body is missing it, it throws a metaphorical temper tantrum and you experience the effects of withdrawal. To make yourself feel better you grab another cigarette, light it up and take a long drag (Cough, splutter, wheeze!), and hey presto! You give your body what it wants and, just like a child, the tantrum subsides.

✔ **Smoking is a habit.** Oh boy! Is smoking a habit! Every smoker knows about this. Every smoker associates their smoking with various activities they carry out during the day. It's not that they need the cigarette at that point, it's just that they always have a cigarette when: they talk on the phone, have a cup of coffee, walk to the station, read a book, sit on the loo, watch television and so on. The list is endless. They do it for no other reason than this is what they have always done at this time. It's a habit. And if they don't do it at these times they feel uncomfortable because they feel something is missing; they don't know what to do with their hands and so on. To fill that missing gap, or give their hands something to do, they light up.

If you ask a smoker to tell you which cigarettes they need to smoke during the day because of the addiction factor, you probably find that there are only a very few. All the other cigarettes are smoked simply out of habit.

Preparing to quit

Okay. You want to quit. And you want to do it through hypnotherapy. So here's some useful advice for you to think about:

✔ **Plan the right time to quit.** Think about a good time to quit. Make sure that you plan to quit at a time when your life is going to be reasonably stable – when you have no major events over the coming month or two such as getting married, birthday parties, exams, holidays such as Christmas, and so on. On the other hand, many people find that quitting just before they go on holiday is a great time to do it, as the change of scenery and lack of all those familiar smoking triggers can reinforce their new non-smoking habit. Fix an appointment with your hypnotherapist and mark it in your diary. Oh, and keep to the date!

✔ **Tell people, who you know are supportive, that you're quitting.** It's always nice to have support and encouragement. These are the people you know you can turn to when your resolve is wavering, or who you know will give you those little words of encouragement just when you need them. Avoid at all costs those who would delight in your failure!

✔ **Get rid of all your smoking paraphernalia just before your hypnotherapy session.** Throw out your ashtrays, your lighters, and your stash of emergency cigarettes. You won't need them any more. Once they are gone they won't be there to tempt you from the straight and narrow. And ensure that your home becomes a strict no smoking zone.

Book IV

Hypnotherapy

✔ **Do something that you know will increase your motivation to quit.** You're motivated, but what else can you do that cranks up that motivation? Half-fill a jamjar with water and drop your old dog ends into it after you smoke each cigarette. Every so often, shake it up and smell the mixture. Nice! That's what's going on in your body each time you smoke. Or take another jamjar and each time you buy a packet of cigarettes put the equivalent amount of money into it. At the end of the week count it up and see how much you are spending on ruining your health. And then think how much you save once you have stopped. Plan to do something nice with that money.

At your first hypnotherapy session your therapist obviously asks you about your smoking habits. It can be helpful to think about these in advance. You can think about:

✔ Why you want to quit.

✔ How many cigarettes you smoke a day.

✔ The cigarettes you feel you need each day.

✔ The cigarettes you have just out of habit.

✔ How smoking affects you.

✔ How you think being a non-smoker benefits you.

✔ How old you were when you first started smoking.

✔ Why you first started smoking.

✔ Why you haven't quit before.

✔ If you have quit before, why you started smoking again.

✔ How much you spend on smoking each week and what you are going to do with all that extra money once you are a non-smoker.

✔ Any fears you may have about quitting.

This last issue often proves to be a sticking point when it comes to helping people quit.

Addressing your fears about quitting

Hypnotherapy for smoking is not just about helping you to stop. After all, you stop smoking between each cigarette you have. No, it's also about helping you to remain a non-smoker. That means it should not only address the process of stopping and keeping you stopped, but also those fears that you may have of what happens when you've done so. It's often these fears and concerns that prompt a person to fall off the healthy wagon and go back into the tarpit of smoking. So it is very important that you talk through any fears or concerns you have with your therapist to enable him to create strategies to help you get around them.

Cessation suggestions and aversion associations

In general, a hypnotherapist helps you quit smoking through the use of suggestion. He gives suggestions that link your desire to quit to the various times of day that you smoke. For example, he may suggest that 'You have no desire to smoke when you first wake up in the morning' or 'You have no desire to smoke after a meal'.

Sounds too easy, doesn't it? Well, it's not that straightforward. What your therapist helps you do is a form of reprogramming. By associating your problem times with having no desire to smoke, the suggestions break the old unconscious associations you have with smoking; they reprogramme you. You may well find that you go through the day and, because of these suggestions, you forget about smoking for long periods of time. Why? Because your mind is no longer focused on the smoking behaviour. The association of various points in the day with smoking has been broken.

Of course, the issue of cravings and withdrawal will be taken into account. Many people who quit smoking through hypnotherapy say they have very few cravings and very little in the way of withdrawal. That doesn't mean to say that everyone gets off this lightly. Your hypnotherapist will give you suggestions to help you cope with any cravings – after all, they only last a very short time – as well as suggesting that you have the willpower to get through any feelings of withdrawal.

Some therapists use aversion therapy as part of the process. In *aversion therapy*, your hypnotherapist reminds you of all the terrible harm smoking does to your body, or perhaps associates the smell and taste of tobacco with something like dog poo in an attempt to scare or revolt you out of the habit.

Your hypnotherapist may even use age progression to let you see how you damage yourself in the long run if you remain a smoker; then show you how great your life will be as a non-smoker. What a wonderful motivator!

Managing your weight

We have a hefty problem with obesity in the Western world. And this means that more and more people are trying to find an effective way to lose weight. They hop onto the passing bandwagon of each and every fad diet that rears its head, only to fall off again later and to then bounce back onto the next . . . and the next . . . and the next! Sound like anyone you know?

The plain and simple fact is that many diets probably do little more than make money for the people who invented them. (Is that the sound of a contract being taken out on our lives for uttering such heresy?). The majority of diets rely solely on restriction of food intake and therein lies a problem.

By relying solely on food restriction, these diets do not teach people to eat healthily, nor do they help them to modify their lifestyle. So, once you are off the diet you return to your old eating habits and the next thing you know all that weight you have lost is piling itself back on. In fact, studies show that around 95 per cent of all people who lose weight through dieting alone subsequently put it back on again! Not good news.

Taking the safe route to the body you want

So, how can you lose weight safely and effectively (and that means keeping the weight off too)? Of course you need to look at what you eat and how much you consume, but weight loss and weight control do not solely rely on restriction of food. For effective weight management, the following should apply to whatever route you take to shed the pounds:

- ✔ **It must not be arduous.** There is nothing worse than having to force yourself to do something. If you are forcing yourself too much it becomes a drag. In the end it is much easier and enjoyable to slip back into your old ways, and any weight you may have lost slips back on. Remember that losing weight is your choice and that means you have to put in some effort to accomplish it. However, with the help of hypnotherapy, the whole process can become something that you can enjoy.

- ✔ **It must be flexible.** Don't be rigid. Just because eating chocolate can make you put on weight doesn't mean you have to give it up completely. Control the amount you eat. Reduce it, but don't ban it. Prohibiting something leads to desire. As the desire grows, you may find that you lose control and end up bingeing on the chocolate.

- ✔ **It must be realistic in terms of weight loss and time.** Most experts agree that 1 to 2 pounds a week is a safe and effective amount to lose.

- ✔ **It must be nutritionally balanced.** Basic common sense here. Ideally you should be eating as much fresh, organic food as possible, but not to the extent that you put weight on. This means that you should be including portions of all the food groups in your diet. Yes, that means fruit and vegetables too. Eating fresh and healthy food provides your body with a quality source of fuel. That means your body runs more efficiently and burns up that fat with more gusto. Oh, and you feel fitter, have more energy, are less prone to illness – the list of positives goes on and on.

- ✔ **It must include exercise.** No, this doesn't mean having to take out a membership to your local gym (though that would be a positive step), but rather it means that you should be prepared to increase your levels of daily activity. The more active you are, the more fat you burn off. Simple steps such as walking more, climbing the stairs rather than taking a lift, and walking up the escalators all help you to lose weight and keep that weight off, not to mention the good it does your heart (you know, that thing in your chest that keeps you alive!).

✔ **It must promote behavioural change.** This means that your lifestyle needs to change. If you take on board all the preceding points, you find that behavioural change occurs naturally and your weight drops. Remember it was your old behaviours and habits that led to that weight piling on in the first place!

If you haven't taken much exercise before and are thinking about starting to work out at the gym, or go running, or whatever, get checked to make sure that you are fit enough to do so. Also, get advice on how much exercise you should be doing. Suddenly going from a sedentary lifestyle to running ten miles a day won't do you, your heart, your muscles, or your joints any good at all. However, with some sensible advice and by building up the amount of exercise you do, you could eventually be running that marathon as you run off that excess weight.

Feeling hungry? Then you must be thirsty! No, you haven't read that wrong, nor have the proofreaders of this book missed a glaring mistake. In this day and age many people don't drink enough fresh water. That means many of us are dehydrated. Unfortunately, your brain sometimes gets mixed up when interpreting those messages from your body that say you're thirsty; and mistakenly registers that you're hungry. Consequently you eat to satisfy a non-existent hunger instead of drinking water to satiate your thirst. In fact, you should be drinking at least two litres of water each day. And that means water alone. Not in a cordial, tea, or coffee. These drinks are all *diuretic*, which means they cause your body to urinate out more water than it should. Drink water and you feel far fewer hunger pangs, eat less and lose more weight.

Eating yourself thin

We've said it before and will say it again – hypnotherapy is not magic. You cannot go in for a hypnotherapy session and come out ten pounds lighter; it just doesn't work that way! What hypnotherapy does is help you make changes to your eating and exercise habits, as well as help you enjoy the process of managing your weight. All in all, it helps you to change your lifestyle to one that keeps you slimmer and fitter and looking great.

Book IV

Hypnotherapy

In order to make sure you get the most out of your hypnotherapy sessions, think of the following before your first visit:

✔ **What weight do you want to achieve?** Make sure it is something sensible for you. Perhaps discuss this with your doctor if you don't know.

✔ **Over what period of time do you want to achieve this?** Again, make sure it is sensible. Remember that experts recommend 1 to 2 pounds of weight loss per week.

✔ **What is your motivation?** Do you have a genuine desire to lose weight for health reasons or your body image – a good motivation – or is someone bullying you into it – the 'I won't marry you unless you drop 2 stone' brigade, which is a not so good motivation. With a good and healthy motivation your chances of success increase.

✔ **How should you be changing your diet?** Examine your diet and see where you can make changes. For example:

   • Grill instead of fry

   • Cut down on portion size

   • Eat more fresh produce including fruit and vegetables

   • Cut down on eating sweets, biscuits, fatty puddings, and so on

   • Drink more water!

✔ **Should you cut down on alcohol?** Sorry folks, but alcohol is *fattening*! We're not saying that you need to cut it out completely – after all, a small amount is good for your heart. Rather, reduce the amount you drink and have a couple of alcohol-free days each week.

✔ **How can you improve on the amount of exercise you take?** Remember to be sensible. Think of times during your day when you can be more energetic (and to put the smutty minded in their place: yes, sex *is* a great calorie burner!).

✔ **What hurdles do you need to overcome?** Let's reality check. There are times when it is difficult to remain in control, at parties for example. How do you want to respond to the situation when temptation rears its fat, ugly head?

✔ **How do you want to look?** Hey, we all have a streak of vanity. Why not pander to it? But again, make sure what you want to achieve is realistic.

✔ **Do you binge on anything?** Are there any foods that when you eat them, you lose control of how much you are eating? You know, opening that box of chocolates and simply having to eat its entire contents!

Armed with the answers to these and other questions that you'll be asked at your first session, your hypnotherapist creates an appropriate plan of action for you. And that plan of action is probably constructed from a variety of techniques that certainly include direct suggestion. For example, ' . . . You have no desire to eat sickly . . . sweet chocolate . . . in fact . . . you only enjoy the wonderful flavours of the right kinds of healthy food . . . that you know are right for you . . . '

Your hypnotherapist may put your imagination to use. For example, he may ask you to imagine that you are shopping for food and that all you buy are small amounts of healthy fresh food. He may take you into the future in your mind, so that you can experience what it's like having lost that weight and maintained its loss too. This mental picture can help you to stop thinking of yourself as a fat person; rather, you can start focusing your self perception on being a thin person. Very motivational!

Some therapists may use analytical tools such as regression or dissociation, though we feel that these analytical tools should be left alone and used only as a last resort. Why? Because for the majority of people coming for weight control it's a simple case of too much of the wrong kind of food into the stomach, and not enough energy out through the muscles! Of course, there are some people for whom being overweight is a symptom of something deeper, and in these cases the use of analytical tools is entirely justified.

However he works, your hypnotherapist aims to help you to:

✔ Take control of your eating habits.

✔ Improve your levels of exercise.

✔ Deal with any issues you may have with regard to losing weight.

✔ Build up and maintain your motivation.

Solving your insomnia

Sleep is something you normally look forward to. A time to rest and recharge your batteries, to take you into the next day alert and full of energy. However, sometimes the process of sleeping may be arduous and less than restful. If you fall into this category, then perhaps a visit to your hypnotherapist is in order.

Most people experience periods when they find it difficult to sleep. Perhaps you're stressed, or travelling from a different time zone, or just don't know why you can't sleep. These times are transitory and are little more than an inconvenience. However, your periods of sleeplessness may become more than transitory and develop into a recurring pattern when you are trying to get to sleep.

There are basically three types of insomnia:

✔ **Initial sleep difficulties:** You have difficulty falling asleep when you first go to bed.

✔ **Intermediate sleep difficulties:** You fall asleep when you first go to bed, but awaken in the middle of the night. Once you awaken you find it difficult to return to sleep.

✔ **Early morning awakening:** You sleep throughout the night, but awaken much earlier than you normally would, feeling unrefreshed and sleepy. Typically you're not able to return to sleep.

Book IV

Hypnotherapy

There could be many reasons why you are experiencing insomnia, but eventually the insomnia becomes a habit – a faulty sleeping strategy, as it were. Hypnotherapy helps you:

- Develop a healthy sleeping strategy
- Deal with any underlying issues contributing to your insomnia

As with any trip to see your hypnotherapist, a little forward thinking goes a long way (and may mean you don't have to see them in the first place!). Think about the following:

- **What was happening in your life when the insomnia first started?** Was there a trigger point for the insomnia, and is this still an issue for you?

- **Do you eat a meal too close to your bedtime?** Going to sleep on a full stomach is not a good idea. You can feel uncomfortable and the process of digestion may interfere with your ability to fall asleep. Ideally, you should not eat for two to three hours prior to going to bed.

- **Do you drink a caffeine drink before bed?** This may seem so obvious, but you may be surprised by the number of people who come for therapy for insomnia who drink coffee or some other caffeinated drink just before going to bed. Remember – caffeine is a stimulant that keeps you awake. If you have a drink before going to bed, make sure that you look at the label of what you are drinking to ensure that it is caffeine free.

- **Do you nap during the day?** If you do, you could be using up your quota of sleep before you get to bed. Try cutting out the napping and see what happens to your sleep.

- **Do you drink alcohol close to your bedtime?** You may think that a little night-time tipple helps you to sleep. Wrong! Even though alcohol is basically an anaesthetic, it can act as a stimulant in small doses. So have your last alcoholic drink a couple of hours before going to sleep. Oh, and don't think that you can drink more alcohol so that you are anaesthetised into sleep! Alcohol-induced sleep is not the same as natural sleep and you still wake up unrefreshed in the morning.

- **Are you overestimating the amount of sleep you think you need?** Try going to bed a little later. See what happens.

Hypnotherapy techniques centre very much on helping you to re-associate bed with sleep. With this in mind your hypnotherapist may give you some advice that could include:

- **Banning anything except sleep from the bedroom.** That means no eating, drinking, watching TV, reading, or sex when in bed. You want to re-associate the bed with sleep and only sleep. Any other activity can be done elsewhere – and that includes sex, so why not spice up your relationship and get amorous in the kitchen or the living room? And don't worry, once you're sleeping well then all these activities can once again return to the boudoir.

- ✔ **Going to bed at the same time each night.** Develop a regular pattern.

- ✔ **Getting up and doing something else if you can't sleep.** If you awaken and aren't able to get to sleep again, get out of bed and go and do something else. The great hypnotherapist Milton Erickson had his insomnia patients polish their kitchen floor over and over again, no matter what the time of night it was! When you're feeling sleepy again, return to your bed. By doing this you associate your bed with sleepiness and eventually sleep.

- ✔ **Writing down any worries or concerns before you go to bed.** This is called *externalising*. Writing down any worries or concerns helps to remove them from your mind, increasing your chance of focusing on sleep, rather than stress.

Controlling your words: Stammering

Stammering (or to use the medical term if you want to, *dysphemia*) is a very common condition that appears in approximately one person in every hundred. It can be expressed in several ways:

- ✔ Some people become blocked when trying to say certain words or sounds.

- ✔ Some people repeat certain words, phrases, or sounds.

- ✔ Some people have long pauses in sentences.

- ✔ Some people prolong the sounds of certain words.

One of the central features of stammering is that the stammer is often accompanied by a sense of a loss of control. This can lead to fear and anxiety building up around the pronunciation of certain words. In fact, many feel that there aren't any words that are impossible for a stammerer to say, only those that they have come to fear!

Stumbling over anxiety

Fear and anxiety certainly promote a stammer. Overcoming these twin hurdles is hard enough for anyone meeting someone new. But for many who stammer, the situation is worsened as the anxiety of the situation increases the worry of saying certain words, which then starts off the stammer. If the person is someone in authority, then the situation gets even worse (something known as *Headmaster Syndrome*). Add time pressure, excitement, or fatigue to the equation and things get completely out of hand.

However, when a stammerer is speaking to someone they know well, many are able to talk quite fluently. Why? Because their levels of anxiety are well down, no longer fuelling the fears that lead to the stammer in the first place.

Book IV

Hypnotherapy

Relaxing your speech through hypnotherapy

Hypnotherapy can help you to speak more fluently, and your hypnotherapist works in conjunction with any advice you have been given by a speech therapist.

The main aims of therapy are to:

- Help you to enjoy a greater sense of self-control.
- Help you to reduce anxiety in general and in specific situations.
- Help you to reinforce your speech therapist's recommendations.
- Help you to interact with strangers more confidently.

In order to do this, your therapist uses a variety of approaches that include:

- **Direct suggestion:** You're given suggestions to direct your attention away from how you're saying a word, and to focus more on what you're saying. You may also get suggestions to help you feel calm and relaxed as you say certain words, or enter into certain situations.

  Where it is appropriate, your therapist also reinforces your speech therapist's recommendations.

- **Self-hypnosis:** This is very useful, because with a regular pattern of practice, self-hypnosis helps you to reduce your general levels of anxiety. Also, you can imagine yourself in a whole variety of situations, speaking calmly and fluently.

- **Ego strengthening:** If you're feeling demoralised, then ego strengthening can help you to feel much better about yourself. Your therapist gives you suggestions themed around enjoying greater self- control.

  Ego strengthening also helps you to cope more effectively with your stress levels and can be directed to help you feel calmer, more confident and relaxed in specific situations.

- **Rehearsal:** If you fear a situation, you almost always think about that situation in advance, imagining all sorts of dire consequences. What you're really doing is practising a form of negative self-hypnosis. The result is that you end up having the bad time you predicted you would have.

  In hypnosis, you can break this nasty habit and start to set yourself up for a good time. Your therapist helps you see yourself coping and speaking much more fluently at these times. By doing this, you set yourself to have a positive experience.

- **Paradoxical advertising:** Many people who stammer often fear that the person they are talking to notices their stammer. By adding this fear, you put yourself under pressure to try and hide your stammer, succeeding only in making the situation worse!

If you fall into this category, your therapist may advise you to advertise the fact that you stammer by saying something on the lines of 'Bear with me, I have a stammer'. By doing so, you immediately reduce one of your concerns and help to improve your fluency.

Reaching a nail-biting conclusion

For someone who doesn't bite their nails, nail-biting can seem quite trivial. However, for those who do, it is an issue that preys on their minds and adds a sometimes considerable inconvenience to their lives. They sit watching TV and munch away at their fingers, they get stressed and dine out on their cuticles, they stop to think and chew away at their problem through their digits! The result is ragged, excessively short nails and, in some cases, bleeding fingers. Not very pleasant.

Biting your nails is a habit that may be associated with some other activity. And, as any nail-biter can tell you, it is often something you do quite unconsciously. It may only be sometime after you have started that you become aware that you are, in fact, biting your nails.

So, your goal is to have fabulous nails. What's your hypnotherapist's goal? Well, obviously the same as yours, but therapeutically he attempts to take your unconscious habit and make it conscious. That means handing you control of your habit. Once it is brought into your conscious awareness and you gain control, you're able to finally stop biting your nails.

Biting off more than you can chew: Why you bite

First things first. Nail-biting is *not* a symptom of some deep-seated neurosis! So you can put your mind to rest; you're not some psycho serial killer because of your habit! In fact nail-biting is simply a remnant of an old childhood behaviour that gave you pleasure: thumb sucking.

To explain this further, we need to take an extremely brief journey into the world of psychology. When good old Sigmund Freud was pondering his theories of psychosexual development, he identified a stage that he termed the 'oral stage'. In fact, it is the earliest developmental stage and lasts from birth to 18 months of age. During this period we are said to gain pleasure and gratification through putting things in our mouth (stop sniggering at the back!). As we develop past this stage, our pleasure and gratification is derived from, er, other areas of our body (we said stop sniggering!). Freud thought that some of us don't fully move on from the oral stage and end up going through life with habits directly linked to gaining gratification through the mouth (oh, come on now!), which could include non-stop chattering, chewing the ends off pens, smoking, eating, and nail-biting.

And by the way, don't expect to hear your hypnotherapist saying '. . . Stop biting your nails . . .' as part of your hypnotherapy session. Why? Because you have probably been hearing that most of your life, and has it ever stopped you? No, we didn't think so. That is why hypnotherapists avoid using this suggestion.

So what do they use? Well, something called *reverse suggestion* – suggestions designed to give you conscious control over a particular behaviour, by suggesting that you can carry out the behaviour – but only if you want to. Your hypnotherapist may deliver suggestions something along these lines: '. . . As soon as your hand moves towards your mouth in order for you to bite your nails . . .. it will instantly and immediately STOP . . . and you will become aware of what you are about to do . . .' This brings the unconscious behaviour to conscious awareness and is followed by the reverse suggestion '. . . In fact . . . you will only be able to bite your nails through a deliberate . . . and conscious . . . act of will . . .' They may then finish off the suggestion with '. . . And you choose to have beautiful . . . healthy . . . shiny nails . . . of which you can be proud . . .'

That sounds straightforward, doesn't it? However, there is a lot more to it than that. Your hypnotherapist also gives suggestions that associate all this with specific times in your day-to-day life, when you know that you bite your nails. And to cap it all off he also wants to take you into the future in your mind, so that you can see yourself enjoying these wonderful new nails. In other words, really firming up a good and strong goal image that motivates you to succeed in your quest for the perfect manicure.

For most people who come to hypnotherapy for nail-biting, this is all that is needed. However, the wonderful diversity of the human mind means that for some, for whatever reason, it may not be this straightforward. If you fall into this category you may also find that your hypnotherapist uses an analytical technique such as dissociation, to help you work with the part of your mind that is responsible for your nail-biting.

Anything else? Well, yes! How about doing something to help yourself along the way. Set yourself up for success by:

✔ Buying yourself a nail file

✔ Buying yourself a decent pair of nail scissors

✔ Booking yourself in for a manicure in a month's time

And yes, that means men too!

Communicating Between Your Mind and Your Body

Many years ago the great French mathematician and philosopher, Rene Descartes, put forward the point of view that the mind and the body were completely separate entities, with neither one influencing the other; a theory known as *Cartesian Dualism*. Unfortunately, the medical and scientific world mainly accepted this idea, ignoring or rejecting the concept that the mind can and does influence the way the body works, and that what happens in your body also influences how your mind works.

Fortunately, a few hardy souls steadfastly researched that very concept, and eventually published convincing research that made the scientific and medical world finally sit up and take notice. The research shows that the immune system, which is responsible for protecting you against infection and disease, also influences your moods. In addition, the research shows that chemical messengers, found in the nervous system, help protect the body against illness.

These findings led to a fairly radical new approach to treating patients. Instead of purely symptom-based treatment, in which the symptom and symptom alone were treated, clued in healthcare professionals now use a more holistic approach that treats not only the symptom but takes the patient's psychological state into consideration as well.

Fitting up the connectors: Your nervous system

In order to perhaps understand how the mind and body can work together, it's useful, first of all, to know a little about the nervous system. Think of it as a very complex and intricate system of wiring, controlled by a very advanced supercomputer. It is divided into two parts:

✔ **The central nervous system:** This consists of the brain (you know, that squidgy lump of porridge in your head), and the spinal cord (an extension of the squidgy porridge that runs down the centre of your spine).

✔ **The peripheral nervous system:** This is made up of the cranial nerves (wires, as it were, that stick out of your brain), the spinal nerves (wires that stick out of your spinal cord), and the autonomic nervous system (the system of wiring that controls all your automatic body functions).

Book IV

Hypnotherapy

Both the central and peripheral nervous systems work together to keep you going on a day-to-day basis, and it's worth having a closer look at how various bits of them work:

- **The brain.** This extremely complex grey matter runs the whole show. If you take a closer look at the brain, you find that it's split up into many different bits, each with their own individual function. Some are very primitive and ancient in evolutionary terms, like the amygdala, which is responsible for things such as emotion and aggression. Some are much more intricate and modern, again in evolutionary terms, such as the cerebral cortex – responsible for consciousness, memory, and thought.

  The brain gives you your intellect, emotions, memories, and so on.

- **The spinal cord.** This is the second part of the central nervous system and dangles from the bottom of your brain, passing down the centre of your spine. Like the brain, the spinal cord is also made up of various bits that all combine together to essentially pass messages back and forth, between your brain and the rest of your nervous system.

  Between them, the brain and the spinal cord control all your body's functions.

- **The autonomic nervous system.** Found throughout your body, this system basically controls all your body's automatic functions, such as the beating of your heart and your breathing. To make things interesting, the autonomic nervous system is divided into two halves that are basically the opposite of each other:

  - **The sympathetic nervous system.** This part of the autonomic nervous system is responsible for you being active. Amongst other things, it reacts to danger and is partly responsible for the effects you feel when you are stressed or afraid (such as increased heart rate and faster breathing).

  - **The parasympathetic nervous system.** The opposite to the sympathetic nervous system, the parasympathetic nervous system is responsible for the effects you feel when you are calm and tranquil (such as slow heart rate and breathing deeply and calmly).

In order to keep functioning properly, both the sympathetic and parasympathetic nervous systems must work together.

- **Nerves.** These carry messages around your body, to and from the brain and spinal cord. They connect your organs, muscles, and skin, to the supercomputer that is your brain, either directly through the cranial nerves, or through the spinal nerves via the spinal cord.

The central and peripheral nervous systems work together. Some of the functioning is under conscious control and some seemingly automatic. For example, if you want to get up out of a chair and walk across the room, your brain makes a conscious decision to do this. Your brain sends messages down your spinal cord and out, via a whole network of nerves, to your muscles, which start to contract to raise you out of the chair. Then your autonomic nervous system kicks in and you start to walk. Your sympathetic nervous system causes some of these muscles to contract (such as those in your thigh and calf), propelling you forward on one leg. Your parasympathetic nervous system then makes some muscles relax as the leg is lifted (such as your calf muscles, because they're not needed for a few moments).

The act of walking is under the control of your peripheral nervous system and your spinal cord, whilst the decision to start or stop walking is under the control of your brain.

A similar process lets you experience emotion. Your peripheral nervous system registers information from the outside world through your eyes, ears, nose, and skin. Those messages are relayed to your brain via your nerves and your spinal cord. Your brain then interprets these messages.

If for example, your brain interprets something as scary, then the amygdala – that primitive part of your brain that is partly responsible for emotions such as fear – becomes active and you feel fear. Messages are sent out via your spinal cord, and the sympathetic nervous system kicks in causing your muscles to tense, your heart rate to rise, and your rate of breathing to increase. When your brain registers that the scary thing has gone, messages are sent to your brain that are interpreted in a way that lets you know not to be scared. The amygdala turns off and you feel calm. Messages are sent out, again via your spinal cord, and the parasympathetic nervous system kicks in and your muscles relax, your heart rate and breathing slow down and hey presto, you are calm again.

Making the connection with hypnosis

Hypnosis happens in the brain, that's for sure. Studies show that the brain wave activity of a person in a trance is very different to when that person is alert, asleep, or pretending to be in trance.

Brain waves are a measurement of the electrical activity of the brain. This activity changes very distinctly when you're sleeping, being alert or experiencing trance. And for those of you who like big words, the machine that measures these brainwaves is called an electroencephalogram. For those who don't, you can call it an EEG!

A number of studies confirm that brainwaves are measurably different when you're in trance. Alpha waves, theta waves, and something with the very grandiose title of the 40-Hertz band, are all altered when we are in hypnosis. These waves and bands have nothing to do with the sea or popular music; they refer to the frequencies at which the electrical activity of the brain is operating. When you are alert the electrical activity is running at a certain frequency, when you are asleep it changes to another frequency, and when you are in trance, to yet another.

Further evidence can be found in PET studies. No, not the study of how Fido is behaving, but something called Positron Emission Tomography. This very interesting technique allows scientists to look at your brain and work out what parts of it are active when you are experiencing something. And guess what? The brain in hypnosis shows different activity than the awake brain or the sleeping brain.

A study was carried out on how the brain reacted to hypnotic pain control. In a non-hypnotised person experiencing a painful stimulus, two areas (amongst several others) were 'lighting up' as it were: the *somatosensory cortex* – the rather posh name for the part of the brain that processes painful stimuli – and the *anterior cingulated cortex* – an even fancier name for the area of the brain that is involved in your perception of suffering. In a hypnotised person being given a painful stimulus, the researchers noticed that the somatosensory cortex was still lighting up; however the anterior cingulated cortex wasn't. In other words, the pain stimulus was being processed, but the brain did not perceive any suffering. Proof positive that hypnosis directly affects the brain.

When you're awake and alert, your sympathetic nervous system is very active. It helps you walk, talk, exercise, and sometimes feel stressed. On the other hand, when you enter into trance, the good old parasympathetic nervous system comes to the fore, turning off the sympathetic nervous system and allowing you to go into a state of relaxation and rest.

So to pull it all together, when you enter into trance, your brainwaves alter, various areas of the brain change their activity, and the parasympathetic nervous system becomes dominant. Small wonder that many patients report that they feel wonderfully relaxed when they are experiencing hypnotherapy.

Considering how your emotions affect you

Everyone experiences emotions. These emotions are products of your brain; they are mental states and as such mean that your brain is active in promoting them. If your brain is active, the rest of your nervous system is too. That means that when you experience an emotion of any kind it will have a knock-on effect in your nervous system. And, by extension, other physical parts of you – remember that the nervous system controls your entire body.

If this emotion that you experience is having an effect on your body, is that a good thing or a bad thing? The answer is that it's a little of both. It all depends on the type of emotion that you are experiencing. The good ones – such as happiness, elation, and joy – have a beneficial effect on your body; helping you to feel relaxed, keeping your immune system healthy, and so on. Positive emotions help you to recover when you're ill by boosting your beleaguered immune system. On the other hand, negative emotions such as anxiety, stress, and depression have a detrimental effect on your immune system.

Your body is quite a resilient thing and can take a fair amount of punishment before it starts to fail. It takes a good old battering from such things as physical knocks, the environment, and your negative emotions. Between these bouts of battering it does need to rest and recuperate. If it is not allowed to do so, then the pressure of keeping you going builds and builds, and if you are not careful, your body eventually starts to fail. It may seem obvious that physical and environmental factors can do this to you, but how do emotional factors figure in this? Read on to find out.

Depressing the effects of low moods

When you are in a good mood your body is in a state of balance in regard to the various biochemicals coursing through it. These biochemicals all have their own specific functions that help to keep your body in tiptop condition.

When you are down or depressed your mind is in a very negative state. You end up having bad feelings coursing through your body, which in turn puts a myriad of hormones and biochemicals out of balance. As a result, your body no longer functions as it should.

For many people these low moods are transitory, you perk up and your resilient body gets a bit of a break – no harm done. In some cases though, these moods persist and your body doesn't get any respite from the imbalance, ending up in a descent into bad health. In fact, studies have shown that people who stay in prolonged low moods, like depression, are more likely to fall ill than those who don't. Now that's a depressing thought! That's because the imbalance in your body is having a negative effect on your immune system – the part of your system that is responsible for keeping you free from infection and disease.

Book IV

Hypnotherapy

Stressing about fear and anxiety

Even the most chilled out people in the world experience anxiety once in a while. It's one of those annoying moods that you can't escape.

In this chapter, we use the words *stress* and *anxiety* to describe the way that your body and mind respond when you experience something that you perceive as threatening to your physical health. You may call this *fear* – we prefer the terms stress or anxiety.

Whatever the word used, your body reacts to this state by releasing a whole host of biochemicals that are usually kept in balance. The quantity of bio-chemicals released determines the strength with which you experience these feelings – the greater the volume, the stronger the feeling. In an ideal world, this response – mild to intense – should only last a short while. However, this is not an ideal world – more's the pity – and this response is often left switched on for long periods of time in many people.

Moderate anxiety is good – without it the human race would probably not exist. No, we haven't lost the plot; all we are saying is that anxiety has a very functional role within your life. It helps to keep you focused on things in your life that need to be attended to. The only time you really need to worry about anxiety is when you experience too much of it, and for too long a period of time. Then it can become a downright liability by increasing your risk of having a heart attack, or lowering your immunity to disease, for example.

Your body has a wide variety of warning and alarm systems that help to keep you safe and out of harm's way. Anxiety is one of them. Anxiety warns you that something is a potential threat to your safety. It keeps you wary and away from harm. Should you decide to explore whatever it is that is poten-tially dangerous, then feeling anxious will mean that you approach whatever it is with caution. What we are talking about here is what anxiety is *supposed* to do for you, and what it *actually* did for your ancestors. You'll see what we mean by going back in time for a few moments.

Fighting or fleeing: Facing the fear response

Experiencing anxiety, stress, or fear is also known as the *fight-or-flight response*.

Several things happen the moment you feel anxious:

- Your sympathetic nervous system becomes overactive.
- Your heart rate increases.
- Your breathing rate increases.
- Your muscles become tense.
- Blood is diverted to the muscles in your arms and legs.
- Your digestion slows or stops.

These physical responses happen whether you're confronted by a bear, or just a beastly boss warning you that your job is at risk.

Unfortunately, the biochemicals that help you to run away and fight also end up damaging your body and immune system if they're left active for a prolonged period of time. If you don't get a chance to take your system off high alert status, the effects of your fight-or-flight response can cause physical damage: an overactive sympathetic nervous system can cause your body to shake; an increased heart rate wears down your heart muscle; increased breathing may end up as hyperventilation, which in turn can lead to a panic attack; muscle tension can cause tension headaches and muscle pain; diverted blood may cause hot flushes; and decreased digestion can result in a number of problems associated with your gut.

Staying alive in caveman days

This response proved very useful to your ancestors! The anxiety response has kept the human race from being eaten into extinction by predators. Imagine one of your ancestors wandering along nonchalantly through a forest, when a sabre-toothed tiger jumps out in front of him with the intention of picking up a caveman takeaway. Your ancestor's immediate response is to fight for his life or to run away: His fight-or-flight response is turned on as a reaction to a perceived personal threat. His body is flooded with a whole variety of chemicals that prepare him for action. After saving his own life (and possibly picking up a sabre-toothed tiger takeaway in the process), his fight-or-flight response is turned off and his body returns to normal.

Just imagine that the human race evolved without an anxiety response. Ah! Nirvana! Or is it? Imagine your everyday caveman hunting for some animal that has the potential for being a pot roast. As he is walking through the forest he hears the sound of branches breaking behind him. Without an anxiety response, he turns nonchalantly around to see what it is that is making the sound, perhaps striding boldly over to investigate. Before he knows it, a bundle of fur, sharp claws, and very long teeth comes hurtling out of the undergrowth and sends him into oblivion.

The moral of this story: no anxiety equals no caution equals no life! Add anxiety back into the equation, and the moral changes: anxiety equals caution equals staying alive (with a nice lunch too!).

During periods of real danger, your stress response can actually save your life by giving you the energy to defend yourself or run away.

Surviving in the modern jungle

You don't meet very many sabre-toothed tigers today, but you do have nagging bosses, threatening bullies, troubling financial concerns, and so on, which are the modern day equivalents. However, in today's society you do very little fighting or fleeing in response to your anxieties (unless you are in a war zone or a dangerous inner city area). In fact, all you tend to do is to let your feelings grow and grow. This is not good, because you have a body that is ready for action, but isn't doing anything.

When your body switches to the fight-or-flight response it prepares to become explosively active. Today, you don't often actually fight and you don't actually run away. As far as your body is concerned, it's a bit like having your foot pressed down on the accelerator and brake at the same time – your engine is revving and going nowhere. The result: breakdown.

All of these responses are like revving your car. Take your foot off the brake and away you go! In this day and age, you tend to keep your foot firmly on the brake, risking damage.

Integrating hypnosis into the mind-body connection

If your mind can affect the way your body functions, and hypnotherapy can affect the way your mind functions, then it stands to reason that hypnotherapy can ultimately affect your body's responses. Using hypnotherapy to change the way you think about and respond to situations and events that affect your life can ultimately change the way your body reacts. This effect can be a by-product of therapy or an actively sought response. For example, if you are coming for therapy to help reduce your levels of stress, a by-product could be better health. Or perhaps you are coming for therapy to help manage and reduce the pain you are experiencing. In this case, you are actively seeking to alter your body's response to whatever is causing the pain (see Chapter 6 to find out more about pain control using hypnotherapy).

Whatever you are seeking therapy for, the hypnotherapy process makes a variety of positive changes to your body. The next sections highlight some of these.

Hypnotherapy does not cure disease and should never be advertised as doing so. Hypnotherapy does help to make changes to the way you think and feel, and the way your body responds in certain situations. De-stressing may, in itself, reduce or eliminate any stress related ailments you may experience such as headaches, ulcers, and rashes. But any effects on a disease state are lucky by-products that may or may not be attributable to your therapy, and can never be guaranteed.

Even though you often don't know how to handle stress, anxiety, or fear, that doesn't mean that there is nothing you can do about it. In fact, you can take a lesson from your primitive ancestors. After any burst of activity that resulted from a fight-or-flight response (have a look at the previous section, 'Fighting or fleeing: Facing the fear response' for more on this), your caveman ancestor would probably seek out a quiet and safe place and take time to rest, to sleep, to perhaps enter into a trance-like state. By doing so, his mind would calm down. As his mind calmed down, it would communicate with his body, which would release all the muscle tensions and turn down the biochemical responses that resulted from the fight-or-flight response. In effect, he would relax.

The key to combating that excess of anxiety, stress, or fear is to relax. How your body responds when you relax is much the same as when you enter hypnosis. The most common body responses are:

- ✔ Your heart rate slows down.
- ✔ Your breathing rate slows down and becomes deeper.
- ✔ The muscles throughout your body become less tense.
- ✔ Blood is evenly distributed throughout the body.
- ✔ Your digestion system works efficiently.
- ✔ Your thoughts become less concrete and more abstract – more image and feeling based.

Of course, you will always have periods of anxiety. It's how you handle that anxiety that is important.

If you can get into a regular pattern of relaxation and exercise, you can minimise the nasty effects of long-term anxiety. It's also worth mentioning that if you stop smoking, eat healthily, and cut down on the amount of alcohol and caffeine you drink, then you will be on tiptop form to beat that anxiety firmly into the ground.

Book IV

Hypnotherapy

Chapter 3

Feeling Good

*I*magine feeling so good that you have that 'I can't lose today' feeling. Everything is going your way for a change. Imagine that the things you want to do seem almost effortless. You begin to surprise yourself with how creative or lucky you are. You feel happy and this feeling runs throughout your body.

When you feel good, the universe provides. When you feel good, you have more energy, you feel healthier, and things just seem to fall into place. Being in a good mood often feeds on itself, meaning things that you want just seem to flow to you.

Feeling good is contagious. People relate to you more positively. It's as if your good energy is being shared in a two-way direction, from you to others and back to yourself. You become more creative and perform better in every area of your life. You may even feel sexier!

But, hey! Maybe you don't feel like this; maybe you want to, but something is blocking the way. Maybe you're asking yourself whether a hypnotherapist can help you to feel like this. Can hypnotherapy help you to feel better? Be more creative? Have more confidence? In a nutshell, the answers are: yes, yes, yes, and yes!

Your mind has awesome potential and through hypnotherapy you can enhance that potential, changing your critical thoughts into something more constructive and supportive. You have the ability to access untapped creativity, which can improve your emotional, intellectual, and physical responses. When this happens, some of the by-products are greater confidence, creativity, and an improved ability to relate to others. From this starting point, you can then combat and overcome a whole variety of problems. This chapter explores exactly how this is possible.

Conquering Performance Anxiety

Have you ever frozen with fear when giving a speech? Ever walked out on stage and dried up on the spot? Ever sat for your driving test and almost driven the car off the road because you shook so badly? If the answer is yes to any of these questions, you have experienced *performance anxiety*. The name says it all and basically means that anxiety has messed up what you are doing in front of others.

Playing the starring role

One thing to get straight, right from the start, is what we mean by the word *performance*. The word may conjure up an image of a stage, an audience, and a performer hoping to make a good impression. This is, of course, a correct interpretation, but the definition of performance can be expanded. Just think of the stage as the world in which you live, the audience are the people with whom you interact, and you are the performer hopeful of showing yourself in a good light.

A *performance* then is any interaction you make with others in which you are likely to feel you're being evaluated. These situations can include:

- Work
- The performing arts such as playing music, dancing, acting, and so on
- Sport
- Public speaking
- Exam-taking
- Sex

Feeling your star fade

You may have been performing perfectly well for some time, or maybe this is your first attempt. Whatever you're doing, it only takes one bad experience to mess up the show. The nasty thing about performance anxiety is that when it happens it just keeps repeating itself. So where does the anxiety come from? The following list offers some possibilities:

✔ **Incomplete or bad preparation:** For any performance to be effective, preparation is paramount.

✔ **A focus on your negative feelings:** For example you may believe that your audience can see that you're nervous.

✔ **Negative criticism:** This can include comments from others as well as your own self-criticism.

✔ **Memories of past bad performances:** You forget your successes and remember only your mistakes or failures. Hypnotherapy can help you to put a variety of positive spins on past bad performances in order to help you focus on raising your game.

The awful thing about anxiety is that it fuels all your fears and doubts and after it's started . . .

In fact, the more you experience performance anxiety, the worse it gets until it forms a nasty and vindictive vicious circle from which you have great difficulty breaking free. Now is the time to call in your hypnotherapist.

Acting your way to a better performance

Consider method actors. Before they perform a role, they begin to live it. They become their character before they even get onto the stage, or in front of the camera. In essence, hypnotherapy helps you use method acting techniques. Through hypnosis, you live your good performance before you have to give it. The more you live it beforehand, the more likely you are to live it when you are up on your stage.

To fully understand a film, you really need to see it from beginning to end. Come in halfway through and you may find yourself getting confused, unable to make head or tail of the plot. The same principle is at work when dealing with performance anxiety. You need to see the whole picture for therapy to be effective. That means you need to be able to view:

✔ The pre-performance period, including your preparation and the buildup to the performance.

✔ The performance itself, with you performing well.

✔ The post-performance period when you're being congratulated, feeling good, celebrating, and relaxing.

Your hypnotherapist guides you through the complete process while you're in trance so that you're able to:

✔ **Prepare yourself properly.** Your hypnotherapist is there to help you with the most vital part of your preparation, which is your mental attitude.

✔ **See yourself performing well.** Envisioning a positive outcome breaks down your negative self-image.

✔ **Experience what it is like** to have the appropriate, positive, and constructive feelings throughout.

✔ **Change your negative self-talk** into positive self talk.

By experiencing the complete process in trance, you get a good understanding of the plot and feel comfortable about how to direct your own performance.

A wise piece of advice to get in trance is to forget about yourself. By following this advice, you can focus on your audience, or your performance, instead of on your negative feelings that may sabotage what you are doing.

Actors respond to cues that prompt them to react in a certain way at the right time. And just as actors respond to cues, so your hypnotherapist helps you respond to cues. These cues are designed to give you appropriate feelings and responses at the appropriate time; before the performance, during it, and after it has been completed.

Summing up your parts

Don't forget that you are the sum of all your parts and that some of these parts can help you give that excellent performance. Some of the resources you have may be hidden from you, some hide away when you need them, some you may not even know are there! Your hypnotherapist will be able to help you get in touch with these parts – confidence, relaxation, clarity of mind, for example – and bring them into play just when you need them.

Your hypnotherapist will give plenty of suggestions that will allow your mind to slip into the method-actor mode, as you start to live your good performance.

The more you rehearse through therapy and self-hypnosis and experience a good performance, the better your performance gets. You'll soon be on your way to winning that Oscar!

Taking the Confidence Trick

Confidence is an elusive thing. You may be surprised to know that some of the people who come to hypnotherapy for confidence building are actually quite successful and are occasionally even well-known celebrities. Both of us have worked on confidence building with clients who are at the top of their professions. The point is that confidence is not something that arrives after you achieve a certain salary or status.

Confidence is extremely subjective, so the techniques your hypnotherapist uses to help you to regain it vary. However, through hypnosis your sense of self-assuredness is easily strengthened.

Feeling ten feet tall (when you're used to feeling like a midget)

Do you know anyone you really envy because they are so confident, calm and cool? If so, you can through hypnosis, 'borrow' some of their attributes and place them into your own personality! This is a really fun technique that can help you achieve your goals. It is priceless to see people rapidly become *genuinely* more confident and happy.

Try it for yourself: *Pretend* you have some positive attribute of someone you admire. Then *imagine* what differences having that attribute would make in how you feel and behave. Speculate about how different people's reactions to you would be. If you really try this exercise – even without hypnosis – you may begin to see how powerful it can be.

Changing your self-talk

If you have read the preceding section and are doubtful – perhaps even thinking to yourself 'It might work for others, but not for me . . .' – perhaps you have a strong critical sense that regularly results in putting yourself down. If you regularly rubbish yourself – think self-critical thoughts or even use humour to put yourself down – you need to work on changing your self-talk.

The common parlance is to refer to this voice as your *inner critic*. Everyone has a self-critical voice or inner critic. This is the part of you that says things like 'I'm bad', 'I'm ugly', 'I'm unlovable', 'I'm stupid', and so on.

But when you become consciously aware of your inner critic, you can bring it under control and actually change your inner critic into an inner mentor. Yes, with a bit of work, the voice that once savaged you can become your ally and coach. Imagine how good it will feel to have a voice that guides and advises you instead of criticises!

Even before you go to see a hypnotherapist about your self-confidence worries, just start noticing all the ways that you undermine yourself or put yourself down through thought, words, or behaviour. Keep a mental awareness of the broad themes that your inner critic uses against you, such as 'I'm dumb', 'I'm poor', 'I'm incompetent', and so on.

Putting your confidence into practice

So you've just been hypnotised for greater self-confidence. You're feeling more optimistic than you've felt in a long time. You go through the whole week feeling great, and for the next few days even your friends can tell you've changed somehow. But one week later, you've lost it.

The trick with sustaining any type of hypnotherapy treatment can be summed up in three words: *act as if*. I sometimes think about putting these on my therapy practice room wall. Why are they so important?

'Acting as if' for any sort of behaviour leads to the creation of habit. If you act as if you are confident for a long enough period of time, you actually *become* more confident. I also say this to people who have just stopped smoking by hypnosis – if you act as if you are a non smoker, then you remain a non smoker.

The important message here is that hypnotherapy is not a passive interaction. The hypnotherapist can provide some of the initial motivation, but the bulk of the work for *remaining* successful is your job. 'Acting as if' is the secret.

Sorting Out Your Anxieties

It has been said that the conscious mind creates most of your problems and if given half a chance, the unconscious can sort out the mess! In fact, some say that 70 per cent of what we worry about never happens and the 30 per cent that does, doesn't happen in the way we thought it would.

Anxiety is a familiar state everyone experiences now and again. It involves a combination of feelings such as fear, restlessness, and worry. It may also be accompanied by physical sensations such as palpitations, chest pain, upset stomach and shortness of breath.

Different people react differently to anxiety, both in how much anxiety they feel and in their reactions to it. If you suffer high levels of anxiety over a long period, you may develop physical ailments as a result. At the extreme end anxieties can be irrational and form a mental health problem.

Bear in mind that appropriate levels of anxiety are functional and desirable. You need a certain amount of anxiety to motivate yourself when things are urgent and have to be attended to. It's when that anxiety runs out of control that problems set in!

A variety of anxieties that people commonly experience include:

- **Panic attacks** are usually one-off experiences, involving intense, brief periods of abrupt, disabling fear. A variety of symptoms such as breathing difficulties, palpitations, and nausea may result.

  A panic disorder is an anxiety disorder involving recurrent, unexpected panic attacks, where the fear of the next anticipated attack becomes itself an anxiety.

- **Obsessive thoughts** can involve a repetitive, anxiety-provoking tendency to dwell on an idea, or series of related ideas. The thoughts can disrupt how you function and impact your quality of life.

- **Phobias** involve a powerful and constant fear of an object, a situation, or individual. Phobias can become disruptive and obsessive to the person experiencing them.

- **Stress** involves physical and emotional reactions that are the opposite of relaxation. Stress can result from either positive or negative events. *Stressors* – anxiety-provoking events – are highly subjective for individuals.

- **Low self-esteem** refers to a negative view a person forms of themselves. Over time, low self-esteem can have detrimental effects on your physical and emotional health.

You may be relieved to know that hypnotherapy has a good track record of resolving many of these types of problems.

With the exception of severe mental health problems, hypnotherapy can help relieve your anxieties. A hypnotherapist can help your unconscious mind calm down and find new methods to cope with current and future anxiety-provoking situations in a variety of ways including:

- Raising your self-esteem and confidence.
- Identifying the themes or patterns of your worries in order to deconstruct them.

> ✔ Finding a healthy way to cope with a legitimate concern. For example, you may be worried about your personal safety; through hypnotherapy you can find practical ways to feel safe.
>
> ✔ Seeing yourself (in trance) in the future without the inappropriate worries, whilst teaching your conscious mind to be that way in the present.

Your hypnotherapist is not there to remove all your anxiety; He is there to help you cope more effectively with it.

Beating the Blues

Part of the human condition involves feeling a bit low from time to time. However, if you have a long-standing problem, it may be that you now have two problems: the original one as well as depression. Having a problem you can't seem to get rid of naturally makes you feel low. Hypnotherapists work with helping people beat the blues on a regular basis.

The way that you think directly affects the way you feel. If you label an experience positive, you feel good, possibly even energetic, not only about the experience but about yourself. If you view an event as bad, you feel horrible and possibly drained. Successful people often have an ability to turn a negative event into a challenge and a crisis into an opportunity.

Your hypnotherapist will work to help you understand how powerfully your evaluation of life events influences both your thoughts and your emotions.

Understanding the different types of depression

Let's clarify some terminology. What is the difference between the blues and depression? There are obviously different levels of feeling low. If you contrast the feelings at receiving a parking ticket with the death of a loved one, you get the picture. The feeling about the parking ticket isn't in the same league as the feeling of bereavement.

It is entirely natural to feel depressed over the death of someone you love or when you have a serious illness, and in similar situations. This type of depression is known as *reactive depression* because your depression is a reaction to events.

Clinical depression, on the other hand, involves a more serious and long-term condition. Psychiatrists label it as a reaction to long-standing depression not necessarily related to a specific event.

The attributes of clinical depression involve:

- ✔ Loss of appetite
- ✔ Inability to sleep
- ✔ Loss of pleasure (also known as *anhedonia*)
- ✔ In extreme forms, suicidal feelings

Clinical depression is very serious and requires urgent medical attention. Psychiatric medication is a common treatment approach, unlike reactive depression.

Working your way out of that black hole

The earlier section, 'Taking the Confidence Trick' deals with ways of making you feel good. A lot of the methods referred to involve the hypnotherapist giving suggestions to make you feel better, also known as 'ego-strengthening'. These can be straightforward suggestions such as, 'You will feel increasingly more optimistic', or 'You will feel happier and healthier than you have felt in a long time'.

Ego-strengthening is a core component with helping you to work your way out of a period of depression.

Stress Busting

Stress, in the true sense of the word, refers to tension. Tension in itself is a neutral condition and not always negative. However, when a hypnotist meets a patient who wants to work on their stress, it is always referred to by the patient as a problem involving an overload or an unbearable tension causing fear, worry, and possibly other health problems such as headaches, or some type of emotional and/or physical problem.

You can think of *stress* simply as the opposite of relaxation. Because hypnotherapy is a marvellous way to induce relaxation, you won't be surprised to read that hypnotherapy is a marvellous stress antidote!

Book IV

Hypnotherapy

Because hypnosis helps you relax, it is an excellent tool in identifying new strategies for stress reductions that feel natural to you.

Cooling yourself off and hypnotherapy

Anger management has become such a buzzword recently that there is even a Hollywood movie about with that title. We haven't actually seen it, as we're too busy helping people to not be angry!

Let's say that you are coming to a hypnotherapist for anger management treatment. Most hypnotherapists begin anger management work by collecting information about how long you've had a problem with anger and how you react. They may also ask you what helps make you less angry and what winds you up the most. These questions help you to start thinking about your own patterns of anger and how you deal (or don't) with it. You may not even be hypnotised in your first session because there will be so much to uncover about you and your way of expressing anger.

Most people with anger issues feel out of control. This lack of control feeds their inner critic and makes them feel awful about themselves. So, early on, your hypnotherapist helps you to build up your confidence. You come to believe that it is possible for you to have greater self-control. At this point, the hypnotherapist can introduce any number of new coping strategies, based on your recently enhanced sense of confidence and control.

Responding with stress

If the source of an alarm hangs around for a sustained period, whether in your mind or in real life, you translate this state of constant alert into what is called a *stress response*. In short, sustaining a fight-or-flight response leads to stress.

However, most people don't experience stress by living for long periods in immediate physical danger (unfortunately, you'd probably get the sack if you physically fought your boss for survival!). More commonly, you produce stress as a product of the way that you think about the external forces affecting you.

The physical consequences of living under stress for prolonged periods can be serious. Stress can lead to stomach ulcers, a heart attack, a stroke, or other physical ailments. Your ancestors would rest after the threat was over (after either fighting and killing a sabre-toothed tiger or fleeing to safety), giving their body biochemistry time to return to normal. Unfortunately, in today's society, many people don't experience this respite from stress; they're under constant stress – a situation that can, and often does, have adverse health effects.

Reframing your stressed-out world

Hypnotherapy can help you find strategies for changing your response to the things that stress you out. Changing your attitude toward your stressors lowers your stress and helps you avoid any detrimental health consequences.

Reframe is a therapy term that simply means viewing something in a new and more positive light. Once you can reframe a situation you view as negative, you improve your ability to cope with that situation.

You're stressed: Your life appears to be on fast forward, and you can't seem to slow down. Work and home life are no longer fun, and you just want to crawl into a hole and sleep. Worry not, because help is on its way in the person of your friendly neighbourhood hypnotherapist. With his expertise, your hypnotherapist can help you stand back and re-evaluate your stressors. How he does that depends on what your particular issues are.

In general, a hypnotherapist can help you to:

- ✔ Take off your blinkers and see that you do, in fact, have options.
- ✔ Look at and change your current reactions to stress.
- ✔ Reframe your feelings towards your stressors and perhaps look upon them as motivational and exciting.
- ✔ Prioritise what is important and what are unnecessary pressures.
- ✔ Ensure that you are putting appropriate effort into the necessities.
- ✔ Access your inner resources and potentials.
- ✔ Relax!

Book IV

Hypnotherapy

Making a molehill out of that mountain

Facing up to stress can seem overwhelming. You can think of stress as a mountain you're standing very close to and need to get by, on your journey through life. Standing so close makes the mountain seem very daunting; you can't see a way around it or through it. The only option appears to be the long, hard slog up its sheer face; a journey that is very tiring and fraught with danger. However, take some time to walk away from that mountain and you start to see it differently. For a start, it doesn't appear so challenging. You notice paths that go around it; tunnels that take you safely through. In fact, you notice that there are many easier options than taking that dangerous route up its side.

Hypnotherapy finds the molehill in your mountains. In trance you can access your unconscious mind and open up new perspectives, which allows you to find easier and safer ways to get by that stress mountain and improve your effectiveness, and your health too.

Schedule in time for yourself. Regularly take yourself away from your stressors and do something that you enjoy. When you return, you return refreshed, invigorated, and able to deal more effectively with what you have to do.

Accessing Your Creativity

Have you ever had a dream and pleasantly surprised yourself? Maybe by telling a funny joke in your sleep and waking up laughing? Or maybe by simply having an astonishing dream that you could never have consciously devised? These simple examples are only the tip of the latent creativity within your unconscious mind. Now think how amazing it would be if you could consciously harness this sort of creativity. Well, through hypnosis you can!

Another way to understand your well of creativity is as an infinite inner oil well reserve. Imagine an oil engineer one day knocks on your door and tells you that you're living on top of an oil well of such immense reserves that it will make you rich beyond your wildest dreams. Sound good so far? You allow him to access your oil by having an oil well constructed that plunges underground and eventually (hooray!) strikes oil! Unfortunately, a few hundred barrels later, the oil well apparently dries up and stops delivering. You call back your now trusted friend, the oil engineer, who promptly identifies the blockage in your oil well and in no time flat, you are producing twice as many barrels of oil as before. You are indeed thrilled!

As if that weren't enough, your now very best friend, the oil engineer, gives you a crash course in DIY maintenance and construction of exploratory oil wells, making himself redundant and allowing you to now access all the oil you want at will! And just before he leaves, he mentions the small fact that, unlike other oil reserves, which eventually dry up, yours is different. Your oil well has infinite resources, which means you will never run out of resources. Nice fantasy, eh?

But the fantasy is real!

You really _do_ possess the metaphorical equivalent of the unlimited oil well we just described. Simply substitute 'hypnotherapist' for 'oil engineer' and 'inner creativity and resources' for 'oil'. Self-hypnosis is the tool you use to access your inner resources whenever you need to. But by now, we have probably pumped this metaphor dry!

Tapping into your endless well of creativity

Your creativity is the storehouse for all your memories. This is like an immense computer that remembers everything under the broad heading of 'creativity' that you have seen, created, experienced or heard. That alone is a staggering concept! Imagine a computer that would allow you to access any of that and we are describing your unconscious mind.

How does a hypnotherapist help you access this type of unconscious creativity? The process involves:

- ✔ **Accessing** your unconscious mind in trance. This is like the computer example in the preceding section. For creative writing, click on your personal drive 'Z:', for a creative strategy to get you out of trouble, click on your personal drive 'Q:' and so forth. (Of course, the 'drives' mentioned are actually your unconscious mind. When given a task in hypnosis, you simply 'go there' without knowing how this happens, or that the info was even stored.)

- ✔ **Releasing** is the process in which your hypnotherapist helps you change your negative thoughts, views, and feelings that are causing a delay in accessing your creativity.

- ✔ **Endlessly releasing** your inner resources when needed. This means finding the previous step increasingly easy to access. The way to make this easier is to learn self-hypnosis and practise it regularly.

Book IV

Hypnotherapy

Some techniques your hypnotherapist may use to help you release your creative side include:

- ✔ Directly requesting your unconscious mind to convince you that you can write/paint/draw/compose easily.

- ✔ Giving your ego a boost to remind you of past successes.

- ✔ Reminding you that your unconscious has infinite ideas.

- ✔ Increasing your motivation and concentration. This can be done through simple suggestions to your unconscious mind that you will find it easier to concentrate and that you will be more motivated.

- ✔ Asking your unconscious to become an ocean of ideas, awash with creativity that flows easily from within, breaking with clarity on the shores of your conscious awareness as and when you need them. (Can't seem to shake this metaphor thing, can we?)

- ✔ Practising self-hypnosis. Your hypnotherapist will probably give you suggestions to keep the well unblocked, and this is where self-hypnosis comes in. It's a good idea to ask your hypnotherapist to teach you self-hypnosis at the beginning of your sessions. Through self-hypnosis, you can turbocharge the results of your hypnotherapy and continue to deepen and maintain the wonderful by-products of an unblocked unconscious for the rest of your life!

Relaxation is the key to unlocking your creativity. No matter what technique your therapist uses, helping you to relax mind and body plays an important role.

Don't get us wrong. We don't mean that in order to be highly creative you have to be so relaxed that you flop about all over the place! On the contrary, it's all about creating the right balance between relaxation and tension. Too relaxed and you won't get anywhere and will probably fall asleep. Too tense and you block your creativity with anxiety, and start fretting over unwanted thoughts. Just the right amount of tension and just the right amount of relaxation keeps your mind alert and focused, and your creativity flowing.

It is down to the skill of the hypnotherapist to help you achieve this balance by using, and teaching you how to use, the very thing you probably have a problem in achieving – relaxation.

Unblocking your creative flow

Whether in art, writing, or music, you may reach a state of impasse in your creative flow, particularly when faced with deadlines or overwhelming self-criticism. Suddenly concentrating becomes impossible and you are unable to supply the creative part of your nature with the necessary ideas. Your flow of creativity just dries up and with every attempt you make to clear it, the blockage just gets stronger and stronger.

The reasons for your blockage can be many and may include:

- Negative thinking about your ability
- Fear of failure
- Fear of success (oh yes, there are many out there who fear this!)

Time then to clean out your pipes and remove that blockage!

So how does this business of using hypnotherapy to access your creative resources actually work? Traditionally, once you are in trance, the hypnotherapist asks your unconscious mind to imagine its creative potential. When your subconscious mind begins to imagine being more creative, the hypnotherapist can additionally suggest that you find it easy to develop new strategies to deal with your problem.

Your hypnotherapist can choose from many techniques, depending on your specific needs. A couple of methods good for helping unblock creativity include asking your unconscious for the answers to questions about the blockage, and creating solutions. Because these solutions come without input from your conscious mind, they feel natural and intuitive. The same system operates when you have a creative impulse, or when your muse inspires you. It is an uncalculated effort and usually feels particularly imaginative and creative because the thinking, analytical part – your conscious mind – cannot take credit for the solution. It is one of the most ethereal, yet real experiences that hypnotherapy regularly produces.

Hey presto, the flow of creativity commences once more.

In many cases, conscious insight is not necessary to remove your block. Oh dear, we hear the sound of many counsellors and psychotherapists preparing the heretical bonfire! Despite what some authorities say, your conscious mind doesn't need to understand why the blockage existed after the unconscious gives permission for it to be removed.

Chapter 4

Touching on Body Matters

· ·

In This Chapter

▶ Understanding how the mind can control pain

▶ Controlling skin problems with hypnosis

▶ Helping your heart

▶ Giving birth the hypnotherapy way

▶ Addressing intestinal issues

▶ Rooting for the dental/hypnosis combo

▶ Coping with physical problems with a psychological component

· ·

*H*ypnotherapists have to restrain themselves when describing the range of physical ailments hypnotherapy can help with. The challenge is to not oversell the incredible variety of treatments possible, nor in any way to imply that hypnotherapy is a substitute for medical care.

Hypnotherapy is a wonderful complementary adjunct to medical care and it can alleviate an amazing range of physical problems. Patients often seek help from a hypnotherapist *after* a doctor has ruled out any physical cause for a complaint and relegated it to the area of 'it must be emotional'.

Common areas of treatment that people come to hypnotherapists with include:

  ✔ Pain management

  ✔ Skin problems

  ✔ Pregnancy related issues

  ✔ Irritable bowel syndrome

  ✔ Bulimia

This is in no way a complete list, but rather the areas of physical treatments we discuss in this chapter.

Letting Go of Pain

Nobody likes to talk about pain – except maybe sadists and masochists. When you're healthy, pain probably never crosses your mind. However, when you experience pain, it takes up some part of your awareness and can affect your mood. If the pain is serious enough or becomes chronic (long-term in duration), it can make you feel irritable and depressed. Chronic pain can even weaken your immune system, making you susceptible to other health problems.

Although the American Medical Association listed hypnosis as an approved treatment for pain as early as 1958, it is a sad fact that medical science has been very slow to acknowledge the powerful pain relief that hypnosis can provide. The evidence of how effective hypnosis can be is available to anyone who wishes to review it.

People who deal with people in pain recognise two types of pain:

- **Acute pain:** Pain that is severe but lasts for a relatively short period of time.
- **Chronic pain:** Pain that ranges from mild to severe and is present for more than three months.

Both acute and chronic pain can involve periods where the sufferer is pain free.

If you have chronic pain that inhibits you from pursuing normal, everyday activities, consult your doctor. Obtain a physical examination from your doctor before seeking any help for pain. It is important to eliminate any medical issues before seeking a psychological cure, such as hypnosis. A qualified hypnotherapist will always gain confirmation and permission from your doctor, prior to using hypnosis, to work with pain-related issues.

Experiencing pain

Simply put, pain is your body's warning system that protects you from hurt or provides a warning that something is wrong somewhere in your body. We all react differently to pain. No two individuals are likely to have the same response to a similar pain-inducing event. But how do you describe something as subjective as pain? The experience of pain can be put into two broad components:

✔ **Sensory pain:** This tells you the location of the pain and its sensory quality – whether the pain is an aching, burning, cold, stabbing, or tingling sensation.

✔ **Affective pain:** This refers to your personal, subjective experience of pain – how much it bothers you.

An athlete may experience injury during her performance but isn't bothered by the pain while she focuses on winning. After finishing the competition, she may gradually, or suddenly, become more aware of the pain.

Perceiving pain

There's a distinct relationship between your perception of pain and how you experience it. If, for example, you're having fun playing football and experience a minor cut on your finger, you are likely not to feel the pain until the fun ends. However, if you are sitting in a quiet office, slightly bored and irritated and a little unhappy when you get a paper cut, the chances are that cut will really hurt because you have nothing to distract you.

The mind perceives pain subjectively. If you are distracted from your pain, you are less likely to focus on it and less likely to register it. For example, you have probably had the experience of suffering some minor injury, like a bruise or a paper cut, without realising it and then, suddenly, when you see it, only then do you begin to feel it. So pain does not necessarily cause suffering. How you perceive pain plays a large part in how you experience it.

Doctors cannot help you to have greater control over your perception of pain. Interestingly, hypnosis can. Your unconscious mind, however, has the power to alter your experience of pain.

Hypnosis can help you manage a variety of pain including headaches, muscular pains, dental operations, and childbirth. Hypnosis can even be used as a supplement to, or complete replacement for, anaesthesia used in surgery!

Book IV

Hypnotherapy

Relieving pain

During hypnosis, you relax and your mind focuses on something other than pain, possibly even something pleasurable. The combination of these two events – lowering your anxiety through relaxation and moving your focus away from the pain – lets your nervous system register less pain, or no pain at all. It is mainly through relaxation and removing fear that hypnosis pain reduction has its greatest advantages.

Theorising about how hypnosis manages pain

There are many theories about how hypnosis is effective with controlling pain. Until recently, it was believed that being in a hypnotic state produced *endorphins* – the body's natural painkillers. This theory now seems to have been disproved, or at least placed in dispute, by a number of researchers. Currently a more popular idea about the theory of hypnosis and pain control involves the 'gate control theory'. This theory was proposed in 1965 by researchers Melzack and Wall, and modified in 1978 by Professor Wall. It states that the brain and the spinal cord pass information about pain in the form of continuously flowing impulses. These pain information messages are sent via the central nervous system to the peripheral nerves.

According to the theory, certain cells and nerves within the body register any signals of injury or pain. These signals are then directed (or not) through a system within the body, not unlike a gate, that lets some message pass onto the brain. The messages allowed through the gate are then received by the brain and interpreted as pain. Because hypnosis can directly influence the nervous system through relaxation, it can decrease the amount of pain signals that are registered.

Research shows that the hypnotic management of pain is not a placebo effect, but has a physiological action that explains its effectiveness. Through PET (Positron Emission Tomography) scans, it has been demonstrated that hypnosis directly affects areas of the brain involved in the perception of suffering (the anterior cingulate cortex). Activity in this brain area decreases during hypnotic pain control.

Two options in dealing with pain management are:

- ✔ **Analgesia** refers to the partial loss of pain sensation.
- ✔ **Anaesthesia** refers to the total loss of any pain sensation.

Analgesic and anaesthetic techniques

Hypnotherapists may suggest using either the analgesic or the anaesthetic approach to your pain control. You may wonder why they don't use anaesthesia in all pain control work. After all, why not lose all the pain instead of just some of it? The reason is that it is usually a good idea to leave just a small amount of the pain behind after a hypnosis session. For example, if you suffered a badly sprained ankle, it probably wouldn't be a good idea to hypnotise all the pain away so that you could go out and run the Boston marathon!

Hypnosis to induce anaesthesia – the total loss of pain sensation – may be useful in a situation such as a surgery, where having an anaesthetic drug is not possible, or unwanted. In such a situation, hypnotherapy can be an alternative where a total absence of pain is required.

Using hypnosis to induce analgesia – the partial loss of pain sensation – may be useful for treating conditions such as migraines. In this situation, the migraines may be occurring for a reason, such as providing an indication of an underlying problem; a food allergy or a yet undiagnosed medical problem. Leaving a trace amount of pain serves as a reminder that more investigation may still be needed. Of course, the approach on whether to use hypnotic analgesia or anaesthesia is negotiable with your hypnotherapist.

Your hypnotherapist may very well avoid the word *pain* and substitute the word *discomfort*. Discomfort sounds much less serious than pain, and by deliberately reframing your perception of pain and subtly changing it, your hypnotherapist encourages your unconscious mind to shift your perception of the pain that your body is registering.

The level of trance directly correlates with how much pain can be made tolerable. Broadly speaking, the deeper the trance you experience, the deeper the pain you are able to endure. However, it's possible to undergo minor surgical procedures even in light and medium-deep trances.

With practise, you can use self-hypnosis to undergo routine dental procedures. Dentists with minimal hypnosis training can use it to perform minor procedures on their patients.

Glove anaesthesia has nothing to do with mittens

Glove anaesthesia is a hypnotherapy technique in which the entire hand is made insensitive – from the fingertips to the wrist. This area is numb, wooden-like, and lacks feeling – as if an anaesthetic had been injected. I (Mike) first saw this demonstrated as a student at the London College of Clinical Hypnosis. Michael Joseph, a master hypnotherapist, used a fellow student on our very first day in class – without inducing a trance. He simply spoke a few words and asked the student if she could imagine wearing a glove on a freezing winter day. The student said 'Yes' and he asked permission to test her hand. He then pinched her skin – very hard. She didn't flinch! But this was for demonstration purposes only. Your hypnotherapist will always work slowly, inducing a trance and being very careful with you!

Glove anaesthesia can be effective in a variety of uses, including treating arthritis and rheumatism, glaucoma, migraine and tension headaches, obesity, and skin disorders. It can be used to ease the pain of dental procedures, childbirth, cancer, and the phantom limb pain amputees feel. Psychological disorders may benefit from glove anaesthesia, and it can be used before and after surgery.

Book IV

Hypnotherapy

The *ice bucket technique* involves your hypnotherapist asking you to imagine placing one of your hands in a bucket full of crushed ice, up to the wrist. The hypnotherapist vividly describes how your hand feels as it gets colder and colder, eventually becoming numb. She then tells you that she's going to test your hand for sensitivity – gently – by pinching your hand with various degrees of strength.

This technique can be demonstrated without trance induction and still be effective. However, for deep and sustained levels of anaesthesia, such as for surgery, trance induction is required. In surgical hypnosis, several hypnosis sessions will typically take place prior to surgery. These will involve helping the client practise self-hypnosis, and experiencing sustained periods of trance and hypnotically induced anaesthesia.

Additionally, the hypnotherapist may inform you that the absence of sensation in your hand will remain even after awakening. She awakens you and tests for sensitivity by pinching the hand, with various degrees of strength. She then re-induces trance and places your 'anaesthetised' hand over your other hand, and informs you that the sense of numbness will be transferred to the non-anaesthetised hand.

You are then told to remove your hand only when the numbness has been transferred. This newly numbed hand is tested as before and then both hands are restored to normal. Your hypnotherapist teaches you self-hypnosis – *while in trance* – and awakens you. Then you are asked to hypnotise yourself, and while in the trance you are asked to anaesthetise one of your hands and then to transfer the numbness to the part of your body affected by pain. The hypnotherapist then suggests that you will be able to do glove anaesthesia at any time in the future, and that you will be able to use it to reduce pain. You are awakened with the new skill of being able to conduct glove anaesthesia on yourself!

Helping Your Skin Look Good

Care to guess what your body's largest organ is? (Men, be very careful with your answer!) Actually, your skin is the largest organ of your body, and what a protective organ it is! Skin acts as a defence against bacterial and viral attack, as well as protecting you from heat, cold, physical injury, and ultraviolet radiation. Skin regulates your body temperature, detects potential harm before injury can occur, provides input to the brain regarding the physical nature of the environment, and even allows you to become sexually aroused.

Since both the skin and the nervous system share a common organ – the *ectoderm* – it is not surprising that stress and anxiety can adversely affect the course of any skin disorder. Conversely, once skin disorders develop, they often produce and prolong the mental and emotional disturbances that can perpetuate symptoms. Hypnosis can be a wonderful adjunct to conventional medical treatments in providing relief from a variety of dermatological problems.

In the following sections we talk about three of the four main types of dermatological problems – eczema, psoriasis, and warts.

Hypnotherapy can't do a lot for someone with acne, the fourth type of skin problem, other than bolster their sense of self-worth. Acne is best treated by dermatologists as it has fairly serious medical implications.

Scratching away at psoriasis and eczema

Both psoriasis and eczema are also known to be stress-related diseases that respond well to reduction in stress levels. Hypnotherapy can help to alleviate stress and thereby factors that may exacerbate both conditions.

Relieving the rash of eczema

A common condition, *eczema* is a very itchy, peeling, thickened, sometimes weepy area of inflamed skin, typically found in the creases of joints and the trunk of the body. The rash may fluctuate both seasonally and over the course of a day. Scratching may lead to bleeding and infection.

Eczema may have physical causes, such as with varicose eczema, in which swollen or twisted veins may influence the condition, but eczema is thought to be a stress-induced condition.

Scaling back psoriasis

Psoriasis is characterised by plaques of red, scaly, easily bleeding skin, often over the knees, elbows, trunk, and back. Finger and toenails may develop pitting. Some people with severe arthritis are prone to getting psoriasis as well.

Book IV

Hypnotherapy

The disease varies widely from one patient to another and in rare, severe cases, may be life-threatening because wide areas of skin are exposed to infection.

The cause of psoriasis is not known, although genetic factors appear to play a role. Environmental factors such as injury, stress, cold climate, and other illnesses are known to adversely affect the condition with some patients.

Stop kissing frogs: Treating your warts

Warts are overgrowths of skin cells caused by the human papilloma virus. The major symptoms are cosmetic, and treating warts is primarily a matter of preference, although warts in certain locations (the sole of the foot, for example) can cause pain.

You can spread warts by person-to-person contact and you can increase the number of warts you have by scratching or picking at them.

Whether you develop warts depends on your immune response to the virus. Though people with known immune deficiencies are more susceptible, most sufferers have a normal immune system.

About 25 per cent of warts go away on their own within 6 months, 50 per cent within a year, and 65 per cent by two years.

Easing skin problems with hypnotherapy

Skin conditions are often exacerbated by anxiety as well as through scratching. Hypnosis – as you know by now – is excellent for lessening anxiety. A hypnotherapist working with someone with a skin disorder would make suggestions to address any emotional problems that may be causing anxiety, and would pay particular attention to the patient's everyday circumstances.

If a client's anxiety is linked to issues of low self-esteem, part of the treatment would include direct suggestions for ego-boosting.

Approaching techniques

For skin problems linked to psychological or emotional problems, your hypnotherapist can choose from a range of techniques, based on your individual needs, such as

- Suggestions to decrease the perception of itching sensations. For example, 'You might still feel itchy, but you no longer have any desire to scratch.'

- Post-hypnotic suggestions providing practical techniques to alleviate the desire to scratch. For example, you may imagine breathing through the itchy parts of your skin with sensations of 'calmness' and 'coolness', and feel relaxed as you do so, or 'You have no desire to scratch'.

✔ Symptom substitution to eliminate scratching. The hypnotherapist may suggest substitute feelings, such as numbness or pressure, instead of itchiness.

✔ Analytical techniques similar to doing counselling or psychotherapy in trance. These techniques may be used when the previously mentioned techniques are deemed ineffective. Analytical techniques are more of an advanced treatment approach and may involve a deeper application, not dissimilar to psychoanalysis. Don't worry – they're not physically painful!

These analytical techniques may involve such approaches as:

- **Regression:** Using hypnosis to take you back in time to before you had the problem. This allows the therapist to demonstrate to you the link between your mind and body, thus giving you control over the symptoms.

- **Dissociation:** This involves working with any unresolved issues that contribute to the skin condition. Dissociation techniques allow you to gain insight into your condition, as well as develop strategies to resolve your problem. Chapter 1 has in-depth information on dissociation.

Glove anaesthesia (see the 'Glove anaesthesia has nothing to do with mittens' section earlier in this chapter) is an effective treatment for burning sensations and can be used to 'freeze' a wart. How does this work? In a word, *dissociation*. The hypnotherapist creates a split between your conscious awareness of pain sensation and the normal response of reacting to pain, thus dissociating your normal reaction to pain. It's like watching a film of yourself having the wart frozen. You wouldn't react with the pain sensation if you were simply watching yourself having the wart removed (although you might cringe!).

Sampling scripts for treating skin problems

In this section are some typical scripts a hypnotist may use for skin problems. The scripts are phrases that broadly represent what a hypnotherapist might say as part of post-hypnotic therapy; that is, after you've been hypnotised and are still in trance.

Keep in mind that these scripts are worded generally, and in a real session would be specifically tailored to your particular problem. Your hypnotherapist won't use the exact words we use; she tailors her words to be meaningful to you and your situation. Still, you can get a good idea of the various approaches from reading the following scripts.

Book IV

Hypnotherapy

Stopping scratching

In this script, your hypnotherapist would identify the specific areas most affected by the rash, to personalise the suggestion for you.

> '. . . and you have no desire to scratch . . . if at any time . . . your hand moves toward your skin in order to scratch . . . the moment your fingers touch your skin . . . you will instantly . . . and immediately become aware of what you are about to do . . . and your hand will move away from your skin . . . and because of this . . . your comfort will increase . . . and your skin will continue to heal . . . and any rash will begin to disappear more and more rapidly . . . even while you sleep at night . . . the moment your fingers touch your skin in order to scratch . . . instantly and immediately your hand will move away from your skin . . . and your skin will continue to heal . . . as you sleep . . . because of this treatment . . . you will be able to exercise enough self-control to . . . allow your skin to heal . . .'

Improving circulation

A hypnotherapist may treat itching by suggesting that your blood circulation is improving. Research shows that the mind can directly affect circulation.

> '. . . your heart will beat more strongly . . . so that more blood will flow through the little blood vessels in the skin . . . carrying more nourishment to the skin . . . because of this . . . your skin will become well nourished . . . it will become healthier . . . and the rash will gradually diminish . . . until it fades away completely . . . leaving the underlying new skin . . . perfectly healthy and normal in every way . . . and . . . as your circulation improves . . . and you become stronger and steadier in every way . . . so . . . the unwanted itching and irritation of your skin will subside . . . and disappear . . . the comfort increasing each day . . .'

The next brief script is for lowering blood circulation:

> '. . . as a result of this treatment . . . you are going to feel fitter and stronger in every way . . . your circulation will improve . . . particularly the little blood vessels that supply the skin . . .'

The above script would actually allow your circulation to improve and allow blood vessels to become healthier.

Solving skin-caused insomnia

If you have a severe skin condition, you may have trouble sleeping, either because of the pain, or the itch. Your hypnotherapist can use your discomfort to ease you into a restorative slumber, through a reverse suggestion:

> '. . . the more you notice the discomfort . . . the drowsier you become . . . until you fall into a deep . . . refreshing . . . healing sleep . . .'

So you can see that the suggestions lead you into a feeling that healing is taking place, even as you become progressively sleepier.

Working on warts

In assisting you in ridding yourself of warts, your hypnotherapist may give you suggestions including:

- ✔ The blood flow to the wart has stopped. You then imagine your wart shrivelling and dropping off, leaving an area of healthy skin behind.
- ✔ Your wart becomes smaller and smaller until it disappears.
- ✔ Your wart is an unwanted building. You then imagine that your immune system is a demolition company, taking apart the unwanted building and carting it away.

Relieving the Pressure of Hypertension

Hypertension (high blood pressure) affects millions of people every year, and is a major contributing factor to coronary heart disease and stroke. Until recently the main treatment approaches involved pharmacological intervention and lifestyle changes. However, more eclectic approaches have been developed involving clinical hypnosis.

Hypnosis can play an important role in maintaining a healthy heart as well as aiding recovery from a variety of cardiovascular diseases. When entering trance, a shift in the autonomic nervous system from sympathetic (responsible for activity) to parasympathetic (responsible for rest) control occurs. When the parasympathetic nervous system is dominant the heart rate decreases, thus reducing the burden on the cardiovascular system.

For anyone experiencing cardiovascular disease, the following lists ways hypnotherapy techniques may be useful:

- ✔ Mastering self-hypnosis for relaxation
- ✔ Using hypnosis to cope better with lifestyle issues such as stress management, weight control, diet, alcohol consumption, and smoking
- ✔ Using hypnosis to engage in appropriate exercise
- ✔ Working with issues of depression related to health problems

Book IV

Hypnotherapy

Relaxation techniques are an important part of helping to alleviate feelings of stress, which are often contributing factors to hypertension.

Let's get things straight, right from the start. Your hypnotherapist will *not* give you suggestions that your blood pressure becomes lower and lower. It just doesn't work that way. However, the very act of going into trance lowers your blood pressure. In fact studies show that people who have regular experience of trance, either with a therapist or through practising self-hypnosis, can achieve a significant lowering of their blood pressure, with some being able to come off their antihypertensive medications. So, when your therapist asks you to practise self-hypnosis, make sure that you practise it. And regularly!

Going into trance isn't the complete story. An important part of managing hypertension is making some important lifestyle changes according to your doctor's recommendation. Many external factors influence hypertension, and working with a hypnotherapist can help you by looking at strategies designed to control these. Your hypnotherapist can strengthen your resolve to carry out your doctor's orders.

These changes are not just for the short term. If you keep them up, you can definitely help to reduce your blood pressure to a much safer level. And if you need a boost in your determination, pick up your phone and call your hypnotherapist!

Never stop taking your medication without your doctor or consultant giving the go-ahead. You're taking it for a reason, and that is to keep you healthy! If you make the required lifestyle changes and stick to them, you have a very good chance that you'll be able to either cut down or stop taking your meds – but *only* with your doctor's say so!

Taking a Pregnant Pause for Childbirth

Hypnosis is useful for a range of issues around conception, pregnancy, and childbirth. Many people are unaware that hypnotherapy can help in this area, but hypnotherapists are regularly involved with helping couples conceive and also get through childbirth with minimum difficulties.

Conceiving options

How does hypnosis help someone become pregnant? Mainly through helping decrease the anxiety associated with having sex with the goal of conceiving. *The Law of Reversed Effect* states that the harder you try to do something, the more likely you are to fail at it. The body works this way too. If you're desperate to conceive each time you have sex, your body may activate hormones that kill off the very sperm that you want to fertilise your ovum. So hypnosis simply helps you to relax, and may offer suggestions of you becoming extremely fertile.

Hypnosis can help only those people who can't conceive due to *psychogenic infertility* – infertility without a physiological cause. Put another way, hypnosis may be able to help if there's no known biological or physical obstacle to pregnancy, and the problem is most likely emotional. Around 17 per cent of all couples experience psychogenic infertility, with psychological stressors possibly playing a central role.

However, hypnosis can help a significant percentage of people with psychogenic infertility conceive. The scientific community is still trying to explain exactly *why* hypnosis is effective in this area, but if you have been unsuccessful in conceiving, and your doctor has found no medical reason why you shouldn't be able to have a baby, you can have hope that there is a good possibility that hypnosis may help you. Given the choice between hypnosis and expensive and complicated *in vitro* fertilisation (IVF) treatments, there really is no competition.

For many people who are having difficulty in conceiving, it becomes an arduous task for both sides of the parental divide: making sure you do the act at the right time, when the woman's temperature is right, having to lie back for 20 minutes with your legs in the air to let gravity do its job, and so on. It takes all the fun out of it and more importantly, on a biological level, it adds stress into the equation.

When you're trying to conceive, stress puts a major biological spanner in the works! When you're stressed, your body's biology switches from long-term survival priorities to immediate survival priorities. And the last thing the body wants at this time is for its all-important biological resources to be drained by having a baby growing inside it! Changing the biological balance of the body makes it a much less welcoming place for the sperm and egg to meet and unite. Think how you feel when you meet someone in a warm and inviting environment. The lights are low, soft music playing in the background, and love is in the air. Turn a couple of spotlights (playing the role of stress) onto the scene and turn the music up loud, and the last thing you think of is romance!

We've all heard the tales of couples who spend years trying to conceive a baby. In the end, they give up and adopt. The next thing you know, the woman is pregnant. The stress of trying to conceive prevented the very thing the parents were after. Take away the stress and the body reverts to long-term survival priorities, the biological lights and music are lowered, and the next thing you know, a baby is on its way!

Book IV

Hypnotherapy

Both the male and female in a couple experiencing psychogenic infertility should undertake treatment. Women who are stressed out because of this problem experience chemical changes in their pH levels that make pregnancy more difficult, and men who are stressed may experience decreased sperm counts.

Hypnosis does not work in cases where there is a known medical problem. A qualified hypnotherapist will always ensure that you have a thorough medical examination prior to seeking hypnotherapy.

Delivering the goods

Many mothers have discovered that hypnotherapy can dramatically improve their ability to enjoy the experiences of both pregnancy and labour. If you are pregnant and considering hypnosis, we encourage you to try hypnosis and enjoy your child's introduction to the world.

In the 'Relieving Pain' section earlier in this chapter, we describe *hypnotic analgesia* – the partial loss of the sensation of pain. Analgesia can also be successfully applied to childbirth, with no problems for you or your child. Many studies consistently show that hypnosis can be effective in pain management, as well as in improving the birth experience.

The main goals for hypnotherapy are to help the mother-to-be achieve control over her pain and develop a greater sense of self-control throughout labour and delivery.

To make this happen you schedule a series of hypnosis sessions when you're pregnant – for you and your birth partner, if possible. Your hypnotherapist takes you through the stages of self-hypnosis – probably during your first session – so that you can practise pain control techniques (Chapter 6 is devoted to self-hypnosis). You may also benefit from visualisations that increase your confidence and ability to relax.

Your hypnotherapist will help you, while in trance, visualise going through the stages of labour and delivery safely and easily, and give you suggestions to enable you to conduct self-hypnosis and induce a loss of sensation of pain as you experience these stages. The hypnotherapist may also suggest that during all this you are in constant, reassuring communication with the child in your womb.

During your sessions with her, your hypnotherapist will take you through all the stages of labour and delivery. Keep in mind that the hypnotherapist will help you and your partner reach a level of skill in self-hypnosis (for the mother), and skills for the partner to make simple, post-hypnotic suggestions to ensure that the mother is relaxed and able to cope with any situation that arises. The following list offers a stage-by-stage approach to how this occurs:

- **Pre-birth stage:** Your hypnotherapist addresses any specific concerns you may have, and helps increase your confidence about the birth and post-birth period. This is when you become familiar with pain control techniques.

  Your birth partner can find out how to cue you on relaxation and trance responses.

- **Birth stage:** Your hypnotherapist will probably suggest that, no matter what level of relaxation or trance you are in, you will always respond to your midwife's or doctor's instructions.

  You will probably also be given suggestions that, no matter what happens, you will remain calm. This will prepare you to cope well with anything unexpected that may arise.

- **Post-birth stage:** For the post-birth stage, you may receive suggestions for healing and recovery. Also helpful for this stage are suggestions for confidence and helping you, as a new mother, to feel able to cope. Further hypnosis pain control techniques appropriate for this stage may also be helpful.

Examples of what a hypnotherapist may say at this stage are:

- *'As the process of bringing your baby into the world begins . . . you will find that the contractions will be weak.'*

- *'You will feel the contractions merely as pressure in your stomach . . . and you will feel calm . . . relaxed . . . and in control throughout.'*

- *'As the contractions continue . . . you will always follow the advice of your midwife or doctor . . . and as soon as you feel the urge to bear down . . . tell the midwife . . . but do not give way until she tells you to . . . when she does . . . take a deep breath . . . hold it as long as you can . . . and push down as hard as you can . . . as long as each contraction lasts . . . if you have to breathe out before the contraction is over . . . take another deep breath as quickly as possible . . . and continue to hold it and push down . . . since it is usually the last part of the contraction that produces most progress . . . you will find that this will greatly reduce any discomfort.'*

Book IV

Hypnotherapy

Improving Irritable Bowel Syndrome

Irritable bowel syndrome (IBS) is a disorder of the intestines. When your gut is working normally, you hardly notice that it moves food through its long passageway, through a series of muscular contractions known as *peristalsis*. Problems with these contractions are classified under the broad heading of IBS.

Hypnotherapy is a recommended treatment for IBS and most people respond rapidly. Usually three sessions are all that are required.

Before going to see a hypnotherapist for IBS treatment, get a proper medical diagnosis of IBS confirmed by a GP. The symptoms may indicate a potentially serious condition, and a qualified hypnotherapist will never work on a patient's self-diagnosis.

Problems with IBS can potentially extend throughout your entire digestive system, which includes the area from your mouth to your anus. Hence, a great number of different conditions come under the heading of IBS.

Some of the symptoms that people with IBS may experience, and that hypnotherapy can help with, include:

- Abdominal distress or pain.
- Cramps or pains in the lower abdomen or rectum (often after eating).
- Variations in bowel movements, including constipation and diarrhoea.

  Bowel movements may alternate between constipation and diarrhoea. Even after a bowel movement, you may feel that the rectum is still full.
- A feeling of urgency. People with IBS often need to rush and open their bowels, usually soon after eating. Incontinence may occur if a toilet is not nearby.
- Bloating. IBS sufferers may experience flatulence or painful trapped wind. You may have rumbling noises in your abdomen.
- Back pain associated with irregular bowel movements.
- Nausea, belching, and vomiting.

Dealing with your IBS anxiety

Many IBS sufferers feel ashamed of their condition. They may experience extreme incontinence, or extreme constipation, or both. This may lead them to feel that this problem has to be kept secret, even sometimes from their own doctors. If their problem is a long-term one, it may lead to psychological problems such as anxiety and depression. Ironically, anxiety and depression exacerbate the symptoms of IBS. Relieving anxiety can be an immense help to IBS sufferers, and confidence and relief from anxiety are areas in which hypnosis excels.

Offering an ice-cold example

Imagine that you come to a hypnotherapist for treatment for IBS. Your session may go something like this:

> *'. . . I would like you to imagine that there is a large bucket of very cold water, filled with lumps of ice . . .'*

At this point your hypnotherapist will vividly describe the bucket to you, using all modalities of sensory representation such as touch, imagined vision, and so on.

> *'. . . and now . . . you are dipping your fingertips into the surface of the water and you can feel the ice against your skin . . . you will notice that the sensation is changing in your fingertips, as they become more and more numb, and you start to lose all feeling in them . . . I now want you to immerse your whole hand into the bucket of water and ice, and notice how the numbness starts to spread over your hand . . . as your hand becomes . . . and continues to become . . . colder and colder . . . you are aware that all sensations are now disappearing from that hand . . . including any response that may arise from a painful stimulus . . . it will seem as if a thick leather glove has been placed on your hand . . . and the colder it gets the more like a piece of wood your hand becomes . . .'*

When the hypnotherapist is convinced that your hand is numb, she instructs you to transfer the numbness to your belly, to help calm your overactive colon. She then gently places your hand on your stomach and tells you that you are going to transfer the analgesia from your hand to your colon.

> *'. . . I want you to imagine that your numb hand is very cold . . . and that this cold is stored in the form of a blue dye . . . and when I count to three I want you to start transferring this dye to your abdomen . . . you may notice how the coldness and numb feeling begins to spread over your abdomen as the dye flows from your hand . . . ready . . . now . . . 1 . . . 2 . . . 3...'*

When the numbness has transferred, the hypnotherapist continues:

> *'. . . Observe how free from discomfort your abdomen is and how your colon is quiet and free from tension . . . and unnecessary contractions . . . it just continues to do very little as far as you are concerned . . . you notice that your hand is now a normal colour and all sensation has returned . . . and . . . the numbness only persists in your abdomen and colon . . . as the days and weeks go by . . . and your unconscious mind is more and more able to control your inner feelings . . . you will feel less bloated as your inner tensions and anxiety flow from your body . . . leaving you calm and able to live your life in a way that is more satisfying to you . . . free from pain . . . free from your problems . . .'*

Before awakening you from trance, your hypnotherapist may teach you to automatically hypnotise yourself, and to use pain control techniques whenever needed in the future. Then they awaken you from trance in the usual way.

Book IV

Hypnotherapy

Conventional medical treatment of IBS involves stress management and dietary awareness, along with pharmacological intervention when needed.

- ✔ **Diet:** Avoidance of foods that irritate the gastro-intestinal tract is recommended, including spicy food, cabbage, turnip, caffeine-containing drinks, and alcohol. Hypnosis can help to maintain good, healthy eating habits.

- ✔ **Pharmacological intervention:** Bulk-forming agents and anti-diarrhoeal medications may be used. Antispasmodic drugs may also be used in severe cases, to regulate peristalsis. Hypnosis can help with overcoming any resistance to following the medication schedule.

- ✔ **Stress management:** Guess what we recommend for an excellent stress management tool? Hypnosis of course! Through hypnosis-based stress management, IBS sufferers may experience significant relief.

Coping with constipation and diarrhoea

IBS sufferers may fluctuate between constipation and diarrhoea. So what exactly does a hypnotherapist do to help?

Depending on the individual, a hypnotherapist can provide a variety of areas of help, including:

- ✔ **Stress management:** IBS is often related to stress and worry. Hypnosis offers other ways to see the problem as not so overwhelming. This can help to provide new coping skills and a sense of managing better.

- ✔ **Relaxation:** A person with IBS invariably associates the toilet with anxiety. A common hypnotherapy approach is to ask the IBS patient to practise hypnosis while using the toilet, in order to be relaxed.

- ✔ **Metaphorical imagery:** While in trance, a hypnotherapist can help to offer metaphorical images that provide relief. For example, to help with constipation, a hypnotherapist may tell you to imagine logs flowing freely down a river; for diarrhoea, imagining logs jamming up a river flow. These can be very effective if given while in trance.

Loving the Dentist!

Hands up those who look forward to going to see the dentist. Hmmm . . . very few hands seem to be appearing! Well, that can all change with a little hypnosis.

Various applications for dental hypnosis exist, including:

- ✔ Controlling pain
- ✔ Treating phobias
- ✔ Controlling excessive salivation or bleeding
- ✔ Controlling the gag reflex
- ✔ Adjusting to orthodontics, such as dentures, braces, and so on
- ✔ Stopping smoking (it adversely affects gums, and so is a dental concern)

I (Mike) work as a hypnotherapist within a London dental practice, and help a range of people overcome various psychological issues prior to receiving dental treatment. Some people fear even the simplest dental procedures, and would otherwise require an expensive anaesthetist to give them a general anaesthetic. Usually a couple of sessions of hypnotherapy can overcome life-long phobias.

Dentists and medical doctors are now beginning to learn hypnotherapy themselves. Since the 1950s and 1960s medical staff – admittedly in small numbers – have used hypnosis, or employed sessional hypnotherapists. Additionally, some training courses exist, such as at the London College for Clinical Hypnosis, aimed specifically for medically trained staff.

Drilling away at your problem

Many people have a fear of dental drills. This is understandable due to the noise, and occasional pain, that may accompany the use of a drill. The fear of drills for some patients can be extreme.

Hypnotherapy can help get rid of the fear of the dentist's drill. Chapter 5 deals with phobia treatments in detail, so here we only briefly mention some of the approaches that a hypnotherapist may use to help you receive a treatment that involves the dentist's drill. Some of these approaches are:

Book IV

Hypnotherapy

- ✔ Hypnotising you to float out of your body during the drilling.
- ✔ Hypnotising you to speed up your subjective sense of time, so that the procedure seems to be over in seconds.
- ✔ Hypnotising you to forget about being afraid.
- ✔ Dealing directly with the fear itself through more extensive phobia treatments.

Grinding down your bruxism: Teeth-grinding and hypnotherapy

Bruxism is the unconscious grinding and/or clenching of the teeth, when a person isn't eating. It's often associated with high stress levels, anger, or rage. Bruxism can happen day or night, though most people experience it while asleep. Problems bruxism causes may include:

✔ Fracturing and/or erosion of the teeth.

✔ Breakdown of the bone supporting the teeth.

✔ Fracturing of the jaw if bruxism is severe.

✔ The jaw may 'click' (frequently audible) when eating.

✔ Problems in the joint connecting the jaw to the skull, which may lead to a condition known as myofacial pain dysfunctional syndrome, a chronically painful condition affecting the face (often only one side).

If you grind your teeth while you sleep, your partner may point out another problem – that you keep him or her awake!

Hypnotherapists usually treat bruxism using very direct methods such as suggesting that, as soon as your teeth touch in order to grind or clench, you stop instantly, relax the muscles of your jaw, and drift into a deeper and more refreshing sleep.

Obsessing About Change: Obsessive-Compulsive Disorder (OCD)

The word *obsessive* is part of everyday parlance, but the psychological condition known as *obsessive-compulsive disorder (OCD)* is an anxiety disorder characterised by:

✔ Recurrent and persistent thoughts, ideas, images, and feelings that are perceived as intrusive and senseless.

✔ Repetitive, ritualised behaviours that the individual feels compelled to carry out in order to prevent the obsessional thoughts and the associated discomfort.

The obsessive thoughts, or compulsive behaviours, are severe enough to be time-consuming – occupy more than one hour per day – or may cause significant distress or impairment to the patient's normal way of life. Often the person with OCD recognises that the obsessive-compulsive behaviour is excessive and unreasonable, but is powerless to stop it. The condition is usually highly secretive and can remain hidden from even immediate members of the patient's family.

For people with OCD, attempts to resist the compulsive behaviour may cause increasing tension and anxiety, which is relieved by giving in to the compulsion.

Of the many compulsive behaviours that can be expressed with OCD, the most common are:

- ✔ **Washing:** Washing or cleaning is the most prevalent compulsion, and is characterised by a fear and avoidance of contamination, as well as elaborate washing, cleaning, or decontamination rituals.

- ✔ **Checking:** Checking behaviours – the next most common – involve elaborate and repeated checking in order to prevent a perceived disaster or dreaded event from occurring. Behaviours that may be expressed include ritual behaviours involving superstitions, and any range of other repeated, or extremely over-cautious behaviours, all intended to make the OCD sufferer feel safer, although often causing great fear and worry instead.

- ✔ **Ordering:** Having to be sequential about items – for example, having specific locations for every item of food and clothing, with no variation or exceptions allowed.

Hypnosis can help with OCD issues. A hypnotherapy approach can view the basis of OCDs as the splitting off of a certain emotional part of the individual. This damaged, split-off emotional content is just out of reach of conscious thought, but is easily recognised in a dream, or in an altered state of consciousness induced by hypnosis. OCD disorders yield successfully to hypnotherapy, or any technique that seeks to reintegrate the split-off component of the personality.

The therapy approach is essentially a two-stage approach involving:

- ✔ **Stage one:** The split-off part is identified and treated.
- ✔ **Stage two:** The symptoms are removed as a separate stage of hypnosis. (Chapter 2 discusses how hypnosis helps change habits.)

Book IV

Hypnotherapy

Beating Bulimia

Bulimia nervosa is an eating disorder characterised by:

- ✔ Episodes of uncontrolled eating or bingeing. During the binge, the bulimic eats enormous amounts of food (often sweet and high in calories) rapidly, until she is uncomfortably or painfully full. For example, a bulimic patient may consume a whole loaf of bread, a pot of jam, an entire cake, and a packet of biscuits in one binge episode. This bingeing provides relief from the tension experienced prior to the binge. Guilt and disgust with regard to the binge rapidly follow. These feelings promote the consequent purge or excess exercise.

- ✔ Extreme and inappropriate measures to control body weight, including taking diuretics and forced vomiting after meals.

- ✔ Distorted ideas concerning body shape. For example, a thin person who believes that they are overweight.

The two distinct subtypes of bulimia nervosa are:

- ✔ **Purging type:** A binge episode is followed by *purging* – self-induced vomiting, the use of laxatives, diuretics, or enemas – to control weight.

- ✔ **Non-purging type:** The person uses excessive exercise or fasting to prevent weight gain after a binge episode. Purging is rarely seen.

Bulimic patients are usually of normal weight. Those who are underweight tend to be diagnosed as having anorexia nervosa of the purging type. Bulimics experience a profound loss of control over their eating behaviour, and may experience *dissociation*. Dissociation experiences involve feeling cut-off from what is happening. Bulimics also cut-off when they are at their most ill and in the process of bingeing on food, or purging what they have eaten.

There may be several bouts of the binge and purge/exercise cycle within one day. The binge and purge cycle is normally secretive. Bulimic patients report complete lack of control during a binge. However, control can return, as the person stops eating if someone enters the room during the binge.

Contrary to popular belief, bulimia is not a 'women-only' condition. Although 90 per cent of all people with bulimia nervosa are female, men can experience it as well. Men who experience bulimia nervosa are more likely to have been obese prior to the onset of the condition.

Treating bulimia through hypnosis

One view of bulimia nervosa says that it's similar to obsessive-compulsive disorders. The binge behaviour is the result of a dissociated part of the individual, with the purge/exercise behaviour becoming a conditioned response to the guilt experienced after the binge.

Low self-esteem, depression, and anxiety disorders are often associated with bulimia nervosa. Hypnotherapy can help with all these conditions. One of the main approaches to helping with bulimia is to educate and address, in hypnosis, the dissociative behaviour involved when bingeing and/or purging. Bulimics are, in a sense, ideal candidates for hypnotherapy as the process of trance involves dissociating the conscious from the unconscious, and bulimics are already skilled at dissociation. Emphasising the conscious awareness of bulimic behaviour gives the patient greater conscious control and awareness over their behaviour.

The hypnotherapist may give direct suggestions, while the patient is in trance, to alter or stop the splitting off, and to become highly conscious of the hand-to-mouth behaviour that occurs during either bingeing or purging behaviour. Suggestions may be given directly to stop. That is an authoritative approach involving a powerful message to simply stop the behaviour.

Making sure hypnosis and medications mesh

When a medical condition could be part of your problem, most professional hypnotherapists will work with you only with the informed consent of your doctor. The general rule is: always go to your doctor first to ensure that all potential physical causes to your problems have been eliminated.

Be open with both your doctor and your hypnotherapist. They both want to help you. Check with your doctor that receiving hypnosis is safe for you. Likewise, always inform your hypnotherapist about medications you take that affect your mood, speech, or ability to concentrate. Other than that, medication is not usually a problem.

Hypnotherapists are often asked how hypnosis interacts with medication, at a first meeting. The question is usually something like, 'I'm on Prozac. Will it be a problem for me to receive hypnosis?' The answer is 'no'. However, it is always a good idea to discuss fully the medications you have been prescribed, and the reasons for taking them.

In general, if you feel clear-headed enough to concentrate and work on your emotional issues, it is fine to undertake hypnotherapy.

Book IV

Hypnotherapy

Analytical approaches can also be used to deal with any of the underlying emotional issues that contributed to the behaviour. These approaches combined – dissociation awareness, direct suggestion and analytical work – can be a powerful therapeutic approach in helping people with bulimia.

Looking at binge eating disorder

Binge eating disorder is found in approximately two per cent of the population, and is predominantly seen in women. Binge eating disorder follows a similar pattern to bulimia, except that patients do not use extreme forms of weight management. Consequently, those suffering from binge eating disorder are obese. Binge eating disorder is treated in a similar way to bulimia nervosa.

Treatment for bingeing behaviour is very similar to the treatment for bulimia: awareness of dissociative behaviour, direct suggestions to stop bingeing and, if deemed useful, analytical techniques to deal with emotional issues. Additionally, for both bulimics and binge eaters, additional lifestyle issues, such as over-exercising, poor diet, and so on, can be addressed using hypnosis.

Chapter 5

Expanding the Reach
of Hypnotherapy

. . . .

In This Chapter

▶ Defining past-life regression

▶ Finding out how to get back to the past before you were born

▶ Getting back to the present

▶ Exploring phobias

▶ Identifying and removing phobias

. . . .

*A*nd now you seemingly enter the world of the mystical to find out how to travel back in time to visit yourself before you were even born. We are, of course, talking about past-life regression (PLR), a therapy technique that many find baffling and many more find exceptionally fascinating. PLR is an approach to helping you overcome your problem, based on the concept of *reincarnation*; a belief that your soul is reborn into different bodies and that you have lived a life (or lives) before your current one.

For many in the Western world, the idea that we have lived other lives before this one is frankly laughable. We have one life and once it's over, that's your lot. End of story. But many millions of people throughout the world, both Western and Eastern, are just as convinced in their belief in the concept of having lived many lives in the past. And it is from this belief that the very powerful hypnotherapy technique of past-life regression has been developed.

Getting Back to the Present

Past-life regression (PLR) is one of the techniques that people often associate with hypnotherapy. PLR is a technique used in hypnotherapy that works with a person's belief in reincarnation. PLR takes you back in time, in your mind, to visit a life, or lives, you lived before. PLR has wonderful esoteric connotations of the mystical hypnotist with staring eyes, lulling his subjects into a trance and then parting the curtains of the mists of time as they travel back to some major historical event. All very nice, and it looks wonderful in those low-budget movies; however the reality of PLR is actually quite mundane.

Beliefs about PLR

Okay. So is PLR real? Who knows? As yet there is no absolute proof one way or the other. Remember, we are dealing with belief systems here and that means, if you truly believe you have lived before, then it is very real . . . for you!

Many people and therapists believe in the powerful therapeutic results of PLR, but don't necessarily believe in reincarnation. So what do they believe PLR is? Here are some of the most popular theories:

- ✔ **PLR accesses genetic memory.** One school of thought believes that certain memories are encoded in our genetic make-up. In other words, somehow memories are stored in our genes. When you experience PLR, these memories are dragged up out of your DNA and once again experienced.

- ✔ **PLR accesses the collective unconscious.** This idea comes from Jungian psychology. Carl Jung was around at the same time as Sigmund Freud. One of the many psychological theories he developed is that of the *collective unconscious*. Jung believed that we all store in our unconscious a whole host of memories that are shared by everyone , and which are passed down to us from our ancestors. PLR provides a means of accessing the collective unconscious and experiencing these memories.

- ✔ **PLR is a dissociative experience.** This theory says that a person experiencing a PLR is creating a new existence in their mind from various pieces of their existing memory. Basically, you create a person and an existence through which you can 'observe' your problem, and its solution, in a metaphorical way – so that you're split off, or dissociated, from the problem. The distance provides a safe way to deal with the problem and the unconscious means to apply the solution.

- ✔ **PLR accesses memories from past lives.** Okay, we're back where we started. In this model, you believe that you've lived before and can access these past lives through hypnosis. As you access past lives, you can also influence them by helping your past self to resolve the unresolved issues that occurred in the life.

Whatever the truth of the matter about what PLR is, when it boils down to it it's *your* belief that is most important. So, if you truly believe that your problem stems from something that happened to you in a past life – and who's to say you are wrong? – then discuss this with your therapist. If she judges that it is right for you to explore this idea, then she will be happy to take you back into your past existence.

Reasons to revisit past lives

So, why do you want to go back and visit your past lives? Usually for one of two main reasons:

- You're simply curious and want to find out about who and what you were before you came into this life.

- You believe that the problems you're having stem from events that occurred in a life, or lives, you experienced prior to this one.

Many therapists happily help you explore your past lives for no other reason than you're interested in who you were. But it is the second reason that explains PLR's most common use in the therapy room.

As you go through life, you have many conflicts and experiences that you need to work through and resolve. However, there are also many that you don't. Obvious so far, but this is where past-life theory kicks in. Past-life theory has it that some unresolved issues may well be so significant, that when you pass into your next life they continue to affect you, creating some of the problems that you may now be experiencing.

That doesn't mean to say that the unresolved issue you had in a past life will manifest itself in exactly the same way in your current life. Far from it, what you're likely to experience is something that is almost a metaphor for the past problem. For example:

- **Weight issues:** It may be that you were starving in a past life, and your weight problem is an attempt to prevent that from occurring in this life.

- **Psychosomatic pain:** It may be that you had a violent accident in a past life where a part of your body was seriously injured. In your current life you experience a pain for which there is no demonstrable cause, in a similar area of your body.

  Psychosomatic pain refers to pain that is purely in the mind. In other words, you are feeling pain somewhere in your body, but there is absolutely no physical cause for that pain.

- **Phobias:** Maybe you were locked in a dark room, or cell, in a previous existence. That experience then filters through to your current life where you have an irrational fear of the dark.

- **Personality issues:** Perhaps you were an oppressed peasant in a past life, always having to hold onto your emotions and feelings. In your current life you vent these feelings by being overly aggressive or emotional.

These are only a few examples of an almost endless list. In order to resolve these problems, you may need to go back to the life where they first occurred. If you can resolve the issue in the past, the likelihood is that the problem in the present fades away too. Of course, after your past-life issues are resolved, you may have work to do on your current life, helping you to adjust to the positive changes that PLR has brought about.

Often, your current problem is an accumulation of unresolved issues from a whole variety of past lives, each needing to be dealt with and resolved.

What to expect during your PLR session

Ready to go back in time, but are a little unsure as to what to expect? Well, read on, because these sections cover what you may find happening during your PLR session.

But wait! Before you go back to a past life, we need to point out one thing. One of the experiences that often take people unawares during a PLR session is that when they get back to their past life they may well find that they are the opposite sex. That means a man may well have been a woman in a past life and vice versa. Let us just point out here and now that this is not a reflection of your sexual orientation, nor does it mean that you have a deep-seated desire for a sex change! It just means that the quirks of time travel do not recognise the gender boundary, and it is entirely possible that you were a member of the opposite sex in many of your past lives.

Setting the scene

During your PLR session, you are not necessarily going to step out of your current life and straight into a full, technicolor awareness of your past life. Your mind may need a little help orientating to this new experience and your therapist helps you get settled in through a process of questioning. She wants to find out from you:

✔ **Who you are.** No, she won't just ask 'Who are you?' Your therapist needs to help you build up your awareness and may ask you:

- What you're wearing

- How old you are

- Your name

✔ **Where you are.** Your therapist may ask you to tell her:

- What you see around you

- The name of the place you're in

- The date

- The time of day

✔ **What you're doing.** Your therapist may ask you to:

- Describe what you are doing (obviously)

- Explain why you're doing it

- Share how you feel about doing it

✔ **If anyone is with you.** Your therapist may ask you:

- If anyone is with you (er, again, obviously!)

- If so, who that person (or persons) is and why they're with you

- How you feel about having that person (or people) with you

This may seem to be quite an interrogation, but it is very important in helping you really get into the character and experience of your past life. Once you are fully there, you can get on with exploring all that it contains. Who knows, you could be an ancient Greek standing on a cliff top, or a Victorian gardener going about his business, or even a proud Mayan mother tending to her children.

If you step into your past life and see nothing or hear nothing, bear in mind that you may be blind or deaf in that life, or perhaps you are in a dark or very quiet room! I (Peter) once carried out a PLR with a patient who reported that they could neither hear nor see anything when we were trying to set the scene. In a moment of inspiration I asked that they reach out and tell me if they could feel anything. A moment later they reported that they could feel a wall. It turned out that in the life they were visiting they were both deaf and blind.

Book IV

Hypnotherapy

In most cases, you experience the past life as if you are there, so don't be surprised if your voice changes a bit and you feel the emotions you felt back then.

Visiting those important times

You're in a past life, so now what? Is this the part of the life you need to visit? Not necessarily. This may only be your entry point to that life; a quite mundane period that allows you to adjust gently. On the other hand, you may step out into the thick of things; right into the heart of the matter, at the point in that life where the problems you're experiencing in this one began.

Wherever you start off, your therapist will ask you to visit the important times in that life relevant to your problem. Keep in mind that there may be more than one event in more than one life. This is an insight gaining exercise, helping both you and your therapist understand how your problem got started. As you visit these times, your therapist may ask you what's happening, how you're feeling, and what you feel you need to do in this situation.

You may find that all your hypnotherapist does is ask you to experience these times. At times, you may feel the need to let out some emotion. If you do, go ahead and let it out. It may be that this pent up emotion has been festering away inside you in your current life, contributing to your problem.

By the way, if the thought of crying or laughing, or even shouting in front of your hypnotherapist is embarrassing, let us reassure you. Your therapist is very used to seeing displays of strong emotion and welcomes them as a healthy release for you. If you don't feel any of these emotions, don't worry – there may be none for you to feel at this time.

Being present at your death

Right, put on your black armband and bring in the doom and gloom brigade, because this is where it gets a little morbid – but for a very good reason. How you meet your end in the life you are visiting, may have a very strong relevance as to why you are experiencing your problem. For example:

- ✔ **Was your death violent?** If it was, it could very well be a contributing factor to your problem. The way in which you shuffled off this mortal coil may be representative of the reason you're seeing your therapist. Maybe you drowned and now have a phobia of water. Maybe you starved to death and now have a weight problem. Maybe you were poisoned and you now have irritable bowel syndrome.

  If your death was peaceful, it may not be a contributing factor to your problem. However, what happened to your body after your death may be, so read on.

✔ **What happened to your body after your death?** In many cases, this can influence a current life problem. Maybe your body wasn't discovered and you have an unexplained sense of being lost in your current life. Or perhaps your body was unceremoniously cremated and you now have a phobia of fire. It could be that your body was misidentified and you were buried under the wrong name, and you now lack a sense of who you are.

✔ **Was anything left unfinished at your death?** Were there things you needed to do, but couldn't as your life was cut short? Were there people you needed to say something to, but didn't get the opportunity to do so? Any unfinished business can follow through and cause havoc in your current life. Maybe you had unpaid debts in your past life and are too frivolous with your money in this one. If you didn't show enough affection to a loved one you may find that you are now too emotional in relationships. It is possible that you were harsh with someone without getting the chance to apologise and now find that you carry a sense of guilt with you wherever you go.

Healing past hurts

You've been through it all; lived and died, and now have an understanding of why your problem started. Is that it? Is your problem resolved? Maybe. For some, the very act of gaining understanding is enough to kick a problem out of their lives forever. However, that isn't true for every person or every problem. Not to worry. There is another step to take in your PLR session to help ensure that your problem is truly dead and buried.

To round off your session, your hypnotherapist gives you the opportunity to 'heal' that past life. In other words, to go through it and make amends, to change what needs to be changed, to say what needs to be said and so on. How can she help you do this? A very popular way is to visit the point of death (here we go with the morbidity again!), and as your spirit leaves your body, allow it to go through the life and to heal whatever it is that needs to be healed.

Book IV

Hypnotherapy

Completing the journey and returning to the present

So that's it, the life is healed and there is nothing left to do. Just wake me up and I'll be on my way then. Wrong! There is plenty more to do. After all, you don't mend the hole in a tyre, but not put it back on the bike. You need to put your past life back where it belongs, and then make sure that nothing else needs fixing:

- ✔ **Sever the tie to the past life.** After you heal a past life, many therapists suggest that you sever the tie you have to that life, so that you can be sure that it will no longer influence you or encourage your problem to return. How they do this depends on the therapist. Some have you imagine cutting a silver thread that attaches you to the life. Some have you imagine that that you are permanently shutting and locking the door to that life. Others may be less specific and have you cut the connection in whatever way you feel is right for you.

  Your therapist should suggest that before you sever any tie, you bring with you all the positive learning that the life gave you into your current existence.

- ✔ **Come out of the past life.** It is important that you are formally brought out of the past life. If you simply emerge from it, you may be somewhat disorientated. Don't worry; the disorientation will pass in time. But to avoid this, the general rule of thumb is that you're brought out of a past life the same way you were taken into it. If you stepped through a door, you step back through a door. If you walked down a tunnel, you walk back up a tunnel, and so on.

- ✔ **Check that there are no other lives you need to visit.** Before you are fully re-oriented back into your current life, your therapist should help you to check that there are no other lives that need to be visited. After all, more than one life may be contributing to your problem, and you want to clear the lot out in order to really ensure that it has been dealt with.

  You may find that you can do this in one session, or it may need to be done over several sessions, depending on how much needs to be worked through in each life.

Whether you are doing it for fun, or using it to solve a problem, you will find that every hypnotherapist will have their own particular approach to carrying out PLR. Whatever your reason is, you will find that a visit to your past selves can be a very interesting, rewarding, and ultimately problem releasing experience for you.

Past lives are not the only ones you can visit. Some therapists will work with you to find out what happens during your inter-life experience. In other words, exploring what happens between each of your lives. Yet other therapists will have you experience future lives – those that you have yet to live after you kick the bucket in this one.

Looking at What a Phobia Is

Are you scared of the dark? Do you freeze with fear whenever a cat saunters nonchalantly across the road in front of you? Do you go apoplectic at the very thought of visiting the dentist? Does the idea of taking a flight to some sunny holiday destination send ice-cold tingles of dread down your spine? If the answer to any of these questions is yes, then you have a phobia!

Phobias are one of the most common reasons people seek hypnotherapy. Many millions of people in this world have phobias. Most manage to get along in life without the phobia interfering too much in their day-to-day existence; in other words, the phobia is mild. However, a significant number of people have phobias that greatly restrict their life in one way or another, and when these phobias get really bad, people seek out therapy.

Phobias are not something you are born with. They are something you learn. You learn to fear an object or situation of some kind, and that fear is accompanied by many irrational thoughts and behaviours.

Explaining phobias

A *phobia* is an abnormal fear of an object or situation, experienced immediately when confronted by the object or situation, directly or indirectly, through seeing it on television, or in a magazine or book, for example. In general, fear makes you avoid whatever it is that triggers your phobia. So, a phobia involves fear and avoidance, but what else makes a phobia a phobia? Well, you may have a phobia if you experience any of the following:

- **Excessive or unreasonable fear:** Some situations may induce just a mild fear response considered normal or non-phobic, something most people would experience in that situation. Your fear is excessive or unreasonable if you find yourself frozen in place, perhaps wanting to escape, possibly trembling or sweating in that situation.

  A fear of heights is a phobia if you are paralysed by fear on the third rung of a ladder, or if simply watching someone standing on the edge of the Grand Canyon on television makes you break out in a sweat.

- **You recognise that the fear is excessive or unreasonable:** You know that what you are experiencing is out of proportion to what you should be feeling. You know, for example, that going to visit your dentist should only give you a mild anxiety, not that 'running down the street shrieking your head off' anxiety you experience when you walk in through the surgery door.

Book IV

Hypnotherapy

- ✔ **The trigger of phobic response always causes anxiety:** You either have the response, or not. You can't be scared of mice one moment and think that they're cute the next.

- ✔ **You avoid whatever causes your phobic response:** All phobics avoid whatever it is that they are afraid of, which is a logical response, really. If you can't avoid it, then you suffer the experience with intense anxiety or stress. For example, imagine that you have avoided flying for years, travelling wherever you needed to go by car, bus or train. However, for one reason or another, you find that you need to travel by plane somewhere. Getting you on the wretched thing may mean that you have to be dragged kicking and screaming, or else you have to be pumped full of enough tranquilisers to stop a rampaging bull elephant in its tracks!

Phobic fear most often causes physical and emotional reactions, including any, or all, the following:

- ✔ Your breathing may become shallow and your heart race, with just the thought of the *possibility* of encountering the object of your fear.

- ✔ You feel tense and anxious, altering your life to avoid any encounter.

- ✔ You feel a sense of shame or embarrassment at harbouring an obsessive fear, which may, in turn, cause you to withdraw from people who don't understand your terror.

As your fear looms large in your mind and in your life, you spend a great deal of your time, energy, and thought on it, which actually fans the flame of your phobia.

Oh, and just so you know, phobias can sometimes be accompanied by a *panic attack*, too. During these nasty episodes, your fear rockets through the roof and rational thought flies out the window, causing your breathing to become very rapid and shallow, which is known as *hyperventilating*. Hyperventilating increases the amount of oxygen in your blood and brain. You may think that more oxygen is a good thing, but too much oxygen in your system increases the symptoms you experience during a panic attack, resulting in more fear, trembling, sweating, weakness and tingling sensations in your limbs, and irrational thoughts that you are going to die.

To stop hyperventilating, put a paper bag over your nose and mouth, and breathe into it. This causes you to breathe in carbon dioxide and subsequently brings down the level of oxygen in your system.

Pointing out triggers

So where do phobias come from in the first place? How do you develop them? After all, no one sets out to deliberately become scared of something. Unfortunately, we don't have a simple answer. The causes of phobias are as varied as phobias themselves.

Starting with stress

When you experience severe stress, such as being stuck on a crowded bus in a traffic jam, or having a project deadline looming at work, your objectivity and ability to rationally analyse the situation may be compromised. The feelings you have as a result of the stress – such as anxiety or fear – can attach themselves to whatever you are stressed about.

Even though this is not always the case, when it does happen that means that if you enter into a similar situation, or come across a similar object, then you experience anxiety or fear. Remember, a phobia can occur to anything, so any situation in which you find yourself stressed has the potential to turn into a phobia.

Going through an extremely rough patch with your significant other obviously causes a lot of stress. This feeling can become attached to any confrontational situation and therefore result in you developing a phobia of confrontation.

However, your mind is a fickle thing and sometimes the fear is attached to something unrelated; you become scared of that and not of whatever it was that frightened you in the first place.

Picking up a phobia from another person

A classic way to assume a phobia is to inherit it from someone who serves as a role model for you. Through witnessing that person's phobic response, you learn to be afraid of whatever it is that they are afraid of.

A mother who is afraid of mice passes on that fear to her daughter. A son picks up his father's fear of spiders. When you witness your role model being scared, you believe that the object that he is afraid of is something that you need to be scared of too. Obvious really, if he is scared of it, then there must be something terrible about it. Unfortunately, this is not necessarily true!

However, you don't pick up phobias only from family members. Anyone you are in close contact with – be it a friend, neighbour, or complete stranger – can transmit their phobia to you. Even witnessing a phobic response on film or television can do the trick!

Building up to a phobia

A single experience of something mildly anxiety provoking may not necessarily end up with you developing a phobia of it. However, if you're repeatedly exposed to the same, or similar, experiences then the anxiety can become cumulative, reinforcing each experience with more and more fear until, wham! – you're slapped in the face with a full-blown phobia. It's as though you didn't see it coming.

Creating a phobia from past trauma

A *trauma* is an event that produces a severely painful physical or emotional experience – and could realistically lead to your death or injury. A trauma can lead to the development of a phobia of whatever it was that caused you that pain. Even witnessing such an event is traumatic and can result in the development of a phobia.

Examining the various types of phobia

Each individual phobia has its own particular characteristics. To be helpful, medical science has divided phobias into the following categories:

- **Animal and insect phobias:** The heading says it all. Any type of animal can be included in this category, from cats and dogs, through to cows and wombats! Insects are traditionally objects of fear, and any of the thousands of species that survive on this planet can become a phobic's worst nightmare.

- **Natural environment phobias:** These are phobias about some aspect of your environment. For example it may be that you are afraid of the dark – typical in children, but also afflicting many adults too. Or maybe you are scared of heights, or water, and so on.

- **Blood, injection, and injury phobias:** It's never pleasant having an injection. However, for some this can prove to be the object of a very severe phobia. In fact, any medical procedure that is invasive can come under this category. The sight of blood too, is often the trigger for a complete freak-out!

- **Situation phobias:** All phobias that are the result of having to do something, or of having to be in a specific place, come under this heading. If you have a fear of flying you belong under this category, for example. Fear being in a lift or elevator? You're here too. Shake and tremble before going to school? This is your category. Get the picture?

    Perhaps the two most famous situation phobias are *claustrophobia*, a fear of enclosed spaces, and *agoraphobia*, a fear of open spaces.

✓ **Miscellaneous phobias:** A bit of a cop out, this heading! Anything that doesn't come under the other headings in this list belongs here. For example, a fear of clowns (honest!), a fear of falling down when standing away from a wall (honest, too!), or a fear of getting ill (now that one you've heard of!), are all included in this category.

You can develop a phobia to anything. So don't worry if you have a phobia you think is strange. It's a dead cert that someone else has had it before you.

Table 5-1 offers a very incomplete list of the variety of phobias out there. (We can't list everything on the planet!) Don't worry if yours isn't there. It doesn't mean that it doesn't really exist, or that you are unique; all it means is that for whatever reason (not enough space, for one thing) we didn't include it.

No matter how strange some of these phobias seem to be, they are very real fears for the people who experience them.

Before we get to the table, one phobia deserves special mention, if only for the sheer audacity of its name. And that is the phobia of long words, ironically known as hippopotomonstrosesquippedaliophobia. Who says scientists don't have a sense of humour!

Table 5-1	Phobias A to Z
What the scientists call it	*What it actually means*
Acrophobia	A fear of heights
Agoraphobia	A fear of open spaces or crowded places. It can also mean a fear of leaving somewhere you feel safe
Apiphobia	A fear of bees
Bromidrophobia	A fear of body smells
Cardiophobia	A fear of the heart or heart disease
Claustrophobia	A fear of confined spaces
Coprophobia	A fear of faeces
Dendrophobia	A fear of trees
Dental phobia	A fear of dentists or dentistry
Emetophobia	A fear of vomiting

Book IV

Hypnotherapy

(continued)

Table 5-1 *(continued)*

What the scientists call it	What it actually means
Erythrophobia	A fear of blushing or of the colour red
Frigophobia	A fear of the cold or of cold things
Gerontophobia	A fear of elderly people or of growing old
Hippophobia	A fear of horses
Ichthyophobia	A fear of fish
Isolophobia	A fear of being alone
Kainophobia	A fear of new things
Koniophobia	A fear of dust
Ligyrophobia	A fear of loud noises
Lygophobia	A fear of darkness
Mechanophobia	A fear of mechanical things
Molysmophobia	A fear of being contaminated
Necrophobia	A fear of death or dead things
Ornithophobia	A fear of birds
Social phobia	A fear of negative evaluation in social situations
Spheksophobia	A fear of wasps
Technophobia	A fear of technology
Zoophobia	A fear of animals

Removing your phobia through hypnotherapy

One thing about phobias is that you can avoid dealing with them for only so long. Eventually you have to face up to the fact that you must sort out your phobia. Why? Because your phobia is making your life unbearable and increasingly interferes with your family, social, and work life. Have no fear (get it? Have no fear?); your hypnotherapist is there to help.

A hypnotherapist can take several approaches to helping you get rid of your phobia. What all approaches have in common is that they bring your fear under control. In fact, hypnotherapy allows you to confront the thing that freaks you out, with a sense of calmness and appropriate relaxation. You no longer avoid whatever it is; in fact, you look it straight in the eye and thumb your nose at it! You put your fear into proper perspective.

This doesn't mean to say that you go from being unable to climb up a ladder to standing on the very edge of the Empire State Building, looking down on New York City below. It simply means that you're able to deal calmly with those everyday occurrences of whatever it was that you were phobic about.

Your therapist won't spring surprises on you. Many phobics come to hypnotherapy fearing that their therapist will suddenly produce whatever it is that they fear. That approach went out with the Ark! You won't suddenly have a spider dumped in your lap, nor will your therapist shut you in a room with his pet canary to cure your bird phobia. Of course, if this is what you want, it can be arranged. However, by far the majority of hypnotherapists don't work this way. If you are at all concerned about unpleasant surprises, ask your hypnotherapist, in advance, about the approach they plan to use. If they intend to do something you don't agree with, say 'Thanks, but no thanks', and find someone else.

Starting with the basics

You've done it. You turned up for your appointment and are about to undergo hypnotherapy. So what can you expect? Well, for a start, your hypnotherapist is going to take a good case history. As part of that case history, your therapist wants to know as much about your phobia as possible. Be prepared to tell your therapist

- **When your phobia first started:** This gives an indication of how your phobia came about in the first place, and may provide a pointer as to the therapy technique your hypnotherapist will use.

- **When your phobia first became a problem for you:** Could you cope with the fear to begin with? What was it that eventually turned your fear into a full-blown phobia?

- **Your worst phobic experience:** This can be important as it may be a major contributing factor to the continuing build-up of your phobia.

- **Your last phobic experience:** How long is it since your last experience? How did that affect you?

- **Whether anyone close to you has the same phobia:** This may indicate whether you picked up the phobia from someone else. If you didn't get it from the person who shares your phobia, perhaps that person could be reinforcing your phobia, because they talk about their own phobic responses in front of you.

Book IV

Hypnotherapy

✔ **Specific information about your phobia:** The specifics are important, and your therapist will want to find out as much as possible about how you experience your phobia.

For a fear of heights, your therapist may want to ask you about the heights you can cope with, whether you cope if there is a barrier between you and the drop, how you feel if you see someone else standing in a high place, and so on.

For a fear of cats, your therapist may want to know if you cope more effectively with black cats or ginger cats, if a sleeping cat is less scary than a moving cat, how you feel when you see pictures of cats, and so on.

✔ **How you want to be after your phobia is gone:** It's no good just focusing on the negatives, your therapist also wants to help you focus on the reason you are sitting in their therapy room. And that means finding out from you just how you want to be when you encounter that phobic stimulus. Remember, you can't make things perfect – you must be realistic. Most spider phobics don't want to have one of their nemeses crawling around on their hand. Rather, they want to feel okay about picking one up out of the bath, on the end of a piece of newspaper, and flicking it out the window.

We'll let you into a little secret. Even though you probably assume that the therapy occurs only when you are hypnotised, the truth is that the taking of the case history information is very therapeutic in its own right. Being able to talk about your problem to a sympathetic pair of ears is a great set-up for the formal hypnotherapy to come. And don't worry; your therapist has heard it all before. No matter how strange you think your phobia is, your hypnotherapist has, more than likely, encountered it at some point. Oh, and he won't laugh, either!

Approaching the trance

So, what can you expect to happen in the trance? Your hypnotherapist may use several different approaches, alone or in combination with each other.

It may take more than one session to help you get rid of your phobia. Be prepared to carry out any homework assignments your therapist gives you to do between sessions – such as self-hypnosis – because these help the therapy process along no end.

Being hypno-desensitised

A very popular approach based on a behaviour therapy technique, created by behaviourist Joseph Wolpe, has the rather posh title of *reciprocal inhibition*. What that means is you can use one feeling to override another. The feeling you get when you experience your phobia is anxiety. Your therapist uses relaxation to override the anxiety. After all, you can't be relaxed and anxious at the same time!

Several approaches to hypno-desensitisation exist. A very common one is for your therapist to help you create something known as an anxiety hierarchy. Simply put, an *anxiety hierarchy* is a series of events you come up with regarding your phobia, ranked according to how much anxiety they produce. You rank these events from 0, which means that you feel no anxiety, to 100, which means that you feel the worst anxiety you can imagine. In hypnosis, your therapist gently takes you through the hierarchy, starting with the events ranked at 0, whilst giving you suggestions that you are calm, relaxed, and in control. He will then question you to find out whether you are indeed calm and relaxed. If you are, he then moves onto the next scene on your hierarchy. If at any point you feel anxious, your therapist will emphasise suggestions for relaxation so that you begin to feel relaxed again.

This is where the reciprocal inhibition really comes in – letting the relaxation wash away the anxiety. Don't worry, your therapist won't force you up the hierarchy too quickly, nor will he take you beyond the point at which you feel comfortable. By creating the association of relaxation with the various images from your hierarchy, you change the way your mind thinks about your phobia. When you encounter it in real life, you find that you cope very well indeed.

Going back to regression

This approach is sometimes used by analytical hypnotherapists who believe that to get rid of a phobia you need to understand and deal with its origin. Your therapist basically takes you back into your past, to the time when the phobia began.

Your hypnotherapist asks you to witness what happened, and perhaps to 'alter' the event in your mind, so that you experience yourself coping well in that situation.

Of course, you won't alter the real event but rather your perception of it. By doing this, you create a domino effect that tumbles into the present, wiping out that irrational fear.

Accessing positive resources

This approach also uses regression, but this time to get resources from your past. These resources are positive feelings that allowed you to cope and feel good before; feelings such as relaxation, confidence, an inner sense of self-control, humour, and so on.

While in trance, you're asked to create an image that represents your phobia. You're then asked to drift back in time and pick up wonderful, positive feelings that help you cope, and bring them forward to the present. You then are guided to fuse your positive resources to the image you created of your phobia.

Book IV

Hypnotherapy

By doing this, the resources overlay the anxiety the image produces (good old reciprocal inhibition!), and helps to alter the way you think about whatever it is you were scared of. When you are out and about and eventually encounter your phobia; you're fine – calm and relaxed and wondering what all the fuss was about.

Chapter 6

Practising Self-Hypnosis

*T*here's something absolutely fascinating about the first time you successfully hypnotise yourself. You feel that you've done something that you thought previously impossible. Then there's the satisfaction of achieving your goal. I'll never forget the first time that I (Mike) successfully hypnotised myself. I had had writer's block on a project for several weeks, and desperately needed to overcome it because a deadline was imminent. I was alone in a hotel room and after ten minutes of self-hypnosis, I immediately began writing – pages and pages!

Most people who learn self-hypnosis from books start by reading generalised scripts. You may have already read some scripts elsewhere in this book. After reading this chapter, you will know how to customise scripts, and even create your own, so that you can specially address your needs.

So, get ready for a step by step explanation of what you need to do to hypnotise yourself.

Connecting to Your Unconscious

Self-hypnosis is a relatively quick and marvellous way to access your unconscious mind, which is where the actual changes take hold in your life.

Your unconscious is the non-emotional part of your mind, which is simply about the business of preserving and protecting you. The intention of your unconscious mind is always to make your life better in some way. It is literally open to suggestion!

But to get there from here, so to speak, and enter self-hypnosis, you must bypass the critical factor of your analytical conscious mind. This simple process, a skill actually, becomes very easy with practise. The moment the critical factor is pushed aside, voila! You're in direct communication with your unconscious mind.

Setting Your Goal

The first step in self-hypnosis involves forming a clear understanding of your goal. Though you may have many goals, it is best to address them one at a time. So make a list if you want to, but focus on only one at a time. Give each goal the exclusive time and attention it deserves.

Think about what you want to achieve or change and state your goal in a single sentence. Making your goal concise and to the point lets you repeat it and remember it easily. That means that your unconscious mind can then absorb the goal and begin to help you seek your own ways of achieving the outcome you want. Stating your goal in a single, simple sentence also helps your unconscious form ways of achieving your goal.

Keep your goals positive and use the present tense.

Some examples of single sentence goals:

- ✔ I am calm and peaceful when I lie down at night, and drift to sleep easily.
- ✔ I remember all I've studied when I take an exam, and can recall the information at will.
- ✔ I have greater public speaking confidence because I am knowledgeable, and the audience wants to hear what I have to say.
- ✔ I honour my health and vitality by selecting foods that are nutritious.

One method helps to clarify goals brilliantly – the *magic wand question*. It goes like this:

> If you had a magic wand and could change one thing about yourself, and one thing about your immediate world, what would be different after you used your wand?

This question immediately forces:

- ✔ A concise focus on the problem.
- ✔ An awareness of the connection between how your perception affects your reality.
- ✔ An ability to focus and visualise the change you want to make.

When I (Mike) ask clients the magic wand question, I can see a slight physical change that indicates they are entering a light trance state.

Use the magic wand question to formulate your goal for self-hypnosis.

Hypnotising Yourself

If you understand the concept of trance (explained in Book 1), you already have a firm grasp on self-hypnosis. And, after you know what trance *feels* like, you can easily hypnotise yourself.

The basic steps for self-hypnosis are similar to those you undergo in a normal session with a hypnotherapist, except that you are the hypnotherapist! The following sections cover what you go through when you experience self-hypnosis.

A couple of tips that can help you establish your self-hypnosis practise include:

✔ **Establish a place to practise:** Choose a place where you can be completely comfortable, whether sitting in a chair or lying down. The environment you choose should be free of distractions and potential interruptions. Your skin becomes sensitive when you are in trance, so be sure that the room temperature is just right (better to be a little warm than too cool). Though not necessary, some people prefer soft lighting, soothing music, or even a scented candle. Self-hypnosis is your gift to you. Whenever possible, indulge yourself in total comfort!

✔ **Set a time limit:** Mentally give yourself the following suggestion: 'Exactly 10 (or 15) minutes from now, my eyelids open automatically and I feel calm, rested, and refreshed. I am ready to take on the rest of the day, or I am ready to drift off to sleep' (whichever you prefer). Don't worry about looking at a clock. Your unconscious mind knows how to measure time and will, with practise, reliably disengage you from hypnosis in the precise time that you allotted.

Dealing with distracting thoughts

Don't be discouraged if distracting or unwelcome thoughts float into your mind during your first few self-hypnosis sessions. Your thoughts are accustomed to bombarding you throughout the day in a rather undisciplined, sometimes chaotic, way. With self-hypnosis, you're retraining your mind so that you can choose which thoughts to attend to and which thoughts to discard.

A helpful technique is to create a mental inbox and outbox. If the thought that crosses your mind is truly important, simply put it into your mental inbox to attend to later. Don't worry, you won't forget about it. If the thought is frivolous, mentally put it in your outbox where you don't have to consider it again.

Inducing your own trance

An *induction* is the method used to put yourself into trance. In self-hypnosis you induce yourself into trance.

You can choose from a variety of induction techniques, many of which you can easily teach yourself. The next subsections offer some induction methods you can try.

As you read more about hypnosis, you may come across induction scripts that use generic phrases that sound harmless, but in certain cases are to be avoided, such as:

- ✔ If you're obese or worried about your weight, avoid the word 'heavy'. Don't think to yourself 'I am feeling heavy and tired', just 'I am feeling tired'.

- ✔ If you are depressed, avoid the word 'down'. Don't say 'I will sink down into trance', but 'I will go into a pleasant trance'.

Progressive relaxation

Using the *progressive relaxation* induction technique, you focus on gradually relaxing muscles over every part of your body. This relaxation helps you to go into trance.

1. **Begin by simply closing your eyes and taking a few deep breaths.**

   Imagine that with each breath you are exhaling bodily tension, which will help you to increasingly relax.

2. **Start progressively relaxing all your muscles, from head to toe, or toe to head, whichever you prefer.**

   Give yourself repeated suggestions to relax all your muscle groups.

   Keep in mind that it is not an anatomy test. Forgetting to relax a specific body part – your knees, or elbows, or toes, or whatever – isn't crucial. Your unconscious will fill in any parts you forget, if you think of your whole body being relaxed, after taking yourself through this script.

   You can use phrases such as 'Let them relax' and 'Let them go limp and slack'. Deliver these quite neutral phrases in a very permissive tone.

   The nearby sidebar, 'Sampling progressive relaxation', offers a script to follow.

The goal of progressive relaxation is to create an overall feeling of comfort from head to toe.

Sampling progressive relaxation

This sidebar contains an example of a progressive relaxation script. You don't have to use it word for word – feel free to adapt it in any way that works well for you.

'I'm now letting go of all unnecessary tension in my body . . . relaxing all my muscles from the top of my head to the bottom of my feet . . . letting them go nice and relaxed . . . my head and face are now going nice and slack . . . my forehead and eyes and eyelids . . . my cheeks, mouth and jaw muscles . . . it's a wonderful feeling as I let my face totally relax . . . I can actually feel the skin settling, smoothing out . . . I'm just letting it happen . . . unclenching my teeth and relaxing my tongue . . . the more I physically relax, the more I can mentally relax . . . my neck and shoulder muscles now . . . becoming completely relaxed . . . the tops of my arms . . . letting all tensions drain away . . . down through my elbows . . . into my forearms . . . down through my wrists and into my hands . . . right the way down into the very tips of my fingers and thumbs . . . just letting all those muscles go nice and relaxed . . . even my breathing is becoming slower as I relax . . . more and more . . . all tension in my chest area is leaving my body . . . relaxing my stomach muscles . . . relaxing my back muscles . . . down to my waist . . . my abdomen . . . down to my buttocks and my thigh muscles . . . becoming nice and relaxed . . . so are my knees . . . down through to my shins and calves . . . all becoming nice and loose . . . allowing all those areas to relax and let go . . . down on through to my ankles, my feet . . . into the very tips of my toes . . . all the muscles of my body beautifully relaxed and easy . . .'

Eye fixation technique

Possibly the simplest of all self-hypnosis methods is to simply choose a spot ahead of you – a picture on a nearby wall, for example – and simply stare at it until your eyes tire. When your eyes tire, relax them by closing them and let your whole body also relax. Then allow yourself to slow your breathing down, and go into a nice relaxed trance state.

Deepening your trance

Once you achieve a light trance state, you need to deepen and maintain the trance. Following is a very easy deepener you can use:

The ten-to-one countdown is probably one of the simplest ways of deepening trance for beginners once a light trance has begun. Basically, you count down from ten to one and tell yourself that with each number you'll become more relaxed, both physically and mentally, and go deeper into trance. The nearby sidebar, 'Counting down' has a sample script.

Book IV

Hypnotherapy

Alternative deepeners may involve

- ✔ Imagining yourself in a relaxing scene.
- ✔ Imagining walking down steps, and at the bottom is a comfortable place to rest.
- ✔ Making a fist, and as you release the fist, imagining a soothing feeling being released throughout your entire body.

You may now even begin to invent your own deepeners!

Trusting your unconscious mind to carry out your suggestion

When you're in a deepened trance state, you start using the goal statement you devised for your self-hypnosis session. (See the 'Setting Your Goal' section at the start of this chapter.) Now you realise why we tell you to state the goal in a single sentence. When in the trance state, you want to minimise words to allow your unconscious – the non-verbal part of you – to work its magic.

At this stage, just remember your single sentence goal statement. Then simply let go. Let the goal statement pass from your conscious mind, just say it a few times before starting the trance, allowing it to sink into your mind, then trust that you have handed it over to your unconscious mind, and that this wise part of you will now solve the problem.

Counting down

This is a sample script for counting down to deepen your trance:

'In a few moments time . . . I will count down from ten to one . . . with each descending number . . . between ten and one . . . . I'll become one-tenth more relaxed . . . ten per cent more relaxed . . . with each descending number . . . and each descending number . . . will help me to go . . . one-tenth deeper . . . into a wonderful hypnotic state of relaxation . . . a light trance state . . . this will become deeper and deeper . . . as I count on . . . and if, while I am counting . . . I will begin to experience a very pleasant . . . physical sensation . . . as if floating down . . . into an ever-deepening state . . . of physical and mental relaxation . . . that will become deeper . . . and deeper . . . as I count on . . . Ready . . . 10 . . . 9 . . . deeper, deeper . . . 8 . . . 7 . . . 6 . . . drifting down . . . ever more deeper relaxed . . . 5 . . . 4 . . . 3 . . . deeper and deeper still . . . 2 . . . 1 . . . and all the way, deep down relaxed . . .'

This is the focal point of self-hypnosis. Don't just think your goal statement – imagine hearing it, seeing it, and experiencing the change actually occurring. Use as many of your senses as possible to incorporate your goal into your trance state. If you can visualise yourself having made the changes, that's even better. The point is to ruminate over your goal and make it as vivid as possible in your imagination. Your unconscious mind will do the work you have given it, if you are clear, focused, and concise on what you want.

Strengthening your ego

Ego strengthening is the icing on the cake after the main therapy. This is where you encourage yourself to feel happier, more confident, and all the other 'feel good' statements. Add these after you've repeated and imagined your goal statement. It can be a very powerful thing to give your unconscious mind positive messages for a change!

Waking yourself from trance

Although you may not feel it necessary, it is a good idea to count yourself awake, and tell yourself that you're no longer in trance. This helps you to disconnect from the self-hypnosis experience and return to a fully alert state.

Try counting *up* from one to ten. Counting up essentially reverses the ten-to-one countdown you use to deepen your trance. Your mind responds to it as it is the opposite of how you entered trance.

You can tell yourself:

> 'As with each ascending number from one to ten, I will become more awake, and confident that my unconscious mind is already seeking new ways to obtain my goal.'

Using awaking scripts helps to come out of trance and back into your normal conscious state. These scripts also give you confidence of success.

A few minutes after awakening from self-hypnosis, you are still in a highly suggestible state. Use that time to reinforce how relaxed and calm you feel, and how pleased you are that your unconscious mind is helping you reach your goal.

Book IV

Hypnotherapy

Examining the Pros and Cons of Self-Hypnosis

One main difference between this book and others is that although we acknowledge the power of self-hypnosis, we still advocate that serious problems are best dealt with in conjunction with a professional clinical hypnotherapist. In the following sections, we describe when self-hypnosis is and isn't appropriate.

When self-hypnosis is appropriate

We want to encourage you to enjoy the amazing benefits of self-hypnosis. Even though you may not have access to a professional hypnotherapist, it doesn't mean that hypnotherapy is out of the question. Self-hypnosis can be an extremely beneficial tool when used appropriately.

Some appropriate goals for self-hypnosis are:

✔ Doing homework assigned by your hypnotherapist.

✔ Boosting your confidence.

✔ Encouraging healthier living and eating choices.

✔ Enhancing your creativity.

✔ Controlling pain.

✔ Lifting your performance in sports, school, the arts, and so on.

Of course you can use self-hypnosis in many other ways, but you may find these suggestions helpful in choosing a goal for your own self-hypnosis.

When self-hypnosis isn't appropriate

It is important to know the limits of self-hypnosis. You should not attempt to hypnotise yourself in certain situations, and it's important to be clear on those occasions.

Following are examples of when not to attempt self-hypnosis:

✔ If you have a serious mental illness (for example, schizophrenia).

✔ If you have issues relating to serious trauma (for example, rape, violence, childhood abuse).

✔ If your problems involve relations between you and other people.

✔ If you have serious phobias.

In any of these situations, we encourage you to work with a professional hypnotherapist. Why? Because with serious problems, it is very difficult indeed to resolve them alone. A professional hypnotherapist has the expertise to help you to achieve your goals and overcome problems that may have roots outside of your conscious awareness.

Developing Your Own Scripts

Hypnotherapy scripts must be individually tailored to be effective.

One of the most exciting things you can do at this stage is to choose a script and rewrite it so the words and message feel natural to you. We present several sample scripts throughout this book that help you understand how hypnotic suggestions are phrased to help you achieve your therapeutic goals.

Take any script in this book that interests you and re-write it in the language that you use when you think or speak to a close friend. Using your own language and phrasing makes it more likely that your unconscious will absorb the suggestions and start searching for change.

Follow these general guidelines for script writing:

✔ Phrase sentences like you breathe – don't be too wordy, and use short phrases.

✔ Aim for the simplest language possible.

✔ Avoid using negatives such as 'no', 'never', 'not', and 'won't' – state goals in the positive.

✔ Avoid being too specific about how to achieve your goal. Trust your unconscious to find its own solution.

✔ Avoid setting deadlines for achieving your goal. Again, trust your internal clock.

✔ Be realistic about your goals.

Believe that you will succeed and you will.

Book IV

Hypnotherapy

Ongoing Self-Hypnosis

How can you best reach your goals? By being true to yourself and discovering the best way that you absorb new information. Hypnosis is a lot like going to school. The difference is that with hypnosis, you are learning a new behaviour.

We are all different, and what works well for one person won't work as well for another. The following subsections offer tips that may be helpful for you to think about when deciding what works best for you.

A great deal of material on self-hypnosis is available, some of it contradictory. The old saying 'be true to yourself' applies here strongly. It is really important to be true to yourself when trying different self-hypnosis scripts and techniques. Don't try a script that doesn't feel right to you. It just won't be as effective as one that you really believe in.

Making your hypnosis work

If you want to be really successful, you should:

- ✔ Try to be hypnotised by a hypnotherapist before trying self-hypnosis.
- ✔ Practise self-hypnosis regularly.
- ✔ Set realistic and simple goals.

As with any newly acquired or desired skill, it is very important to persevere with your practise. Praise yourself for practising regularly, and don't punish yourself if you miss a practise session; just keep persevering!

Establishing a routine

If your hypnotist teaches you self-hypnosis, she will give you direct advice about how often to practise, and tips for how to get the most with your practise.

As a beginner, you first need to prove that you can induce trance. At this beginning stage, you can keep the hypnosis brief – maybe two or three times a day for 10 to 15 minutes at a time.

Just before bed, and after waking up, are excellent times to practise self-hypnosis.

As you get better at hypnosis, you will get quicker and be able to hypnotise yourself in seconds. But be patient, this takes a good deal of practise.

At the risk of sounding obvious, the secret is to practise as much as you can without overdoing things. If you practise too often you don't give your unconscious enough time to process your previous self-hypnosis session. You must trust that even if you don't get instant results, your unconscious self is working on your goal on its own timetable.

Regular practise, over a period of time, is more effective than huge gaps of time with no practise and then overdoing it in a single day to compensate.

Improving your effectiveness

The main way to deepen your trance is to read scripts, and to see a variety of approaches to the problem, or goal, that you are trying to work on. The Appendix can point you to books and other resources that offer a broad range of techniques.

A technique called *pseudo orientation in time* helps you visualise yourself in the near future, having achieved your goal. Using an hypnotic trance to see yourself in the future without the problem greatly increases your chances for success.

To use the pseudo orientation in time technique, you hypnotise yourself to go into the near future, with the change having been made sometime ago. Then you simply experience the feelings and changes made after achieving your goal. You then return to the present with these feelings of change embedded in your unconscious. (This technique is the bedrock of much hypnotherapy, and was one of the most frequent components of the work of Milton Erickson.)

Book IV

Hypnotherapy

Practising seeing your problem in the past under hypnosis activates your unconscious to move you towards the solutions and goals you want to achieve. This is one of the most tangible proofs that your hypnosis is working – when you find that you have suddenly solved your problem, without actually mapping out a conscious strategy to do so!

Considering the Limits of Hypnotherapy

When you go for your hypnotherapy session, you need to be realistic about what it can achieve. Even hypnotherapy has its limitations.

Setting yourself up for success

As with anything, many factors determine the outcome of hypnotherapy:

✔ **Your symptom:** Hypnotherapy can help resolve many different symptoms. However, it cannot help with everything. The earlier chapters in this part of the book give you a good idea as to the type of symptoms that can and can't benefit from hypnotherapy. For example, cigarette addiction can be treated, whereas the treatment of heroin addiction should be left to the medical profession.

Your symptom itself often determines the length of time you spend in therapy. Smoking cessation can take as little as one session to complete. However, if your symptom is more involved, such as bulimia, you can expect a longer course of treatment because of the deeper issues involved with this condition. Obviously if your symptom is as complex as this, you should seek professional help; self-hypnosis should only form part of your treatment.

✔ **Your expectations:** Are you expecting too much from hypnotherapy? Do you think it is a magical panacea that will get rid of your symptom at the click of a finger?

The 'I want to lose two stone by Friday' mindset is doomed to failure. Your expectations must be realistic from the outset. Hypnotherapy is therapy, not magic!

Highlighting the importance of your motivation

The most important thing you can do to ensure success for your hypnotherapy sessions is to look at your motivation and make sure that it is correct. The motivations for therapy are many and varied. For some, the motivation is positive, helping them along the path to change. For others, the motivation is negative, and can actually hinder that process. A couple of examples of the negatives and why they hinder:

✔ **Because someone said you should:** So someone in your life is urging you to try hypnotherapy. Take a look at why that person is pushing you toward therapy. Is it because they have a genuine concern for your welfare, such as not wanting you to die from lung cancer because you smoke, or wanting to help you get over the turmoil you experience when public speaking – or is it because they are trying to manipulate you? Do you feel that you need therapy because if you don't they are going to leave you? Do you feel that they're using emotional blackmail to get you to try hypnotherapy for their own selfish ends?

If you're undergoing therapy only because someone else wants you to and you have no real desire to change, then the chances are it won't make the slightest bit of difference. Even if change does happen, the likelihood is that you will be back to your old ways faster than you can say 'therapist'! Why? Because you never really wanted to change in the first place. By the way, if someone urges therapy on you out of genuine concern, perhaps you should take a little time to listen to them. After all, if you act on their concern and try therapy, it could very well improve your life no end – if not save it!

✔ **Because you don't want to make any effort:** This applies to the lazy amongst us! If you're trying hypnotherapy because you think it's the easy option, you aren't going to get very far. Sure, hypnotherapy can certainly speed up and ease the process of change, but this only happens if you put some effort into it too.

If you don't put any effort into the process you aren't going to get anywhere. Imagine wanting to push a stalled car. You need to put some effort into pushing, in order to get it to move. Simply rest your hands against it and you will be standing there all day getting nowhere fast!

So, in order for therapy to have the greatest chance of succeeding, you need to have the appropriate motivation. Your chances for success are much greater if your motivation:

Book IV

Hypnotherapy

✔ **Genuinely comes from you:** You are trying therapy because *you* want to make the change.

✔ **Is realistic:** You understand that change may take time and that hypnotherapy is not a magical panacea for all ills, and you're prepared to put some effort into the process.

Letting go may be harder than you think

Sometimes giving up your problems isn't easy. Okay, tell us something new! Perhaps you are thinking this is a bit of an understatement. After all, you're probably reading this book because you want to get rid of a problem that's proving difficult to shift. However, some problems can be very easy to get rid of, so why is it that others prove to be difficult blighters?

The human mind can be as fickle as the human being to which it belongs. So, even though on one level you are desperate to get rid of your problem, on another level there really might be a good reason for you to keep it. This is known as a *secondary gain*: your problem has something of benefit to give you.

Oh yes, your problems can be beneficial, even though you may not be aware of what that benefit is! That benefit may be misplaced and dysfunctional and can be achieved by other, healthier means; but the problem is still serving some important function. You may find, for example, that your problem keeps you away from a job that you don't like, or perhaps it's stopping you from having to do tasks you dread, such as shopping, ironing, or picking the kids up from school.

Of course, you may be able to resolve an issue without the need to address the secondary gain. However, you may find that you develop new and equally dysfunctional symptoms in order to provide the same benefit! In this case there would be little point in therapy in the first place.

Book V
Life Coaching

The 5th Wave   By Rich Tennant

"We're looking for someone with a high level of self-confidence, Mr Anthony. Unfortunately, I think you're overqualified."

In this part . . .

Life coaching can help you find the right balance, enjoyment, and meaning in your life. It encourages you to look at every aspect of your life, to take the time to question and challenge your own assumptions, to focus on working out what your own life is really about, rather than what you or others think it *should* be. The end goal is to get more balance, enjoy yourself more, and work out the meaning of life for you.

Here are the contents of Book V at a glance:

Chapter 1

Introducing Your Coaching Journey

*P*reparing for coaching helps you to enjoy the process of achieving your goals. Getting ready for coaching is partly about getting into the right mindset and feeling confident about your promise to yourself to achieve a certain goal. But it's also about getting the little things right and understanding some of the stages you go through on your journey to achieving your goal.

Getting Ready for Your Coaching Session

If you decide to work with a professional coach, your coach will discuss with you at the outset how to get the most out of your sessions. If you're self-coaching, you can benefit from setting up some ground rules for yourself to help you get into a good coaching pattern. Here are some general guidelines to consider:

> ✔ **Schedule your coaching time in your diary or calendar and treat it as a priority.** You may be guilty of putting your own needs last – don't! You'll be better prepared to face the emergencies of your life if you give yourself the calm space of coaching. (Okay, at times you really will have to cancel the session because of unforeseen events, but thinking of your coaching as a major priority in your life helps you to challenge yourself when you're tempted to sacrifice the coaching time for something else.)

✔ **Ensure you have a quiet physical space for your coaching session.** If you have a telephone session with a professional coach, you need to know that you won't be disturbed and that nothing will distract you. You may want to have some soft, calming music playing very low in the background and light a candle to create a special atmosphere.

✔ **Take a few moments to review your goals from the last session and the actions you've completed or attempted.** You usually discuss these early in the session with a coach, but reflecting quietly to yourself beforehand makes this part of the coaching more focused and gets you into the right frame of mind. If you're self-coaching, you can close your eyes and review your goals for a few moments.

✔ **Keep a journal between your coaching sessions to keep track of your progress.** You can use your journal to make notes of what you discuss during coaching or to complete exercises and record answers to powerful questions.

✔ **Complete your assignments between sessions.** Many professional coaches like to suggest ideas for 'homework' between sessions. This may be as simple as reflecting on an idea or new belief, or it may involve a specific exercise or piece of research to help you move closer to your goals. If you're self-coaching, you may want to complete some of the activities in this book, or have a stockpile of inspiring resources to dip into to keep your motivation high.

✔ **Spend a few moments after the session drawing your thoughts together and refining your actions.** If you're working with a professional coach you can drop him an email confirming the actions you agreed, and if you're self-coaching, send the email to yourself! Simply confirming your commitments in this way is a fantastic way to make them feel real and significant.

Beginning Your Coaching Journey

You may be quite familiar with concepts of personal development, having read other books, attended programmes, or worked through your own goals. Or maybe this is the first time you've had much exposure to the idea of personal development. But the great thing about coaching is that you enter into the process at the level you're currently at. Coaching works as a mechanism for harnessing everything you have learnt about yourself so far and all the great self-development ideas that other people have found to work.

Seeing the big picture

Your coaching journey isn't a straight line. Take a look at Figure 1-1. Central to life coaching is building your self-awareness. This begins with seeing how and why you behave in certain ways and how you can adapt and change that behaviour to improve your life. Moving to the second ring, you then begin to think about what makes you uniquely you – your beliefs, needs, and values.

Armed with a clear idea of yourself, you can enter into the journey at one of the three stages of the third cycle. Perhaps you begin by noticing the results that you have achieved in your life so far; by working out what's working. Maybe you then move on to exploring your options. Then you're ready to take action, which leads you back into noticing your results, and so the cycle continues. All of this activity is surrounded by the outer ring – the skill of asking yourself searching and empowering questions that assist you in the journey and feed back into your self-awareness.

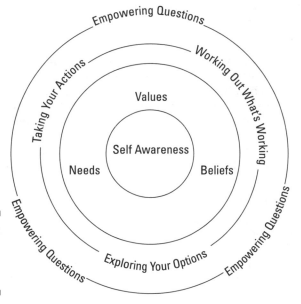

Figure 1-1:
The life coaching circle.

Packing your survival kit

To begin your journey, you need a kit bag of qualities to develop and hone along the way. These qualities will sustain you on your journey and help you navigate the twists and turns of the road. Your particular kit bag will be stuffed full of self-awareness, positive self belief, motivation, and an impressive array of powerful questions to help you reach your destination.

Stocking up on empowering questions

Coaching takes you back to the habit you developed as a child of questioning everything around you. As an adult you may be out of the habit of questioning and exploring, because you get into the habit of thinking that your questions should be intelligent and sensible – no one wants to look stupid. And you find that you get by in the world even though you sense that you don't know quite enough about some stuff. Life coaching helps you to recapture your child-like curiosity so that you can get to what's really going on for you. Stock up on questions to empower you, such as 'What will happen if I don't make this change in my life?' And check out Chapter 6 for how to frame the questions that will prove to be powerful navigation aids for you.

Choosing your beliefs

You have helpful beliefs about yourself but also destructive beliefs. For example, I think of myself as good with words but tend to hold a belief about myself that I'm hopeless with numbers. The positive belief gave me the confidence to write this book – great outcome! – but the negative belief causes me to procrastinate on doing my accounts – disastrous outcome! Life coaching helps you to increase the power of your positive beliefs and minimise or reject the negative, limiting ones, breaking free of any self-doubt that stops you from getting what you want in life. I talk more about beliefs in Chapter 3.

Building your motivation

Values, as well as beliefs, are in the second inner ring of the coaching circle (refer to Figure 1-1). The values you hold about what is important to you, and, to a great extent, the needs you have, drive you forward. You create this motivation inside you as you seek to shape your world. Understanding how your values and needs work for you is a powerful tool to propel you forward.

Becoming self-aware

At the centre of the coaching circles is *self-awareness*, an understanding about yourself and how you respond to your world. The more self-aware you become, the more you're able to understand others, which helps you in many ways. You work more effectively with colleagues, and your personal life benefits too, because you have a better idea of how people tick.

Achieving the highest level of self-awareness is the most beneficial outcome of all personal development, and coaching is the very best medium to achieve this. Through self-awareness you can begin to change aspects of your behaviour that don't serve you well, you can identify what it is that truly makes you happy, you can become realistic about what you're not prepared to sacrifice, and you can ultimately achieve inner peace and harmony with who you are and what your place in the world is. Chapter 3 has more about understanding yourself, your preferences, and your attitudes.

A client of mine said to me at the outset of a coaching programme that her goal was to work out a way of balancing the demands of her career and family life, or to accept that she needed to make a small sacrifice somewhere and to be happy with that decision. Sometimes you have to recognise that you can't always have your cake and eat it, and be at peace with your decision, and this too is a form of self-awareness.

The stages of your journey

Kit bag packed? Good. Time to take the first steps. This section provides an overview of the stopping off points of your journey. Remember that the journey is circular. In general though, you start by thinking about what you want to change, move onto considering your options and choices, and then you take your actions.

Working out what's working

During coaching you spend time thinking about what's working well in your life, as well as what's wrong. Shifting the focus in this way still allows you to see what you don't want, but puts you in a more powerful frame of mind to take action. Do more of what you do well and enjoy, and you discover that many other things fall into place. You still encourage yourself to change and adopt new behaviours, but your focus is on identifying positive new habits, not condemning yourself for old, bad ones.

Exploring your options

On your life coaching journey you encourage yourself to experiment and try new approaches to reaching your goals. Acting in the same way as you always do generally results in the same outcomes, so flexibility, creativity, and imagination become your new friends as you step outside your comfort zone a little and try new options.

Taking your actions

Having identified what you want more of or a specific goal, and explored ways of achieving that, you can begin to take actions that move you, one small and significant step at a time, towards your goals.

Marking Your Progress

Coaching often produces results that are hard to measure because they are qualitative (measuring quality) rather than quantitative (measuring quantity). If your goal is to get a promotion, you know you're there when you're holding the new contract. But what if you take a year to get there? You can always find ways to mark your progress so that you can look back at any stage and see how far you've come, which particularly helps you when the going gets tough.

As you change and develop you set ever higher standards for yourself, so sometimes it's easy to forget where you started from. Have you ever been involved in a house renovation project? The work can get more frustrating as you get closer to completion and you have to look at the photos of digging the foundations and clearing all the dirt and rubble to get a sense of the transformation.

Using milestone goals to celebrate success

When you set yourself a significant goal you probably won't be able to achieve it overnight. Start thinking early on about how you'll celebrate success along the way. Getting fit, working towards a promotion, tackling an unhealthy habit – all these goals produce benefits for you during the journey as well as when you reach your destination, so why not celebrate these milestone benefits? Your milestones are individual to the task you set yourself. They may be tangible, such as going down one dress size (even though your ultimate goal is three sizes smaller!), or completing a great CV to submit for a new job. Your milestone goals can be process goals – maintaining your commitment to staying alcohol- or cigarette-free for a month.

Attaching rewards to milestone goals helps you to keep a focus on the here and now, not just the future, which bolsters your commitment.

What is a reward for you? Naturally, achieving your goal is a great reward, but perhaps you set a long-term goal. Waiting months or even years to breathe a sigh of relief and congratulate yourself for a job well done isn't really the best way to sustain your motivation. Instead, you can set milestone goals that you link to smaller rewards to sustain your enthusiasm.

Choose milestone rewards that don't go against your ultimate goal. If you want to lose weight, allowing yourself to binge on your favourite food every time the scales show a loss is likely to be detrimental. Aim for rewards that are healthy and nurturing for you. They needn't be expensive either, although you can push the boat out a bit when the milestone you achieve is especially significant. Here are some examples:

- ✔ A couple of hours with a good novel.

- ✔ A long, relaxing bubble bath.

- ✔ A round of golf.

- ✔ Watching your favourite sports on television.

- ✔ An evening at the theatre or cinema.

- ✔ Buying yourself something special that you've had your eye on for ages.

- ✔ A weekend away with a friend or loved one.

- ✔ Something you haven't done before that will get the adrenalin going and energise you such as a helicopter ride, trip in a hot-air balloon, or a day spent go-carting.

Think about the treats that you tend to put off because other responsibilities come first. A reward feels more like a treat when it's something you don't do every day or don't always make time for.

Why not introduce an element of surprise to your rewards? Ask a friend or partner to hold your list for you and choose items off it at random for you at the appropriate milestone. Or write out each reward on a separate card, and post it in a box that acts as your Rewards Bank. Every time you decide to celebrate a milestone achievement, take out a card at random and treat yourself.

Giving yourself a pat on the back

One of the simplest ways of marking your progress is simply to notice when you move forward and take a few seconds to give yourself a pat on the back. A former boss of mine is one of the happiest people I know and his secret is that he makes a point of looking out for small things that he's proud of during the day and mentally saying to himself, 'Well done!'

Most people are unused to paying themselves compliments and you may have to do battle with your inner critic. But try it – anything from finding a parking spot in a crowded high street to pulling off a brilliant presentation to a client deserves a quiet acknowledgement to yourself that you have added to the smooth running of your day. As patting yourself on the back becomes a habit, you find it easier to take those few moments of reflection to celebrate the small and significant steps you make towards the big goals in your life.

Paying it forward

You may have read the book or seen the film *Pay It Forward*, in which a young boy transforms the world through an idea he generates during a school project, to pay forward three good deeds for every one that you receive.

Recent research on happiness suggests that a key factor in personal wellbeing is helping to make other people happy – one reason why volunteers report great personal satisfaction despite putting in time and effort for no pay. I'm not suggesting that you should spend all your time in the service of others (unless that's what

you want), but in preparing for coaching think about not only ways in which you can get support but also how you can start looking beyond yourself. Small daily random acts of kindness not only benefit the recipient but have a way of coming back to the giver in spades. A key element of coaching is finding new and better ways to exist in your daily life, and adopting this subtle change in your approach can produce amazingly powerful shifts in how you perceive things. See www.helpothers.org for inspiration.

Anticipating setbacks and relapses

Take a long view and accept that you experience setbacks when attempting change. Gridlock and deadlock aren't disastrous when you think through in advance the keys to unlocking them. Seven helpful guidelines to bear in mind when you anticipate the challenges ahead are:

- **Remember that change requires effort and can cost more than you think.** Shaping the life you want is worth the investment so think about the resources, especially of your time, that you are putting into your change programme. Trying to take short-cuts may result in longer periods where you stay stuck.

- **Choose the methods that are right for you, not the latest 'get rich and happy quick' theory.** And if something you try doesn't work, be prepared to reflect on the reasons and try something different.

- **Realise that willpower is over-rated!** Almost no one can sustain strong willpower in the face of temptation. So avoid actions, no matter how small, that may jeopardise your goals, such as keeping tempting foods in the house when you're working to lose weight (even if you tell yourself that the biscuits are for unexpected visitors!).

- **Accept that you almost certainly don't make it first time every time.** If you're training for a race you expect to reach your best time after preparation, practice, and experimentation – not on the first day of your training programme. Of course, you easily achieve some goals at your first attempt, and you feel exhilarated at your 'hole-in-one', but they may be the exception.

✔ **Expect the unexpected.** The journey to change isn't a straight line. You may encounter surprises, go back on yourself, zigzag around, lose your way in the dark corners, and suddenly find you're back in the same spot – but armed with a lot more knowledge and maybe a level up from where you started out.

✔ **Don't forget that your emotional state matters.** Sometimes you need to retreat and recuperate because you feel somewhat battered by events. Perhaps the struggle has got you down a bit, or maybe an upsetting life event has thrown you off course emotionally. Whatever the reason, you must anticipate that you need to let yourself off the hook at times and take care of your emotional state to gather strength for the next phase of the journey.

✔ **Stay curious!** Lapses do not mean that you've failed; they simply indicate that some reflection and adjustment are needed. Stay open to the lessons you can learn from your relapses and you begin to develop a helpful curiosity that allows you to step beyond gridlock and deadlock and move to the next stage.

Keeping a record

As you work through activities in this book you may find that the simple act of writing down your thoughts and reflections really helps to clarify your understanding of your goals. Consider starting a coaching diary or journal to record your progress. Your journal can take many forms. Some clients push the boat out with leather-bound, handmade journals and write with an expensive pen. Others prefer a simple ring binder. Still others carry around a small notebook to jot down ideas and reflections as they go about their day, while the technology lovers tend to deploy their PDAs or laptops.

Writing in your journal enables you to:

✔ Capture your reflections on what you learn from your coaching sessions, helping you to build up a bigger picture over time and make connections between your thoughts, feelings, actions, and behaviours. You'll see trends developing that aren't always obvious until you write them down!

✔ Track your goals and results so that you can look back on what you have achieved. This alone can be a significant motivator in your journey.

✔ 'Write out' inner critic attacks. Sometimes just seeing the nonsense that your inner critic comes up with in black and white on the page is enough to break the spell and restore your confidence in yourself.

A record of your progress need not be expressed only in words. Many people get more meaning from pictures and images. Consider collages, scrapbooks, or drawings that represent the stages of your journey. If you have a room of your own you can even create your own timeline on one wall, representing the stages you go through. Or why not invest in a flip-chart pad and get creative on a large scale?

You can also use objects to remind yourself of goals and reflections.

Assessing the Benefits and Challenges of Coaching

One of the most surprising things about life coaching is that you don't have to know at the outset exactly what it is that you want to fix or improve in your life for the magic to work. Having a specific goal in mind (such as getting fit) or at least an area of your life that you want to improve (such as your relationships) does help the coaching process. But you can also use coaching to help you identify that vague, nagging feeling of dissatisfaction that you have and what needs to change in your life to restore your vim and vigour. In fact, sometimes having too fixed a goal in mind distracts you from enjoying the many benefits of the process. I've (Jeni) found that many clients who had a very clear objective about change in a specific area of their life, later identified that what they thought was the problem or goal either wasn't at all, or was secondary to something else. So if you're worried that you don't have a clear enough idea of what's wrong or could be better – relax! Whole life coaching is the perfect medium for exploring what's really going on.

Because coaching has a wonderful way of giving you many more goodies than you set out to acquire, keeping a completely open mind helps you appreciate those goodies when they pop up. Life coaching shows you how connected your life really is. Maybe you have a specific goal to use coaching to improve your assertiveness at work, but you'll almost certainly discover that, as a result, you find new ways of improving your personal relationships too. Or, in taking a close look at the 'problem' you have getting fit and healthy, you may discover fresh resources of motivation that result in better work performance and perhaps even a promotion.

You can use the ideas in this section to help you to get a feel for some of the main benefits of coaching so that you can begin your journey with a sense of what you want to achieve, and equally, so that you can prepare for some of the consequences of the process. It helps you work out the best way for you to go about coaching, and prepares you for the commitment you're about to make to yourself and your life.

All coaching gets results but not all coaching results look the same. You get more out of the process if you have the right expectations about what you want to achieve. Your coaching results may be very tangible and visible – a new job, or a trimmer waistline. Or your results may be reflected in changes in the way you think and behave that make you happier in your daily life. The biggest benefit of coaching is that it brings more self-awareness and makes you at peace with your life choices. Think about the following benefits of coaching and decide which are priorities for you.

The act of reaching for your goals creates a great deal of the enjoyment in your life.

Attaining goals

Coaching is a very effective mechanism to support you as you identify and attain your goals. Perhaps you're aiming for a specific outcome or outcomes from coaching, such as wanting to:

- ✔ Change your job or embark on a new career
- ✔ Establish your own business
- ✔ Improve a personal relationship
- ✔ Get fit and healthy
- ✔ Become a non-smoker
- ✔ Increase your personal wealth
- ✔ Become more self-confident

The list could go on and on. You can tackle anything tangible that you want to change or improve in your life through coaching. If you have a long list of goals, decide how they stack up on your priority scale, because you can't achieve everything all at once. Coaching can help you decide on these priorities too – and what you think is the compelling issue may turn out to be rather less critical after you've turned the spotlight on it through coaching.

Think about some broad outcomes that you hope to achieve through coaching:

- ✔ What goals do I want to focus on?
- ✔ How do I feel about my whole life balance?
- ✔ Do I have a sense of purpose, and if not, is this a key area for me?
- ✔ How do my thought and behaviour patterns get in my way?
- ✔ How often do I question myself and my actions without being self-critical?
- ✔ How focused am I on enjoying the present moment in my life?

When you have some answers, even though they may not yet be very specific, ask yourself which of these areas are the most compelling for you. What benefits may you get if you choose to focus on these areas? What challenges do you think lie ahead?

Growing through self-awareness

All coaching offers you the possibility of growing through becoming more self-aware. Think of yourself as an onion with many, many layers to uncover (not a very flattering image, we know!). As you peel back the layers you reveal more of your true self, until you get to the fullest understanding of who you are and what you're capable of. Some people describe this as a feeling of 'coming home to themselves'. This understanding is like spending a long time away travelling, soaking up new experiences, and finally arriving home richer for your travels. Home is still the same, yet you see it with new eyes because of all the things you have seen, done, and learnt.

Throughout this book you discover how coaching allows you to reflect and take new meanings from the things that are most important to you.

Coaching is a combination of getting the results you want and taking steps to get those results. Sometimes the goals in themselves may turn out to have limited power to make you happy. Have you ever worked really hard to achieve something and then found that the reward at the end was somehow not as satisfying as you'd hoped? Often the *challenge* of attaining your goals makes you really come alive, as you stretch yourself and your abilities. The joy you experience as you cross each finishing line is more likely to be lasting if you've been fully engaged in everything leading up to that moment. Coaching can become addictive, because the process of setting and reaching for your goals in a way that's meaningful to you gives you the most benefits as you begin to see and experience all that you're capable of. The great results then become a wonderful bonus!

Finding a meaningful way to achieve your goal is especially important if your goal is to 'give up' a bad habit. The successful non-smoker who makes a determined plan to focus on being a new, healthy version of themselves and use the savings from their old habit to fund a gym membership will enjoy the challenge and stick with the goal. Someone who doesn't replace smoking with a positive distraction mopes around thinking about how much pleasure they're giving up. Being realistic in your coaching journey means knowing that you need a massive effort to get to your goal, as well as appreciating the pleasure of the process that gets you there.

This book focuses on getting your expectations of coaching right, and prepares you for the ups and downs of the road to your new self.

Not all the results of coaching feel positive at the time. Like any process of self-development, you need to prepare yourself for hard work and effort, and perhaps some frustration and disappointment along the way. Perhaps you have to let go of something that has acted as a comfort blanket for you, and maybe you also face up to some tough facts about yourself and your choices to date. Don't think that these challenges are depressing – there's way more on the positive side to make your life coaching journey all worthwhile. Knowing in advance that a few thorns lie in the bed of roses helps to keep you grounded.

Making a Promise to Yourself

You may be wondering if you'll be able to maintain the commitment to your goals that you feel right now. You've probably experienced the disappointment of setbacks before and know how hard it feels to maintain motivation long after the mood in which you first made your commitment has gone. Why are things different for you now?

For the things that are really important to you, think in terms of making a serious promise to yourself about the changes you want to make. This is different to a simple commitment, which you can measure in milestones and outcomes. The promise you make to yourself in coaching may involve allowing yourself to learn and grow from the process, to persist despite setbacks, to be honest with yourself about what is truly important, and to stop beating yourself up when you get it wrong. Within this promise you make commitments that you aim to fulfil. But the big picture of your promise is to commit to making the changes and choices that are best for you and that move you forward.

Checking out your current life conditions

Are your current life conditions right for you to begin your coaching journey? Coaching can be challenging and you should only begin if you're already feeling pretty strong and capable. Everyone suffers from low self-esteem and a lack of confidence at times, but if your current emotional state is very negative, or even depressed, you may want to consider a different kind of help, such as counselling, to get you to the point where you're ready for coaching.

Perhaps a lot is going on in your life at the moment and you're under an unusual amount of pressure. You may be tempted to look on coaching as the answer to your prayers, but if your life balance is so out of kilter that you can't make time for coaching and find that you cancel appointments – with yourself or your coach – then it's time to ask yourself some hard questions.

Ask yourself if you're ready for coaching now. Maybe you want to take a session with a coach to discuss and decide this. A half-hearted commitment can be worse than no commitment at all, and you needn't feel bad if your current life conditions don't allow you to be whole-hearted about coaching yet. You may simply have to go with the flow of what's happening in the here and now for a while. Think about what other support mechanisms are around for you, read this book to get you into the right frame of mind, and make a promise that when the time is right for you, you will take the first step.

Framing your coaching promise

You can make a real commitment to coaching by framing your own coaching promise. Think about the traits that, in your heart of hearts, you know have most held you back in seeing through commitments in the past. Now take yourself back to the feeling you had when you last made a solemn promise. What was it that gave you the conviction that you would see that promise through? How can you access that feeling of conviction again?

Here are some examples of coaching promises that you can make:

- ✔ I promise to take responsibility for discovering the solutions that are right for me and that allow me to be the best I can be in my life.
- ✔ I promise to be open and honest with myself and trust that as long as I am taking positive action, I am making progress.
- ✔ I promise to commit to developing my awareness of myself so that I can replace habits and behaviours that are destructive with ones that are creative and productive.
- ✔ I promise never to accept second best for myself.
- ✔ I promise to seek to learn from all my experiences and actions.

What is your promise?

Chapter 2

Visualising Your Whole-Life Goals

*Y*our life changes whether you want it to or not. Choosing to stand still means that in fact you go backwards, because your world changes around you. And when your world changes, even in small ways, you eventually get dragged along, sometimes kicking and screaming because not everyone embraces change. Just recognising that change is inevitable can be a relief. Putting yourself in control of the changes you experience makes the journey a lot more enjoyable. You may have tough work to do along the way, and a fair sprinkling of discomfort to accompany the exhilaration and accomplishment, but *you* are in the driving seat, focused on the road ahead. And while you're moving up the gears, you need to see what's going on clearly and objectively so that you can make the best possible choices for your route.

Practising Awareness

We're sure that some things that are going on for you are pure, unalloyed success. Others are mixed blessings. Yet others seem to be clearly big, bad mistakes. When you analyse your life without supportive awareness, you can tend to feel like prosecuting counsel and defence lawyer at the same time – imposing the death penalty on yourself while being convinced that you're really the innocent party! Your inner judge rushes into sentencing before really seeing what you are getting out of the situation, good and bad, in an objective and calm way.

Redefining success

Think for a moment about what success means to you. You may choose to reflect quietly, write in your journal, paint, draw, or find some other way of representing your definitions. Choose whichever means of expression seems to you to be the most natural and compelling as you consider the following questions:

- ✔ What does true success mean to you in your life? Is it achieving material goals, enjoying the moment, building wonderful relationships? What will your life look like when you've achieved your vision of success?

- ✔ What has to happen for you to be and feel successful? How will you know when you're successful? Perhaps you realise that you need the assurance of others to feel successful? The more your success depends on other people's approval, the trickier success is to achieve and maintain.

- ✔ What are the consequences to you and your loved ones of holding this meaning of success? You may feel that your success must come at a price – a coveted promotion versus less time with loved ones, for example. Think about how your definition of success fits into the rest of your life. What tensions may be created by holding values that are at odds with each other?

After you identify your answers to these questions you can summarise your vision in a single statement, for example:

> *Success for me is setting and achieving personal goals that stretch me, both at home and work. I measure my success by asking for feedback and by recognising the inner satisfaction I get for a job well done.*

Focusing on outcomes

Being self-aware allows you to see the results of your life objectively and in perspective. You may have a tendency to label certain events that happened to you 'good' or 'bad' based on how you felt about them at the time. In reality, events are mixed, and you even change how you feel about them over time. For instance, you may look back and smile about an embarrassing first date where you seemed to say all the wrong things, although at the time you wanted the ground to swallow you up.

The following activity gets you to think differently about some significant events in your life to practice getting curious about outcomes of your actions.

Think of some events in your life that were significant for you. Start by considering an event that has happy associations for you and where you got a result that pleased you. Perhaps passing an exam, getting a promotion, accepting a job offer, or taking a trip abroad. Ask yourself the following questions:

✔ Were there any results from this action that were less than satisfactory?

✔ What other options did I rule out for myself by the action that I took?

Now repeat the exercise with an event that didn't turn out well for you. Maybe a poor performance at a meeting, failing your driving test, or even a relationship ending. Ask yourself:

✔ What came out of this experience that turned out to be good?

✔ What did I learn from the experience that has stood me in good stead since?

Curiosity never killed anyone – not even the cat. Thinking about the choices you make in your life in a curious way doesn't mean that you always have regrets that your actions can never produce 100 per cent good results. It does mean that you begin to relax, knowing that whatever choice you make, you always open up for yourself the possibility to choose again and perhaps choose differently. When you focus on outcomes you find that you automatically start to become interested in the puzzle, curious about how it's going to be solved, and fascinated by the new end result. This is a great state to be in, because it's almost always a better way of getting the answers you need than agonising that you messed things up – and it's certainly a lot more fun.

Become more curious in your own life. Stand back a little as if you were a benevolent observer and take a look more often at what's really going on for you.

Focusing on the results or outcomes of your life is a great technique of life coaching. What happens when you do it? Lots of positive things:

✔ You take the emotion out of things for a while. It's like being your own best friend – you're interested and engaged but not self-obsessed about the highs and lows of your life.

✔ You get to play detective on your life, looking for clues and trends that help you build up a picture to guide you.

✔ You start to see your life as a whole – a constantly changing balance sheet, where your assets and liabilities shift around and develop. You realise that, as in the corporate world, even going out of business for a while doesn't stop you from refinancing and getting back in the game.

✔ You discover surprises and make connections that are simply not possible when you're intent on adding up your running scores as if you were sitting the final exam for passing your life.

✔ You begin to realise that many possible interpretations of events exist and you can see the right solutions when you open yourself up to changing your perspective.

Talk to people you know who have to use and develop curiosity in their jobs and professions. Thinking like a scientist, inventor, detective, or trouble-shooter can add intriguing dimensions to how you approach the big issues in your own life. How do these different job roles employ curiosity? How can you find ways to harness these methods of discovery in your life?

Tapping into your intuitive self

Curiosity is a wonderful thing to have in your life coaching toolkit as you develop supporting awareness. It's a free, enjoyable way of analysing your results. You can take curiosity to a new level by taking steps to find out just how intuitive you are and how powerful intuition can be in helping you see what aspects need addressing in your life.

Everyone has intuitive powers. Mostly you pick up evidence through your five senses – you consciously notice the clues in how you feel, and what you see, hear, touch, and taste. But have you ever had that 'aha!' moment where your conscious mind is distracted from the task in hand? Maybe you are taking a shower, waiting for the kettle to boil, laughing and joking with friends. But suddenly, out of nowhere, you get a new insight that helps you solve a problem you've been chewing over for ages!

Intuition is incredibly valuable for supportive awareness and can provide you with solutions that are light years better than some of the solutions you analyse and agonise over. Trusting your instincts, living with a light touch, and tapping into the power of relaxed focus are some of the most effective ways to become more intuitive and can really benefit the quality of the decisions you make in your life.

Trusting your gut feeling

In his book about developing intuition, *Blink: The Power of Thinking Without Thinking*, Malcom Gladwell talks about the concept of *thin-slicing*. Thin-slicing is the way in which humans often instinctively come to make decisions and judgements within seconds. Thin-slicing means that you quite unconsciously make intuitive assessments about something or someone from tiny bits of information, often in what feels like a nano-second. For example, you meet someone for the first time and know that something isn't quite right, that you don't quite trust that person. You pick up cues that you don't even notice on a conscious level and later you may find the tangible evidence that backs up your intuitive flash. Of course, that doesn't mean that you should always trust your first impressions – whole romantic dramas warn you of *that* danger! But it does mean that listening to what your instincts tell you may often work better for you than trying to analyse and gather facts.

How can you develop intuition? It's one of those elusive traits that defies a structured approach but you can become more aware of how finely-tuned your intuition is with these suggestions:

✔ Start to predict who's on the end of the phone when it rings and note how often you're right. You may find your hit rate starts to improve for no reason other than that you're focusing on it.

✔ Intuition is strongly linked with creativity and playfulness. Take a hop and a skip to these chapters to find out more about how to become more creative and playful in your daily life.

✔ Becoming more present-centred assists you in tuning out conscious thought and tapping into what's going on in your unconscious – the source of your intuition. See the section 'Visualising your whole-life goals' in this chapter for more on living in the present.

✔ Finally, simply notice what results you get over time when you 'go with your gut' compared to the times when you carefully weigh up evidence. Do you see any trends developing?

Living with a light heart

Life can be a serious old business at times, but taking every little setback to heart drains your energy. Laughter is truly one of the best medicines, and after you've done what you can to resolve a bad situation, you can help yourself best by seeking out ways to lighten your mood. Your brain works more efficiently when the negative emotions of worry and anxiety aren't weighing you down. You can see what's going on in a difficult situation far more easily if you're able to tune into the lighter side of your day. Situation comedy is so popular because it gives people just this kind of release. Watching the antics of ordinary people going about their daily lives and being able to laugh at, and with, them is incredibly therapeutic.

How can you find ways to introduce a lighter touch to your day? Sharing a laugh or joke with work colleagues, or catching up with friends at the end of a busy day is great for lightening the mood. And when your day threatens to become tense and over-serious, you can recall a time when you enjoyed a good old-fashioned belly laugh to help you recapture a sense of perspective.

Cultivating a relaxed focus

Have you ever been in the middle of a task and lost all track of time? Not only that, but you know that your thoughts, actions, and emotions are in tune with each other as you go about the task. You feel as if you are in slow motion, yet you are working effectively, even speedily, and without effort. You're in what athletes call *the zone* and it's a wonderful state to be in. You are totally absorbed in what you're doing and your awareness of everything else going on around you seems heightened at the same time. Your conscious mind is utterly absorbed in the task in hand, and your unconscious mind is free to play along, providing all sorts of unexpected insights and knowledge. Your inner critic is dozing and your inner coach is proudly cheering you on from the sidelines! At these moments you feel invincible and you get a sense of how powerful and talented you really are. This kind of relaxed focus helps you perform better, make better decisions, and enjoy your life more.

How can you harness a relaxed focus in your life? Start by thinking of the times when you've experienced a relaxed focus. Be specific. What sort of things were you doing? Was it work, or play? What were the feelings and sensations that went with the experiences? If you think about these experiences, can you recall those feelings and sensations? If so, you already have a great tool for changing your state of mind.

You may be able to recreate this feeling of relaxed focus, or being in the zone, during the following activities:

- ✔ Driving or cycling
- ✔ Running or jogging
- ✔ A special hobby you are passionate about
- ✔ Reading
- ✔ Meditation and contemplation
- ✔ Yoga, Pilates, t'ai chi, and many other mind/body practices
- ✔ A long walk outdoors

If recapturing those feelings and sensations doesn't come easily to you, look for ways to recreate the experiences that created them in the first place. As you get more practice at recalling your resourceful states, you find you can enter into relaxed focus at will, instantly allowing you to notice what's going on with alertness and a sense of calm.

Knowing What You Really Want

What does your awareness of now tell you about where you're heading in your life? If you carry on doing the things that you're doing, will you be able to look back and see a life that you have designed, with all its joys and challenges?

When you're clear on what you're getting from the actions you take and the decisions you make, you find it much easier to answer the big questions of what you really want in life. You can be more objective about the bad habits that get in the way of your full enjoyment, such as procrastination, negative self-talk, or always running late. And you can prepare to replace them with habits that enhance your life. Yet even when you are crystal clear on the most important things in your life, it can be tricky to sort out the ones that form the biggest goals. You may have achieved a big goal and felt somehow a little flat and empty afterwards – a kind of 'what now?' feeling. Perhaps working towards your goal was more enjoyable than actually attaining it.

These feelings are normal, and in fact the most compelling reason to set goals is to propel you into action, which is where the real rewards in life often come. In fact, the more you coach yourself to set and achieve your goals, the more you're likely to find that the feeling of forward movement and progress gives you the most satisfaction. This is one reason why starting to think about your next big goal before you've completed the one you're currently working towards is a great idea.

Sometimes the things you thought you really wanted turn out to be not so wonderful after all, which can be confusing. A coaching client of mine focused obsessively on her forthcoming house purchase – a significant symbol of her corporate success. However, on the day she moved in, her enthusiasm fell to rock bottom. She discovered that the thrill of the renovation project was what she really wanted, although she'd mistaken it for the end goal itself. This realisation caused her to rethink her career direction and five years later she's carved out a stimulating sideline in property development.

You're creating your future now

In the very first *Back to the Future* film, the character Marty goes back in time to before he was born to ensure that his parents meet and fall in love, despite the odds against them, or he simply won't exist in his own future. As he takes actions that move him by turn towards and then further away from his goal, you can actually see the images of Marty and his sister fading in and out of the family photograph that Marty carries with him. Marty was able to adjust his actions because he had a very clear idea of what he wanted to achieve and could clearly see how certain things were taking him off course.

Although you don't have a crystal ball about how your life will turn out (or a Hollywood scriptwriter!) you can keep a focus on the kind of future you want to create. This focus can act like a beacon that helps you walk your chosen path. Is one of your long-term goals to create enough wealth so that you can retire early and run a small hotel on a fabulous tropical island? If so, the avoidance habit you may have in the here and now of never opening your bank statements isn't going to help you create that future.

The action you take in the here and now creates the many possible futures that can exist for you.

Enjoying the journey

Think of your future life goals as if they are features on a far-distant horizon. You can see, way ahead of you in the distance, the shapes and colours of a mountain, or a lake, or a village. But nothing is in sharp relief because you're too far away. You can choose to head towards the mountain, or the lake, or the village – whichever seems the most appealing to you from where you are now. As you get closer, you begin to see the terrain on the mountain, the eddies and whirls of the lake, the houses and buildings of the village. You get a stronger sense of whether your choice to head for the mountain was the right one, or whether, now that you can see a little more in focus and have gathered speed along the way, the lake or the village seems to be a better destination. You can still change course, even quite late in the day, and make your final decision about your destination. You may even notice something that you couldn't see from your starting point. Just around the corner from the mountain is a valley that looks appealing. And when you finally reach the destination that you've chosen, you have no regrets because you've had the most amazing journey along the way.

Achieving what you really want depends on creating some kind of vision for yourself that you can begin to shape into tangible goals with a clear route to reaching them. At this stage your vision for your life may be clear, but equally it may be quite general or vague. Now that you're truly getting in touch with knowing your values (refer to Chapter 6), you can describe many of the things that have to be present in your future life. You can also get clearer on some other details too.

The following activity helps you to get your whole-life goals clearly in sight.

Imagine that you turn on your computer one morning and pick up a series of emails from your inner coach. Remember that your inner coach exists now, in your present, and at all stages of your life in your future. Your inner coach wants to tell you all the things you've accomplished in your life and so has decided to write you emails from five, 10, and 20 years in the future.

Look at the following list of different areas of your life. Maybe some areas are more of a priority to you than others, so you may choose to focus on just a few for now. You may want to work through the activity for each key area in turn, or alternatively discover that looking at your life as a whole is the right way for you. Both approaches work very well. Where do you see yourself in five, 10, and 20 years time in terms of your:

✔ **Health.** Your physical, mental, and emotional wellbeing and health.

✔ **Career.** Your job, work, or career, paid or unpaid.

✔ **People.** The relationships and people in your life.

✔ **Money.** Financial security and lifestyle choices.

✔ **Growth.** The way you learn and develop as a person.

In terms of people, you may see yourself as a parent in five years. In the area of growth, your inner coach may tell you that you've travelled the world. In 20 years you may be enjoying a comfortable retirement.

Happy writing and happy reading!

Placing your whole-life goals on your horizon

After you have a vision of your whole-life goals, you can frame them into a desire statement in preparation for generating options and an action plan. A *desire statement* is a simple expression of a vision for yourself for your future.

What did you see when you emailed yourself as your inner coach? Perhaps you saw yourself running your own business? Maybe you got a vision of a wonderful family life? Or did you see yourself using a talent or passion in a certain way?

Time to place your goals on your horizon with the following activity so you know where you're heading!

1. **Take each of your whole-life goals and condense them into a short desire statement.** Your desire statement for wealth may look something like this example:

   I want to be a successful and talented businessperson, creating the wealth that I need to provide my family with the lifestyle that we all want.

2. **Think of the time period in which you want to achieve your whole-life goals – it could be a year or 20 years – and choose an image to represent your path.** You may like the idea of a mountain range to represent your ultimate destination, or perhaps the point where the sea and sky meet in a coastal landscape. Maybe you'll choose the night sky and focus on the furthest star.

3. **Place each of your whole-life goals on the terrain ahead of you, approximately where you think they'll be in the time when you achieve them.** As you place them, think of the images and feelings associated with each goal and repeat your desire statement to yourself. For example, you may get an image of your perfect home that represents for you a goal of family life, or a trophy to symbolise a sporting achievement like running a marathon.

4. **Recall this visualisation regularly to keep your own big-picture vision for your life sharply in focus.**

This activity may already get you thinking about how you are going to fulfil your whole life goals.

Planning Effective Action

After you've decided on the goal(s) you want to aim for you're ready to formulate and take the specific actions that move you towards achieving your goals in life. The saying 'well begun is half done' is true – planning well and considering all the possible outcomes gets you off to a flying start. Taking action is so much easier when you've really looked at what you believe is possible for you, you're aware of the resources and options you have, and the values that guide you.

You also need to ensure that the circumstances you're in when you're taking these actions are those that make it easiest for you to succeed. This chapter takes a look at how you can build an effective action plan to sustain you through the ups and downs of your journey.

Smarten up your goal setting

You already have some compelling whole-life goals sitting on your horizon. At the moment, these goals are a broad vision of how you want your life to be at some point soon. You also have some possible options in mind to get you there. The first stage of taking action is to bring those whole life goals into full sight and apply the SMARTEN UP goal setting guidelines to the whole process (we explain this acronym in a moment). This process means getting up close and personal with the what, how, where, and who associated with your goals.

Your brain needs clear instructions about what, how, and when to achieve that which you want. The SMARTEN UP goal-setting model is a great method to help you on your way.

To be realistically achievable your goal (or in some instances, you) must be:

- ✔ Specific
- ✔ Measurable
- ✔ Achievable and appealing
- ✔ Realistic
- ✔ Timed
- ✔ Enthusiastic
- ✔ Natural
- ✔ Understood
- ✔ Prepared

Here are all the elements of cast-iron, can't-fail SMARTEN UP goal setting in more detail.

Specific

Your goal must be specific. Saying that you want to 'get fitter' isn't enough because your brain has no clear way to interpret that type of instruction. Fitness for you may be getting slim, being more energetic, getting more toned, growing stronger, or becoming free of disease. Or perhaps all of the above!

When you formulate your goals, think carefully about the aspects of each goal that are most important to you. You can give each aspect a priority ranking to keep you focused on what really works for you, or to help you pinpoint your hot buttons. Designing your plan to get fit then allows you to major on the options that generate the most important results for you. If energy is vital, look at how you eat and the exercise you do to get the maximum impact in this area.

Measurable

Your goal must be measurable. If you want to tackle your smoking habit, you must quantify what you want to achieve. For example, this may be to cut out smoking completely from your life, or to reduce the number of cigarettes you smoke by a stated amount. Again, your brain needs a clear instruction or it doesn't know where to start, and procrastination sets in.

Achievable or appealing

The A in SMARTEN UP can be 'achievable', but 'appealing' is often a more meaningful measure to apply to your goals. So, is a goal achievable because other people have done it? In the example of buying a French farmhouse, the fact that many other people have successfully moved abroad can be a great impetus for you. On the other hand, you're not 'other people' and thinking too much about this as a measure can sometimes get in your way. You may even prevent yourself from going for a goal that you can achieve because you lack a precedent. Think of Roger Bannister running a mile in 4 minutes – if he had applied the 'achievable' measure he never would have attempted to set this record because the whole world was telling him it was impossible.

Your goal must also be attractive and compelling for you. Focusing on the undesirable effects of continuing to overeat as a motivator for action only goes so far, and you may find that all the negative associations make you feel worse, not better. Instead, find a positive vision for yourself of all of the benefits of eating in a healthy and controlled way – focus on how much you're likely to enjoy your new lifestyle and your slimmer, healthier body shape.

If you don't find your goal appealing you can't get anywhere with it because the goal doesn't motivate you. If your goal is to lose weight because you think that your partner wants you to, but you're pretty happy with your body shape, you may well find getting fit a struggle. Either make your goal appealing or find a new goal that makes you want to start the journey.

Realistic

External measures of what may be achievable, such as comparing your circumstances with those of others, may not be very helpful to you. Nevertheless, you must still ensure that your goal is realistic for you, in the current circumstances of your life and for your current level of ability. Having a big, stretching goal is wonderful and you can always give yourself permission to reach way beyond your comfort zone, in the knowledge that really wanting to reach your goal helps you to succeed. But you need to ensure that you set yourself up for your own *success*, so take into account any constraints that you may be working with that may mean a longer journey or an adjustment to your plan.

Perhaps you have other commitments that you want to honour so your goal of travelling the world on horseback has to wait a while or be scaled down. Perhaps you have to look at a series of smaller goals to get you to the point where you have the resources you need to set up your own business.

Being realistic doesn't mean you have to set limits on yourself, it simply means that you need to figure out how to walk before you can run.

Timed

Your goal must be time bound or you may find you never quite make it. If you want to get a promotion at work, you succeed more easily if you set your sights on timed milestones to get to that point. You can start out by identifying the skills you want to develop and agree on certain dates when you can attend training or work with a mentor. Then you can set your sights on a role that is available to you and set yourself dates by which to prepare a new CV or practise your interview technique. You can always adjust these times as you gather more information, but the presence of timed milestones helps you to focus on the deadlines that are right for you. Having a time-bound goal is one of the best cures ever for procrastination.

Enthusiastic

As well as your goal being appealing to you, you must also be enthusiastic about the entire journey you take to it. You may want the end result very badly, but if the process of getting you there is too tough and painful, you may find it hard to keep going. You don't have to subscribe to the glib mantra of 'no pain, no gain'. OK, achieving your goals may well involve some discomfort and sacrifice, but don't make it extra hard for yourself by never letting up. If you have explored your options well you're always able to find a way of getting to your goal that increases your chance of success by boosting your enthusiasm along the way.

Give yourself regular small rewards – even making a call to a friend to celebrate an achievement along the way can give you a boost. Or approach the journey in a way that's fun for you – perhaps map out your progress on a large sheet of paper, pin it somewhere prominent, and mark off with coloured pens as you go along. And whatever you do, ensure that you think of ways to celebrate your success as you take each significant step of the way. You make the rules, no one else!

Natural

Your goal must work with your natural instincts. Harness your self-awareness and check all your goals against your intuition. Is this goal really for me? Is it someone else's goal that I think I *should* want? Or is my goal so fundamental to me that putting off taking action is simply not an option? If you can't answer yes to that last question, check out your needs, values, and beliefs and see what changes you can make to your goal to make it fully your own.

Understood

Your goals must be clearly understood by your significant others, whoever they may be – partner, friends, children, work colleagues. They need to know what you are trying to achieve and how they can support you. This doesn't mean you have to tell *everyone* your private thoughts and dreams. But you can help yourself by identifying the key players in your life and telling them what they need to know so that they can cheer you on your way. If other people play a big role in getting you to your goal, you need to make sure that they understand what you need from them and are able to support you or work with you.

Prepared

And finally, despite making sure that everyone is rooting for you, you must be prepared for setbacks and perhaps even for negative reactions from others. Even though your nearest and dearest want the best for you, they may find it unsettling to see you racing towards a stretching goal, especially if they wish they were doing so well with the goals in their own lives. Your loved ones may not mean to sabotage you, but they may quite unconsciously pull you back with a stray comment or a small temptation at just the wrong time.

Even if everyone around you is being incredibly supportive, you still may encounter some setbacks along the way. You need to be prepared for the fact that other people may not always be able to offer you the encouragement you need to pick yourself up and carry on. Your loved ones may want you to 'give yourself a break' and ease off your efforts for a while. That may be good advice, which you can choose to take. The key is to be prepared for the fact that other people are never so invested in you getting results as you are.

To see exactly how SMARTEN UP can work for one specific goal consider the following objective that you might set yourself:

> I want to sell my house and buy a farmhouse in France by May of next year.

- ✔ **Does the statement contain a specific goal?** Yes, you've expressed your goal as a plan to move to a specific place in a specific manner, rather than as a wish simply to 'move abroad' for example.

- ✔ **Is your goal measurable?** Can you know when you have achieved it? Yes, when you're the proud owner of a French farmhouse!

- ✔ **Is your goal achievable?** Yes, many people have done this kind of thing before. And appealing? Yes, you can really see yourself moving in!

✔ **Is your goal realistic?** Yes, you've investigated the property market on both sides of the Channel, and it seems to be perfectly possible for you to make the move in the current market and in your circumstances.

✔ **Is your goal timed?** Yes, you want to do this by May of next year, and you've checked that the timescale seems quite realistic.

✔ **Are you enthusiastic about the journey towards your goal?** Yes, you've already taken steps and started your research. And you've planned to spend two hours a week working towards your goal.

✔ **Is the goal a natural one for you?** Yes, you've spent many happy holidays in France, know the language quite well, and feel at home there already.

✔ **Is the goal understood by the key people in your life?** Yes, your family is up for the change and look forward to spending long holidays there.

✔ **Are you prepared for the journey to your goal?** Yes, you've considered different contingency plans if your ideal farmhouse is out of your budget. You've thought through how you may need to adjust your strategy if the sale takes longer than expected or falls through.

Putting theory into practice

You can now write out your whole-life goals in Figure 2-1. Keep each whole life goal as simply worded as possible – you want to be able to recall these statements quickly as you go about your day to keep your vision clear in your mind.

	Specific	Measurable	Appealing	Realistic	Timed	Enthusiastic	Natural	Understood	Prepared
Health									
Wealth									
People									
Career									
Growth									

Figure 2-1: SMARTEN UP goal setting.

Smartening up to lose weight

The following is another example of how to apply SMARTEN UP to your whole-life goals.

Louise had two young children under 5 and her lifestyle had changed so much as a result that she had acquired quite a lot of excess weight for the first time in her life. This added weight felt unhealthy to her and she wanted to regain the energy levels that she had when she was slimmer. A secondary, and quite important, issue for her was that she wanted to wear a certain special outfit for a family wedding that summer. She decided to use coaching as a means to keep her focused.

Louise stated her whole-life goal for her health as follows:

> *Over the next 9 months I will reach my natural body weight through a healthy eating programme and regular exercise. This will result in reaching my target dress size for the family wedding while building up my energy levels on a daily basis.*

This goal checked out against SMARTEN UP! as *specific*, *measurable*, and *timed* – Louise felt she didn't need to put an absolute end measure on her energy levels because she would be able to see that change through what she felt on a daily basis. Louise decided to focus on a specific dress size because that felt very real to her – she was able to see and touch the outfit she wanted to wear and this was a significant factor in making the goal *appealing* to her and maintaining her *enthusiasm* for the journey.

Louise's goal was *realistic* because she could lose weight slowly and this felt very doable in the context of her busy life. Her goal was a *natural* one for her because she had always hated the idea of having to crash diet and liked to eat well without depriving herself. And Louise made sure that her family *understood* what she wanted to achieve and that they were ready to support her. At the same time, she was *prepared* for the sustained effort that she needed to maintain, as well as the possibility of setbacks, and she had engaged a coach to support her through the process.

Matching Your Options to Your Goals

So you have clearly defined your whole-life goals, and you have considered some of the options for getting you there. Now's the time to map out the stages of your route and the very first step is to match up specific ways of moving forward to the goals you've set yourself. Having applied SMARTEN UP to your goals it may now be very clear that some options are better than others for your circumstances. But you can check this out by looking at your options in the context of SMARTEN UP as well.

Louise matched her options to her goals in the following way:

Louise was happy with her whole-life health goal and now needed to look at the options she had generated for getting there. She planned two aspects – losing the excess weight and becoming more energetic through regular exercise. For the weight loss she considered two main options: joining a local slimming group and following their recommended diet plan, or asking her local GP to suggest a healthy eating programme that she could follow herself. For the fitness aspect, she decided that some kind of aerobic exercise would generate the most energy for her. She had two main options: she could have access to a friend's exercise bike or she could join the local gym and follow a programme there. All her options passed the SMARTEN UP check in terms of being *appealing* and *enthusiastic* (and she could also check them out against *specific*, *measurable*, and *timed*), so she now needed to decide which were most *realistic* and *natural* for her.

Louise considered her natural preferences. She liked the idea of following her GP's suggestions slightly more than joining the slimming group because doing so would gave her more flexibility of time. She also chose the option of going to the gym over using the bike because the option of the bike felt just a little too loose to keep her on track.

Setting milestones for your journey

Having a clear goal and preferred options mapped out is probably enough to propel you into taking the first step towards achieving your goal – maybe you need to book an appointment with someone, or check out times of a fitness or educational class. Making a start as soon as you can is key to getting momentum. But you also want to think about *milestones* now. Your milestones are the stopping-off points on your journey where you can celebrate your success so far. You can think of these stopping-off points as an oasis, where you can recharge your energy and enthusiasm for your whole-life goals and take a quick check of your coordinates to make sure you're still going in the direction you want to go in.

During the course of Louise's nine-month programme she set herself alternate milestones every six weeks. Every 12 weeks she was able to see a big result in either fitness and energy levels or inch loss. This period of time between milestone goals worked well for her because she felt that she was never that far away from an opportunity to monitor and celebrate her progress and because the big changes were very motivating.

Taking baby steps

You may be tempted to race towards your whole-life goals and try to achieve them as quickly as possible. Sometimes that's the right approach and you gain lots of momentum. However, most people find that lasting change comes about through small, incremental progress to your goal.

Here are some advantages of following the tortoise strategy for making it to your goals rather than joining the hare on his racetrack:

- You can fit your goals into the rest of your life without sacrificing other things that are also important to you.

- You can make small and significant adjustments to your route as you go along, instead of finding that you have to do a rapid U-turn at speed if something doesn't turn out as you wanted.

- You enjoy the journey much more because you have time to build in rewards and celebrations.

- You build habits that stay with you for longer and become part of who you are, making the change much easier to sustain after you've reached your goal(s).

- You take out a lot of extra stress and pressure from your life that could have undesirable effects for you.

- You are more likely to sustain progress because you aren't behaving in an extreme or uncomfortable way for your natural preferences.

Louise achieved better results from taking baby steps rather than racing ahead – her slow weight loss was better for her body's health overall and her skin adjusted along the way so she wasn't left with sags and wrinkles.

If you simply must join the hare, apply this racing-ahead approach to goals that cause minimum disruption to everything else in your life and take you a relatively short time to attain, where you know you can maintain your momentum. Getting fast results in this way may well kick-start your motivation but is unlikely to be sustainable. You need to consider the healthy option for you in the long-term, especially if you have a weight loss goal. Some people even put a hold on other activities and go on a form of retreat or sabbatical to focus on their specific objective. This approach can have advantages, but you usually need a lot of time and money, and you still need to consider how you're going to sustain your progress after the period of focus. We're talking about *your* goals and *your* life – only you can decide what works best for you.

Keeping Your Promise to Yourself

Congratulations on setting out on your journey with a well-stocked kit bag and clear coordinates! If you continue to review your progress at each milestone, achieving your whole-life goals seems easy and effortless.

When events test your resolve, remember the promise you made yourself to achieve your goals. In this section we show you some simple things you can keep in mind to help you see your promise through.

Thinking like a hero

You don't have to scale mountains or fight dragons to be heroic. You are the hero in your own life. Your unique brand of heroism lies in living your life with your own sense of integrity in the way you want to live it. That may mean huge goals or small adjustments, yet the courage and commitment you need to do either is of the same quality. Your promise to yourself is ultimately accountable only to you, even though you may also choose to share your goals with others to garner support. All true heroes know that they have the highest standards for themselves.

Part of the deal of being a hero is that you are probably tested along the way and sometimes you may falter. This quality of courageously reaching for your goals over and over again marks you out as the hero in your own life, a quality that is a long, long way from any absolute standard of perfectionism. Thinking like a hero in this way can sustain you at the toughest of times.

The following activity is a fun way to help you think about your heroic qualities.

Imagine your favourite movie director has phoned you up with the great news that he or she wants to make *The Film of Your Life*. You get first option on how the script is written and who plays you.

How does *The Film of Your Life* play out? Is it an action adventure with lots of cliff-hangers? A warm romance? A joyful comedy? A thoughtful reflection on serious issues? Or a mind-expanding fantasy/sci-fi extravaganza?

If you could choose anyone, famous or not, to play you, who would you pick? What qualities do they have that you see in yourself? What would be the peak performances, the scenes that take your breath away? What advice would you give to the main actor about how to approach the role?

What does this activity reveal to you about how you approach the drama of your life?

When life gets in the way of living

Taking steps towards your goal feels easier when life goes on around you in a fairly predictable manner. You've prepared well, so you have contingency plans for lots of eventualities along the way and you find that not a lot can deflect you from your course. And then you have One of Those Days. Every crisis you can possibly imagine rains down on you all at once – you collect parking tickets from nowhere, final demands turn up for bills that you thought you had dealt with, and the people around you seem unwilling or unable to help you out with any of it. On top of that your energy levels are low because you've been working hard and missed out on your usual quota of sleep and you're coming down with a nasty bug that makes you feel weak, fed up, and sorry for yourself. The final straw is finding that you can't get a signal on your mobile to warn an important new client that you're stuck in traffic and are running late for the presentation.

Everyone has these days – sometimes they turn into weeks or even longer – and when you're in the middle of a challenging goal sustaining your efforts is tough. Something has to give. Trouble is, if your goal gets sidelined, you find it really easy to beat yourself up and that can create an even bigger setback.

At times you're playing the long game in your life. If you have to put aside your big goal in order to get through a bad run of luck or unusual series of events, then so be it. Accept that setbacks are a normal part of any change and keep focused on what you can do to deal with your current crises as best you can and get out the other side to the clear open terrain of your journey again. Think about ways to make progress, even in very small ways, such as looking for any unexpected opportunity in the situation.

During her nine-month journey to health and fitness, Louise encountered several setbacks and temptations along the way as other aspects of her life provided distractions. During the times when she had to miss her gym sessions to deal with other priorities she kept her focus by writing in her journal for five minutes a day, considering a different benefit of maintaining her goal each time.

Exploding the myth of willpower

Suppose your setback happens because you succumb to temptation. You can often give in to temptation when you're making a change in your health – quitting smoking, getting fit, losing weight – but it can also happen in your other goal areas. Perhaps you're focused on getting a promotion at work but suddenly you find yourself slipping back into old, comfortable habits of pro-crastinating on essential tasks. Again, your inner critic is happy to berate you for your lack of willpower and causes you to wonder, 'What's the point in trying for this new role?'

You may be surprised to discover that the people who are most successful in achieving their goals in life often don't believe in willpower. Successful people often behave as if they have *no* willpower at all and make sure that they set up conditions around them to avoid temptations most of the time. When they do give into temptation, they shrug their shoulders, enjoy the moment of indulgence, and get straight back on track without any self-recrimination.

Think of willpower as a trait you can develop as you gain momentum and start to see results. If you're blessed with strong willpower then that will certainly help to get you started with your goals. For most people though, seeing great results helps them to maintain their enthusiasm and progress.

Accept that you're human, and that you're going to 'fail' from time to time. Don't accept that one failure is an excuse to carry on with a habit that takes you further away from your goal.

Dealing with jealousy from others

Setbacks can occur when people around you withhold approval or even express disapproval about you coaching yourself to achieve a goal. Sometimes this stems from jealousy that you are doing so well with your goal and it can be very unsettling.

When this happens, look for the positive intent behind the jealousy from the other person. She is probably afraid that by achieving your goal she may lose something valuable that she got from you. Perhaps you were the one who joined her for a cigarette at break time and she is unsettled by your new non-smoking conviction. Or it may be a family member who has got used to joining you as a couch potato in front of the television and feels bereft because you're spending more time down the gym. Maybe you used to be the person in the office who always seemed to sympathise when a colleague wanted to have a good old whinge about the boss, and now you're taking a different atti-tude to being a team player – your new approach takes the fun out of it for your colleague.

In all of these examples, the people close to you miss the rapport they for-merly had with you and the sense that you were 'in it together'. Your new habits *are* changing your behaviour and change is what you want. It may take a little time to readjust the relationships you had before you started making these changes. Some of those relationships may never be the same again and you can take the lead in changing your relationships for the better too.

Chapter 3

Becoming Your Best Self

· ·

In This Chapter

▶ Putting your best foot forward

▶ Assessing your competencies

▶ Expanding your range of behavioural skills

▶ Making your beliefs work for you

▶ Keeping your fears in check

· ·

*I*n this chapter you take the first steps of your coaching journey by developing your self-awareness. You start to think about your strengths as valuable resources you can draw on at will and you see why those traits that you perceive as your weaknesses are far less significant than you may think. You find out more about some of the behaviours that you may like to adopt, such as becoming more organised or having the confidence to deliver a speech, and start to experiment with trying out new approaches. Above all, you'll begin to recognise that you really do have your own unique style and you can develop this to become your most authentic, and best self.

Considering Your Unique Gifts

When you were a child learning to walk you didn't think for a minute that, just because you were exceptionally good at crawling, you were destined to crawl for the rest of your life because, well, crawling was your major strength. Even if when learning to walk you fell over more than most of the toddlers in your playgroup, you didn't let that put you off for long. Sooner or later you developed the ability to walk just as competently as you could previously crawl, and chances are you were a lot less anxious about the whole experience than your fond parents were.

Trouble is, most people get rather bogged down in attaching labels (such as 'I'm a hopeless speller') to themselves as they get older. You start noticing things that seem to come easier to you and begin to ignore the stuff that is a bit harder. Other people, perhaps your teachers and parents, reinforce this behaviour by telling you how good you are at music but maybe art isn't your *thing*. And because you learn early on that doing things well gets approval and rewards, you tend automatically to shoot for maximum points in the areas that feel most comfortable to you.

Nothing wrong with that, of course, and it's probably got you a lot of goodies so far in your life. Passing an exam in your best subject with flying colours? Winning at your favourite sport? A rapid promotion through using your natural abilities at work? Hardly results to be sneezed at!

But you've probably also had a few frustrations along the way, feeling that some things just seem to be out of your grasp. Maybe, no matter how hard you try, you still feel like a nincompoop around computers, or you're on your seventh driving test and it's not funny any more. People are very good at adapting, though, so you come up with solutions that mean you don't have to do the things you don't like or find tricky. You leave the computing to your partner, and get to know the bus timetable by heart. You can avoid and evade, and often other people don't even notice. But you don't fool yourself, right?

Now imagine if you could feel able to tackle anything and everything? Picture yourself with loads of things you are really good at and also some other things that are as yet undiscovered talents. Envisage that your 'weaknesses' are just an aspect of you, and not the most significant aspects by a long way. You can begin to change your mindset by thinking about the following:

✔ There are many more things that you *can* do than things you can't.

✔ The things you can't do are often simply skills that you haven't yet mastered or prefer to avoid. You have the choice to put in the time and the effort to become competent at almost anything, within the bounds of what's realistic and achievable for you.

✔ By focusing on your positive unique qualities you make more progress than trying really hard to excel at something you're less strong at. And the confidence this gives you makes tackling those trickier challenges easier because you're in a more relaxed and productive state of mind.

Boosting Your Competencies

Apart from being a good way to boost your reserves of confidence, taking a close look at the times in your life when you achieved great results is an effective way to find out more about yourself in all areas of your life. A great result certainly doesn't have to mean winning the Nobel Peace Prize. What you need to focus on is any event that turned out the way you wanted it to, as a result of *something you did*.

Take a look at this list of accomplishments. You may be able to add some or all of them to your own list:

✔ You passed your driving test.

✔ You got a job offer from an interview.

✔ You asked someone out on a date.

✔ You learned to ride a bike.

✔ You mastered a foreign language.

✔ You made a successful sales call.

✔ You became computer literate.

✔ You wrote a complex report for your boss.

✔ You navigated your way round a new city on a walking holiday.

✔ You cooked a fancy three-course meal from scratch for the first time.

If you were to tell the story of exactly how you did anything on that list, your story would be different to anyone else's, although the nuts and bolts of the task may be pretty much the same. Even the simplest of these examples can take an impressive array of skill and knowledge. But *how* you go about getting and using that skill and knowledge is what makes the difference.

As well as skill and knowledge, *competency* – the behaviour or 'how' of carrying out an action – is the magic third ingredient you need to achieve a great result in whatever you put your mind to. Writing that complex report? Maybe you already have enough technical knowledge but you've never written a formal business report before. So you might apply your competency of persuasion to get the help of a team member who's done this before.

Your competencies can often compensate for shortcomings in your skills and knowledge. Knowing how to apply your competencies can help you find new ways to hone any skills and knowledge you think you lack. The really great news about competencies is that, far from being qualities that only get dusted off at your annual work appraisal, they apply to all the different areas of your life with just a few tweaks here and there. Table 3-1 gives some examples of using competencies.

Table 3-1	Examples of Using Competencies	
Competency	*At work*	*At home/socially*
Communication skills	Writing a report	Giving your opinion about a news item to friends
Getting results	Winning some new business	Completing a do-it-yourself project in time for a housewarming party
Team work	Working on a departmental budget with others	Cooking a big family meal together

(continued)

Table 3-1 *(continued)*		
Planning and organising	Drawing up a staff rota	Organising a family party
Flexible/ adaptable	Taking on additional work duties	Adapting to a major change in your life circumstance
Developing others	Training and coaching staff	Teaching a child to ride a bike
Problem solving	Fixing a jammed photocopier	Arranging some private space in the house for a teenager
Building relationships	Meeting new clients	Joining a club or society

Other competencies include:

- ✔ Creativity
- ✔ Determination
- ✔ Initiative
- ✔ Self-reliance
- ✔ Persuading and influencing
- ✔ Negotiating
- ✔ Empathy

Make a list of your competencies. A good way to begin to get at your 'competency list' is to ask a friend or family member to describe you. Your friend or family member is very unlikely to tell you what they think you *can* do and much more likely to talk about *how* you do it. (Beware of asking this question when she is just a *teeny* bit annoyed with you for leaving all the washing-up in the sink overnight . . .)

Life coaching involves looking for ways to develop your inner resources to create the results you want. When you try out new things it sometimes feels scary, because you know you don't have the appropriate knowledge or skill yet. But armed with a well-developed set of competencies you can truly tackle anything.

Follow these steps to find out more about the resources of skill, knowledge, and competency you already have in the area of getting results in your life.

1. **Create your own Great Resources list by thinking of 10 examples of things you have accomplished.** Remember to include examples from your work, home, and social life.

2. **Now choose one of your examples and think about what skills you used to accomplish it.** For becoming computer literate, maybe you already had good keyboard skills. What new skills did you learn? Perhaps you learnt to surf the Web. What knowledge did you have to start, and what did you know at the end? What competencies did you apply to the task? List as many different examples as you can think of.

3. **Do the same with the other nine items on the list.**

4. **Stand back and admire the impressive array of skills, knowledge, and competency that you already have!** And that's from only 10 accomplishments! Imagine what the list would look like if you did this activity on all of your accomplishments?

5. **Consider what you want to do with this knowledge about yourself.** You can look at the skills you have in certain areas that transfer to other parts of your life. And you can consider the goals you have and which of your unique qualities will best help you achieve them.

Noticing Your Preferences

Have you noticed how easily you fall into a familiar pattern of behaviour, or *comfort zone*, as you go about your daily tasks? You may, for example, always take the same seat round the table at your team meeting. Maybe you have a certain routine for getting out of the house in the morning and feel mildly panicked whenever that gets disrupted? Life can often be so chaotic that, consciously or unconsciously, people like to have certain things that they always do in the same way. Following patterns of behaviour is a very effective strategy for dealing with times when you feel under stress or have to make difficult decisions that take you into unfamiliar territory.

These 'preferences' are a bit like a comfy woolly cardigan that you pull on for a day home alone when you don't want to think about picking out coordinated clothing. And like the comfy cardigan, your preferences are right at home in that situation but not always appropriate for other circumstances of your life.

Looking out or looking in?

The two basic behavioural preferences are *extraversion* and *introversion*. Extraverts like to experience their world externally, through thinking aloud and interaction with others, while introverts prefer to make sense of their world through inner reflection, independent of others.

Just in the same way that everyone possesses some element of every competency, everyone has aspects of their personality that they express in an extraverted way and other aspects that are more introverted. Perhaps you are by preference more extraverted than introverted. You love meetings where lots of people talk through ideas and brainstorm, generating high energy but not much in the way of paperwork. But part of your role is to prepare a detailed budget report that means you have to lock yourself away in a room by yourself for a day a month and concentrate. You may really dislike this part of your job and feel that it isn't your strongest area. To improve the results you get at work you can adapt your approach to ensure that you develop the introverted skills, even if they are not as strong as your more extraverted qualities.

You can take yourself out of your comfort zone from time to time, which helps to build your flexibility muscle. Doing so stops you from only achieving results in certain areas.

Changing the hand you write with is a simple example of stepping out of your comfort zone and trying something you're less comfortable with. Try the following activity.

1. **Take a pen and write your signature as you normally do.** How does that feel? Comfortable? Automatic?

2. **Now change hands and write your signature holding the pen in your other hand.** What's the difference? The action is probably a lot less comfortable. You're certainly going to be more conscious of what you're doing. How does your signature look? Would you get away with it as a forgery?!

3. **Now try again, six more times, changing hands each time.** What differences do you notice? You are probably beginning to feel more comfortable and the results are starting to look a bit better. If you carry on practising this every day, you eventually start to get results that are equally good and feel almost as natural as writing with your leading hand.

The more you do a certain job or activity, or use a particular character trait or competency, the more comfortable you become because you *already* have some ability in the area. You always enjoy the comfy cardigan, but the feelings of comfort between that and the smart suit start to feel more similar. And you make a much better impression on a new client in the smart suit!

Finding your behavioural styles

There is another dimension to your preferred behaviours besides favouring either introversion or extraversion (refer to previous section). You may gravitate more towards the *task* in hand or the *people* who are involved. For example, you have a strong focus on task if, as a manager of a business, you tend to think first of the business results, and you consider the people in the business as part of the systems and the processes that get those results. A people-focused manager, on the other hand, thinks of people first and then considers how to make the systems and processes work with those people. Both approaches have advantages and disadvantages at the extremes, and a good manager works to compensate for their own strong preference by adapting their behaviour and/or ensuring that other team members can balance it.

When you add the preference you have for extraversion or introversion together with your preference for tasks or people, you get a certain style or way of being that you can also recognise in other people. Knowing your style is invaluable in working out which of your behaviours you want to develop, as well as predicting how people around you might respond to your behaviour and actions. Awareness of these behavioural styles is helpful in three key ways:

- ✔ You can come up with action steps for your goals that fit with the way you like to do things, which means that you can accomplish these goals more effortlessly and enjoyably.

- ✔ You can identify people who have a different behavioural style to you. You can model how these particular people accomplish their goals in areas in which you may not feel strong.

- ✔ You can better understand why people around you react in certain ways to your behaviour, and you can deal with resistance and conflict as you make your life changes.

You can find many ways to help you understand your particular behavioural style. The following activity is a very simple exercise that will give you a quick sense of your main preferred behavioural style.

1. **Look at columns A and B in Table 3-2. Tick the extreme of each pair that you're most like.** For example, you may sometimes take risks and sometimes avoid them, but if in general you tend to be more risk averse than risk attracted, tick the response in column A. Enter the total number of ticks for each column underneath.

2. **Now do the same for columns C and D.** If you see yourself as 'relaxed and warm' rather than 'formal and proper' most of the time, tick the response in column C. Again, enter the total for each column.

3. **Take your total score for column B and make a cross on the horizontal line at the appropriate number in Figure 3-1.** This score shows your tendency towards an extraverted or introverted behavioural style.

4. **Take your score for column D and make a cross on the vertical line.** This shows your preference for task or people.

5. **The intersection of the two crosses shows you which of the four behavioural styles you tend to feel most comfortable in.**

Table 3-2	Working Out Your Behavioural Style	
Column A	**Column B**
Avoids risks	Embraces risks
Slow to decide	Quick to decide
Indirect	Direct
Easy going	Impatient
Prefers to listen	Prefers to talk
Reserved	Outgoing
Keeps opinions to self	Expresses opinions often
TOTAL A SCORE:	
TOTAL B SCORE:	
Column C	**Column D**
Relaxed and warm	Formal and proper
Opinion oriented	Fact oriented
Open	Reserved
Time flexible	Time disciplined
Relationship focus	Task focus
Shares personal feelings	Keeps feelings to self
Intuitive	Analytical
TOTAL C SCORE:	
TOTAL D SCORE:	

If your style is Mountain:

- ✔ You like to focus on tasks and results in an outgoing (extroverted) way.
- ✔ You favour taking action, decisiveness, effectiveness, and getting results

If your style is Sun:

- ✔ You like to be around people and prefer to behave in an outgoing (extroverted) way.
- ✔ You favour spontaneity, enthusiasm, having fun, and collaboration with others.

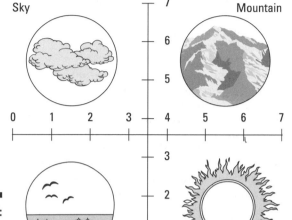

Figure 3-1:
Find your
behavioural
style.

If your style is Ocean:

- ✔ You like to be around people and tend to be more reflective (introverted) in your style.
- ✔ You favour patience, sensitivity, and support.

If your style is Sky:

- ✔ You like to focus on tasks and results and prefer to be more reflective (introverted) in your style.
- ✔ You favour thinking things through, structure, planning, and being thorough.

What did you notice when you did this activity?

- ✔ Perhaps it was difficult making a choice between the pairs. Sometimes you feel you are spontaneous, sometimes cautious. You are a complex human being and all your responses vary to a degree. Variety is what makes you unique.
- ✔ If you had very high total scores that placed you squarely in a certain style, did you feel quite dismissive about the opposite style? Did you feel that your style is definitely the 'best'? Being your best self certainly means celebrating your unique positive qualities – and it also means being aware of those that you can develop. Opening your mind to the benefits of your opposite qualities can be extremely liberating!

> ✔ In contrast, did you look at your opposite style with some regret, wishing you were more like that? Other people may well be doing the same with you – start to value the great qualities you have, knowing that you can expand your range if you choose.

This exercise gives you a sense of the general behavioural arena that you prefer to operate in. If you meet other people who also like that general arena, they may seem different to you in some respects yet you probably have quite a strong rapport with them because they are, in essence, rather more like you than some other people you meet. And you may struggle to get rapport with people of the opposite style to you for the same reason. On the other hand, many successful marriages and partnerships are formed on the basis of 'opposites attract', because we instinctively seek out those aspects of our style that are different to us, perhaps as a way of achieving a complete whole.

Knowing your preferred style is a great starting point for self-awareness. You can look at some of the behaviours of your opposite style and begin to experiment with ones that you think may serve you well, much like the idea behind practising writing with your left hand if you are normally right handed. Try reflecting a little more before you give an opinion perhaps, or speaking out even if your idea feels not quite fully formed. You can do this because you already have in you some element of the whole range of behaviours and you can make an informed choice that you are going to step into another style and see how that changes the results you get. Flexibility is the key!

Adding New Behaviours

Being your best self doesn't mean that you have to change how you do things, but it usually means that adapting some of your behaviours will help you get even better results.

In fact, a willingness to develop yourself is a fundamental part of coaching – but are some people *unable* to change? You probably know people who've made major changes in their lives yet appear to have ultimately reverted to their old behaviour. Examples are the smoker who quits for a decade and then suddenly starts again, or the calm and controlled individual who reverts to anger after years of managing their unhelpful emotions. This seems to be pretty discouraging evidence that a leopard never changes its spots!

The process of change is often tough and challenging. However, even repeated relapses into old behaviour patterns do not in any way mean that you are unable to change. Indeed, every fresh attempt simply provides new information about what's working and what's not, so you get ever closer to lasting change. Think of the legend of Thomas Edison and the invention of the light bulb – it's believed he made close to 10,000 attempts, and he still refused to see any of them as proof that he couldn't succeed, choosing to regard each 'failure' as a step closer to success by eliminating what *wasn't* going to work.

Fundamentally, the essence of *you* never changes. Alcoholics Anonymous works on the premise that someone may always *be* an alcoholic, but that they always have the power to change their behaviour so that they do not *live* as an alcoholic. Although this might seem depressing on the face of it, it's a pretty encouraging fact – you can choose your best life and be your best self and that's when your real strength shines through.

Start to think of the change process a little differently. See yourself *adding* new habits rather than fighting to eradicate old, unhelpful ones. Anyone who has ever successfully lost weight will tell you that simply cutting out favourite foods only goes so far, whereas building regular exercise into your schedule not only promotes weight loss but also cuts down on the times when you're available to snack on unhealthy foods (unless you are very adept at slurping ice-cream while you're on the treadmill!).

Think of your state of mind when you choose to do something that is positive, enjoyable, and easy for you. Then think of the opposite of that – the feeling of deprivation you get when you're trying really hard to kick a bad habit. The truth is that *doing* something is almost always more enjoyable than *stopping* something.

As you open your mind to *choosing* new behaviours rather than stifling old ones, you begin to *want* to choose the new, empowering behaviours over any old, destructive habits that have been restricting you from living your best life.

Choosing Your Beliefs

Perhaps you have a pretty clear idea of what you want to change or improve in your life, such as becoming more assertive, or starting your own business, and you've had a good look at your options. You may even have formulated a plan but somehow you never really got going with it. You feel frustrated, because the plan's a good one, and you really want to put it into action. But you find yourself procrastinating, thinking of reasons not to start, or getting discouraged along the way. You say to yourself that you don't have time or that you need to do other things first.

What's going on? Are you simply weak, or lazy? I'd guess you've beaten yourself up on this count a number of times in your life. The good news is that the reason you're blocked may have nothing to do with weakness, or laziness, or any other nasty trait you choose to label yourself with. You may well be blocked because, deep down, maybe you don't believe you're capable of executing your plan. Or even worse, you don't really believe that you deserve to be happier than you are at the moment.

In this section we talk about having the power of a strong belief system to catapult you into action. We show you how you can choose the beliefs that will support you and how to turn down the volume on the beliefs that hold you back.

Understanding how your beliefs shape you

You can lack resources and your plan can be no more than a few random scribbles on the back of an envelope, yet if your motivation is right and you really believe you can do it, you can make your plan happen. History is full of men and women who have defied the odds and overcome seemingly immovable obstacles to reach their goals, and these people all have one thing in common – an unshakable belief that they are exactly the right person at exactly the right moment in time to achieve whatever they set out to do, be it scaling an impossible mountain or winning a marathon.

In life coaching, a *belief* is simply a feeling of conviction about something, specifically about yourself – and strong positive beliefs about something are the foundation for action. Holding negative beliefs or beliefs that no longer serve you well has the opposite effect and keeps you stuck. Your inner critic specialises in these destructive beliefs and can produce them at the drop of a hat.

Beliefs are tricky things; they always appear to be logical and watertight – that's their nature – but whole communities have built their worldview based on beliefs that were later proved wrong. For example, the world isn't flat, but people used to believe that it was, and wasted a lot of energy in elaborate strategies to avoid falling off the edge.

What are your beliefs and where are they from?

Some of the beliefs you hold go right back to your childhood. When you were very young you genuinely believed that your parents knew the answer to everything. And what about your belief in Santa Claus or the Tooth Fairy? Some beliefs you picked up in childhood are harmful. What about the school report that left you with a belief that you're lazy and easily distracted? Okay, you sometimes behaved that way in class, but these kinds of labels have a habit of sticking with you as part of your identity long after you've also become hardworking and focused. Beliefs learnt, or given to you, in childhood can be very powerful indeed, and if the beliefs are negative, they can really hold you back from seeing and then fulfilling your true potential.

But sometimes beliefs can be overturned in an instant. Do you remember the film *The Matrix*? Neo, the main character, is stunned to discover that the world is not what he thought it was, that it has been elaborately constructed in a certain way, for a sinister purpose. His *inner* world, his whole frame of reference, is certainly never the same again after he starts to hold his new beliefs. And in the real world, scientists are constantly making surprising discoveries about 'facts' that have always been held to be true about our external world and the internal workings of the human consciousness.

Have *you* ever experienced a time when something you utterly believed in turned out to be different to what you thought? Perhaps you've read true stories where someone discovers that their partner of many years has been leading a double life for decades. Having a core belief overturned like this cuts to the quick of your belief system, and makes you begin to question many things you've always held to be true.

Sometimes beliefs you pick up may be incomplete or misleading. Perhaps you formed ideas about someone from what a friend told you and then found out that there was a lot more to the situation than met the eye. What do you believe about the stories you read in the newspapers? The media can be very compelling and authoritative and yet can only reflect a tiny proportion of the whole truth of the matter, or even be a distortion.

Realising that your beliefs can be wrong doesn't mean that you need to walk around in some kind of conspiracy theory state, challenging everything that comes your way. But you can see how strongly held beliefs propel you into acting with conviction, for good or ill. Choosing different beliefs that move you forward isn't being naïve, or 'thinking positive' – it's simply plain good sense.

The belief that's holding you back is no truer than a belief that spurs you into positive action, so choose to focus on the beliefs that get you great results!

Many of your beliefs are so much a part of you that you rarely have a good, objective look at them. A quick glance isn't always enough, because on face value all your beliefs may look perfectly reasonable to you. Building a strong positive belief system starts with dusting off your beliefs and pinning them up on your mental washing line to let some air get to them.

They said it couldn't be done

Some of the greatest achievements in history have been things that were considered impossible. Whenever you feel that you can't overcome your limiting beliefs, remember:

- Thomas Edison persisted in his many thousand attempts to invent the light bulb in the face of sceptics who said that gas-light was the only feasible option.

- Roger Bannister ran the 4-minute mile despite the medical experts who said that the human body was not capable of the feat.

- Neil Armstrong walked on the moon.

And from modern business, in the face of overwhelming market evidence and belief:

- James Dyson created a vacuum cleaner that never loses suction.

- Sony created the Walkman, the first pocket-sized music system.

- First Direct pioneered 24/7 banking without branches.

What do your beliefs give you?

All the beliefs you hold are likely to feel very real to you. Even negative and destructive beliefs exist for a reason. At some point you've gathered evidence that supports everything you believe. If you're convinced that you're hopeless at sports, that's because you've got a stack of compelling examples, such as missing an easy goal, or coming in last in a race. You have more negative examples than you have instances where you performed well, so you get used to looking only for the evidence that supports your negative belief about your sporting ability. Holding on to this belief protects you from failing or looking stupid, because by doing so you can choose to avoid sports. In reality, you're almost certainly able to become very good at sports if you want to do so badly enough and are willing to put in the practice and effort required.

Your most limiting beliefs about yourself get in the way of the action you need to take. But many people are surprisingly attached to their limiting beliefs and are reluctant to let them go. That's because all your beliefs serve you in some way. If you believe that you're not bright enough to get a promotion, then you can give yourself permission not to try. If you believe that all the men or women you date are selfish and untrustworthy, you can build up a comfortable protective armour so that you don't get hurt. Your limiting beliefs have a function, but a very limited one. Your empowering beliefs, on the other hand, serve you far better by helping you to expand the range of what is possible in your world.

Changing your beliefs

Sometimes, simply by recognising a limiting belief, you take all its power away. You then are able to see it for the false friend it really is. Whatever you believe about yourself ('I am deceitful', 'I am unattractive', 'I am stupid') you can always find plenty of evidence to support that belief if you look hard enough. Your brain seems to actively seek out that evidence and ignore the contrary evidence that says you are truthful, attractive, and smart.

You are a complex human being who at times may behave in a deceitful way and at other times in a truthful manner. But what defines the essence of *you* isn't your behaviour. Nevertheless, your behaviour does tend to define the results you get, and those results determine how good you feel about your life. Changing your beliefs allows you to act in different ways more of the time. The more you choose positive behaviours, the better the results you get, and the better you feel. It's a virtuous circle.

Can you simply decide in an instant that you no longer hold a limiting belief, even if you feel as if you're playing mind games with yourself? Yes, absolutely!

You can defeat your limiting belief through regularly repeated *affirmations and mantras*, powerful, positive, present-centred belief statements that help to change your thinking patterns. For example, 'I radiate energy and vitality' is a great affirmation to use if you're working to cut out unhealthy foods that make you feel sluggish. Your brain believes what you tell it. So a great starting point is to experiment with simply switching the language that you use from negative to positive. You may feel a little as if you're kidding yourself, but over time, the new belief becomes embedded and you begin to gather more evidence to support it than you previously had for the old limiting belief. So instead of always seeing the evidence that you're lazy (spending all afternoon on the sofa) you begin to notice and focus on the contrary evidence (when you take a walk, clean out a cupboard, or knuckle down to a work task).

The following activity helps you to zap those limiting beliefs about yourself.

1. **Take your list of negative limiting beliefs and decide which ones you want to eliminate (hopefully all of them!).**

2. **Write out your negative beliefs again on the left side of a sheet of A4 paper.** Keep the sentences simple, such as 'I am stupid' or 'I am deceitful'. You already know that these statements are at best partial truths. Seeing them written in black and white like this, can't help but make your brain protest a little!

3. **Now think of the opposite statement to each negative belief and write it on the right side of the page.** Use the first person ('I') and again keep the statements simple and unqualified, such as 'I am intelligent' or 'I am honest'. Take care to write the positive statement larger and bolder than the negative statement; use coloured pens if you like.

4. **Go back to the negative statements and strike through all the negative words one by one, with a thick black pen, leaving incomplete sentences.** This helps your brain to demolish the negative association.

5. **Read your positive statements again. Then read them out loud, 10 times, hearing your voice get stronger with each repetition.** Have some fun with this. Imagine you're at a rock concert and you're swept along with the elevated mood of the crowd. Ten thousand other people are shouting out your positive beliefs along with you and you feel great!

6. **Refer to your list daily for at least the next 15 days.** Take time to find a few moments each day when you can shout out your new beliefs at the top of your voice. (Don't try this in company unless they have been to the same metaphorical rock concert as you!)

Book V

Life Coaching

You need time and practice to embed a new habit. Research suggests that you need to do something 15 times before it becomes a part of you. This varies according to what it is you are trying to do and how deeply ingrained your old habit is. The best approach is to keep practising the new habit until you catch yourself doing it three times in a row without having to *make* yourself do it. And then carry on!

Managing Your Fears

All limiting beliefs stem from some kind of fear. Strange as it seems, fear is often a good thing. The physical symptoms you get when you're scared silly are exactly the same ones that accompany extreme excitement. Compare the butterflies in your stomach before you're about to speak in front of a crowd of people with the butterflies you get when you meet the person of your dreams on a date. The *meaning* you attach to the feelings can cause the poor outcome. Athletes and stage performers have long learned to channel their natural fear into excited anticipation before they're required to perform at their peak. And having no fear of any kind in your life isn't as great as it sounds. People seem to love the thrill of the chase and are hardwired to respond to challenges. So even when the feelings are unpleasant, your mind and body may choose a state of fear over that flat feeling that nothing exciting is ever going to happen to you.

Fear gets in the way when you allow it to stop you from taking action and achieving things. Managing your fear stands you in good stead as you coach yourself to your own success.

Fear of failure

Most people can relate to this one. Perhaps your biggest fear is failing and so proving that you're not good enough. Certainly failure often has undesirable consequences, and most people enjoy being successful much more. But your real fear may be that not being good enough means that you won't be loved. Conquering this fear means embracing some or all of the following new beliefs:

✔ Failure is simply part of my discovery process and success comes from being willing to gain knowledge.

✔ I am always good enough, even when the things that I do don't work.

✔ I always succeed when I try my best with good intention.

✔ Avoiding failure means closing myself off to new possibilities I may never otherwise experience or know.

If you fear failure because you're worried you'll let people down, remember that self-love is the best starting point for being all that you can be to yourself and others.

Fear of embarrassment

Sometimes you avoid things because you don't want to look stupid or exposed. Perhaps you hold back from speaking up at a meeting with a different point of view because you fear ridicule. You may avoid speaking in public because you worry that you'll literally fall flat on your face as you take the stand. We learn in childhood that not everything we do is universally applauded and we are made to feel foolish instead of creative and innovative. So it's easier to stay out of the limelight in case we feel embarrassed again. Fight your fear of embarrassment with the following self-talk:

- Everyone admires someone who has the courage to say what they think, even if they don't agree with it.

- What's the worst that can happen? If I make a fool of myself it breaks the ice and people warm to me.

- There are no stupid questions – I bet everyone wants to know the answer and is afraid to ask.

Fear of rejection

Fear of rejection is connected with the deep desire we all have to be loved and liked by everyone we meet. Successful salespeople find ways to overcome this basic fear in order to make the hundreds of calls that generate the one sale they need. Accept that rejection is an inevitable part of life – you can't be loved and liked by everyone you come into contact with and even if it were possible, you would make yourself miserable trying to be all things to all people. Make it easier on yourself to handle rejection by adopting the following attitudes:

- When my ideas get rejected I get the benefit of more information about what isn't going to work, and that takes me closer to a successful outcome.

- Nothing people do to me is personal – they have their own reasons and anxieties that make them behave badly towards me at times.

Fear of achievement

Fear of achievement seems an odd fear to have, yet it holds everyone back at some point in their lives. Doesn't everyone want to achieve things? Often you don't do something that you know you're capable of because you want to fit in with the crowd and, even more importantly, you don't want to be left alone and isolated because of your success. Being good at something can seem like a lonely place to be and the expectations that people have of you sustaining your success can seem overwhelming. Sometimes you find it easier and more comfortable to avoid being the best you know you can be.

Fear of achievement can be the trickiest fear to recognise in yourself because it seems quite unselfish – don't blow your own trumpet, be modest, avoid pride. But it's a false friend. Marianne Williamson, in her book *Return to Love*, says: 'Our deepest fear is not that we are inadequate. Our deepest fear is that we are powerful beyond measure.' Get comfortable with your own success with the following thoughts:

- ✔ Holding myself back doesn't help others and only harms me.
- ✔ I'll develop the skills of dealing with my success as I go along.
- ✔ I can be a shining example to others and will experience much more joy from this than pain.
- ✔ I'm worth going the extra mile for.

Minimising your fear foes

Ironically, reducing the impact of fear in your life means inviting it in to play and taking a good look at it. You can eliminate fear over time by experiencing the reality, rather than what your imagination conjures up. As you gain confidence, you start to realise that, more often than not, you don't fail, get embarrassed, get rejected, or end up lonely and alone. And you begin to appreciate all the great things that come out of having a go, taking a risk, and trusting in yourself.

Try to perceive fear as just another powerful emotion that can serve you in some way – if you let it. In fact sometimes fighting against things increases their resistance. You can think of your fears as comic book monsters. Why not have some fun by creating your own personalities – be inspired by the wonderful un-scary scary monsters in the Pixar film *Monsters Inc*. Seeing your fears in this way takes a lot of the power out of them. Do your 'fear foes' have names? Does giving them a personality that's faintly ridiculous allow you to laugh them out of existence, just as the monster moguls in the film discovered when they saw that laughter generated far more power than fear ever did?

Chapter 4

Focusing on the Elements of Your Life

In This Chapter

▶ Making proactive lifestyle choices

▶ Understanding the power of focus and feedback

▶ Creating productive relationships

*Y*ou probably spend a large proportion of your time 'at work'. Or, if you're not currently employed, you may spend a fair bit of time and energy searching for work. If you're retired from a career or job, you may be in the process of redefining what can fill the gap that your work used to fill in your life. But the paid work that you do, or have done in the past, is only one aspect of what constitutes work for you over your lifetime. Your work as a parent, caregiver, volunteer, and even your hobbies or interests are all facets of your natural drive to be involved in purposeful activity for your own or others' benefit.

A helpful definition of 'work' is that it is the context in which you use your skills and talents in some way to give and (often) receive something of value, whether monetary, in kind, for your own satisfaction, or as a duty of care. Having a 'career' on the other hand, means that you also make choices that allow you to build on the skills and abilities you use at work so that you can take on bigger and/or more demanding roles. These roles are usually associated with pay rises and improved benefits because you're stretching the range of what you can offer and as an employee you can command more value in return. Building your career may include self-employment and consultancy work where you create and generate opportunities for yourself in a broader market-place.

Not everyone wants a career in this sense and you may be happy to consider the work that you do as a lower priority in your life than, for example, your family or your commitment to your health. You may work simply to get enough money to fund the lifestyle that you want and so choose to invest most of your energy in areas that are more important to you than work. In reality, you're likely to alternate between thinking 'it's just a job' and having your work take centre stage.

Setting Your Work in Context

Adjusting the balance on your work areas helps you to identify ways to ensure that you get what you need from all aspects of the work that you do. The next few sections of this chapter focus on improving what most people classify as work: your paid job.

Even if work is just something you do to pay the bills, you probably spend a fair amount of time doing it, so considering how work fits into your life and preferences as a whole makes sense. To what extent does your job match your natural abilities, fit with your beliefs about your world, and support the values that you hold most dear? Why should what you do best in terms of skills determine the most natural choice of work for you? Would you get even more personal satisfaction in an environment where you were developing skills that are currently less strong for you? For the work that you choose to do most of the time – whether that be paid or unpaid – this section helps you to find your unique balance between being comfortable using your best skills and stretching yourself to your natural potential.

Making a conscious choice

Think for a moment about how you ended up in the role you currently hold, or the jobs you have formerly performed. What made you choose the work you currently do? Did happy or not-so-happy accidents result in your career choices? Were you influenced by a parent or an older adult? Did you get swept along by an interview process and suddenly find yourself accepting an offer? Would you choose your job again knowing what you now know?

Perhaps you're struggling with work issues, or you're in the wrong job, or you're not using your skills to best advantage, and you can't see how to get to the work that you're meant to do (or even decide what it is). All of that experience, however uncomfortable, is preparing you in just the right way for what's around the corner. Whichever route you take – either being open and flexible to opportunities or planning every move – use the detachment and questioning skills of coaching to ensure that you're heading in the right direction. You may choose to stay where you are for the moment, knowing that you need to gather strength (maybe a strong sense of self-belief and confidence) and resources (skills, knowledge, and experience) to make a change. Making that choice in itself is part of the process of moving forward.

Evaluating your job

You may find that you get so caught up in the detail of your work, for good or ill, that before you know it another year has passed and you wonder what's changed for the better. You can adapt to almost anything and you may find yourself settling for a role that you've long outgrown, or that imposes unhealthy pressure on you, simply because you haven't taken the time to ask yourself some searching questions on a regular basis. A high proportion of workplace stress is caused by the accumulation of lots of small irritations piled on top of each other and left to go unchecked. If you're ambitious and want to progress your career, you need to carefully assess where you are and where you're heading.

You can assess whether your skills and natural preferences are best suited to what you currently do by putting yourself in the role of someone who is evaluating the requirements, ups and downs, and perks and potholes of your job. See how you measure up against this evaluation. Don't think about your official job specification – often the things that aren't written down cause the most frustration or offer the most joy. Try the following activity and feel free to add other questions to tailor it to the context of your own work. (You may want to refer to Chapter 3 to explore your specific skills prior to completing this activity.)

✔ What is your main purpose for doing the work you do?

✔ What do you spend 80 per cent of your time doing at work?

✔ Which of your best skills do you use at work?

✔ Which of your skills do you never or rarely get the opportunity to use at work?

✔ What proportion of your time do you spend

- Feeling stressed?

- Feeling bored?

- Feeling stimulated?

- Enjoying your work?

✔ To what extent do you feel in control at work?

✔ How often do you stretch your capabilities?

✔ How often do you coast along at work?

✔ How would you describe your working environment on a scale of 1 (= your worst nightmare) to 10 (= your idea of heaven)?

✔ Finish the following statement: 'I choose the work I currently do because . . .'

- Choose the statement that best describes how you feel about your work:

  - 'I'm living my work dream – I don't even think of it as "work".'

  - 'I feel challenged, stimulated, and valued most of the time, and this carries me through the difficult bits.'

  - 'Some days are better than others and on the whole, I can take it or leave it. Work is not a priority area for me.'

  - 'I often get frustrated, anxious, or bored at work and this affects my enjoyment of the good bits.'

  - 'I have to drag myself in every day; I'm ready to quit.'

As a result of this activity, what have you discovered about your work that needs to change? Perhaps you found that you spend 80 per cent of your time doing tasks that bore you or use skills that you least enjoy? Or you may have discovered that you feel bored half the time and stimulated the other half, and that overall the stimulation outweighs the boredom. Or perhaps you've identified that your attitude to your work is in the middle ground – 'take it or leave it' – and that this means you can put up with day to day irritations because work is a low priority for you. Look for common themes and links in your answers to the activity. Is your main purpose the same as the reason you choose the work you do?

Making adjustments at work

From the previous activity, you can identify the main areas that need change. Work often needs adjustment as a result of undesirable impact in the following areas:

- **Beliefs.** Your beliefs about your work may be holding you back. Perhaps you think that you're 'entitled' to be stimulated by what you do and need to re-think that belief so you can be more proactive about finding ways to increase stimulation for yourself.

- **Motivation.** Your motivation may need re-adjusting by making a change in the way you approach work.

- **Freedom.** You may feel the need for more freedom and autonomy in your work.

- **Support.** You may require more support and recognition from those around you.

- **Pressure.** Your work may overload you and cause you unhelpful stress.

✔ **Responsibility.** You may feel disconnected from your work and want to take more responsibility in order for you to become more engaged in what you do.

✔ **Environment.** You may be unfulfilled with your current environment – from a simple issue of 'same desk, same four walls' to having really out-grown your current job and company.

Improving Your Current Job: Keeping Your Focus

If evaluating your job has made you realise that your current work isn't meeting your needs, you may now be formulating a plan to make radical changes. You may decide that although you want to change certain aspects of your current role, it basically meets a lot of your requirements for a satisfactory work situation. On the other hand, you may feel ready to take a deep breath and search elsewhere for a new position. But you probably have to serve notice, meet obligations, and hand over projects before you can cross the next threshold. Even if your change is relatively organic – such as acquiring or developing a new skill so that you can progress to the next level in your current organisation – a shortfall remains between your ambitions and where you are now.

You need to work out how to focus your attention on the here and now at work while setting your sights on your next goal. And in the process of 'making the best' of your current situation you may also discover some new wisdom to inform your next step. You may realise that you can make changes in your current job that improve your situation.

Senti started coaching with one clear objective – to escape from her current role before she got fired! Although she admitted that she probably wouldn't really be fired (she was a careful and conscientious manager), she hated the relationship she had with her boss so much that she *felt* as if it were true. She was intensely unhappy because although she knew where she *didn't* want to be, she had no clue about the next best step.

During coaching she worked through the steps she needed to take to resolve her stalemate. She realised that deciding exactly on her next career move was not the most urgent priority. She faced the fact that some of her own beliefs about herself were contributing to the poor relationship she had with her boss. Unless she found more assertive ways of behaving, she would find herself in a similar position in any new role she undertook.

Senti set herself two main goals – to identify and begin to take action to secure the job of her dreams, and to address her relationship with her boss. The second goal was hard work because part of her had already written off her current position and was focused on the future. She worked hard on her self-esteem and confidence, which allowed her to stop taking her boss's style personally. In turn, this helped her boss to see Senti's talents clearly at last. Three months later, he offered Senti a promotion to manage a new project.

After some thought Senti accepted the new role. It would enhance her skills considerably and was in an exciting area of the business that interested her. Her biggest surprise was that she found that her new role took her pretty close to the dream job she'd begun to identify for herself. Using coaching, Senti's new-found self-confidence gave her the courage to identify business needs that she was uniquely fitted to address.

Like Senti, you may discover through coaching that the external factor that you think is the problem with your current work role – the pay; the way you're managed; the pressures of deadlines – may be secondary to the internal factors that you can control by applying and developing your natural skills. Here are some suggestions that can help you to improve your enjoyment of work:

- ✔ **Practise assertive communication.** If you feel frustrated at work, your needs are not being met. Be clear with yourself about what you need from your role – is variety more important to you than a fixed routine? You may find ways of creating a more varied structure to what you do but you may need the okay from your boss to make changes. State what will work best for you clearly and directly as early as possible rather than fuming quietly over a situation. This helps you avoid any tense confrontations further down the line when the boredom has really got to you.

- ✔ **Remember what motivates you.** When you're clear on your values, you can link all that you do to these motivating forces. If elements of your job feel stressful at times and you wonder why you stick with it, think about what your job gives you that helps you live your values. Perhaps your salary supports the lifestyle you want, or the recognition you receive for meeting deadlines feeds your sense of accomplishment and self-belief. Keeping a focus on the end result helps you put your job into a whole-life perspective.

- ✔ **Catch yourself 'being in the moment'.** A sign that you're performing well is when you get absorbed in what you're doing and lose track of time. With a little practice, you can place yourself 'in the moment' even when you're bored or frustrated. Simply focus on what you are doing as if your life depended on it, or as if it were the most fascinating thing you've ever encountered, or try to recall the feeling you had when you completed this task for the very first time. This trick won't always turn a boring task into the highlight of your day, but making the effort to switch your mental state is often enough to jolt you out of negativity and help you deal effectively with the routine so you can move on to more interesting tasks.

✔ **Remember that the only things that are ever fully in your control are your own thoughts, behaviour, and actions.** No matter how little you deserve it, you sometimes fall foul of the bad mood of a colleague or boss. You can allow this to throw you off course or you can put yourself in their shoes and decide on a course of action that accommodates the unfavourable circumstance and still gets you where you need to be. Sometimes that means tackling the behaviour and sometimes it means giving the other person space to work through their bad mood without you taking it personally. Focus on what you can control – your *own* mood and behaviour – and you're more likely to help the other person get back on track too.

✔ **Take a rain check with yourself every couple of hours.** If you know you tend to prefer the company of others rather than working alone, how can you inject some human interaction into your task to help you regain energy to continue? Think about the different ways you can carry out simple or routine tasks that increase your enjoyment. If you have a mailing to pack up for the post can you get some other people involved to make it more fun? Or would you prefer to sit by a window with a nice view and let the routine task act like a calming meditation? These little choices can make a huge difference to how you feel about what you do and help to put you more in control of your work.

Looking to the Future

What are the trends you see developing in your work choices? You may feel you have to run to keep up with the pace of change, but if you regularly coach yourself through your work choices you can set your own pace, and establish your own standards of excellence.

Progression in your work life need not always equate to promotion up the ranks. Progression may be more about finding ways to remain stimulated in what you do, perhaps taking a sideways move from time to time to re-energise yourself and your skills. Or progression may mean that you move to a different role in a new company every few years. If you've found the work that you feel you were meant to do, making progress may be easy.

Generally, you feel a sense of making progress when you're living your values at work and being your authentic self. And while all jobs have an element of routine in them, you usually feel more inspired if you're able to find new things to learn about yourself and your skills through work.

Here are three things that you can contemplate on a daily basis to measure your progress:

- ✔ **What were my 'wins' today?** This could be successfully negotiating with a supplier, or achieving a deadline.

- ✔ **What have I learnt today?** Maybe you added to your skills, picked up some new knowledge, or discovered a way not to do something!

- ✔ **What can I change as a result of today?** Perhaps you want to revisit your time management strategy as result of experiencing a bit too much stress meeting that deadline, or you decide that you're going to step into future negotiations more readily to take your confidence to another level.

Write down your answers so that you can reflect back on them and witness the cumulative power of these small daily successes, learning points, and significant steps that you've integrated into your working life.

When you think about the work you plan for the future, how prepared are you for it? Do you have a dream to be your own boss, or to create a working life that is independent of your source of wealth – by investing in property for example – so that you have more freedom to choose your work on its own merits? You can think about your future work in the context of a SWOT analysis – considering your strengths, weaknesses, opportunities, and threats – as follows:

- ✔ What are my **strengths** at work?

- ✔ What **weaknesses** am I aware of and how am I working on them?

- ✔ What **opportunities** do I have at work that match my whole-life goals?

- ✔ What **threats** at work may hold me back from meeting my whole life goals?

Coach yourself for your future work by working through the following coaching questions:

- ✔ **Powerful opening question:** What attitudes do I want to develop about work to fulfil my potential throughout my career?

- ✔ **Personal style:** What kind of work am I naturally drawn to? What do I thrive on? What demotivates me? What kind of environments suit me best? Where do I feel most at home when I am working?

- ✔ **Beliefs:** What negative beliefs do I have about work that prevent me from preparing for future challenges?

- ✔ **Motivation:** What image of myself at work is most appealing as my future vision? What would I reach for if I knew that I couldn't fail?

- ✔ **What's working:** What am I doing now to prepare myself for my future working life? How can I develop these behaviours and habits? What's getting in the way of fulfilling my potential? What trends do I see developing now that either propel me forward or hold me back?

✓ **Exploring options:** What options do I have to expand my working range? What is the easiest route? What is the most challenging route? What more information do I need before I decided on my options?

✓ **Taking action:** What's my first step? How much time can I allocate to planning my approach? How do I know when I am making progress? What can I do to celebrate?

Being Financially Secure

Money and wealth aren't necessarily the same thing. Most people have to work to earn enough money to buy the basics that they need and the luxuries that they want. Whether you have a little or a lot of money, your relationship with wealth is probably a significant factor in how content you are in your life.

However, money doesn't always produce more happiness. Some interesting research looked at lottery winners and people who had been severely handicapped in serious accidents and found that a year later, the lottery winners reported the higher levels of unhappiness. But, of course, many deliriously content multimillionaires live in this world too. What you do with your money and your personal relationship with it are what create or destroy some of your potential for happiness.

Wealth issues usually centre on the degree of basic financial security you have, the extent to which you can live the lifestyle you want, and the provision you're making for the future. This section helps you put money in its rightful place, assists you in identifying what real wealth is for you, and encourages you to explore how you can create your own sense of abundance. If you focus on what you want to have, do, and be in your life and arrange your financials around those goals, you may well find that the money then flows far more easily than those times when you put the money cart before the wealth horse.

First things first – life coaching to get to abundance starts with developing your basic financial common sense. Enjoying life is pretty hard if you're wondering where to get the money to pay the bills or put food on the table. You may be familiar with the anxiety that goes with tough times, when outgoings completely outstrip income. Just starting out on your own and taking on rent or a mortgage for the first time, not to mention losing your job, experiencing a business failure, or even going bankrupt all contribute to a feeling of financial insecurity. You don't always feel that you have much control over whatever financial hit is lying in wait.

The constant worry that you may lose your financial security can hold you back from fulfilling your dreams, and not fulfilling your dreams can in turn stop you from generating the wealth and ultimately the security you most want and deserve. You can avoid this vicious circle by putting in place your own lifetime strategy that allows you breathing space and the knowledge that you can always survive financially, no matter what's round that corner.

Drawing up your financial ground rules

Do you know the critical things you need to do on a regular basis to ensure that you are always financially secure? (You can find lots of detailed information on this subject in *Sorting Out Your Finances For Dummies* by Melanie Bien, published by Wiley). To get you started in coaching yourself to a new financial plan, here are some tried-and-tested guidelines that can help you think about exactly what's going to work for you:

- **Be honest with yourself.** Get out of denial. Do you know how much you actually spend? A client of mine decided to de-clutter and clear out six months' worth of accumulated paperwork. She was horrified to find that the only envelopes that were unopened were her bank statements. Spend a month writing down every penny that you spend instead of comforting yourself that you only indulge in the occasional bargain impulse buy.

- **Work out your budget.** Happiness is possible even on a reduced budget, but unhappiness seems almost guaranteed if you lose control of your spending, even if you have lots of money to start with. Your budget is a simple formula – your outgoings should never be more than your incomings – so start with two columns and list every item under each.

- **Aim to spend less than you earn each month.** After you set your budget, you can decide on your regular safety margin. By spending a little less than you earn each month, you know that you have some money left at the end of the month to act as a rainy-day contingency. You can then, at the end of the month choose to spend some of the extra cash on a treat or reward if you'd like. By holding back a little you reduce the worry that can turn money into an obsession that gets in the way of other, more significant life goals.

Reducing your spending may not sound much fun but you can take a positive mindset to this and turn it into a challenge or game. Consider the choices you make in the supermarket – do you always go for certain brands when you could select own-label products? You could make a policy of visiting the shop at the end of the day when many products are reduced in price. Make a game out of finding the best bargains and see how much you can shave off your weekly shopping bill.

- **Try to save 10 per cent of everything you earn.** Instead of using the extra cash to indulge yourself at the end of the month, you may choose to let it work for your future financial security by saving or investing the money. Decide what proportion of your income is possible for you to save and aim for that. Stashing away a certain amount each month often works better than a feast-and-famine approach where you save like crazy when you get a big bonus and then abandon saving at other times. Make the transaction automatic so that you aren't tempted to change your mind and simply 'forget' what you promised yourself.

Write down your new financial ground rules in your journal so you can refer to them easily and reinforce your commitment.

How do you feel about developing a budget, spending less than you earn, and saving a set amount of money each month? Perhaps you relish the idea of getting in control again. Or perhaps you recoil in horror at setting such constraints around yourself. Ask yourself what's causing this recoil. Is it that you value spontaneity and freedom where money is concerned and feel that budgets and savings plans would stifle this? What impact does having this freedom then have for you? If you experiment with a more structured approach, what can it give you that's better than what you currently have? You can find other financial ground rules that suit you and your life – rules that give you the same sense of freedom yet don't leave you panicking about final demands and unexpected bills. If other options exist for you, what are they? Whatever option you choose, you need some element of discipline to ensure that your spending stays in control over the long term.

Developing your financial survival plan

Coaching yourself in matters of money may result in a major decision to change your lifestyle or work. Or you may find yourself suddenly bereft of a major source of income through redundancy or business failure. What's your survival plan? Do you know how much money you need to get by and how long you're going to need to get things back on track? Financial advisors usually recommend having six months' salary in savings to tide you over in an emergency, but this figure will differ depending upon your spending habits and your circumstances. You'll almost certainly need more if you're thinking of setting up in business unless you're certain that your new venture will pull in cash for you very quickly. If you've already worked out your everyday budget, determining your contingency fund is a lot easier. Here are a couple of suggestions to get you motivated about drawing up your ideas:

✔ **Think of doing this as a 'freedom strategy' rather than a 'survival plan'.** If security is a strong value for you then imagining yourself safe and secure when that rainy day comes is very compelling. But you may already be pretty financially secure and not feel the same drive to amass this contingency resource. If so, then allow yourself to daydream about the possibilities your savings give you if/when you wake up one morning and know with certainty that this is the perfect time for you to enjoy that sabbatical from work, go travelling for six months, or take advantage of a business opportunity that has fallen into your lap.

You can always think of your nest egg as both a 'freedom strategy' and a 'survival plan' – focus on whatever beliefs support you to take positive forward action.

✔ **Get help to design your plan.** A trained financial adviser or an accountant can discuss tax and investment issues with you. A trusted and level-headed friend can help you check your budgeting assumptions.

When Shami was considering establishing her own business, she had a figure in mind of what she needed to see her through the first year of trading when she didn't expect to be making much money. This was a pretty tidy sum and was beginning to sap her motivation. Exploring the issue with her coach helped her to look more closely at her figures and assumptions. Shami discovered that she didn't need nearly as much as she thought because of the savings she'd make on travel costs and expenses directly bound up with her current role at work.

Living Your Chosen Lifestyle

No matter how much you enjoy your work, you probably hold the belief that you'd rather be enjoying more leisure time. You look forward to eating out in nice restaurants, or playing a round of golf, or lazing by the pool – and often these activities really do enhance your life. Sometimes though, your leisure pursuits don't give you what you expect. You may have occasionally experienced that flat feeling when you're on holiday, surrounded by the good things in life, willing yourself to have fun but in reality bored, restless, and discontented.

Your lifestyle is an aspect of your wealth; you may need money to enjoy a certain lifestyle, but your enjoyment of your lifestyle doesn't have to be directly related to how much money you spend. How and where you get enjoyment are like drawing money out of a bank. If you choose wisely and build a lifestyle that connects with what fires you up inside, your leisure time is well spent and pays dividends, creating a feeling of richness to your life. If you focus on things that 'should' make you happy but never really fully engage with them, true wealth doesn't get a chance to grow. You feel empty and cheated. Think hard about your leisure pursuits and the money and time you spend on them. Perhaps you shell out your hard-earned cash on a gym membership that you never use. A weekly run in the park with your best friend would do the job of getting you fit just as well, while feeding the inspiration and energy you get from your friend's company.

Counting the true cost of your lifestyle

Like all tangible resources, money is not usually unlimited. If you fall into the trap of believing that the more money you spend on immediate gratification the happier you'll be, you end up being disappointed. And you'll deplete the financial resource that could be directed to areas to enhance your happiness, such as saving for your dream holiday home. You can probably remember the thrill of your first really big-ticket purchase – a car, a down payment on a house, a holiday abroad – but the truth is, you get used to things. That thrill may have been a little less intense with the second car, the third house move, or the fourth exotic holiday. You may feel that you need to spend even more money to recapture that thrill. On the other hand, you may find that you continue to get a real buzz from trading up possessions, and that's fine too – don't be guilty because you love the material things in life and get real pleasure from acquiring the money to buy them.

Consider what you lose out on, or jeopardise, by choosing the lifestyle that you have. You may have convinced yourself that you aren't at all materialistic when secretly you'd love a fancy sports car but don't think you deserve one and couldn't possibly afford it. If so, perhaps you need to face up to the fact that money and what it can buy *is* pretty important to you and start to put strategies in place to attract more money into your life. Or you may swan around in the latest swanky car looking enviously at the couple strolling hand in hand to the bus stop to go shopping. Maybe in this situation you realise that material possessions don't make up for the lack of a loving relationship in your life, and you may decide to direct some of the energies you currently place in creating money wealth into securing relationship wealth.

Peace of mind concerning money issues often comes down to knowing where to direct your resources and when to recognise that 'retail therapy' is often just a sticking plaster.

When you consider the things that are important to you, coaching reminds you to look beneath the tangible possessions that you have, such as money, to what that possession gives to you. If you love money, you no doubt love the security it offers you, or the joy you get from owning beautiful objects. Few people actually love money for itself – unless they have a passion for coin collecting.

Coach yourself to financial awareness by working through the following coaching questions:

- ✔ **Powerful opening question:** What is the true cost of my lifestyle?

- ✔ **Personal style:** How much money do I need to live my life according to the way that suits my natural preferences and my needs? How can I test how much money I need?

- ✔ **Beliefs:** What limiting beliefs do I have about money?

- ✔ **Motivation:** What does money buy me? What does the pursuit of money give me that I don't want?

- ✔ **What's working:** What's good about my attitude to money? What do I want to change?

- ✔ **Exploring options:** What ways of being around money help me to achieve my whole-life goals?

- ✔ **Taking action:** What's my first step towards using money to achieve my whole life goals? How much time can I allocate to planning my approach? How do I know when I am making progress? What can I do to celebrate?

Permitting yourself to be rich

What assumptions about money do you hold? You may hold beliefs that stop you from generating the wealth you deserve. Do you think being poor is virtuous? How you manifest that virtue is what really matters and you can find some pretty mean-spirited poor people out there as well as some wildly generous and philanthropic multimillionaires. Do you think you don't deserve to be wealthier than you are? What cash price do you put on yourself that limits you? Or do you think you don't have the talent, the commercial acumen, the persistence, or the drive to go out there and seek a glittering prize? Where is the evidence for your belief and what contrary evidence do you have? Where do your beliefs about money come from?

Ask yourself these questions:

- ✔ Can I allow myself to be rich? (Consider your beliefs.)
- ✔ Can I be rich and remain wealthy in all other areas of my life? (Consider your whole-life implications.)
- ✔ Can I be rich and keep my integrity? (Consider your overall contribution to your world.)

If the answer to all three questions is yes, you've given yourself permission to take the steps you need to take to pursue riches *if* that's what you really want. In the case of riches, the old adage to be careful what you wish for lest it come true contains much wisdom. Acquiring riches isn't actually the hardest part of the process; deciding why you want money, what you're going to do with it, and then unblocking the thought processes that are holding you back from attracting it into your life constitute the real ground work. After you're clear on what you want and why, you're then ready to do the hard work and make the sacrifices that are required to make money.

Enjoying Loving Relationships

When I (Jeni) worked in recruitment and the going got especially tough we'd joke, 'If only we didn't have clients or candidates . . . or colleagues – this job would be perfect!' You can probably relate to this sentiment when you've had a particularly bad day and everyone seems out to get you, reject you, or complicate your life. Really bad days are when the most meaningful relationship you want to have is with your DVD player or personal stereo so you can escape from everyone!

Hopefully, most of the time you don't really want to escape from everyone. After all, many of your most precious and enjoyable moments stem from being with people you love, who stimulate you and you have fun with. Getting the balance right between give and take in relationships is tricky and is one of the biggest causes of discontent in life when the balance is askew.

Relationships fall into three main categories – your family and your partner if you have one, your friends, and the wider networks around you at work and in your community.

Creating a relationship with yourself

When it comes to relationships, the only constant you have is the relationship that you build with yourself. Family members and friends may not always be there for you; you may never find 'the one', or you may be together for a while and then separate. Your children grow up and your relationship with them may change. Your wider networks may not always support you. You can deal with all of this and you can accept that everything changes over time – as long as the certainty of your self-esteem remains.

If your self-esteem is strong, you're comfortable in your own skin, and you don't feel the need to fill your time alone with distractions that may not enhance the overall quality of your life. If you don't manage to develop self-esteem, no matter how hard you try to please the important people in your life – and sometimes because of your efforts – you often find that real connection with them remains just out of your grasp.

Finding your soul mate

If you're meeting your own needs and building your own self-esteem as a single person, finding a soul mate becomes a much less anxious pursuit. You're already presenting your best self to the world, which is naturally attractive and gives you the best chance of finding someone who is attracted to the real you. When you have high self-esteem you can make relationship choices that feel healthy and mature. You don't fall prey to flattery or insincerity that feeds your vanity, and you can enjoy each other's company without wondering if this is 'the one' relationship to bring you happiness – because you're already happy.

Are you holding on to an ideal of romantic love that may not be realistic? Do you feel that you're looking in vain for Mr or Ms Right? If this search is a source of unhappiness for you, think honestly about what a relationship can give you that you don't already have or can't get elsewhere.

If you find yourself alone after a separation or bereavement, you may feel uncertain about how to fill what feels like a big hole in your life. Certainly, people need people but not always in the way they think. The more clarity you have about why you want to meet someone, and the consequences of the choices you make, the better placed you are to forge the right kind of relationship with the right person for you. So quickly getting back into the dating game may be just the boost to your confidence that you need. But you also need to take account of the fact that you may not be ready to start a serious relationship for a while and may benefit from some alone time to sort out exactly what you want from your changed lifestyle.

Here are some suggestions to consider if one of your whole-life goals is to meet someone you can share your life with:

✔ **Check out your beliefs carefully.** Are you holding on to a romantic dream that only one person is out there for you and that you'll know instantly when you meet your soul mate? What pressure is that belief putting on you and the friendships you're building right now? Would changing that belief help you to see clearly your potential soul mate who lives right next door, or works in the next office?

✔ **Consider where you're looking for your soul mate.** For example, Internet dating works wonderfully for some people and for others it's an unmitigated disaster. Notice the patterns that occur for you and if you always seem to get the same kind of poor results, consider that you may be fishing in the wrong pool. Try different waters for a change.

✔ **Your soul mate is going to share some of your most important passions, so make it easy for them to recognise the passion in you.** If you love reading, you can join a book club. Maybe you won't meet a romantic partner there, but you may discover some great friends. And who knows who they may introduce you to?

✔ **Don't think that all your attached friends are gloriously happy while you are still single.** Every life choice has ups and downs, and your coupled friends may envy the freedom and fun of your single life. Remember that a true zest for life is one of the most attractive qualities around, whether you are looking for love or friendship.

Building Productive Networks

Your wider networks are unique to you and taking the time to build productive relationships with people outside your immediate circle of close friends and family can really pay off. Casual acquaintances, neighbours, and work colleagues can turn into good friends – even if they don't, a little investment in the people around you helps to oil the wheels of your daily life.

Widening your circle of influence

The more people you have access to in a positive, mutually beneficial relationship, the more support you have when you need it. Not everything you want to accomplish in your life is within your power to complete alone, no matter how self-sufficient you are. If information is power, other people often hold the information you need.

Your *circle of influence* contains all the people you have contact with in your life, from those who are closest to you, to your casual acquaintances. You touch or influence the lives of all of these people in some way and they do the same for you. Consider for a moment the areas where your circle of influence is already extensive. Perhaps you already make the effort at work to get to know people in other departments or divisions, or you're particularly good at building relationships with customers and suppliers. Do you maintain personal contact with some of these people when you move on from that job or do you invest all of your energies in a new circle of people? You have a limited store of time and energy so it may be impossible and unrealistic to stay in touch with everyone, but you may be able to keep in contact with a few key people who you've established rapport and respect with. How can you continue to benefit from their influence and support over the years?

What about your neighbours? Communication breakdown with neighbours can lead to painful disagreements and strained relationships that become difficult to repair. How satisfied are you with the quality of your connections with your neighbours? What opportunities do you have to play a bigger role in your community, perhaps at a local school, a neighbourhood watch group, or a social club?

This activity homes in on what your circle of influence looks like. Grab a large sheet of paper – maybe flip-chart size – and map out your circle of influence (see Figure 4-1). Put specific names on it. Stand back and look at your world of people. What areas need focus? How can you widen your circle of influence if you want to?

Figure 4-1:
Your Circle
of Influence.

Getting into the networking groove

Networking – the process of meeting new people and adding them to your circle for mutual benefit – isn't just for finding business opportunities. You can apply networking skills to any new social situation – a party, a fundraising event, or chatting to other parents during the school run. Try out these tips for successful networking:

- **Be interested rather than interesting.** Use your coaching skills to ask open questions and really listen to the answers. Don't be tempted to cut in with a 'me too' story too quickly. People find you fascinating if you show that they fascinate you.

- **Look for ways you can help one another.** This might be in very small areas – perhaps passing on a useful article on an area of mutual interest – but it can be something pretty significant, such as a skill, resource, or business introduction.

- **Play the host.** If you're among a group of strangers and want to break the ice, try to find ways of carrying out simple tasks that make people warm to you. Maybe you can offer to get them a coffee, or fill up their glass.

Chapter 5

Physical, Mental, and Emotional Wellbeing

*B*eing in great health is about much more than physical fitness or freedom from disease. To feel on top form, you also want to be in good mental health – managing the stress and pressures of everyday life. Wellbeing in a life coaching sense means taking note of your emotional health, and keeping a check on your emotions instead of letting them overwhelm or incapacitate you. Health matters include both taking care of your physical body and building your mental and emotional resilience. In this chapter you discover that the small steps you take to integrate a holistic approach to your health can make the most difference in how you look and feel on a regular basis.

Health and wellbeing is a critical area for coaching, because really big changes in other areas of your life are often more possible when you have good health as a foundation.

Choosing Your Health Goals

How have your feelings about your health changed over the years? Much depends on how healthy you used to be and how healthy you are now. If you were a strong, healthy child, you may feel that you'll always be strong and healthy. But if you experienced a life threatening or debilitating illness as a child, you may not take good health for granted. When you consider family members, the fact that your loved ones live long and remain disease free may comfort you. Or you may be very conscious of the sad losses you've experienced due to heart disease, cancer, or other fatal illnesses. Your previous experiences affect your current attitude to your health, and you need to take account of this in defining your health goals and focusing your motivation.

In choosing your health and wellbeing goals, you can ponder the following:

- **What's really important to me right now about my health?** Which areas of health have taken priority for me up to now? For example, your energy levels may be the priority right now. You may be looking for a way of being that promotes this rather than a short-term focus on losing weight fast for a forthcoming holiday.

- **What has to happen for me to feel healthy?** How has my definition of good health changed over the years? Good health at one time in your life may have meant having the stamina to burn the candle at both ends. Now, good health may mean giving your body rest, and taking care of your mental and emotional wellbeing through gentle exercise and meditation.

- **How much time do I want to allocate to my health and wellbeing?** Reaching and maintaining fitness takes time and effort. Consider whether you want to devote a regular daily time slot to your health goals or if a weekly commitment is better. Planning your goal and preparing the ground also takes a little time, so consider how you want to schedule that.

- **What old beliefs may be getting in the way of my current health goals?** Perhaps you think that because everyone in your family smokes, giving up is impossible for you? Challenge this belief and seek new ways to build better ones.

- **What may I be 'in denial' over in relation to my health?** Perhaps you always dress well to hide the excess pounds you carry, and avoid having your photo taken so you don't have to face the reality.

- **How do I want to feel when I think about my health?** You can translate this desire into a positive affirmation such as 'I feel strong, energetic, and full of vitality every day.'

- **What do I want for my future health and wellbeing?** Perhaps you want to be able to take your children swimming and play football with them, or simply want to be disease-free and able to enjoy life.

Looking After Your Body

As far as your physical body goes, most people tend to underrate the positive attributes they already have and focus on the body bits that displease them. Unless you decide that radical cosmetic surgery is part of your strategy (and we say 'radical' for a reason) you simply can't change parts of your body. The body you were born with is sufficiently miraculous in its form and function without too much user interference. Your body deserves respect and loving care, so a great starting point for *holistic health* (the concept that physical, mental, and emotional health are all connected and impact on each other) is getting used to being comfortable in your own skin and changing the way you think and feel about your body for the better. Substitute the negative thoughts about your body that pop into your head for positive ones. Instead of giving yourself a hard time about those love handles, think about your strong arm muscles. What can you already do, have, and be as a result of the body you inhabit?

Coaching in health and wellbeing issues usually works best when you focus on what's already working and figure out how to do more of that or enhance what you already have. Focusing on how big you think your nose is compared to other people's only makes you more conscious of your nose. And plenty of people with tiny button noses wish they had more striking features like you!

Avoiding illness and disease

Suffering the occasional cold in winter or minor attack of hay fever in summer is annoying. But when it comes to debilitating illnesses that you or your loved ones have to cope with, you really begin to appreciate what it means to have good health.

Coaching works best by focusing on positive goals, but in areas of illness and disease you may need to imagine the consequences of becoming ill while you are relatively fit and healthy. By the time the problem is severe enough to cause you to want to make changes, the road to recovery can be an uphill one (literally and figuratively).

Hereditary and environmental factors on your health are not within your full control to affect. But whatever your gene pool is like and no matter what kind of air you have to breathe, you can actively coach yourself on improving your diet and the exercise you get. Diet and exercise can make a massive difference to how healthy you are now and will remain throughout your life.

Filling your body with the best fuel

How should you eat for optimum health? The government and media offer such a bewildering array of (often contradictory) advice on food choices that you may opt to ignore it all and enjoy your food the way you want to. Alternatively, you may become a diet junkie and career from one 'holy grail' eating plan to the next.

Weight loss is only one aspect of preventing illness and disease and is an important one if you're a long way beyond a healthy body weight. But think about other considerations. The food choices you make can affect your mood and your energy levels, and can be connected with allergies or have an impact on conditions such as asthma. Food can act as nourishment or poison, depending on what the food is and how you use or abuse it. If you plan your life, why not also take the time to design your approach to the fuel that enables you to live your life to the full? You wouldn't expect your car to run on below-par fuel, and because your body is a lot more valuable than any car, take the same care when making food choices to keep you healthy.

Most nutrition experts agree on avoiding processed foods, drinking lots of water, eating a balanced diet, and practising moderation in your diet. (Take a look at *Nutrition For Dummies* (Wiley) for lots more practical advice on the options you have for healthy food intake.) You need to make the right choice of fuel for your body, within the context of the lifestyle you want. Consider the following:

- ✔ **What makes you choose to eat certain foods that you know are unhealthy for you?** Do you reach for heaps of chocolate when you're feeling emotionally low? Or is alcohol a way for you to get in the party mood? What else can help fuel a feel-good factor apart from these things?

- ✔ **What habits do you have that support a healthy attitude to food?** Do you take time to enjoy meals without the distraction of the TV? Do you take time over cooking nice meals?

- ✔ **Do you use food and drink as a reward?** That's fine, as long as it doesn't go too far for your own good. What other rewards can sustain you in better ways?

- ✔ **Do you have to get into a mentality of 'going on a diet' in order to lose weight?** How can you change your attitude so that you permanently adapt your eating habits and integrate good choices into your life?

Building energy, strength, and fitness

If you're already fairly healthy, you may want to coach yourself on taking your fitness to the next level. If this is your health goal then you need to move up a gear and commit to a sustained programme that allows you to participate in your chosen exercise for 30–60 minutes for five out of seven days to achieve a real change in your fitness level.

Why do you want to be fitter? Is it to have more vitality on a daily basis, to strengthen bones and joints, to become more toned, to look and feel younger, to reduce stress, to be able to join in games with your children, to have a great posture? All these aims and more are within your grasp through a well-chosen fitness strategy. If you want to achieve all of these benefits, bear in mind the following:

- Choose a number of different forms of exercise

- Set yourself realistic long-term goals

- Accept that you need to spend a high proportion of your time pursuing your health goals, perhaps at the expense of other priorities

- Choose the form of exercise that works for you and inspires and motivates you to keep going with it

Taking Care of Your Mental and Emotional Wellbeing

Recent research on happiness suggests that 20 per cent of what makes us happy in life comes from personal characteristics such as our outlook on life, flexibility, openness to change, and resilience. A 'hardy' personality bounces back from setbacks quickly and generally remains positive. You have inherited some of your attitude to life from your gene pool, but you can do a great deal to develop your mental and emotional health. Coaching forms a great foundation for improving your emotional wellbeing, because you're constantly questioning unhelpful thought patterns and behaviours, as well as setting yourself challenging goals that help you to stay motivated and fulfilled in your life.

Managing your emotions

Do you feel comfortable expressing your emotions or do you bottle things up only to find they explode at just the wrong moment? Do you notice what your emotions are all the time, or do you find you sometimes feel upset but can't really put your finger on why? Knowing your emotional range takes practice, and being able to describe how you feel to others can be tricky until you become clear on exactly what these feelings are for you. Marshall Rosenburg, a specialist in conflict resolution, pioneered an approach called *non-violent communication*, which advocates speaking from the heart in all interactions. Doing so helps you to become more assertive, to say what you really mean and need in a factual way that doesn't threaten other people. The starting point to non-violent communication is working out what your heart feels. Think of how you feel when your needs are being fulfilled – glad, joyful, proud, inspired, motivated, amazed, eager, thankful. Each emotion feels slightly different to you, but you may be used to attaching a single label to many of them, such as, 'I'm feeling happy today.' Now think about how you feel when your needs are not being fulfilled – angry, frustrated, puzzled, annoyed, lonely, bitter, disappointed.

The more specific you can be in identifying what you're actually feeling, the clearer you can be in expressing what you need out of a situation to move yourself to a more positive emotion. The following activity helps you to identify specific emotions:

1. **Write down as many positive emotions as you can think of. Recall some times when you've experienced these emotions and describe what the physical feeling is for you.** Perhaps 'joy' is like 'pride' for you and for both you feel a warm sensation at the back of your throat? Or 'motivated' feels like a pleasant tension in your abdomen? Notice the similarities and differences between each positive emotion.

2. **Do the same with the negative emotions that you experience.** Maybe 'anger' causes your shoulders to tense while 'lonely' gives you an empty feeling in your stomach?

3. **Recapture some of the pleasant emotions you've identified by focusing in on the thoughts and memories that trigger the physical feelings for you.** As you recall the moment when you felt 'pride', notice how you can recapture the same warm sensation at the back of your throat even though you experienced unpleasant reactions only a moment before. Notice how quickly you can begin to affect changes in your body that directly affect your mood. Keep practising this – sometimes you need some time to really tune into managing your state in this way.

4. **Armed with this awareness, catch yourself as you go about your day and notice your feelings.** When someone cuts you up on a roundabout, what do you feel? Angry? Frustrated? Rejected? You might be surprised at the real emotion behind the trigger, and that it can change depending on the mood you're in to start with.

Recognising your emotions is half the battle. Expressing them in a way that gets the message across clearly and moves the situation forward in a positive way is the next step to healthy emotional wellbeing. Think about the last time you were in a heated argument with someone close to you. Did you say – and hear – things that were hurtful and hard to forgive? In a calmer mood you realise that you didn't really mean some of what you said. Although getting things off your chest is good, letting strong emotion exaggerate the drama of a situation is rarely helpful.

Take some of the sting out of arguments by staying mindful of what your needs really are. Perhaps you feel neglected or frustrated in a relationship. Choose to express yourself by describing the specific reasons that make you feel that way, without resorting to a blanket accusation such as 'You never have time for me'. Help the other person by explaining what action they can take to resolve matters.

Don't forget to celebrate your happy and positive emotions. You can make a big impact on your emotional wellbeing by simply noticing the things that make you feel good and going out of your way to make sure they're part of your life. Those mornings when you wake up full of enthusiasm for no particular reason don't come out of nowhere. Certain triggers help you to feel that way – maybe a smile from a stranger or a supportive email that you didn't really notice at the time. If you can work out what those triggers are, it's like bottling up your own personal happiness formula for your future use.

Developing mental resilience

Everyday emotional health stems from your level of mental resilience and how quickly you can bounce back from setbacks. If you feel that you're wobbling on the edge of breaking down due to external pressures and feeling out of control, you're not alone. Many people who seem to be very good at coping have at some time or other suffered from stress and depression.

Dancing for happiness

A team of six social science professionals conducted a fascinating experiment for a BBC documentary called *Making Slough Happy*. Fifty volunteers were given their own Happiness Manifesto (a kind of mission statement of how to be happy) to incorporate into their lives. Some of the top tips for action that came out of the experiment were very simple ones, such as enjoying nature, setting aside time to have a good natter with a friend or partner, and enjoying a small treat every day such as 30 minutes of 'me-time' or an inexpensive impulse buy.

Interestingly, the top negative factor that reduces happiness was watching too much television. Although a pleasurable activity for many people, watching the box for long periods of time is passive and makes people feel sluggish and fed up.

A surprising result on the activity front is that barn dancing was found to promote a lot of happiness. Perhaps some of the reasons behind this discovery are that barn dancing is highly physical, everyone can join in, and it's almost impossible to get through an evening of barn dancing without having a good laugh. So take your partners by the hand, it's time to dosey-do . . .

People are a lot less open about emotional and mental instability than they are about physical illness. Spotting the signs of stress that can lead to depression or physical illness is the first step towards dealing with the problem.

What gives you mental strength? If you're living the life you want and are in control of what you are doing, you're likely to feel strong and resilient. What drains you mentally and how can you reduce the impact of this?

Developing mental resilience begins with four basic strategies that can help you grow stronger:

- ✔ **Get support.** Talk to people who can help you when you hit problems. Sometimes you simply need a friend who can be there for you. You don't get a bravery award for going it alone. Enlist the advice of a doctor or trained counsellor if your low feelings become persistent and overwhelming.

- ✔ **Keep a focus on your priorities.** You may need to practise saying no from time to time. When you feel less mentally resilient you may try to please people more, or go in the other direction and get angry at the demands they place on you. Knowing your goals and reminding yourself of them often can be the sanity check you need to assert your needs.

- ✔ **Schedule a regular activity that builds your mental and emotional muscles.** Take note of activities that leave you with a sense of peace and perspective and make sure that they have a priority in your life. The activity may be meditation or an active sport.

- ✔ **Take the performance pressure off yourself.** You are the most important person in your world, but everyone around you is far too caught up in their own performance anxiety to notice yours. Remember that you don't have to be perfect – be content with being good enough.

Finding Your Balance

In life coaching, having *balance* means that you have a sense that all the parts of your life form a harmonious whole. Balance is different for everyone and even different for you at various stages of your life. You may work long hours, but if that produces your desired rewards and allows you enough time to enjoy some leisure pursuits, then you're likely to feel balanced and stable. When you're off-balance, on the other hand, the smallest thing, such as an unexpected deadline, can send you over the *tipping point* – when things get overwhelming and you lose your balance point.

Balance can be a tricky thing to catch and hold onto in your life. Simply trying to stand firm and hoping that you can keep all those plates spinning isn't really going to work for long, because something is sure to come along, knock you over, and send the plates crashing to the ground. The key to balance is to be in control of yourself and your goals, to keep moving in a forward direction, and yet to accept that sometimes you need to take a backwards or sideways step to maintain your momentum.

Your sense of balance changes with your life priorities, as the excitement of new roles begins to fade a little and as you become more comfortable with who you are. You may be prepared to put lots of energy into your work and social life when you're a young adult because it may be very important to you to prove yourself, to earn the money you want, and to have fun. In your forties and beyond you may well have achieved a lot of your material goals and find you want to spend more time rediscovering yourself and trying out new things. You may consider money with fresh eyes and you may change the ways you go about having fun. Coaching yourself regularly to identify the overall impact that your daily choices have on your whole life will help you find your balance point at any point in time.

Integrating the Goldilocks theory of balance into your life

Goldilocks, the heroine of the *Three Bears* fairytale, was a great natural self-coach on the subject of balance. She took a long, hard look at the three bowls of bears' porridge in front of her and made quite sure she tested them all out thoroughly before she settled down to enjoy the one that was 'just right'. She knew instinctively that trial and error was the best approach to making sure that she got exactly the right quantity and quality of porridge for her, and guesswork just wasn't an option.

Do you find yourself making assumptions about balance in your life? Here are some thoughts you may carry around with you:

✔ Not enough money

✔ Too much stress

✔ Not enough time

✔ Too many demands

✔ Not enough fun

Many of these assumptions may well be true for you at certain times in your life, and often you instinctively know what changes can improve your sense of balance. But you may find that you make the adjustment (by freeing up some time or dropping a hobby that demanded too much of your attention) and things don't improve. Or perhaps you discover an unexpected negative consequence of your adjustment that outweighs the benefit you have gained. You may actually miss the adrenaline rush and sense of achievement you got from handling all those demands at work. You won't always get your balancing actions right first time – quite often it's the process of making adjustments that tells you exactly what and how much you need of certain things in your life.

Think hard about whether you have too much or too little of something in your life. In fact you may have good reasons why you made the balance tip in a certain direction. You may thrive on the adrenaline you get from your demanding job and feel you 'should' want to spend more time with your family. But if the quality of the time you do spend with your family is good for all concerned, maybe you can let yourself off the hook a little? And you may love the role of the giver in your social group – the one who always has time for other people's problems – but feel that you 'ought' to be more assertive and less willing to drop what you're doing for a friend in need. Be honest about what you want and don't want in your life.

This activity provides you with a visual way to check how balanced you are right now.

1. **Take a sheet of paper and draw a circle in the middle of the bottom of the page.** Label this circle 'My Centre of Balance'.

2. **Draw two arms coming out of the circle, one to the left and one to the right.** Label the left arm 'Too Little and Not Enough' and the right arm 'Too Much and Too Many'.

3. **Load up the two arms with things that are 'too much' for you and things that you have 'too little' of in your life.** Load up your arms as if each separate thing was a box, and stack them on top of each other. Not having enough of something feels just as heavy as having too much.

4. **Now draw a triangle at the top of the page, in the middle, above your Centre of Balance.** Call this triangle 'My Ideal Life'. Imagine that this triangle contains all of your whole-life goals. You can get creative by deciding on a symbol that represents this for you. Perhaps you choose a heart, a star, a tree, or a house – pick whatever best represents your life at its most balanced. Imagine standing in your Centre of Balance, with your arms stretched out to your sides, and your sights firmly set on your Ideal Life.

5. **Write 'Just Right Zone' below your Ideal Life triangle.** The space in between your Centre of Balance and your Ideal Life is the Just Right Zone. Things that are just right for you feel light and airy, like wispy clouds that let you see through them to a clear view of your ideal life. Draw clouds in your Just Right Zone and within the clouds write down the things that are just right for you at the moment.

6. **Look at the balance between Too Much and Too Little.** If you have too much or too little of a lot of things, your focus is probably on the balancing act itself, keeping your energy from moving forward and preventing you from focusing on your ideal life.

7. **Consider what action you could take from each arm that would move something into the Just Right space and take the load off one or both of your over-burdened arms.** Maybe you have too much time spent on housework and not enough fun?

8. **Write out your actions in your journal and redraw your balanced whole life as it now looks.**

Take a look at Figure 5-1 for an example of a completed Centre of Balance activity.

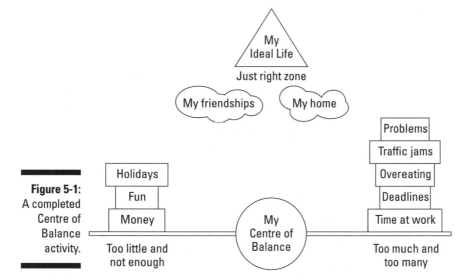

Figure 5-1:
A completed Centre of Balance activity.

Checking out your daily energy balance

Remember the old chestnut: 'It's better to wear out than to rust out'? You'd probably prefer to be active and fully engaged in all that you do rather than feel lethargic and bored. So you may instinctively push yourself that little bit harder on a regular basis in order to avoid feeling rusty. But actually the opposite of rust-out is burn-out, so don't push yourself too far.

Take a look at the Balance Curve in Figure 5-2. Generally, you experience high levels of energy when you're fully engaged in what you're doing. This energy is sometimes created by 'good' stress – feelings of excitement, the sense of adrenalin pumping to help you meet a deadline, a target, or other desired goal in your life, especially a goal that has a time critical factor. This 'good' stress only becomes 'bad' stress when the pressures reach a tipping point – when you feel that you're not coping so effectively and maybe begin to doubt your own judgement. The tipping point may be an actual event or simply your own state of mind. Beyond that tipping point you feel stressed, and your energy often dips, which compounds the feeling of stress.

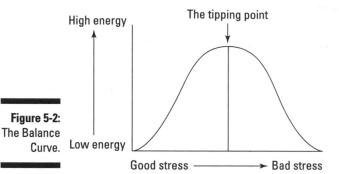

Figure 5-2:
The Balance
Curve.

Imagine a 'typical' work day. You start off pretty calm perhaps, having enjoyed a good night's sleep. As you race around the house preparing yourself for the tasks ahead, your energy picks up and the 'good' stress starts to rise. You negotiate the traffic, get to your destination, and start ploughing through your task list. You tackle challenges, work towards deadlines, and solve problems. Your energy matches the rise in good stress that you feel, so you see some good results.

Then you hit a real puzzle that halts you in your tracks. Perhaps you have a genuine project crisis, a perceived immovable obstacle, some unpleasant feedback, or a call from home to say the boiler has exploded. Whatever the trigger, it's just enough to send you over the top of the curve and now you're feeling 'bad' stress – out of control, unsure what to do for the best, beginning to doubt your own opinion and actions. And your energy levels start to drain as you begin to feel paralysed by the situation. In reality the trigger event may be no different to all the other stuff you've handled well up to that point, but just the little bit of overload pushes you over the curve – your tipping point.

This type of thing won't happen every day, of course. Often, you stay just the right side of the curve so that you're firing on all cylinders, harnessing your adrenaline to help you maintain your energy and get lots done. And sometimes the 'bad' stress keeps you focused on something very important just long enough to pull it off.

But have you ever revisited something you did when you were on the wrong side of the curve? Your work may be below standard because your productive energy levels were dissipated and all that anxiety got in the way of your creativity and vision. Think also of the harmful effects of stress on your physical and mental health.

Where is your tipping point? Think back to days when you felt out of balance and identify your external and internal triggers, which may include:

- ✔ An unexpected time-critical demand
- ✔ A crisis you didn't foresee
- ✔ Something someone said to throw you off track
- ✔ Starting to doubt yourself
- ✔ Something taking too long to complete

Adjusting your daily balance often starts with changing your attitude to the stress trigger before going on to take whatever action you need. Try these seven simple steps when you feel overwhelmed or out of kilter during the day:

1. **Ask yourself** *exactly* **what you're feeling and what** *specifically* **is the trigger.**

2. **Think about where you are on the balance curve.** Sometimes momentary anxiety can be set in context very quickly as you focus on the good energy you still feel.

3. **Change your physical state rapidly by taking a few deep breaths, a brisk walk round the room, or having a long stretch.**

4. **Imagine yourself standing back from the anxiety you now feel.** Ask yourself, what would this feel like if it was curiosity instead of anxiety? Changing your state of mind from anxiety to curiosity helps you get into the mindset of problem-solving and reduces the tension in your body.

5. **Consider what you need to do now**. Do you need to act, explore, or reflect on the challenge?

6. **Take your first small step towards resolving the challenge.**

7. **Review your feelings and position on the balance curve and repeat Steps 1 to 6 if you need to.**

Centring yourself

Finding your sense of balance can result in doing things that initially feel like going against restoring order. You're running up against a crucial deadline, you're tired, irritable, and panicky because you have three hours to finish something that would normally take six. The last thing you can afford to do is take a break, and yet a balanced approach suggests that having a quick rest is vital to give yourself the best chance of delivering a quality piece of work.

Do you know what it feels like to be centred? Think of a strong-rooted tree with its flexible branches waving in the wind. Grounding yourself physically gives you clues to understanding your emotional and mental balance. Notice what your body does instinctively when you're not in motion. Do you slouch, lean on one leg, cross your arms, or even find yourself contorting your body into a combination of all three? Standing tall, firm, and straight feels quite weird if you're used to slouching. But not only does making like a tree help your body physically, it can also act as a gentle meditation and a reminder of the importance of staying grounded.

The following activity is a 5-minute balancing act that you can carry out at any time.

1. **Stand with your feet a shoulder width apart.** Check that your toes point forward and not to either side.

2. **Let your arms drop loosely to your sides, leaving a little space between them and your body.** Pull your shoulders back comfortably.

3. **Take a few deep breaths so that your chest expands.**

4. **Look straight ahead of you, keeping your chin up as you do so.**

5. **Bring your attention to the strong physical centre of your body, just below your navel.** You may want to repeat an affirmation or mantra to yourself, such as, *'I am strong, centred, and balanced.'* Imagine the strength of the roots that support you and the resources that sustain you.

6. **Continue to stand centred for a few moments, breathing deeply and with control, until you're ready to reach out to your next challenge.**

Managing yourself and your time

Time seems so rigid and finite and yet I'm sure you've experienced the strange way that time seems to speed up or slow down in contradiction to what the clock actually says! You can't 'manage' time, but you can manage yourself and what you want to do in each 24 hours. Every day you have 24 hours available to you and you have choices about how you're going to use them. Ask yourself the following question regularly throughout each day to bring yourself back on track:

'What can I let go of right now so that I can regain my balance?'

Your answers may surprise you. Sometimes you can drop a tangible thing such as an item on your 'to do' list that you can easily delegate. But often you can simply let go of a feeling of tension and anxiety that you've built up without realising. Reflecting on what you can lose may help you to let go of that feeling, knowing that you're capable of whatever challenge you face.

Don't worry – you don't need to be firing on all cylinders every second of the day, with no time to take a break. Sometimes you want to be full steam ahead, taking action on your goals, and other times you want to be still, calm, and quiet, or having fun at a party.

You can find loads of tools to increase your effectiveness in managing yourself and your time, but before you race to book yourself on a time management course or invest in more books, consider the kind of person you are:

- Do you enjoy working with the same systems or processes or do you get excited by new time management tools (a different diary system, the latest personal digital assistant, colour-coded task lists) but then find you lose interest quickly? You may be the type of person who needs to chop and change their time management systems to get the best out of your time.

- What times of the day do you usually get the most done? You may be an early bird lark or a night owl, so play to your body clock strengths and adopt a system that encourages you to be most proactive when your energy levels are highest.

- Do you prefer to spend a block of time working to complete a big task, or is it better for you to break it up into digestible chunks? Time yourself on a big project and see when your attention and productivity start to wane. People usually need some kind of break every 45 minutes, even just a few moments staring into space, but your own clock may work to a different rhythm.

- Are you a self-starter or someone who needs to be prodded – do you respond better to the carrot or the stick? Some people are spurred on by rewards and others need a 'push' to propel them into action. As a rule (although you create the rules, remember) you are best served by 70–80 per cent pull motivation versus only 20–30 per cent push tactics. Some tasks may need more push, especially if they're tough ones for you to get really motivated about, in which case remember to play to your attention span strengths and get more support.

- Are you an optimist or a pessimist when it comes to the amount of time you have available to complete tasks? Do you often under- or over-estimate how much time you need, potentially causing yourself too much pressure on the one hand or too little challenge on the other? Some people believe that it's better to under-promise and over-deliver and this might earn you a few brownie points at work (until your boss gets wise to the technique). However, the most respected approach, and the healthiest one for your own balance, is to become more skilled at making accurate estimates of the time you need for a task. This takes practice and close observation, so keep trying.

Think about your daily choices in the context of being either *reactive* (responding to events and people) or *proactive* (taking the initiative and thinking ahead). Usually when you're aiming for your goals you work proactively. But how much time do you spend being reactive to tasks that you're given? You can't avoid being reactive sometimes; you simply have to do certain things because you have responsibilities you must fulfil. But because this reactive approach is so much a part of everyday life you may find it hard to get out of autopilot. Ask yourself if you can add anything a little more proactive to the process to move you further towards your goals.

Khan was responsible for the hour-long morning school run for his two young children. He enjoyed the time he spent in the car with the young ones, but found that their high energy levels at that time of the morning were distracting. In addition, he expressed a concern during coaching that he was rarely finding time in his busy days to reflect on his goals and build on them. During the morning drive Khan's mind was full of the things that he needed to put on his task list for that day, which, combined with the two boisterous forces of nature bouncing around, didn't help him arrive at work calm and collected. He decided to write out his task list for the next day just before he went to bed instead of when he arrived at work.

For Khan, this small proactive change had a remarkable effect. Instead of his head buzzing with all the problems he needed to solve that day, possible solutions started popping up during the drive. It was as if his brain had processed all the challenges during the night and was now delivering neat outputs into his brain. This enjoyable outcome nearly matched his children's energy because it felt positive and upbeat.

Managing Longer-Term Stress

Good stress is the fuel that helps you to deliver your great results. This good stress is more a feeling of excitement, a sense of urgency, and a willingness to push out of your comfort zone, despite the butterflies in your stomach or your fears of failure. The kind of stress that you need to manage is really *di-stress*, when you feel overwhelmed by the enormity of what you have to do and your energy recedes instead of grows. You can often deal with distress on a daily basis, but at other times, no matter what you do, you seem to be under the kind of sustained pressure that dissipates your enjoyment of life for a while. Don't allow yourself to come to boiling point slowly, without even realising the cumulative effect of pressure piled on pressure on a regular basis. Learn to spot your danger signs and have a plan of action ready to put in place.

Spotting your danger signs

You have your own danger signs that warn you when you're under too much pressure. Spotting these signs at an early stage is vital for your physical, mental, and emotional wellbeing.

Your danger signs may include:

- ✔ Not sleeping well
- ✔ Feeling anxious
- ✔ Always being tired

✔ Having lapses of concentration

✔ Experiencing extreme mood swings

✔ Feeling low

✔ Having trouble with memory

✔ Eating for comfort or drinking to excess

✔ Noticing unpleasant physical symptoms (headaches, stomach pains, cold sores)

Many of these symptoms can have other underlying causes, but if you're experiencing several of them at the same time, you're probably living on the wrong side of your balance curve.

You can start regaining balance by changing your attitude to the stress in your life, but that may have limited impact. The only effective long-term solution when matters get to this stage is to change the situation in some way. A sign that you really need to change the stressful situation can be when you're adamant that you can't implement change or deny that you need to, so be honest with yourself. Extreme stress, the kind that leads to depression and other diseases, is often accompanied by a feeling of being locked into the bad situation and bereft of choices.

Apply the following three-point plan to launch yourself into action:

1. **Ask yourself what options you have that can reduce the ongoing stress without increasing negative stress in another area.** Imagine an ideal solution, even if at this stage you don't really believe it's possible. If your job is causing you stress, these ideal solutions may include working part-time, taking a sabbatical, finding a new job, giving up work entirely, or getting extra support in your role. For each solution ask yourself, 'What will happen if I do this?' and 'What will happen if I don't do this?'

2. **Ask yourself what further information you need to move forward.** You may find you need more information from your boss or the human resources department. Perhaps you can get information on your contract of employment via a Web site or need to check out with your bank manager if you can secure a loan to fund a sabbatical.

3. **Ask yourself what resources and support you need and what's stopping you from enlisting that help.** Apart from the people you need information from, you may want to consider who can lend a supportive ear and help you think through your options. If you're having professional coaching, your coach is a great start, and so are family members. Perhaps you need to start with your boss but worry that you'll come across as uncommitted to your job? You can approach this conversation by thinking through the benefits for the organisation of getting to a better working situation for you.

Don't hesitate to get more help in stressful situations. This isn't a time for going it alone and your energies are best employed pulling in other resources and fresh perspectives.

The Web site of the International Stress Management Association has some great resources on the topic of stress and time management. Check out www.isma.org.uk.

Coaching your way through stressful situations

Stressful situations have a habit of driving out logical thought and creating panic. Taking the time to coach yourself through these occasions pays dividends because the next time stress hits, you'll find making the best choices for you a little easier. The following tips focus on the use of powerful questions to help you stand back from the panic and get some perspective.

Ten Daily Balancing Acts

Taking ten short moments through your day to balance your energies pays dividends out of all proportion to the effort you expend. And doing so is the fastest way to build self-coaching into your life. Try out these simple tips and see how your daily life improves:

- See a clear vision – the simple act of enjoying the luxury of seeing, hearing, and feeling your ideal future helps you to relax, refocus, and get back to the fray of your everyday life.

- Take a gratitude tonic – good, strong, positive feelings stay in your emotional bloodstream.

- Do a kind and thoughtful act – balance your own needs and goals with random acts of kindness.

- Soak up wise words – collect inspiring quotes and affirmations and keep them to hand.

- Seesaw between action and reflection – take time out for reflection and action to provide balance.

- Take a deep breath – deep breathing instantly revives you, calms you, and centres you.

- Share a smile – a simple smile can dissolve tensions and create ripples of harmony.

- Give yourself a treat – your busy routine benefits from the injection of the occasional spontaneous gifts to yourself.

- Stretch out – do a 2–5 minute stretch every morning to have a positive effect on your balance for the day.

- Get natural – take in the beauty of the natural world. Enjoy the smell of the earth after rain, a lungful of fresh air, or the sight of a plant or flower.

Here are some rules of engagement for when stress attacks you:

✔ **Be clear on your values, your vision, and your goals.** Take time to see the clear vision of your life and measure every choice you make against this vision.

Powerful question: What do I really want now in my life?

✔ **Hold your goals lightly and be mindful that changing circumstances may change the goal and the steps you need to take to get there.** Accept that stressful times do occur and give yourself permission to make the adjustments to your goals that you need.

Powerful question: Where can I be more flexible now?

✔ **Ask yourself frequently what you can let go of, and what you don't need any more.**

Powerful question: What's getting in the way of my best interests?

✔ **Take only actions that enhance your self-esteem and personal integrity.**

Powerful question: How does this action or decision make me stronger?

✔ **Understand that you will have situations you can't change, people you can't help, and results you can't achieve.** You can win other battles instead.

Powerful question: What can I accept with graceful humility?

✔ **Tap into the goodwill of others.** Don't let your ego stand in the way of joining forces with your best allies.

Powerful question: Who can support, encourage, or inspire me?

✔ **Have a contingency plan, or two, or three.** Get into the habit of thinking through your contingency plans for the really key areas of your life, or really stressful situations.

Powerful questions: What are my options? What else can I do? What option can't I yet see?

Chapter 6

Developing and Growing

. . . .

In This Chapter

▶ Developing yourself through change

▶ Understanding your powerful brain

▶ Putting play and purpose into your life

. . . .

*T*he changes that you make through coaching not only give you better results; they help you grow as a person. In fact, even without the goal of improving your life situation, you constantly need to find new ways to grow, adapt, and change, otherwise your enjoyment of life over time can diminish because you become used to the status quo. Coaching is a fantastic mechanism for personal growth. You can apply coaching to the process of your personal development, enhancing your ability to acquire new skills faster and more effectively, so that becoming wiser and more self-aware in itself becomes a whole life goal.

How well you take on board new information and ideas, how much you seek to gain from fun and leisure time, and your focus on your spiritual wellbeing are all aspects of personal growth. This chapter focuses on how you can accelerate results in all areas of your life by harnessing your natural talents to soak up new experiences and integrate them into your world – and how you can discover what truly has meaning and purpose for you.

Thriving on Learning

Get one thing clear for starters – learning in the context of your whole life has very little to do with anything you may have experienced at school. Learning is simply a cycle of assessing the information available to you, making decisions, taking action, and reflecting on your results to take better steps next time.

Over the last 20 years, research into *accelerated* or brain-friendly learning has identified some fascinating stuff that may explain why so many people 'switch off' and don't get as much out of their early schooling as others seem to do. *Accelerated learning* (also known as *whole brain thinking*) means you employ the strengths of both the left and right sides of your brain (the later section 'Harnessing your brain power' has more). Exciting times are ahead as schools, adult learning, and the workplace begin to integrate these new theories fully. The potential of accelerated learning has massive implications for improving the quality of lives and the effectiveness of organisations.

Being your best

Is it really important for you to aim to become competent at everything you do, to stay at that stage, and to enjoy the fruits of your labours? Well, becoming competent at something is a great goal. But a higher level is always ahead and, sooner or later, if you want to grow to become your best self, you have to come to terms with letting yourself become incompetent on a regular basis – allowing yourself to struggle at the higher level for a while. This process is like a spiral taking you to ever higher levels, as shown in Figure 6-1.

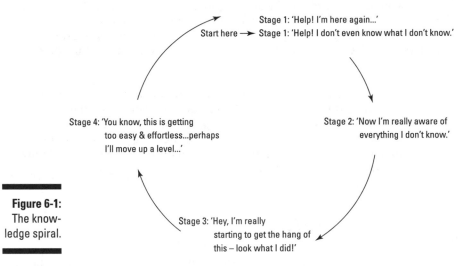

Stage 1: 'Help! I'm here again...'

Start here → Stage 1: 'Help! I don't even know what I don't know.'

Stage 2: 'Now I'm really aware of everything I don't know.'

Stage 4: 'You know, this is getting too easy & effortless...perhaps I'll move up a level...'

Stage 3: 'Hey, I'm really starting to get the hang of this – look what I did!'

Figure 6-1: The knowledge spiral.

Try applying the knowledge spiral to taking driving lessons. You may experience some of the following:

Stage 1: You're enthusiastic, ready to learn, and blissfully unaware of the scope of the challenges ahead. Anyway, other people make it look so easy. You don't yet know what you don't know!

Stage 2: You start to feel a bit panicky and confused, and are suddenly conscious of how clumsy or ignorant you feel. You have a lot to study and remember – both theory and practice – and you wonder why you thought driving was going to be easy. You are all too aware of the things you don't know and can't do properly.

Stage 3: You're gaining confidence now and feeling proud of your progress, although you may still crunch the gears or forget a road sign occasionally.

Stage 4: A good while after passing your test, you can now spend long stretches not thinking at all about how you drive the car but just doing it. You feel great most of the time, but you do wonder sometimes if you're as good a driver as you were the day you passed your test. Time to enrol in an advanced driving course maybe?

Getting to Stage 4 is often a mixed blessing. You feel comfortable because you're so good at what you do, but if you stay too long at that stage, bad habits can creep in, as well as boredom and complacency. Think about the different areas of your life now. What stages are you at? If you're in a brand new work role you may be experiencing the heady optimism of Stage 1 – but how are you preparing for the potential frustration of Stage 2? Are you in a long-term relationship where you think you know everything about the other person? Perhaps Stage 4 complacency has set in – how can you take your relationship to the next level and discover new things about each other? Or you may be working hard at your fitness goals and honing your technique in a new sport. What can you do to accelerate yourself to Stage 4 so that you can have the feel-good factor that comes from being unconsciously competent?

Harnessing your brain power

The choices you make and the actions you take determine the results you get in life, and your choices and actions stem from how you think and use your brain power. You naturally develop preferences and grooves of thinking that work well most of the time, so you may not see the need to stretch yourself. Unless you change how you think, you continue to get pretty much the same results as you always have because you probably choose the same actions and behaviours. But you can develop different ways to think and get different results by engaging other parts of your brain.

In very simple terms you can think of your brain as two halves of a whole that work together to produce your best results. Table 6-1 summarises the differences between your left brain and your right brain.

Table 6-1	Differences between the Left and Right Sides of Your Brain
Your left brain focuses on:	*Your right brain focuses on:*
Detail first then big picture	Big picture then detail
Fact	Intuition
Logic	Imagination
Theories	Experiments
Structures	Patterns
Organisation	Spontaneity
Seeing what's tangible	Asking what's possible

The left side of your brain is brilliant at processing small bits of data, working out sequences and structures, coming up with theories, and applying logic and analysis to problems. Your left brain is really handy for a task such as doing a 5,000-piece jigsaw. You separate the pieces out, look for the edge ones first, assemble the frame, then begin to put small pieces together. Then (five months later) you finally succeed in assembling the big picture. Your left brain gathers together information logically from the parts to the whole. Left brain activities tend to dominate most traditional schooling, in part because they're easier to measure than right brain activities.

The right side of your brain is fantastic at glimpsing the big picture and making those intuitive leaps that seem to come from nowhere. Your right brain helps you stand back, look at the half-completed jigsaw for a second or two, pick up a new piece seemingly at random, and somehow know exactly where it goes. Your right brain breaks down information intuitively from the whole to the parts. If you have a strong preference for using your right brain you may have been the kind of child at school who learned best from imagination and unstructured activities and you may have found it difficult to tune into the logic and order of left brain learning.

Relying on intuition (right brain) alone doesn't get the jigsaw completed any quicker than using your left brain. Ideally the parts of your brain work together, so you apply logic and process along with those flashes of intuitive brilliance.

Just by comparing the two lists in Table 6-1 you can probably see which of the two sides your brain tends to favour, and areas you can now focus on to get enhanced results. Do you want to get all the facts before you make a decision about something? Maybe you can coach yourself to listen to your intuition from time to time to see how that affects the results you get. Or you may prefer to dive into a task and go with the flow. Try applying more organisational structure to improve your results.

An ability to handle facts, data, and logic, and to pass exams, is only one aspect of being successful. Accelerated learning leads to balanced behaviours that get significantly better outcomes for you overall.

Coaching yourself means opening up options for yourself, trying out new things, and exploring different routes. In doing so, you discover better ways of getting what you want and need in your life. Harnessing the sleepy side of your brain and getting it up to speed with the side that's happily whirring away means that you can achieve at least twice as much as you ever did before.

How can you develop your whole brain capability to help you get better results, in coaching and in your life? Here are a few suggestions:

- ✓ **When you formulate your goals, take time to write them down (left brain activity) and also to visualise or draw them (right brain activities).** This helps your whole brain to recognise the instruction you're giving it.

- ✓ **Take up crossword puzzles or su doku to train your whole brain.** Cryptic crosswords in particular are very whole-brain friendly because they make you apply logic and language as well as leaps of intuitive thinking. And su doku isn't just about numbers (left brain) but about pattern recognition (right brain). Take a look at *Su Doku For Dummies* by Andrew Heron and Edmund James (Wiley) for some real brainteasers.

- ✓ **Build in rest periods for your task.** The optimum period to concentrate fully on a task for your whole brain efficiency is around 90 minutes, after which your brain needs to 'rest' for 20 minutes. (A change really can be as good as a rest, so this doesn't mean a quick snooze at your desk!)

Playing in the Game of Life

Can you remember how you used to play as a child? You'd be fully absorbed in what you were doing, engaging with others, freely moving from one activity to another, coming up with all sorts of imaginative approaches that defied logic. Play enabled you to socialise and interact with others and it also helped you acquire new skills without feeling anxious and under pressure.

Humans learn at the most concentrated level in their first seven years. When formal education begins, you start to learn other skills – how to reason and apply logic. Both play and logic are helpful in life, but developing through play is much more right brained and hard to measure, so the education system favours measurable left-brain activities. You leave behind childish things as you grow, and feel a little foolish if you go back to them. Even though you may secretly still love joining your niece or nephew with crayons and paints, you may feel you can't possibly whip out your own colouring book when no children are around!

Play can bring you back to life

Some fascinating research among a group of orphans indicates that, far from being a frivolous activity, play is crucial to human development and maybe even survival. In 1999 the Sighisoara Paediatric Hospital in Romania secured the services of the country's first playworker – someone trained in enabling children to learn through play – who trained at Leeds Metropolitan University's innovative Playwork programme. The children at the hospital had all suffered such terrible trauma and neglect that they were used to spending all of their time sitting and rocking, trapped in their own solitary worlds. Indeed, all the children had been diagnosed as severely retarded and were destined for a children's mental hospital.

Through the playworker engaging with the children in play activities over a few short months, all of them made the sort of progress that many experts had asserted was impossible with such severe cases of disturbance. A very high proportion of the children were subsequently adopted or fostered, and it seems clear that their rapid transformation was primarily due to the introduction of purposeful play activities.

If play is so important to a child's development think about what it can do for your adult development.

What did you love to do as a child that you have 'grown out of'? What have you lost as a result? In what ways can you integrate this back into your life? You may have replaced simple activities such as cycling with friends with more 'adult' pursuits such as trips to the gym – all well and good, but recapturing the sense of fun you had in child-like activities can bring unexpected benefits.

Benefiting from a playful approach

Coaching yourself to a more playful approach to life has practical benefits, including:

- ✔ **You enjoy enhanced creativity in the solutions you come up with for your life.** Apply a little childlike imagination and ask yourself a nonlogical question from time to time. For example, 'If this problem were a colour/animal/city, what would it be?'

- ✔ **You begin to see things more clearly.** Children are often brutally honest about what they see in their world. However, they quickly learn not to point out to Great Aunt Ethel that she's got a very wobbly bottom, so they discover diplomacy and how to keep quiet. This develops into telling little white lies to avoid hurting people's feelings. You may have become so used to the truth being a bit of a chameleon that seeing what's going on clearly is sometimes tricky. Young children are generally honest with themselves until they learn otherwise. This innate talent can help you take anxiety out of everyday mishaps and problems. Ask yourself, 'What's really true for me here? In what way am I glossing over the truth to avoid facing something?'

✔ **You enjoy your journey more.** Ask yourself 'Am I having fun yet?' from time to time to stop you from taking yourself or your task too seriously. Look for ways to liven up whatever you're doing.

✔ **You begin to probe beneath the surface more often.** Play the Game of Five Whys with yourself from time to time. This game (inspired from the eternal question children ask) simply means that you explore an issue for yourself by asking 'why?' five times in a row, to really get to the heart of the problem. For example: *Why* am I still doing this job I hate? To earn money. *Why?* So I can have more holidays. *Why?* So I enjoy myself more. *Why?* Because I feel miserable most of the time. *Why?* Because I keep turning up to this job I hate!

Making the most of your leisure time

The habits you get into during your leisure time have a lot of impact on how much you enjoy your life as a whole. Weekends and holidays may be the main way that you rebalance the frantic pace of the rest of your life. You may feel that the last thing you want to do is take on more challenges. Your perfect vacation may be lazing by the pool – this may be just the thing to send you back to your daily routine relaxed and recharged.

But check your assumptions once in a while. What's the best holiday you've ever had and why? Do you go back to the same resort or have a similar holiday every year because that's what feeds your soul or because that's become a habit? Do you find that you need or want to take longer and longer to recharge? Do you find that a week or so of inactivity leaves you feeling less, not more, energised? You may be reaching a tipping point where the stress in certain areas of your life is getting to be a little more than is good for your healthy balance.

Your lack of energy may have another explanation. Do you know people who never seem to stop doing things? They take on numerous projects at work and at home and then spend their holidays learning to sky-dive or climbing minor mountain ranges. Sometimes, the more you do, the more energy you have.

Look closely at your leisure time and see how you can get the best of both worlds, relaxing *and* action packed. So you've been promising yourself to learn another language? Rather than sign up for an evening class that may be hard to schedule into your busy week, you can investigate joining in with some classes on holiday abroad, spending the morning having fun 'in school' and the afternoon sightseeing or relaxing. In terms of variety, for example, if you usually holiday with your family, consider taking a solo short break to reconnect with your own sense of self.

Your leisure time is a great opportunity for personal growth as well as a blissful space where you can 'simply be' for a while, before you get right back into the thick of the action.

Find a quiet spot and ask yourself these questions to coach yourself to more enjoyable leisure pursuits:

- **Powerful opening question:** What role do I want leisure to take in my life?

- **Personal style:** Am I naturally active or reflective? Do I favour left- or right-brain activities? What gives me energy?

- **Beliefs:** What beliefs do I have about 'time out' that may be restricting my enjoyment? What constraints do I put around holiday time? How do I reduce the priority of leisure in my life?

- **Motivation:** What can I achieve in my personal time that supports my key values? What is a compelling goal to aim for that enhances my enjoyment of my core interests?

- **What's working:** What's good about the choices I make to spend my leisure? What compromises do I make that I resent having to make?

- **Exploring options:** What ways can I find to experiment with different approaches to my leisure time? How can I test the choices that are right for me?

- **Taking action:** What's my first step? How much time can I allocate to planning my approach? How do I know when I'm making progress? What can I do to celebrate?

Getting in Touch with Your Spiritual Side

Part of gaining knowledge and growing is getting in touch with and developing your spiritual side. One of the greatest benefits to come out of coaching is a growing sense of self-awareness. You begin to accept yourself as human, unique, capable, sometimes flawed, and yet endlessly resourceful. You become comfortable in your own skin, you accept yourself, and you begin to get a feeling for what is really important for you.

What is spirituality for you?

Here are some of the things that you may associate with spirituality:

- Feeling touched by something you see or experience – perhaps a glorious sunset, the wingspan of a bird in flight, or a baby's smile.

- Sensing that you're contributing to something bigger than yourself.

- Being willing to connect with others openly for no other reason than that they share the same air as you.

✔ Feeling in flow with what you're doing at that exact moment and that your attention is fully focused.

✔ Wondering at the ultimate mystery of the world around you.

✔ Noticing how often the opportunity to have what you most want presents itself to you unexpectedly without you actively seeking it.

What are the characteristics of spirituality for you? Spirituality may be connected with your religion or faith. The two concepts are not the same, although for many people religion is a powerful mechanism to access their spirituality.

Accessing your spirituality

Coaching helps you to realise that you can deal with anything. Having a strong sense of self enables you to handle even the worst events and you begin to learn the truth in the saying 'what doesn't kill you makes you stronger'. You create your world through what you choose to focus on and do. Coaching can result in changes in your thoughts, behaviours, and actions to build a life that sits well with your authentic self. And that can lead to a search for your true role in the world, whether on a big or small stage. For many people all of this self-discovery in itself can become a spiritual journey.

How can you access your spirituality? Here are some ideas:

✔ Meditation relaxes you, helps you to feel grounded, and is a great way to empty your mind of everyday concerns so that you become more open to the big questions and connections that form the basis of spirituality. Sitting comfortably and gazing at a candle is a simple form of meditation.

✔ Get out in the natural world and take a good look around. Think about how long the oak tree in the woods has stood, when the hills were formed, and how often the waves crash against the shore. Your head will soon start to spin but you'll get some perspective on the challenges in your life.

✔ Take up a physical practice such as yoga, Pilates, or t'ai chi. Or combine your spiritual quest with a fitness goal through running and jogging if that's more your style. By giving the body purposeful movement you also free up your mind.

✔ Read as much as possible. Fiction, poetry, humour, philosophy – read whatever takes your fancy as long as it challenges you a little and broadens your horizons.

✔ Feast on art, music, and dance whenever you can. All great artists express their bigger purpose in some way through their art and you can catch some of their magic dust as you appreciate the beauty of their work.

Asking the Right Questions

A surprising amount of the success you create for yourself as an adult comes from the times when you think carefully about the questions you ask of yourself and others around you, and then listen hard for the right answer.

Think of using questions as you use a good search engine – the right keywords get you to the result you want. You still have to be discriminating with the information you get, but you can master the skill of knowing how to phrase your request with the help of this chapter, and you're then better placed to sort out the wheat from the chaff.

Questions are an open invitation for more information or a call to action. Closed questions – those that generate a yes or no response – aren't 'bad' questions at all – in the right place closed questions have a vital role to play. In general though, work with a kind of funnel approach, where you start off with broad open questions (generally beginning with who?, what?, how?, where?, or why?). Then move on to probing questions to find out more; perhaps ask a few clarifying questions to check your understanding; and finish off with closed questions to confirm action. The idea is to funnel your thinking so that you cover all possibilities and get to the best solution as quickly as possible. Figure 6-2 illustrates the question funnel.

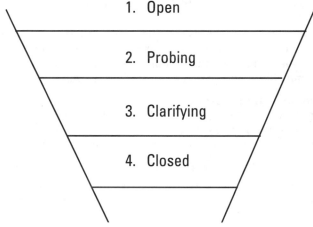

Figure 6-2:
The question funnel.

1. Open

2. Probing

3. Clarifying

4. Closed

Moving down the funnel

You don't have to be rigid about using the question funnel by starting at the top with open questions and finishing at the bottom with a closed question. More likely you'll experiment with moving up and down the funnel to get the results you need. The trick is to make sure that you've covered all the levels before proceeding to action.

Open questions

Think about getting fit. The first open question you ask yourself may be:

What does getting fit mean to me?

Your answer may include gaining energy, strength, looking good in your clothes, avoiding illness and disease.

Probing questions and statements

Probing questions invite you to explore more about the situation or objective. You may examine your priorities for getting fit:

Which of these health objectives are most important to me and for what reasons?

You may discover that 'looking good' is connected to a need to feel attractive and that avoiding illness and disease is associated with living a full life with your children. Knowing the value you place on these two things helps you sort out your motivation.

Clarifying questions and statements

A good clarifying question or statement can keep you on track and stop you from wasting time:

So, what I really want from my fitness programme is . . .

Although it may sound odd, asking yourself a clarifying question just as you're about to go on to action planning can make you stop, think, and re-consider. Your plan of action may not be what you really want after all. Asking a clarifying question is a way of re-stating your objectives and checking if anything is missing.

You may be surprised at how often your objective or action gets tweaked at this stage. Clarifying moves you nicely onto closing.

Closed questions

Closed questions are great for closing the funnel with a commitment or action. A closed question often generates a yes or no answer so you may simply ask yourself if you're 100 per cent committed to the action. In coaching, a closing question also means a specifically focused question designed to generate that action, for example:

What's my best first step?

When will I make the call to the gym?

Closed questions are directed towards a clear decision rather than options.

Finding your most powerful questions

The right questions asked at the right time are always empowering, but some questions have even more impact. *Reflective* and *pre-supposing* questions are two special types of questions that effectively challenge your thinking when you coach yourself.

Reflective questions

A reflective question is a probing or clarifying question used very frequently in coaching because of its almost magical properties in getting to the heart of a particular issue.

Reflective questions allow you to reflect inwards and consider possibilities in a certain way. By crafting a tightly focused reflective question and thinking about its context, you can often gain a real light bulb moment when something just clicks into place.

Pre-supposing questions

Pre-supposing questions are a form of probing or hypothetical question and fall mainly into the context of generating solutions. These coaching questions pre-suppose that you can form a bridge over a limiting belief and they show you what you can achieve on the other side. They give you the safety of simply putting aside for a moment the need to believe in whatever may be holding you back and imagining what your world would look like. Here are some presupposing questions:

> If I knew that I couldn't fail, what would I do next?
>
> If I could have my perfect state of health, what would that look and feel like?
>
> If it were possible to combine the security of my current job and the freedom of self-employment, how would I be working right now?

Working with my clients, I (Jeni) find this type of question to be the most powerful in helping them set aside their limiting beliefs. Even if a client has a deeply embedded belief, their attitude towards that belief always changes after answering a pre-supposing question so that they can approach the limiting belief with new, more effective strategies.

Listening to the Answers

If questioning is one of the most important skills you can apply in your life coaching journey, listening is the most under-rated! The quality of your life improves dramatically if you spend more time listening both to other people and to yourself. Everyone loves to be listened to. You've probably met someone who is a good listener and thought afterwards what an interesting person they were – even though they may have said very little. The truth is that they were allowing *you* to be interesting, so you naturally warmed to them.

Turning that charm on yourself works in the same way. It feels wonderful to ask yourself empowering questions and really listen to the answers, as long as the voice you hear is your inner coach and not your inner critic.

When you don't know the answer

One frustration you may have when you start to use your communication skills in an advanced way is that you sometimes feel you really *don't* have the answer. No matter how hard you try to get yourself into a resourceful frame of mind, no matter how well framed your questions to yourself are, no matter how willing you are to believe that the answer is inside you – sometimes you simply draw a big fat blank. Don't worry. That's okay, and sometimes it just means that you need to search around for a different question, or try again another time, or go off and do something different to change your state of mind. The answer sometimes comes when you least expect it.

What do you do if the answer doesn't come to you? Try out this very simple technique and amaze yourself at the number of times it gets you unstuck. When you have asked yourself a question and you really, truly, don't seem to know the answer, ask yourself this:

> What would the answer be if I did know it?

This question may sound daft to you, but be reassured that it works in almost all cases. Why it works is a bit mysterious, but it has something to do with reaching down a level to your unconscious thoughts and knowledge. And on a superficial level, it also lets you step back from the anxiety of 'not knowing' to the possibility of 'what if?' You can also think of it as the answer that your inner coach provides for you.

You can try this out on other people too and watch their expression change from confusion to delight as they come up with the answer they really didn't think they had in them.

Tuning into energy levels to find the answers

Your energy levels contribute significantly to how good you are at making sense of your answers. You can ask yourself great questions and even generate great answers, but if your mood is low, or you're tired and worn out, or feeling particularly stressed, you may not hear those answers for the gift they really are. Your inner critic loves those days when you are drained of energy and takes every opportunity to beat you up for not even having the spirit to make the changes you say you want.

Recognising that you're feeling low or stressed is the first stage of solving this problem. At certain times in your life you get caught up in one long vortex of stress and activity and never seem to find the time and energy to really listen to yourself. Because you are strong and resilient you can cope with this in the short term but sooner or later you need to call a halt and find some mental and physical refuge – the second stage of solving the problem. Your refuge can be as simple as a quiet hour alone with yourself or as extensive as a long holiday or sabbatical.

Thankfully, most energy lows are short-term and you can plan times to coach yourself when you feel strong, positive, and alert.

Making Your Best Decision

You've finally decided that a radical decision must be made. Perhaps you've decided that an unhealthy or painful relationship or a job that's stifling the best of you has to change. You know you have to act, soon, and in a big way. What are your options? Take a look at the pros and cons of tackling your decision from a problem-based view first.

Fixing it or fleeing from it

Fixing a bad situation does have huge benefits to you. First, and most obviously, doing so solves your problem. Secondly, and maybe more importantly, fixing a bad situation does wonders for your self-esteem. You get to be the hero in your own life who draws on all your reserves of strength and talent to come up with resourceful options for saving your own world. The benefits will continue, because you discover so much in the process of change that you can apply your problem-solving skills more widely. Yet you may also reach a point at which trying to fix something indicates stubbornness or even low self-esteem rather than wisdom. Staying in an abusive relationship that shows no signs of changing despite all your efforts is an extreme example of this.

Ask yourself the following powerful positive questions about fixing a bad situation:

- What would my life be like? If a miracle happened overnight, what would the situation look like?
- What would I gain and what sacrifices would I need to make?
- What impact on my whole life would fixing it have?
- What support do I need?
- Where can I start and how can I maintain my commitment?

Fleeing from an unpleasant situation sometimes seems like the only viable option and it's often an agonising choice to make. If you're in a bad relationship, have tried to fix it to no avail, but can't bear the thought of finally ending it, you may be tempted to seek out the catalyst for change in the form of another person. So you may think about or actually start an affair, which then becomes the excuse to leave your bad relationship without actually resolving the underlying problems. Of course, people do fall in love and as a result may choose to end existing relationships; that's a bittersweet fact of life. But falling in love with the right person is easier when you've had a chance to work out why things went wrong before.

Ask yourself the following powerful challenging questions about fleeing from a bad situation:

- What am I escaping from?

- What am I using as a distraction from facing the real issue?

- What impact is this choice having on my self-esteem?

- What would it be like to move away from this situation?

- What beliefs do I have that cause me to take the line of least resistance at present?

- How can I learn from this bad situation?

- What environment can best support me to grow from my experience?

Building on strength

Often the most constructive approach to making your best decision is to take your focus away from the problem and begin to draw out the elements of what's working for you in your current situation as a starting point for major change. You don't want to throw out the baby with the bathwater and this is a real danger when you're contemplating brand new horizons, whether for negative or positive reasons. Think about a major change, such as becoming self-employed and consider the following example of a coaching conversation you might have with yourself:

Q: What's great about my current situation that I want to retain?

A: I have financial security, great team relationships, and fixed working hours.

Q: What is my dream for my working life?

A: To add in greater freedom and autonomy. I want to make more of my own decisions, choose how to spend my budget, and develop my creativity in new markets.

Q: How can I design a new working life that combines the best of both worlds?

A: If I begin to identify potential working partners now I'll be ready to trade at a profit in a year's time when I plan to resign my current role. I can begin to develop ideas for products and services in my spare time, which will help me identify my learning needs in the new market. If I work towards reduced hours within 6 months I'll have more time to consolidate these beginnings so that I'm ready with a solid foundation financially and personally.

This positive approach, based on a coaching technique called *appreciative inquiry*, can help you move away from problems and into the more fertile land of possibilities.

When a major change seems big and far away you can measure your ongoing progress by the following questions:

✔ On a scale of 1–10, where am I now in relation to my goal?

✔ What would move me closer to a 10?

✔ What positive attributes are helping me to achieve the number I'm at?

✔ How can I enhance these positive attributes?

Letting Go and Integrating the New

A major change can occur at any stage of your life, whether self-motivated or through external, largely uncontrollable factors such as redundancy or bereavement. You may be on the receiving end of someone else's major life change, and if you're not at the same stage, separation and divorce can result, which will of course throw you into radical change as well.

Whether you choose your life change or have it imposed on you, you need to make sense of it all.

Working through the change

Even when your radical change is positive and you have actively chosen it, you actually go through a grieving process similar to bereavement. You're saying goodbye to a part of your life and even when you feel relief and happiness, you can also feel deeply uncomfortable and sad.

Think about the following scenarios:

- ✔ Vimla has just heard rumours that the company she works for has been bought out by a competitor who has a cut-throat, highly commercial approach to business.

- ✔ Peter's partner of many years reveals she has fallen in love with someone else and wants a divorce.

- ✔ Maria is deciding whether to leave her career as a corporate lawyer and secure a qualification to teach English as a foreign language to fulfil her ultimate goal of living and working in Portugal.

- ✔ Jonathan is about to hand in his notice on his well-paid managerial role in a big company so that he can set up in business for himself for the first time.

Now consider how each person manages the bereavement process of denial, anger, emotional negotiation, sadness, and acceptance:

1. **Denial:** Vimla is horrified at the takeover news and initially can't believe it's happening. She thinks of all the reasons why the takeover news can't be true and can't accept that the board of directors has sold out in this way.

2. **Anger:** After his initial shock and denial, Peter feels extreme anger towards his partner for the betrayal of trust. He is furious that she has been having an affair behind his back and finds it difficult to see past this to discuss options calmly and clearly.

3. **Negotiating:** Maria initially fought against both her need to retain her status and her urge to start again in a new career. She experienced anger that she couldn't 'have it all' before arriving at a negotiating stage where she accommodated both options in her mind. She comes round to the idea that a break from the law profession is going to be best for her in the long run so that she can really focus her energies her new goals.

4. **Sadness:** Jonathan went through denial about how he could ever set up his own business and anger in the form of extreme frustration at his unhappiness. He also experienced negotiating as he attempted to weigh up his real options clearly. He now feels sadness that he is saying goodbye to a feeling of security that has served him well for a long time. Handing in his notice feels like a huge step and he is not yet ready to look forward to the next stage.

5. **Acceptance:** All four finally arrive at acceptance and are ready to let go of the old path for the possibilities of the new. Even negative outcomes – Vimla does lose her job, and Peter does get divorced – are easier to bear because the people concerned have accepted and processed those outcomes during their acknowledgement of the changes that are occurring.

Evolving to the next stage

After you accept that a major change is inevitable and work through the stages of loss to arrive at acceptance, you then begin yet another journey. The following steps walk you through the period of transition.

1. **Start with closure, or the end.** Accept the passing era of your life. You may choose to symbolise it in some way, either visually or by a clear out or bonfire of paperwork or objects you no longer need that are associated with the passing phase. You now distance yourself from the past, in order to embrace the future. You're probably relieved that you're free to move on, but may also be fearful of what is to come.

    Vimla, who lost her job as a result of a company takeover, moved through to acceptance with the help of supportive friends and family networks. She realised that she had stayed with her old company out of fierce loyalty, even though she now saw that she had been quite bored by the routine. She was getting excited about fresh fields, although she hadn't a clue how she was going to find the confidence to get back on the interview circuit.

2. **Flow through your transition.** The transition from old to new may be chaotic, as you adjust and discover the consequences of your new choices. Your energy rises as you grow in confidence that you're on the right path, even if you don't have all the answers quite yet. You may be tempted to stay in this phase for a long time without making a definite commitment to the new start as you explore rather than make commitments to action.

    Vimla spent her transition period working with a career coach. At first she was surprised that the coaching focused less on interview techniques and writing a great CV than on exploring what she really enjoyed about her work, and what helped to build her confidence in all areas of her life. Vimla quickly got into the flow of her transition and was soon picking up the phone and researching potential new employers.

3. **Begin the new.** You arrive at a position of certainty and realign yourself with your new goals. This is a time of high energy, commitment, and action. You feel strong and empowered and can look on your past self, your struggles and challenges, with acceptance.

After quite a short time, Vimla secured a number of interviews and got two job offers in one day! On the day she started her new job she wrote a short note to the new owner of her old company, thanking him for making her redundant and giving her the opportunity to spread her wings.

Appendix

Personal Development Resources

• •

*T*his appendix contains blank forms for you to use. You can photocopy these blank forms and fill them in, using the instructions provided within specific chapters.

Well-Formed Outcome Checklist (Book II, Chapter 1)

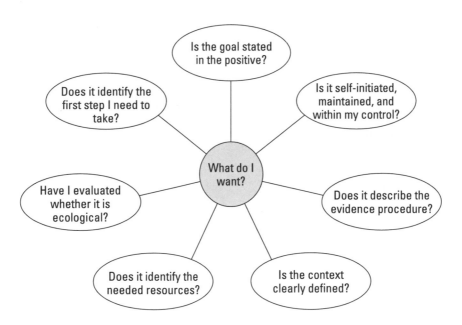

Submodalities Worksheet (Book II, Chapter 4)

Visual Submodalities	Describe What You See
Location	
Colour/black–and white	
Associated or dissociated	
Size	
2- or 3-dimensional	
Brightness	
Still or moving	
Shape	
Framed or panoramic	
Focused or fuzzy	

Auditory Submodalities	Describe What You Hear
Location	
Words or sounds	
Volume	
Tone	

Pitch

Mono or stereo

Constant or intermittent

Rhythm

Tempo

Tune

Kinaesthetic Submodalities   **Describe What You Feel**

Location

Shape

Pressure

Size

Quality

Intensity

Still or moving

Temperature

Constant or intermittent

Texture

ABC Forms (Book III, Chapter 1)

The ABC Form #1

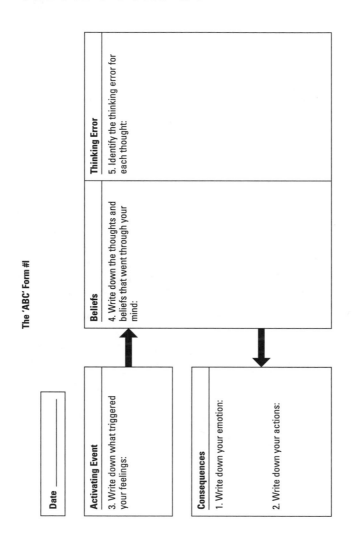

The 'ABC' Form #

Date _____

Activating Event

3. Write down what triggered your feelings:

Beliefs

4. Write down the thoughts and beliefs that went through your mind:

Thinking Error

5. Identify the thinking error for each thought:

Consequences

1. Write down your emotion:

2. Write down your actions:

The ABC Form #2

Date _____

The 'ABC' Form #II

Activating Event (Trigger).	Beliefs, thoughts, and attitudes about A.	Consequences of A+B on your emotions and behaviours.	Dispute (question and examine) B and generate alternatives. The questions at the bottom of the form will help you with this.	Effect of alternative thoughts and beliefs (D).
2. Briefly write down what triggered your emotions. (e.g: event, situation, sensation, memory, image)	3. Write down what went through your mind, or what A *meant* to you. B's can be about you, others, the world, the past, or the future.	1. Write down what emotion you felt and how you acted when you felt this emotion. **Emotions** e.g: Depression, guilt, hurt, anger, shame, jealousy, envy, anxiety. Rate intensity 0–100.	4. Write an alternative for each B, using supporting arguments and evidence.	5. Write down how you feel and wish to act as consequence of your alternatives at D. **Emotions** Re-rate 0–100. List any healthy alternative emotion e.g: Sadness, regret, concern.
		Behaviour e.g. Avoidance, withdrawing, escape, using alcohol or drugs, seeking reassurance, procrastination		**Alternative Behaviour or Experiment** e.g. Facing situation, increased activity, assertion

Disputing (Questioning and Examining) and Generating Alternative Thoughts, Attitudes, and Beliefs: 1. Identify your 'thinking errors' at **B** (e.g. Mind Reading, Catastrophising, Labelling, Demands etc.). Write them next to the appropriate 'B'. 2. Examine whether the evidence at hand supports that your thought at **B** is 100% true. Consider whether someone whose opinions you respect would totally agree with your conclusions. 3. Evaluate the helpfulness of each **B**. Write down what you think might be a more helpful, balanced and flexible way of looking at **A**. Consider what you would advise a friend to think, what a role model of yours might think, or how you might look at **A** if you were feeling OK. 4. Add evidence and arguments that support your alternative thoughts, attitudes and beliefs. Write as if you were trying to persuade someone you cared about.

Zigzag Form (Book III, Chapter 4)

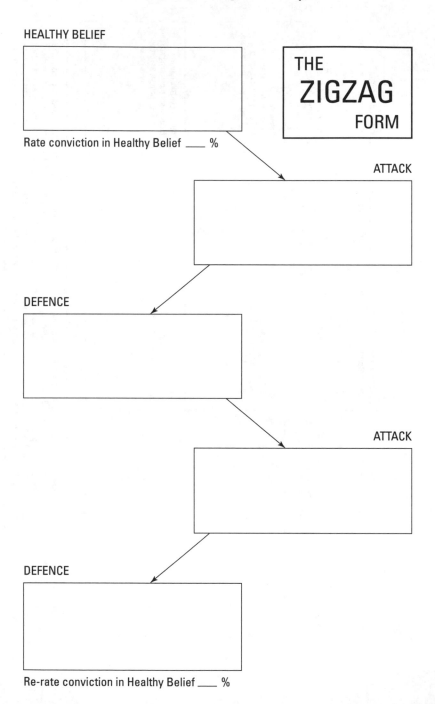

HEALTHY BELIEF

Rate conviction in Healthy Belief _____ %

THE
ZIGZAG
FORM

ATTACK

DEFENCE

ATTACK

DEFENCE

Re-rate conviction in Healthy Belief _____ %

Index

indirect hypnotic
   suggestion, 300–301
indirect metaphors, NLP,
   104–105
induction method, trance,
   404
inner coach, life coach,
   37–40
inner critic
   hypnotherapy, 347–348
   life coaching, 39, 423
inner resources, and
   creativity, 354–357
insomnia, hypnotherapy,
   327–329, 368–369
inspiration to change, self-
   acceptance, 231–232
integration
   CBT, 259–261
   hypnosis, 307–308,
   340–341
   life course, 522–524
interactions, core beliefs,
   252
internal event, ABC self-
   help form, 23, 528–529
internal mapping, NLP,
   15–18
internal metaprograms,
   82–83
internal resources, NLP
   presuppositions, 17
internal smile, 150
International Stress
   Management
   Association
interpersonal triggers,
   depression, 291–292
intimacy, goal setting,
   285–287
in-time diagrams, NLP,
   152–153
in-time line, NLP, 151–153
intrinsic life coaching gifts,
   37, 40, 451–453

intrinsic self-worth,
   223, 226
intrinsic value of human
   beings, 223, 226
introversion, 456–460
intuition
   right brain, 510
   visualisation, 434–435
irritable bowel syndrome
   (IBS), and
   hypnotherapy, 374–376
isolation
   acting out, 23
   as acting out, 23
   depression, 213
   emotional problems, 285
   rapport, NLP, 23
isometric metaphor, 105
(IVF) *in vitro* fertilisation,
   hypnosis, 371

• J •

James, Tad (Time Line
   Therapist), 145
jealousy, 193, 200, 450
journal writing. *See* writing
Jung, Carl (psychoanalyst),
   384

• K •

keywords, in question
   funnel, 516
kinaesthetic modality
   anchors, NLP, 131–132
   sense of, hypnotherapy,
   314
   submodalities, NLP, 111,
   113, 115, 121–122, 527
kindness, acts of, 424
knowledge spiral, 508–509
Korzybski, Alfred (linguist),
   11, 15

• L •

labelling
   gifts, 451–452
   versus self-acceptance,
   223–225
   self-esteem, 221–222
   self-talk strategies, 233
   thinking errors, CBT,
   170–171
language
   Meta Model, NLP, 87–107
   metaprograms, 81–86
   other people's NLP logical
   levels, 144
   rapport, NLP, 76–77
   resisting self-abusive,
   232–233
   words of rigid demand, as
   thinking error, 171–172
The Law of Reversed Effect,
   370
laziness and hypnotherapy,
   413
leadership, NLP rapport,
   72–73
learning, knowledge spiral,
   508–509
learning theory, and NLP, 10
left-brain learning, 508–512
leisure time, 283, 513–514
LFT (low frustration
   tolerance), 174, 230
life coaching. *See also* life
   coaching, visualisation
   attending to inner
   coach, 40
   balance and harmonious
   life, 494–502
   becoming your best self,
   451–468
   belief choices, 461–466
   benefits/challenges,
   426–429
   big picture, 419

FOR DUMMIES®

Do Anything. Just Add Dummies

PROPERTY

UK editions

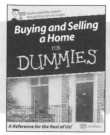

Buying and Selling a Home For Dummies

978-0-7645-7027-8

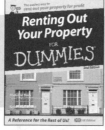

Renting Out Your Property For Dummies

978-0-470-02921-3

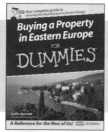

Buying a Property in Eastern Europe For Dummies

978-0-7645-7047-6

PERSONAL FINANCE

Investing For Dummies

978-0-7645-7023-0

Personal Finance & Investing All-In-One For Dummies

978-0-470-51510-5

Bookkeeping For Dummies

978-0-470-05815-2

BUSINESS

Starting a Business For Dummies

978-0-7645-7018-6

Marketing For Dummies

978-0-7645-7056-8

Business Plans For Dummies

978-0-7645-7026-1

Answering Tough Interview Questions For Dummies
(978-0-470-01903-0)

Arthritis For Dummies
(978-0-470-02582-6)

Being the Best Man For Dummies
(978-0-470-02657-1)

British History For Dummies
(978-0-470-03536-8)

Building Self-Confidence For Dummies
(978-0-470-01669-5)

Buying a Home on a Budget For Dummies
(978-0-7645-7035-3)

Children's Health For Dummies
(978-0-470-02735-6)

Cognitive Behavioural Therapy For Dummies
(978-0-470-01838-5)

Cricket For Dummies
(978-0-470-03454-5)

CVs For Dummies
(978-0-7645-7017-9)

Detox For Dummies
(978-0-470-01908-5)

Diabetes For Dummies
(978-0-470-05810-7)

Divorce For Dummies
(978-0-7645-7030-8)

DJing For Dummies
(978-0-470-03275-6)

eBay.co.uk For Dummies
(978-0-7645-7059-9)

English Grammar For Dummies
(978-0-470-05752-0)

Gardening For Dummies
(978-0-470-01843-9)

Genealogy Online For Dummies
(978-0-7645-7061-2)

Green Living For Dummies
(978-0-470-06038-4)

Hypnotherapy For Dummies
(978-0-470-01930-6)

Life Coaching For Dummies
(978-0-470-03135-3)

Neuro-linguistic Programming For Dummies
(978-0-7645-7028-5)

Nutrition For Dummies
(978-0-7645-7058-2)

Parenting For Dummies
(978-0-470-02714-1)

Pregnancy For Dummies
(978-0-7645-7042-1)

Rugby Union For Dummies
(978-0-470-03537-5)

Self Build and Renovation For Dummies
(978-0-470-02586-4)

Starting a Business on eBay.co.uk For Dummies
(978-0-470-02666-3)

Starting and Running an Online Business For Dummies
(978-0-470-05768-1)

The GL Diet For Dummies
(978-0-470-02753-0)

The Romans For Dummies
(978-0-470-03077-6)

Thyroid For Dummies
(978-0-470-03172-8)

UK Law and Your Rights For Dummies
(978-0-470-02796-7)

Writing a Novel and Getting Published For Dummies
(978-0-470-05910-4)

FOR DUMMIES®

Do Anything. Just Add Dummies

HOBBIES

Poker
978-0-7645-5232-8

Sewing
978-0-7645-6847-3

Drawing
978-0-7645-5476-6

Also available:

Art For Dummies
(978-0-7645-5104-8)

Aromatherapy For Dummies
(978-0-7645-5171-0)

Bridge For Dummies
(978-0-471-92426-5)

Card Games For Dummies
(978-0-7645-9910-1)

Chess For Dummies
(978-0-7645-8404-6)

Improving Your Memory
For Dummies
(978-0-7645-5435-3)

Massage For Dummies
(978-0-7645-5172-7)

Meditation For Dummies
(978-0-471-77774-8)

Photography For Dummies
(978-0-7645-4116-2)

Quilting For Dummies
(978-0-7645-9799-2)

EDUCATION

Cooking Basics
978-0-7645-7206-7

The Koran
978-0-7645-5581-7

Anatomy & Physiology
978-0-7645-5422-3

Also available:

Algebra For Dummies
(978-0-7645-5325-7)

Algebra II For Dummies
(978-0-471-77581-2)

Astronomy For Dummies
(978-0-7645-8465-7)

Buddhism For Dummies
(978-0-7645-5359-2)

Calculus For Dummies
(978-0-7645-2498-1)

Forensics For Dummies
(978-0-7645-5580-0)

Islam For Dummies
(978-0-7645-5503-9)

Philosophy For Dummies
(978-0-7645-5153-6)

Religion For Dummies
(978-0-7645-5264-9)

Trigonometry For Dummies
(978-0-7645-6903-6)

PETS

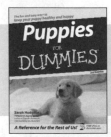

Puppies
978-0-470-03717-1

Dog Training
978-0-7645-8418-3

Cats
978-0-7645-5275-5

Also available:

Labrador Retrievers
For Dummies
(978-0-7645-5281-6)

Aquariums For Dummies
(978-0-7645-5156-7)

Birds For Dummies
(978-0-7645-5139-0)

Dogs For Dummies
(978-0-7645-5274-8)

Ferrets For Dummies
(978-0-7645-5259-5)

Golden Retrievers
For Dummies
(978-0-7645-5267-0)

Horses For Dummies
(978-0-7645-9797-8)

Jack Russell Terriers
For Dummies
(978-0-7645-5268-7)

Puppies Raising & Training
Diary For Dummies
(978-0-7645-0876-9)

Available wherever books are sold. For more information or to order direct go to www.wiley.com or call 0800 243407 (Non UK call +44 1243 843296)

FOR DUMMIES®

The easy way to get more done and have more fun

LANGUAGES

978-0-7645-5193-2

978-0-7645-5193-2

978-0-7645-5196-3

Also available:

Chinese For Dummies
(978-0-471-78897-3)

Chinese Phrases
For Dummies
(978-0-7645-8477-0)

French Phrases For Dummies
(978-0-7645-7202-9)

German For Dummies
(978-0-7645-5195-6)

Italian Phrases For Dummies
(978-0-7645-7203-6)

Japanese For Dummies
(978-0-7645-5429-2)

Latin For Dummies
(978-0-7645-5431-5)

Spanish Phrases
For Dummies
(978-0-7645-7204-3)

Spanish Verbs For Dummies
(978-0-471-76872-2)

Hebrew For Dummies
(978-0-7645-5489-6)

MUSIC AND FILM

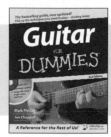

978-0-7645-9904-0

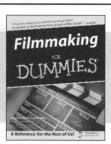

978-0-7645-2476-9

978-0-7645-5105-5

Also available:

Bass Guitar For Dummies
(978-0-7645-2487-5)

Blues For Dummies
(978-0-7645-5080-5)

Classical Music For Dummies
(978-0-7645-5009-6)

Drums For Dummies
(978-0-471-79411-0)

Jazz For Dummies
(978-0-471-76844-9)

Opera For Dummies
(978-0-7645-5010-2)

Rock Guitar For Dummies
(978-0-7645-5356-1)

Screenwriting For Dummies
(978-0-7645-5486-5)

Songwriting For Dummies
(978-0-7645-5404-9)

Singing For Dummies
(978-0-7645-2475-2)

HEALTH, SPORTS & FITNESS

978-0-7645-7851-9

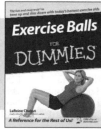

978-0-7645-5623-4

978-0-7645-4233-6

Also available:

Controlling Cholesterol
For Dummies
(978-0-7645-5440-7)

Dieting For Dummies
(978-0-7645-4149-0)

High Blood Pressure
For Dummies
(978-0-7645-5424-7)

Martial Arts For Dummies
(978-0-7645-5358-5)

Pilates For Dummies
(978-0-7645-5397-4)

Power Yoga For Dummies
(978-0-7645-5342-4)

Weight Training
For Dummies
(978-0-471-76845-6)

Yoga For Dummies
(978-0-7645-5117-8)

FOR DUMMIES®

Helping you expand your horizons and achieve your potential

INTERNET

The Internet FOR DUMMIES
978-0-7645-8996-6

Search Engine Optimization FOR DUMMIES
978-0-471-97998-2

Creating Web Pages FOR DUMMIES
978-0-470-08030-6

Also available:

Building a Web Site For Dummies, 2nd Edition
(978-0-7645-7144-2)

Blogging For Dummies
(978-0-471-77084-8)

eBay.co.uk For Dummies
(978-0-7645-7059-9)

Web Analysis For Dummies
(978-0-470-09824-0)

Web Design For Dummies, 2nd Edition
(978-0-471-78117-2)

Creating Web Pages All-in-One Desk Reference For Dummies, 3rd Edition
(978-0-470-09629-1)

DIGITAL MEDIA

Digital Photography FOR DUMMIES
978-0-7645-9802-9

iPod & iTunes FOR DUMMIES
978-0-470-04894-8

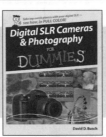

Digital SLR Cameras & Photography FOR DUMMIES
978-0-7645-9803-6

Also available:

Photoshop CS3 For Dummies
(978-0-470-11193-2)

Podcasting For Dummies
(978-0-471-74898-4)

Digital Photography All-In-One Desk Reference For Dummies
(978-0-470-03743-0)

Digital Photo Projects For Dummies
(978-0-470-12101-6)

BlackBerry For Dummies
(978-0-471-75741-2)

Zune For Dummies
(978-0-470-12045-3)

COMPUTER BASICS

PCs FOR DUMMIES
978-0-7645-8958-4

Laptops FOR DUMMIES
978-0-470-05432-1

Windows Vista FOR DUMMIES
978-0-471-75421-3

Also available:

Macs For Dummies, 9th Edition
(978-0-470-04849-8)

Windows Vista All-in-One Desk Reference For Dummies
(978-0-471-74941-7)

Office 2007 All-in-One Desk Reference For Dummies
(978-0-471-78279-7)

Windows XP For Dummies, 2nd Edition
(978-0-7645-7326-2)

PCs All-in-One Desk Reference For Dummies, 3rd Edition
(978-0-471-77082-4)

Upgrading & Fixing PCs For Dummies, 7th Edition
(978-0-470-12102-3)
